the art and craft of fiction

A WRITER'S GUIDE

"This is the perfect text on narrative technique and story writing for college fiction writers. Honestly, I can't see how Kardos might improve it. The minute you guys publish this book, I'm ordering it—and requiring it—for my students."

~ STEPHEN WATKINS, *University of Mary Washington*

"What I like best, and what is too often missing in other writing texts, is the practicality of instruction. Kardos wisely focuses on the 'nuts & bolts' that can be taught and demonstrated."

~ RANDALL SILVIS, *Edinboro University of Pennsylvania*

"Kardos's instruction is clear and down-to-earth—and the prose is as informative and enlightening as it is interesting and fun to read. I look forward to teaching with this book as soon as it is available."

~ WILEY CASH, *Bethany College*

"Kardos gives students uncomplicated access to the mysterious process of fiction making."

~ JOHN HOLMAN, *Georgia State University*

"The strength of this book lies in Kardos's easy, frank presentation. This is a 'how to write' book that distinguishes itself with a friendly, conversational tone."

~ ALYCE MILLER, *Indiana University*

"I was sold on this book as soon as I read the first few paragraphs of the Mechanics chapter."

~ BETTY WIESEPAPE, *University of Texas at Dallas*

"Kardos gives a thorough overview of the most important ideas and techniques on the craft of fiction. Even advanced writers will find new insights and new angles on old challenges."

~ LAURA VALERI, *Georgia Southern University*

"Kardos touches upon the very problems I have seen in the stories my students write. I love this book!"

~ PATRICK BIZZARO, *Indiana University of Pennsylvania*

"I like Kardos's approach of singling out the landmarks of the story arc and examining their variations. The text is comprehensive, examples well-chosen, and user-friendliness exemplary. I am impressed."

~ BARRY LAWLER, *Oregon State University*

"This is the kind of stuff I wish I'd been taught in grad school, and it's what I try to teach my undergrads: specific techniques that can enhance their stories. I wish I'd had something like this book as a beginning writer."

~ STEPHANIE VANDERSLICE, *University of Central Arkansas*

"I've been looking for a book like this for years. It's refreshingly different in organization, with an emphasis on not just the elements of fiction, but on mechanics, openings and endings, and structure. The brevity and price are also strengths. I absolutely would adopt this book."

~ LIZA WIELAND, *East Carolina University*

"The content supports the kind of work my students aspire to."

~ MARC NIESON, *Chatham University*

the art and craft of fiction

A WRITER'S GUIDE

Michael Kardos
Mississippi State University

BEDFORD/ST. MARTIN'S

Boston • New York

FOR BEDFORD/ST. MARTIN'S

Executive Editor: Ellen Thibault
Senior Production Editor: Lori Chong Roncka
Production Supervisor: Samuel Jones
Marketing Manager: Stacey Propps
Editorial Assistant: Amanda Legee
Production Assistants: Laura Winstead and Elise Keller
Copy Editor: Linda McLatchie
Indexer: Mary White
Permissions Manager: Kalina K. Ingham
Senior Art Director: Anna Palchik
Text Design: Jonathon Nix
Cover Design: Donna Lee Dennison
Cover Photo: Corgi and Chihuahua looking out a screen door,
   © Vincent Sandoval/Funk Zone Studios/Corbis
Composition: Westchester Book Group
Printing and Binding: RR Donnelley and Sons

President, Bedford/St. Martin's: Denise B. Wydra
Presidents, Macmillan Higher Education: Joan E. Feinberg and Tom Scotty
Editor in Chief: Karen S. Henry
Senior Executive Editor: Stephen A. Scipione
Director of Marketing: Karen R. Soeltz
Production Director: Susan W. Brown
Associate Production Director: Elise S. Kaiser
Managing Editor: Elizabeth M. Schaaf

Library of Congress Control Number: 2012941069

Manufactured in the United States of America.

7   6   5   4   3   2
f   e   d   c   b   a

For information, write: Bedford/St. Martin's, 75 Arlington Street, Boston, MA 02116
   (617-399-4000)

ISBN 978-1-4576-1390-6

ACKNOWLEDGMENTS

preface for instructors

Many of us who teach creative writing have struggled at one time or another with choosing a textbook. The challenge is to find a book that is pedagogically effective, practical to work into a syllabus, and written in a style that will engage students.

With those considerations in mind, *The Art and Craft of Fiction* is intended to

- provide a practical introduction to writing and revising fiction
- fit fluidly into the day-by-day schedule of both the fiction-writing workshop and the multigenre workshop
- be clear, concise, and engaging

There's also a fourth consideration: price. Students, instructors, and university administrators have quite reasonably become highly attuned to the cost of textbooks. So everyone involved in the creation of this book has kept affordability in mind.

How the book is structured

You'll notice right away that this book isn't organized around the elements of fiction. As discussed in Chapter 4, the reason is twofold. First, I wanted this book to emphasize the interdependence of elements, rather than to imply that each element stands alone. Second, I believed there had to be a way to organize a book about story-making that would more closely align with the actual process of writing and revising stories.

So instead of the elements-of-fiction approach, these chapters focus on the major issues that beginning writers face *as they're working on their stories* (the use of relevant detail, the nuts and bolts of scene-writing, the mechanics of fiction) as well as the issues that all fiction writers face (where to start, where to end, how to be clear, how to make stories compelling, and how to revise). The chapters are ordered in such a way that they build on one another, but the book can be taught in any order.

All told, these chapters comprise an introduction to the writer who wishes to bridge the gap between his or her desire to tell a story and the ability to do it effectively. In the process, students will also learn about literature "from the inside"—an important goal in any creative writing course.

Speaking of mechanics

Chapter 11, "The Mechanics of Fiction: A Writer's Boot Camp," began years ago, when as a graduate student I created a handout for the first fiction-writing classes I ever taught. The handout contained exactly one thing: instructions for punctuating dialogue.

I've been expanding and updating the handout ever since.

The purpose of that chapter is to provide, in one place and without going on too long, some of the most common technical issues that students will face as fiction writers. The chapter introduction explains exactly why it's critical for them to master these technical points: "One of the writer's most important jobs is to gain the reader's trust. Earning that trust is hard work. Losing it is easy—and one of the easiest ways to lose a reader's trust is by paying too little attention to mechanics."

This review of the mechanics of fiction has proven to be very useful to my students over the years. They can refer to it as they write and revise, and I can expect them to know and use these important tools of the craft.

We placed this chapter in its own section, knowing that different instructors will want to assign it at different points in the term. (I typically assign it about two weeks into a term—once it's already under way, but before students begin to hand in their finished drafts.)

The exercises & checklists

The exercises in this book reinforce specific lessons and develop particular skills. There are far too many exercises to assign in a single semester and, we hope, more than enough to suit any instructor's needs. Some exercises may be assigned as homework, others as in-class writing assignments or group activities. Checklists remind students of key concepts and appear in a convenient list—along with a list of the exercises—on pages xxiv–xxv.

The mini-anthology

The fifteen stories in the anthology (1) demonstrate key elements of the fiction-writing craft, (2) represent diverse storytelling approaches, and (3) have been well received by students. They are all contemporary. (The oldest story is from 1961; the most current ones are from 2010.) The decision to include only contemporary fiction in the anthology is in no way meant to challenge the importance to a writer's apprenticeship of reading older works. Many of the chapters do, in fact, bring in excerpts from such writers as Poe, Chekhov, Fitzgerald, Welty, and others. But an equally important part of the fiction writer's apprenticeship is becoming familiar with contemporary writing and developing a sense of what it looks and feels like.

Most of the examples in this book draw from the anthologized stories. Many of the stories are discussed in more than one chapter. For that reason, the stories appear at the end of the book, alphabetized by author, rather than within the individual chapters. (As a student, I always liked being able to browse an entire anthology; when I teach a class, I dislike having to page through a book hunting for a particular story.)

The stories can be assigned in any order, though for convenience here is a listing that pairs each chapter with the stories that are discussed in them:

CHAPTER 2, THE EXTREME IMPORTANCE OF RELEVANT DETAIL

Jill McCorkle, Magic Words
Percival Everett, The Appropriation of Cultures
John Updike, A & P
Sherman Alexie, This Is What It Means to Say Phoenix, Arizona

CHAPTER 3, STARTING YOUR STORY

Kevin Brockmeier, A Fable with Slips of White Paper Spilling from the Pockets
Sherman Alexie, This Is What It Means to Say Phoenix, Arizona
Tim O'Brien, On the Rainy River
ZZ Packer, Drinking Coffee Elsewhere
Karen Russell, St. Lucy's Home for Girls Raised by Wolves
Becky Hagenston, Midnight, Licorice, Shadow

CHAPTER 4, WORKING WITH THE ELEMENTS OF FICTION

Jhumpa Lahiri, This Blessed House
Tobias Wolff, Bullet in the Brain
Tim O'Brien, On the Rainy River
Lorrie Moore, How to Become a Writer

CHAPTER 5, CREATING SCENES: A NUTS & BOLTS APPROACH

Becky Hagenston, Midnight, Licorice, Shadow
Tobias Wolff, Bullet in the Brain

CHAPTER 6, ORGANIZING YOUR STORY: FORM & STRUCTURE

John Updike, A & P
Tim O'Brien, On the Rainy River
Kevin Brockmeier, A Fable with Slips of White Paper Spilling from the Pockets
Jill McCorkle, Magic Words
Sherman Alexie, This Is What It Means to Say Phoenix, Arizona
Barry Hannah, Water Liars

CHAPTER 7, WRITING A COMPELLING STORY

Tim O'Brien, On the Rainy River
Richard Bausch, Tandolfo the Great
George Saunders, CivilWarLand in Bad Decline

CHAPTER 8, ENDING YOUR STORY

Becky Hagenston, Midnight, Licorice, Shadow
Jhumpa Lahiri, This Blessed House
Richard Bausch, Tandolfo the Great
Tobias Wolff, Bullet in the Brain

CHAPTER 9, THE POWER OF CLARITY

ZZ Packer, Drinking Coffee Elsewhere
Jill McCorkle, Magic Words

CHAPTER 10, REVISING YOUR STORY

Becky Hagenston, Midnight, Licorice, Shadow

Acknowledgments

My sincere thanks to the fine folks at Bedford/St. Martin's who made this book possible. Ellen Thibault is a writer's dream editor — she was my trusted guide and unflagging champion from initial concept to finished book, and I'm grateful for her wisdom and generosity. I'd like to thank Joan Feinberg and Denise Wydra for making this book possible, as well as Karen Henry, Steve Scipione, Lori Roncka, Anna Palchik, Jonathon Nix, Linda McLatchie, Amanda Legee, Laura Winstead, and Elise Keller.

We are who we are because of our teachers, and I would like to thank mine. Lee K. Abbott, Michelle Herman, Trudy Lewis, Lee Martin, Erin McGraw, Speer Morgan, and Marly Swick: These pages are dripping with your pedagogy. Thanks, too, to Becky Hagenston, Richard Lyons, and Catherine Pierce, my creative writing colleagues at Mississippi State, whose knowledge and friendship I rely on daily.

I would like to thank the following reviewers, who were kind enough to read parts of this book during its development and help make it stronger: Abby Bardi, Prince George's Community College; Nicky Beer, University of Colorado Denver; Patrick Bizzaro, Indiana University of Pennsylvania; James Braziel, University of Alabama, Birmingham; Stephanie Carpenter, University of Michigan–Flint; Wiley Cash, Bethany College; Tony Grooms, Kennesaw State University; John Holman, Georgia State University; Barry Lawler, Oregon State University; Alyce Miller, Indiana University; Chloe Yelena Miller, Fairleigh Dickinson University; Keith Lee Morris, Clemson University; Marc Neison, Chatham University; Anne Panning, State University of New York, The College at Brockport; R. Clay Reynolds, University of Texas at Dallas; Susan Jackson Rodgers, Oregon State University; Randall Silvis, Edinboro University of Pennsylvania; Laura Valeri, Georgia Southern University; Stephanie Vanderslice, University of Central Arkansas; Stephen Watkins, University of Mary Washington; Liza Wieland, East Carolina University; Betty Wiesepape, University of Texas at Dallas. Thanks, too, to Christopher Coake, University of Nevada–Reno, for our many discussions over the years about what might go into a book such as this, and to Michael Piafsky, Spring Hill College, for his generous feedback and consistent encouragement.

Thanks to my students—all of them, but especially to those who test-drove the manuscript and contributed the student examples.

Finally, one more hearty thanks to Catherine Pierce—when you're married to your colleague, you get to thank her twice—for her constant support (I'd have written "tireless support," but with a newborn we were often tired) and valuable advice at every stage of this book. I couldn't have done this without you.

Michael Kardos
Starkville, Mississippi

Resources for *The Art and Craft of Fiction*

The Art and Craft of Fiction doesn't end with a print book. Online you'll find both free and affordable premium resources to help students get even more out of this text and your course. To learn about or order any of the following products, contact your Bedford/St. Martin's sales representative, e-mail sales support (sales_support@bfwpub.com), or visit **bedfordstmartins.com/kardos /catalog**.

This book is available as a Bedford e-Book to Go
This PDF-style e-book matches our print book page for page and is ready for your tablet, computer, phone, or e-reader device. You and your students gain access to the e-book at this book's companion site (see below) and can take it with you wherever you go. To order the e-book for your course, use ISBN 978-1-4576-3783-4. At roughly half the cost of the print book, *The Art and Craft of Fiction e-Book to Go* is convenient and affordable.

It also comes with a free & open companion site
Our companion site for *The Art and Craft of Fiction* adds value, not cost. Here, students can access our premier collections of author videos and multimedia resources, including:

- **A tutorial: "Publishing Your Work: How, Where, and When," by Michael Kardos.** It's only natural for aspiring writers to wonder who might read their work. In this tutorial, author Michael Kardos gives an introduction to literary publishing as well as insight into researching publications, drafting a cover letter, submitting work, and dealing with rejection. He also explains the roles of agents and editors.
- **A bibliography: "For Further Reading," by Michael Kardos.** Kardos's annotated bibliography of books, magazines, blogs, and Web sites is a handy resource for fiction writers looking to further their craft.
- **Anthology author interviews, plus biographies and links.** Read the full texts of interviews that Michael Kardos conducted with several authors whose stories appear in the anthology. Find out more about the writers' lives and works through our annotated collection, *AuthorLinks*.

Packaging options

Take advantage of our collection of author videos—and a course space and e-portfolio tool available at a discount with student copies of *The Art and Craft of Fiction*.

This book comes with video

Bring today's writers into your classroom. Hear from T. C. Boyle, Ha Jin, Jane Smiley, and others, on character, voice, plot, and more. Questions, biographies, and transcripts make each video an assignable module. To package this collection, free with new student copies of this book, use package ISBN 978-1-4576-5315-5. bedfordstmartins.com/videolit/catalog

Our online writing studio: *CompClass*

CompClass gives students the tools for reading and writing, discussion and response, and drafting and feedback that will make them better creative writers. With *CompClass*, students never have to ask you what their grade is, where to find course material, or how they can find a space to draft, revise, and get organized. Preloaded with autoscored exercises, a commenting and peer review space where students can annotate one another's work, the first-ever peer review game, and our library of writing resources, *CompClass* is ready for you to customize and make your own. To order *CompClass* with the student edition of *The Art and Craft of Fiction*, use package ISBN 978-1-4576-5189-2. **courses.bfwpub.com/yourcompclass**

The Bedford e-Portfolio: simply flexible—and coming in fall 2013
Select. Collect. Reflect. The Bedford e-Portfolio makes it easy for students to showcase their writing and other coursework—whether for their class, for their job, or even for their friends. With flexible assessment tools, the Bedford e-Portfolio lets you map learning outcomes or just invite students to start their collections. **bedfordstmartins.com/eportfolio**

Get teaching ideas you can use today

Are you looking for free and open professional resources for teaching literature and writing? How about some help with planning classroom activities?

LitBits: **ideas for teaching literature & creative writing**
Hosted by a team of instructors, poets, novelists, and scholars, our *LitBits* blog offers fresh, regularly updated ideas and assignments for teaching creative writing, including simple ways to teach with media. Check out **Michael Kardos's posts** on teaching fiction writing at **bedfordstmartins.com/litbits.**

TeachingCentral: **all of our professional resources, in one place**
You'll find landmark reference works, sourcebooks on pedagogical issues, award-winning collections, and practical advice for the classroom—all free. **bedfordstmartins.com/teachingcentral**

Add value to your course

Could your students use some help with style, grammar, and clarity? Have you ever wanted to put together your own custom anthology? Would you like to teach with longer works by adding a trade title or two to your course?

Add a handbook & save your students 20%
Package *EasyWriter* by Andrea Lunsford or *A Pocket Style Manual* by Diana Hacker and Nancy Sommers with this text at 20 percent off. **bedfordstmartins .com/easywriter/catalog** or **bedfordstmartins.com/pocket/catalog**

Create your own fiction anthology

The Art and Craft of Fiction includes a brief anthology of fifteen terrific stories, but are you looking for more? Choose your literature, select a cover, and publish at **bedfordstmartins.com/select.**

Save 50% on hundreds of trade titles

Package a trade book for half off with new student copies of *The Art and Craft of Fiction*. **bedfordstmartins.com/tradeup**

brief contents

contents

anthology

12 a mini-anthology: 15 stories   185

✳ exercises, checklists & tips

exercises

checklists

tips

the art and craft of fiction

A WRITER'S GUIDE

art & craft

1 thinking, reading, & writing like a writer

SEVERAL YEARS AGO, my wife and I went on vacation to Niagara Falls. After a full day of walking, we decided to ride the gondola up a hillside back to our hotel's street. With us in the gondola were a mother and daughter. The girl was about four years old.

As our car climbed, we all watched the scene below: the falls in the distance, the *Maid of the Mist* returning to its dock, cars trolling for parking spaces, people walking the footpath beside the river. We were fairly high up when the girl smiled and said, "The people look like broken toothpicks!"

What did the mother do? She corrected her daughter.

"No, honey," she said, "they look like ants."

The girl looked down again at the footpath. "The people look like ants," she said.

But the people didn't look like ants. They looked like broken toothpicks.

BEING A WRITER MEANS PAYING ATTENTION

In his 1888 essay "The Art of Fiction," Henry James famously wrote that to be a writer one should "try to be one of the people on whom nothing is lost."

But what does that mean, and how does one become such a person?

It means being attuned to the world around you — closely looking (and smelling and tasting and touching and listening) — rather than being satisfied with viewing the world through the fuzzy lens of conventional wisdom.

One on whom nothing is lost knows that people seen from high above don't always — or ever — look like ants. Sometimes they look like broken toothpicks. But we'll never know if we don't pay attention.

Being a writer, then, means honing your ability to closely observe and carefully consider *everything*, taking nothing for granted.

Then, of course, you need to find the right words to describe what you see.

WHY A TEXTBOOK? (AND WHY *THIS* TEXTBOOK?)

In his book *On Writing* (2000), Stephen King has this to say:

> If you want to be a writer, you must do two things above all others: read a lot and write a lot. There's no way around these two things that I'm aware of, no shortcut.

On the one hand, yes, absolutely. A writer isn't someone who talks about writing, or imagines writing, or tells people that he's a writer. A writer is some-one who writes—and, as we'll discuss shortly, someone who reads.

On the other hand, books like King's presume that study and practice can go a long way toward instilling good habits that will shorten the fiction writer's long apprenticeship.

Now, study and practice are, in a sense, just other words for reading and writing. But they imply *focused* study and *guided* practice, rather than the mere churning out of pages in the hope that productivity alone will develop the writer.

This book is intended to provide exactly that focused study and guided practice. It's a book that will get you going and, I hope, one that you'll find yourself returning to as you continue to develop your craft.

RULES OF THE ROAD

Rather than repeat it over and over in every chapter, I'll say it once now, up front: *If you try hard enough, you will find exceptions to nearly every rule in this book.*

This is as it should be. Fiction is an art, not a science with inviolable laws. Other than the chapter devoted to mechanics, this book contains very few rules anyway. Rather, it contains principles of narrative and aesthetics that many writers, over time, have come to find effective in telling their stories.

So here's the deal: Just like in the game of "maul the guy with the ball" that my friends and I used to play as weird kids, *The rules are, there are no rules.*

But here's the catch: As someone interested in furthering your development as an artist, you need to learn the principles of your craft—because they tend to work.

Flannery O'Connor, one of America's great fiction writers, put it this way:

> It's always wrong of course to say that you can't do this or you can't do that in fiction. You can do anything you can get away with, but nobody has ever gotten away with much.

READING LIKE A WRITER

Not every reader writes, but every writer reads—and usually a lot. Quite simply, in order to become a good writer, one must become a good reader. That means reading not only for what a work means but also for how it was done.

Every chapter in this book will discuss fiction in this mode, looking closely at the technical choices that the authors made in writing their stories.

As you read the anthologized stories (and any other fiction), remember to be greedy. Ask yourself what, specifically, each work of fiction has to teach you. What technique can you apply to your next story?

checklist » read like a writer

Some questions to ask of the stories you read include the following:

» Why does this story begin when it does?

» What is different about the day when the story takes place?

» When you close your eyes, what part of the story do you picture most clearly in your mind? Why might that be?

» What is the main character's underlying problem, and how does the story bring this problem into sharper focus?

» Why does the story focus on this main character, as opposed to another character in the story? How do you think the author intends readers to feel about him or her? How do you feel?

» If the story is told from more than one character's perspective, why do you think this choice was made?

» Why is this story in the point of view that it is?

» Which parts of the story are dramatized through scenes? Which parts are summarized? Why?

» How would you describe the story's voice? What does the voice do for the story?

» Is the writing ever less clear than it could be?

» How is the story structured? How else could it be?

» Why does the story end when it does?

» How is this story different from other stories you've read?

» What details make this story especially vivid or unexpected?

And once again, perhaps the most important question of all:

» What specific technique(s) would you most readily take from this story and try in your own story?

In asking this final question, you ensure that you're learning to identify and apply particular techniques that fiction writers use. We aren't talking about plagiarism—we're talking about skills that, once learned, will stay with you.

Here's an example. The second half of Tobias Wolff's story "Bullet in the Brain" (see p. 366) takes place over one split second (actually, a fraction of a fraction of a second). How does Wolff go about enlarging such a minuscule time period into several pages of story? How might you go about doing something like that? And what sort of situation, other than the one that Wolff describes, might warrant such slowing down of time?

When you read Wolff's story—and the others in the anthology—like a writer, you discover choices that you never knew existed. You expand your notion of what stories can do, and then you get to try to do those things.

THE HABIT OF WRITING

There's always a big exam to study for, laundry piling up, a series finale or playoff game to watch, a friend or family member in need of a favor, or any number of things that demand your attention.

There are always reasons not to write—sometimes very good reasons. And yet a writer finds the time to write anyway. Discipline means doing the thing you set out to do not when it's easy, but when it's hard.

We all love inspiration because inspiration requires little time or conscious effort. Bursts of creative fervor get the heart pumping and make us feel good about ourselves. A story or novel that we read can inspire and motivate us, as can a caring, knowledgeable teacher and a classroom of motivated peers. (A class can also give you deadlines.) A textbook like this one can give you plenty to think about. But ultimately, only you can make yourself sit down and write.

Not that writing happens only at the writing desk. By all means, think about the story you're writing when you're in the car, in the grocery aisle, in bed as you're falling asleep at night. Keep your story in mind, and your mind will keep working on your story. Still, there's no substitute for sitting down and writing.

checklist » sit down & write

To make the habit of writing a little easier to acquire and maintain, consider the following:

» If at all possible, designate a particular time and place to write every day. Doing so will not only help you schedule your writing time but will also train your brain to start thinking creatively at that specific place and time.

» I include this remarkably obvious advice only because it can be so hard to follow: Stay offline. Forget Facebook. Forget email. If you have fact-checking or research to do for your story, save it until the end of your writing session. Otherwise, keep your workspace Internet-free.

» Turn off the phone. No calls. No texting.

» Designate a certain amount of time each day to devote to your writing, or a certain number of words per day that you must add to your story before you quit. (When working on a longer piece of fiction, I prefer trying to meet a words-per-day quota. When I'm working on a short story, or revising, then I prefer to work for a set amount of time.)

» Ernest Hemingway used to stop writing every day not when he was out of ideas, but when he knew exactly what he was going to write next. That way, he knew that the next day when he sat down to write, he wouldn't waste any time before he got going.

» Learn what works for you. Do you work better with music or silence? A window with a view or sensory deprivation? A crowded public space or your own little private corner? Do whatever works so that you can develop the habit of writing. Indeed, whatever you choose might well *become* what works best for you.

FINDING IDEAS FOR STORIES

A character? A setting? An image? A situation? An appealing sentence?

Yes, yes, yes, yes, yes.

The end of this chapter contains several prompts to get you going, but whatever captures your interest is the right way to start thinking about a story.

I've never been a journal keeper, but many other writers swear by their journals, in which they record their thoughts, dreams, and observations—the raw material that might later find its way into a story.

Even though I don't keep a journal, once I start writing a story I take plenty of notes away from the computer. I sketch out character details and make plot connections. Then I return to the computer and write. Then I go away from the computer again. Then back. That's my way of working. It might not be yours.

The chapters in this book contain detailed advice that will help you craft your stories. For now, consider what intrigues you or puzzles you or keeps you awake at night. Try to recall something from your day that stopped you cold. Write it down. That's a good way to start.

Borrow freely from your own experience, but bear in mind that the aim of fiction isn't autobiography. Rather, the purpose of "writing what you know" is to use the details and emotions that you're familiar with to tell a *new* story. Our biographies might well be useful, but only if they spark, rather than supplant, our imaginations.

From the time you first start thinking about a story to the final revision, remember to play the "What if" game: "What if this were to happen?" "What if she were to say this, or do that?" "What if this scene were set *here*, instead of *there*?" What if, what if, what if. Learn to play that game, and you'll surprise yourself with the discoveries you make about your own stories. (In Chapter 10, Becky Hagenston describes how she played the "What if" game while writing her story "Midnight, Licorice, Shadow.")

Be skeptical of looking to television, movies, and video games as influences. Unlike literature, those other media are primarily visual and follow different narrative principles. They also often rely on formulaic, contrived plots and character types—though to be fair, there are good and bad television shows, just as there are good and bad books. The important thing is to learn to recognize, and assiduously avoid, clichéd writing.

checklist » beware of clichéd writing

Learn to recognize and avoid the following:

» Prepackaged ways of describing the world—people far away who look like ants, or someone whose heart breaks or who has butterflies in her stomach

» Hackneyed plot conventions—the multiple-personality serial killer; the story that was all a dream; the story about a novelist with writer's block (Of course, the more you read, the more you'll learn just what is hackneyed and what isn't.)

» Simplified or generalized depictions of people (the "strong, silent type," the "jock," the "nerd," the "prostitute with a heart of gold") and places (the "unfriendly big city" or the "idyllic small town")

The guiding principle is to root your story in what is particular and original, rather than in what is typical or rehashed.

Another way to say this is that if you are someone on whom nothing is lost, then you know that every person, place, or thing is replete with nuance. Your job is to find it.

A WORD TO THE NOVELIST

This book, like the majority of college courses in fiction writing, is tailored to the production of short stories rather than novels. The reasons are practical. The typical semester-long workshop makes it difficult for, say, fifteen people to read one another's novel-length manuscripts. It would also be rare for all the students in a class to have finished drafts of novels ready for discussion, and partially written novels are often difficult to workshop.

That said—novelists, don't fret. While our examples draw mainly from short stories, this is a book about *fiction writing*. The novelist will benefit from all of this book's discussions, and the accompanying website will refer you to several books tailored specifically to writing novels.

WHAT'S THE POINT OF ALL THIS?

We read fiction to be entertained and enlightened, to learn about other people and places without going anywhere, and to see a slice of our own world reflected back to us in a way that we find emotionally, intellectually, and artistically satisfying. Reading fiction is a way to pass the time engaged in a kind of active imagining, a way of forgetting ourselves for a while.

A well-told story makes us pay attention. It reminds us what it feels like to be human.

When we write fiction, we also engage in an act of empathy. Writing fiction requires seeing the world vividly through others' eyes. Even villains don't believe they're villains—rather, everybody is the hero of his or her own story. That doesn't necessarily mean finding the good in every character, but it means finding the stories that our characters, even the minor ones, tell themselves *about* themselves in order to get up in the morning and face the day as beleaguered and misunderstood heroes.

This intense act of empathy means that what you're doing when you write stories is important. No matter what your career is or ends up being—writer, zookeeper, accountant—you'll only benefit from imagining life from other people's perspectives and searching for the most precise language to describe what you see.

The main characters in the anthologized stories are plenty flawed: a drunken, gambling-addicted children's magician; a woman determined to cheat on her husband; a vicious book critic; an accessory to an amusement-park rampage. Just as real people are more than the items on their résumés, however, so too are the people in our stories—provided we try to understand them as thoroughly as we try to understand our mothers and fathers and siblings and romantic partners and children.

And if we can do that, then we might just be able to remind ourselves — and others — what it feels like to be human.

So pay attention, and get writing!

✳ exercises: draw on experience

1. Describe a time when you told somebody a lie. Include the details that explain why you felt the need to tell it.

2. What is the worst job you ever had? Describe in detail what made it so terrible.

3. Walk outside. What's the first thing you see that you don't expect? Describe it.

4. Draw a map of your childhood neighborhood, labeling every place you can remember. Where would the most interesting story take place?

5. What would you be convinced to do for $100 million, but not for $1 million?

6. If you were to put three meaningful — but interesting — possessions into a duffel bag, what would they be? (Avoid photographs, journals, and jewelry passed down from parents/grandparents.) What if you left this duffel bag on a train — what sense might someone make of this find?

7. The last time you called in sick from work when you were not actually sick, why did you do it? Describe what you did instead. If you can't remember, make it up.

8. What is the worst present you ever received? Describe it, and explain what made it awful.

9. If you could apologize to one person from your past, who would it be and why? Write the imagined meeting between you and that person.

the extreme importance of relevant detail

2

IMAGINE THIS SCENARIO: You were out late with friends until 2 a.m. Now you're tired, so you decide to skip class on the day a major project is due.

The next time you see your instructor, what will you say?

I couldn't make it to class because my car broke down.

A statement like that is sure to generate some eye-rolling from your instructor, who's heard it before. This is why you'll add a few embellishments:

"I was on my way to school when some idiot was texting and drifting into my lane, and when I swerved I ended up in that ditch with mud from all the rain. You know the ditch I'm talking about? At the intersection of University Boulevard and Court Street? Well, that's where I got stuck until campus police . . . the tall officer with the red hair—I don't know his name—he and I were able to push the car out. But by then, class was almost over, and I was too muddy to go anywhere anyway."

DETAILS AND BELIEVABILITY

When we lie, we know instinctively to supply details because the details lend credibility to our story. The red-headed officer serves as evidence in the case we're making.

Jill McCorkle's short story "Magic Words" (p. 262) depicts a character, Paula Blake, about to embark on an extramarital affair. Knowing that a believable alibi requires the right details, McCorkle's character has prepared them ahead of time.

> "Where are *you* going?" Erin asks, mouth sullen and sarcastic as it has been since her thirteenth birthday two years ago.

"Out with a friend," Paula says, forcing herself to make eye contact, the rest of the story she has practiced for days ready to roll. She's someone I work with, someone going through a really hard time, someone brand-new to the area, knows no one, really needs a friend.

But her daughter never looks up from the glossy magazine spread before her, engrossed in yet another drama about a teen star lost to drugs and wild nights. Her husband doesn't even ask her new friend's name or where she moved from, yet the answer is poised and waiting on her tongue. Tonya Matthews from Phoenix, Arizona.

Liars, cheaters, and con artists—the good ones, anyway—know the value of a well-chosen detail. So do fiction writers.

✳ exercise: write a letter & a diary entry

Write a one-page story, in the form of a letter, that explains to the recipient why the writer has quit something important (a job, school, a marriage). Then write a one-page diary entry that explains the *real* reason(s) that the writer actually quit.

DETAILS AND ENGAGING THE READER

On the first day of the semester, I explain to my Introduction to Fiction Writing class that if they are to learn just one thing about writing this semester, it should be this—and in large letters, I write on the board:

relevant detail

And I tell them that if they are to learn just two things this semester, the second thing should be this—and underneath the words "relevant detail," I write:

relevant detail

Finally, I tell them that if they are to learn just three things this semester . . . You get the idea.

I'm being humorous—or trying to be, anyway—but I'm not kidding. The ability to write with specificity—to write concrete, vivid, sensory details—is absolutely fundamental for the fiction writer. A simple reason is that writing is communication, and the more precise you are, the more clearly you communicate.

Example: I say "animal." You think "giraffe." I mean "dog." The communication has failed.

While "dog" is more specific than "animal," "golden retriever" is more specific than "dog." More specific still would be "golden retriever with a dry nose and a meek bark like it was asking for a raise it knew it didn't deserve." One could conceivably take things too far, though newer fiction writers usually provide too little detail, rather than too much.

Details do more, however, than provide clarity. They also engage the reader. In their classic guide *The Elements of Style*, William Strunk and E. B. White emphasize the importance of using concrete details:

> If those who have studied the art of writing are in accord on any one point, it is this: the surest way to arouse and hold the reader's attention is by being specific, definite, and concrete. The greatest writers—Homer, Dante, Shakespeare—are effective largely because they deal in particulars and report the details that matter.

Some beginning writers intentionally avoid specificity, believing that the use of concrete details would prevent their stories from having broad appeal. However, writing that avoids specificity tends to be vague or coy, and appealing to no one.

Only writing that dwells in the realm of the specific will "arouse and hold the reader's attention." *Moby Dick* might be a timeless novel with universal themes, but first it's a book about a particular ship captain obsessed with hunting down a particular sperm whale.

✳ exercises: recall details

1. Write down the name of a favorite novel or story. After the name, write down as many details from it as you can remember. (In "A & P," these details might include Queenie's dirty pink bathing suit or the can of Kingfish Fancy Herring Snacks that she is buying.) Why are these the details you recall?

2. Repeat this exercise with four more works.

SHOWING AND TELLING

Perhaps the most common advice given to creative writers is to "show" their story rather than "tell" it. This advice, while basically sound, can also be misleading. Doesn't all writing involve "telling"? Unless we include illustrations, we never actually show anything.

So what does it mean to "show," and why are writers so often urged to do it? Think of "showing" as writing the kinds of sentences that paint a picture for readers, causing the story to occur before their eyes. It's the kind of writing that results when you use concrete, relevant details.

Consider this sentence:

Curt broke his ankle playing baseball.

Although informative and concise, the sentence doesn't come alive in our minds. It summarizes, or "tells," a fact. Compare it with a sentence that describes in sensory detail exactly what happened:

Curt slid into second base underneath the shortstop's glove and came to a sudden, ankle-popping halt when his cleat hit the bag.

Unlike the first sentence, the second one paints a picture; it "shows" Curt breaking his ankle.

Which is the better sentence? It all depends. Despite the oft-given advice to "show, don't tell," the truth is that stories require both showing *and* telling—just examine any story in the anthology. An important skill to develop is learning when to show and when to tell, and how each type of writing contributes to the story. For instance, Percival Everett's story "The Appropriation of Cultures" (see p. 218) begins with a sentence that "tells":

Daniel Barkley had money left to him by his mother.

This sentence quickly provides the reader with necessary information, so there really is no reason to "show" it:

~~The estate attorney, seated at the end of the conference table, opened up his leather briefcase and handed Daniel Barkley a notarized copy of his mother's will . . .~~

Everett's story isn't about the *process* of being willed money. All the reader needs to know is that Daniel is living off his mother's inheritance—hence, the brief "telling" sentence of exposition.

Beginning fiction writers, however, tend to tell too much and show too little. Therefore, they need to develop and practice the techniques that writers use to show their stories unfolding. (That is why Chapter 5 is devoted entirely to scene-writing.)

Everett's story contains a scene in which Daniel, an African American man, goes to a white family's house to see about buying their truck. To write "Everyone watched Daniel warily as he arrived" would be to summarize—to "tell" rather than "show." While the statement might be accurate, the lack of details prevents us from seeing Daniel's arrival clearly in our minds.

Here is what Everett actually writes:

> A woman in a housecoat across the street watched from her porch, safe inside the chain-link fence around her yard. From down the street a man and a teenager, who were covered with grease and apparently engaged in work on a torn-apart Dodge Charger, mindlessly wiped their hands and studied him.

Rather than write a sentence that summarizes Daniel's arrival, Everett provides the raw sensory data that invites the reader to imagine the scene and arrive at his or her own conclusion.

In fact, a common mistake is to provide conclusions or explanations rather than the raw data itself. Compare these sentences that "tell" (which I've written) with the raw data that "shows," found in the actual works.

CONCLUSION	RAW DATA
Gatsby, a wealthy man, threw extravagant parties each weekend.	Every Friday five crates of oranges and lemons arrived from a fruiterer in New York—every Monday these same oranges and lemons left his back door in a pyramid of pulpless halves. There was a machine in the kitchen which could extract the juice of two hundred oranges in half an hour if a little button was pressed two hundred times by a butler's thumb.
	~ F. Scott Fitzgerald, *The Great Gatsby*

CONCLUSION	RAW DATA
Ever since the accident, Leroy and Norma Jean have been drifting apart—or rather Norma Jean has been drifting away from Leroy, spending less and less time at home.	Before his accident, when Leroy came home he used to stay in the house with Norma Jean, watching TV in bed and playing cards. She would cook fried chicken, picnic ham, chocolate pie—all his favorites. Now he is home alone much of the time. In the mornings, Norma Jean disappears, leaving a cooling place in the bed. She eats a cereal called Body Buddies, and she leaves the bowl on the table with the soggy tan balls floating in a milk puddle. ~ BOBBIE ANN MASON, "Shiloh"
The grandmother put a high premium on how people appeared; she therefore made sure always to dress with class, even on a car trip.	The children's mother still had on slacks and still had her hair tied up in a green kerchief, but the grandmother had on a navy blue dress with a small white dot in the print. Her collars and cuffs were white organdy trimmed with lace and at her neckline she had pinned a purple spray of cloth violets containing a sachet. In case of an accident, anyone seeing her dead on the highway would know at once that she was a lady. ~ FLANNERY O'CONNOR, "A Good Man Is Hard to Find"

In that last example, my "conclusion" *almost* reads like detail. The first half of the sentence makes a claim, and the second half of the sentence gives an example to support the claim. Still, the sentence is unnecessarily abstract, especially the phrase "with class." We can't visualize "class" (or what the grandmother considers "class"), but we *can* visualize a navy blue dress with a small white dot in the print and white organdy collars and cuffs trimmed with lace.

Don't take my word for it, though. Here are Flannery O'Connor's own words on the matter:

> The first and most obvious characteristic of fiction is that it deals with reality through what can be seen, heard, smelt, tasted, and touched.

✳ exercises: show with raw data

Now it's your turn. For each conclusion provided, write an alternative sentence (or paragraph) in which you provide the raw data that makes the conclusion unnecessary.

1. My sister was always the favorite child.

2. Edna's parents wasted their considerable fortune on frivolities that, in time, they would come to regret.

3. The train terminal looked as if it hadn't been open for years.

4. Jack threw the worst New Year's Eve parties.

FICTION WRITING AS TELEPATHY

Open any of the anthologized stories to just about any page, and you'll find examples of details that produce images in the reader's mind. In *Writing Fiction*, Stephen King refers to this image transfer, beginning with the writer and ending with the reader, as a form of telepathy.

> Look, here's a table covered with a red cloth. On it is a cage the size of a small fish aquarium. In the cage is a white rabbit with a pink nose and pink-rimmed eyes. In its front paws is a carrot-stub upon which it is contentedly munching. On its back, clearly marked in blue ink, is the numeral 8.
>
> Do we see the same thing? We'd have to get together and compare notes to make absolutely sure, but I think we do.

In his 2001 novel *Atonement*, Ian McEwan's precocious young character Briony marvels at the effect of fiction in these same terms:

> A story was a form of telepathy. By means of inking symbols onto a page, she was able to send thoughts and feelings from her mind to the reader's. It was a magical process, so commonplace that no one stopped to wonder at it.

Well, that's exactly what we're doing now. We're stopping to wonder at it.

tip: remember all five senses

Most of us tend to describe the world visually. But a story with only visual details will be a flatter fictional world than one that also includes smells, tastes, sounds, and tactile sensations. Here is Paula Blake observing her household's typical disarray in Jill McCorkle's story "Magic Words" on page 262:

> And now she looks around to see the table filled with cartons of Chinese food from last night and cereal boxes from the morning, and the television blares from the other room. Her son is anxious to get to his sleepover; her daughter has painted her toenails, and the fumes of the purple enamel fill the air. Her husband is studying a map showing the progression of killer bees up the coast. He speaks of them like hated relatives who are determined to drop in, whether you want them to or not. Their arrival is as inevitable as all the other predicted disasters that will wreak havoc on human life.

✳ exercise: describe an event

In a paragraph, describe an event at which many people are present, such as a parade or a sporting event. Appeal to at least three senses, and ideally to all five.

WHICH DETAILS TO INCLUDE?

If you were to walk outside for ten seconds, whether you were in a bustling city, a suburban street, or a pasture, your brain would absorb enough sensory detail for a thousand-page book. Every day contains an infinite amount of raw data. Although writing a story feels like an act of creation, in a sense you're always omitting far more than you could ever hope to include in the fictional world.

This is where the "relevant" part of "relevant detail" comes into play. What do you include?

Report what is newsworthy (the strange or unexpected)

Were I to describe a dog in a story, I wouldn't mention that it had four legs because four legs on a dog isn't news. What if it had three legs, however, or whipped up a decent soufflé? That I'd mention.

In Stephen King's example of telepathy, the numeral 8 marked in blue ink on the rabbit's back is strange and therefore newsworthy.

Sometimes newsworthiness is all about context. In John Updike's story "A & P" (p. 359), after some extremely detailed descriptions of three teenage girls in their bathing suits, Sammy explains what makes the girls' clothing newsworthy and therefore worth describing:

> You know, it's one thing to have a girl in a bathing suit down on the beach, where what with the glare nobody can look at each other much anyway, and another thing in the cool of the A & P, under the fluorescent lights, against all those stacked packages, with her feet paddling along naked over our checkerboard green-and-cream rubber-tile floor.

Report details that represent other details

Well-chosen details also tend to represent other unstated details. Karen Russell's story "St. Lucy's Home for Girls Raised by Wolves" (p. 324) chronicles a pack of girls, the children of werewolves, who are attending a boarding school at their parents' insistence in order to acquire the social skills they'll need to live among humans. Jeanette is progressing faster than the others, causing the pack to turn on her. Here is a detail that Claudette, the story's narrator, provides so that we'll understand just how much Jeanette has changed:

> She was the most successful of us, the one furthest removed from her origins. Her real name was GWARR! but she wouldn't respond to this anymore. Jeanette spiffed her penny loafers until her very shoes seemed to gloat.

Once we have that detail about the penny loafers, we really don't need much more. We understand exactly why the other girls have come to hate and fear her.

✳ exercises: choose relevant details

1. Go outside and, for fifteen minutes, quietly observe your surroundings, writing down everything you observe. Then circle the descriptions that (a) are unusual or surprising and (b) feel representative of other details.

2. Write a paragraph that captures the feel of the place, emphasizing and expanding on the details you circled.

NOTHING MORE THAN FEELINGS

Isn't that one of the main reasons why we read fiction—to feel something? The conveyance of feelings from writer to reader just might be the highest order of fiction. And this, too, comes down to the details.

Raymond Carver, one of the most influential short-story writers of the twentieth century, explains:

> It's possible, in a poem or short story, to write about commonplace things and objects using commonplace but precise language, and to endow those things—a chair, a window curtain, a fork, a stone, a woman's earring—with immense, even startling power.

There's a moment toward the end of *The Great Gatsby* that perfectly illustrates the emotional power of the well-chosen detail. The scene takes place after a car accident, when Tom and Daisy Buchanan are back at home and Gatsby is loitering outside, keeping vigil, convinced that he's protecting Daisy from a potentially violent husband. He still believes—or at least is holding out hope—that Daisy is going to leave Tom for him. Yet the scene, described by narrator Nick Carraway, gives a different impression:

> I walked back along the border of the lawn, traversed the gravel softly, and tiptoed up the veranda steps. The drawing-room curtains were open, and I saw that the room was empty. Crossing the porch where we had dined that June night three months before, I came to a small rectangle of light which I guessed was the pantry window. The blind was drawn, but I found a rift at the sill.
>
> Daisy and Tom were sitting opposite each other at the kitchen table, with a plate of cold fried chicken between them, and two bottles of ale.

He was talking intently across the table at her, and in his earnestness his hand had fallen upon and covered her own. Once in a while she looked up at him and nodded in agreement.

Witnessing this scene, we know better than Gatsby that this is no breakup, but rather a reconciliation. The moment is quiet, domestic, even cozy. Tom and Daisy have acted wildly irresponsibly, their behavior made possible because they are superrich, yet their reconciliation is understated and ordinary—at their kitchen table, picking at leftovers. In Nick's words:

> There was an unmistakable air of natural intimacy about the picture, and anybody would have said that they were conspiring together.

We know that Daisy and Tom will stay together because of those two bottles of ale and that plate of cold fried chicken. We contrast this simple snack to the orgiastic events that Gatsby has thrown all summer in an attempt to impress Daisy—and we can't help feeling sorry for Gatsby, whose efforts were all in vain and who is now maintaining his pointless vigil outside, still holding on to that last bit of hope, not yet allowing himself to see that his dream is over.

Two bottles of ale. A plate of cold fried chicken. And, if there was any doubt left, Tom's hand casually covering Daisy's as they talk. Those three details convey—show—everything a reader needs to know, and evoke everything a reader needs to feel.

✳ exercises: use details to convey emotion

1. a. Write a paragraph depicting a character leaving a place he loves. Don't mention his feelings toward the place or the other people there. Rather, let the details convey his emotions.

   b. Now write a paragraph depicting a character leaving a place that he can't stand. Again, don't mention his feelings toward the place or the other people there. Rather, let the details convey his emotions.

2. Write a brief scene in which two characters observe something together (for example, a couple eating in a restaurant, a police officer who has

pulled over a motorist). Narrate the scene from the perspective of the character who draws the *correct* conclusion from the observed details. Then have the other character, who has observed the same details, announce his or her *incorrect* conclusion to the narrator.

DETAILS AND THE WRITER'S SENSIBILITY

Writing details requires thinking in details—having trust, or faith, in the physical world's potential to carry meaning and emotion. So by all means, jump right into the details when writing a first draft. You'll need them, because the details will lead you to character development, to plot, to setting . . . to just about everything.

In Sherman Alexie's story "This Is What It Means to Say Phoenix, Arizona" (p. 185), the ashes of Victor's father are placed into two receptacles:

Victor's father, his ashes, fit in one wooden box with enough left over to fill a cardboard box.

This particularly unceremonious depiction is made more overtly comic by the line that follows:

"He always was a big man," Thomas said.

Despite the comedy, the detail of the two boxes of ashes later becomes important: When the young men arrive back home at the reservation, Victor tells Thomas to keep one of the boxes "that contained half of his father." Victor's offer (and Thomas's acceptance) cements their ties both to Victor's father and to each other and repairs, symbolically, some of the tribal ties that have been severed in their community.

This key moment in the story is made possible by the seemingly minor detail of there being two boxes of ashes.

Not only do details help you to express your story, but they also help to define what it is you're trying to express. So as you write, be as specific as you can, and remember that details aren't an adornment to your story. They *are* your story.

✳ exercises: use details to tell stories

1. Describe in detail a character performing an activity that you know about but that most people don't (for example, throwing out a runner at home plate, playing "Stars and Stripes Forever" on the piccolo, repairing a lawn mower).

2. Make a list of thirty facts about yourself: physical attributes, hobbies and interests, specific fears, family history, or anything else. Stay away from any abstract words. (No writing "I'm honest," for instance, or "I'm a good friend.") When you are done, circle the five facts that, if you were a character in a story, would be most useful in giving the reader a clear sense of that character.

3. Find four unusual objects in your home. Make all four objects "relevant details" in the same story.

4. Describe an ordinary object (a telephone, a lamp) from the perspective of a character who has never come across it before.

5. Describe a familiar place from the perspective of a character who has just arrived there for the first time.

6. Find a photograph of someone in your family and write a detailed physical description, based on the photo, that evokes a sense of the person you're describing.

3 starting your story

THERE'S AN OLD Head & Shoulders shampoo ad campaign with the tagline "You never get a second chance to make a first impression."

And what's true for shampoo is generally true for fiction.

The beginning of a story presents a world of possibilities for a writer, and each beginning will make a different first impression. The first sentence matters because a story has exactly one of them. The same is true about a first paragraph and a first scene.

WHAT BEGINNINGS DO

Beyond making a favorable first impression on the reader, the beginning of a story typically needs to complete certain narrative tasks. Before long, a story must

- Introduce the characters and the relationships among them
- Present the underlying situation and the beginning of conflict
- Establish the tone, voice, and point of view (its storytelling approach)
- Establish the setting
- Give us a reason to keep reading

This might sound like a lot—and it is—but it needn't be overly complicated. Consider fairy tales. The Brothers Grimm began many of their fairy tales by conveying just this sort of information:

> Once upon a time, in a large forest, close to a village, stood the cottage where the Teddy Bear family lived. They were not really proper Teddy Bears, for

> Father Bear was very big, Mother Bear was middling in size, and only Baby Bear could be described as a Teddy Bear.

Right away, we're told the story's setting—its time (the past, when magical things happened) and place (the cottage, the village, the forest). We're introduced to the Bear family, their relationships, and their key characteristics. We're also introduced to the storytelling approach—it is being told to us by an all-knowing third-person narrator, in a fairly formal storytelling voice.

Here's another one:

> Next to a great forest there lived a poor woodcutter with his wife and his two children. The boy's name was Hansel and the girl's name was Gretel. He had but little to eat, and once, when a great famine came to the land, he could no longer provide even their daily bread.

As with "Goldilocks and the Three Bears," the beginning of "Hansel and Gretel" lays out its setting as well as its principal characters and their relationships to one another. It also immediately reveals the family's predicament: A famine has made this already poor family desperate for food.

Notice the similarities between the storytelling approach taken by the Brothers Grimm and Kevin Brockmeier in his 2008 story "A Fable with Slips of White Paper Spilling from the Pockets" (p. 211):

> Once there was a man who happened to buy God's overcoat. He was rummaging through a thrift store when he found it hanging on a rack by the fire exit, nestled between a birch-colored fisherman's sweater and a cotton blazer with a suede patch on one of the elbows.

Here, too, we're introduced immediately to the main character (the man), the story's initial setting (a thrift store), and its time ("once"—like the Grimm fairy tale, some unspecified time in the past). The narrative voice is somewhat less formal than in the Grimm tale. The phrase "who happened to buy" sounds casual, and even a little comic in the way it downplays what a reader would assume is an extraordinary event. We also get a sense of the story's underlying *situation* and its *conflict*. A man has bought God's overcoat. Surely this fact must lead to something.

Brockmeier's beginning illustrates one other thing that story openings do:

▸ The beginning of a story gives the reader a sense of what *kind* of story the story is going to be. It lays out the rules of the game.

When I was growing up, most board games printed their rules on the inside of the box. Nowadays, board games usually come with instruction manuals. In any event, when you buy a new game, first you learn the rules and then you play the game.

Stories don't work that way. Stories—all stories—have "rules," but the rules get revealed *as* the game is being played. As we read the beginning of a story, we come to understand the story's rules—what sort of things are permissible in the story's world, and what aren't. We also start to determine such things as whether the story will be sincere, or ironic, or comic, or somber, and whether the prose will be lyrical or workmanlike.

This laying out of a story's own rules is sometimes referred to as a "contract"— that this, the story establishes a contract with its readers. A highly realistic story in which, on page 10, the mother ship lands and beams all the characters aboard would be said to be *violating the story's contract.*

From Brockmeier's first two sentences, we anticipate a story that in terms of content and tone will resemble a fable or fairy tale ("Once there was a man . . ."), but one that also is rooted in the real, modern-day world of thrift stores with fire exits. A story like Brockmeier's includes highly realistic characters and also fantastical elements, such as God's overcoat, without violating the contract or breaking the rules, whichever phrase you prefer.

REVEAL KEY INFORMATION (SPILL THE BEANS)

The opening sentence of "A Fable with Slips of White Paper Spilling from the Pockets" is a wonderful example of the following maxim: *It's a good idea to reveal key information, especially hard-to-swallow information, as soon as possible.*

By telling us immediately that this is "God's overcoat," we, the readers, aren't allowed to argue the point. We can't say, "No, it isn't." Because it is. We're told it is and must accept that fact as part of the story's premise.

Perhaps the best example of front-loading hard-to-swallow information is the first sentence of Franz Kafka's 1915 novella *The Metamorphosis*:

> Gregor Samsa awoke one morning from unsettled dreams to find that he had turned into a giant cockroach.

When we begin reading Kafka's novella, we don't think: "No, Gregor didn't. People can't turn into cockroaches." Of course we don't. Rather, we accept the situation as presented and keep reading. Why? Because we're told about it up front. The author is making a first impression that says, "My story features a man-cockroach. Deal with it."

So one answer to the question "How do I begin?" is to begin with whatever information the reader needs most in order to appreciate—or simply believe—your story.

The corresponding advice is that you shouldn't withhold vital information as a secret until the end of your story. Sometimes new writers like to "surprise" the reader at the end with shocking facts. The two characters are really a single character with multiple personalities! The whole story was actually just a dream! These sort of "surprises" (I put the word in quotation marks because they rarely surprise) will disappoint all but the most naïve reader.

Rather than mislead or trick the reader, give us the important information up front. Make us care, and go from there.

✳ exercise: inform & convince

Go online and find a weird news story, something that is factually true but doesn't seem plausible. (You can even Google "weird news.") Then write the first paragraph of a short story, based on the news piece, that readers must believe.

Even stories that do not feature heavenly outerwear or giant, sentient insects often front-load information that the reader needs in order to appreciate and care about what happens. Here is how Sherman Alexie begins his story "This Is What It Means to Say Phoenix, Arizona" (p. 185):

> Just after Victor lost his job at the BIA, he also found out that his father had died of a heart attack in Phoenix, Arizona. Victor hadn't seen his father

in a few years, only talked to him on the telephone once or twice, but there still was a genetic pain, which was soon to be pain as real and immediate as a broken bone.

    Victor didn't have any money. Who does have money on a reservation, except the cigarette and fireworks salespeople? His father had a savings account waiting to be claimed, but Victor needed to find a way to get to Phoenix. Victor's mother was just as poor as he was, and the rest of his family didn't have any use at all for him. So Victor called the Tribal Council.

Notice how this opening quickly establishes its characters, setting, and tone. But beyond that, it gives us the story's underlying *situation* (Victor must deal with the practicalities of the death of his father, with whom he didn't have a close relationship, a problem compounded by his lack of funds to get to Phoenix). Finally, this paragraph ends with the promise of immediate *conflict*, specifically an uncomfortable meeting between Victor and the Tribal Council. Surely the council won't simply agree to give Victor all the money he needs. That would be too easy.

    Notice, too, that in revealing certain information, Alexie arouses our curiosity. We know that Victor hasn't seen his father in a few years, but we know nothing of the nature of their rift. We know that Victor's family "didn't have any use at all for him," but we don't know why that is. By providing us with information, Alexie causes us to ask questions about the story that we hope will be answered before long.

    The opening to Richard Bausch's story "The Man Who Knew Belle Starr" looks, at first, like a relatively straightforward paragraph of exposition in which basic information about McRae's situation is revealed. Yet the story withholds just enough information to create little mysteries that make us want to keep reading:

> On his way west McRae picked up a hitcher,[1] a young woman carrying a paper bag[2] and a leather purse, wearing jeans and a shawl—which she didn't take off, though it was more than ninety degrees out and McRae had no air-conditioning.[3] He was driving an old Dodge Charger with a bad exhaust system and one long crack in the wraparound windshield. He pulled over for her, and she got right in, put the leather purse on the seat between them, and settled herself with a paper bag on her lap between her hands.[4] He had just crossed into Texas from Oklahoma. This was the third day of the trip.

This opening raises a number of questions:

[1] Why is McRae heading west? And why does he pick up the hitch-hiker?

[2] What is in the bag?

[3] Why won't she take off her shawl?

[4] Seriously, what's in the paper bag? It's been mentioned twice already. She sure is protective of it. Must be important.

✳ exercise: spark curiosity

Write the opening paragraph or two of a story. Reveal necessary information about your character and his or her situation — but in doing so, see if you can plant little mysteries the way that Bausch does in "The Man Who Knew Belle Starr." If you don't already have a story in mind, here's a prompt: A character arrives at work convinced that he or she is about to be fired.

ESTABLISH THE STORY'S STAKES

Readers need a reason to keep reading. They need to see fairly quickly why what they're reading matters. A story's stakes are what make a story matter to the story's characters and to the reader.

"This Is What It Means to Say Phoenix, Arizona" immediately provides reasons to care about Victor and to understand why he wants what he wants. The story matters to us because it matters to Victor, and because we sense that Victor's quest will not be an easy one. I'm not just referring to his lack of money. I mean that already, in the story's first paragraphs, we see Victor's ambivalence. On the one hand, he and his father weren't close. That should make the man's death a little easier on Victor. On the other hand, Victor feels "a genetic pain, which was soon to be pain as real and immediate as a broken bone." Before the end of the story, Victor will have to deal with his conflicting feelings about his father — and that internal voyage is what pulls us into the story at least as much as the prospect of his trip to Phoenix.

checklist » set the stakes

» What does your main character have to gain or lose in your story? What is at stake for him or her?

» How can you introduce the stakes early in your story?

Tim O'Brien takes a different approach toward presenting the stakes at the beginning of his story "On the Rainy River" (p. 287)—a direct appeal to the reader:

> This is one story I've never told before.

Quite simply, this sentence appeals to our desire to know somebody else's intimate secrets. After reading that sentence, we naturally want to know (1) the story that's been kept secret and (2) why it's been kept secret.

But the paragraph doesn't end there. The stakes get raised:

> Not to anyone. Not to my parents, not to my brother or sister, not even to my wife. To go into it, I've always thought, would only cause embarrassment for all of us, a sudden need to be elsewhere, which is the natural response to a confession.

So the narrator isn't simply revealing a long-held secret—he's making a confession. Confessions, as we know, tend to be juicy and worth sticking around for. The paragraph continues:

> Even now, I'll admit, the story makes me squirm. For more than twenty years I've had to live with it, feeling the shame, trying to push it away, and so by this act of remembrance, by putting the facts down on paper, I'm hoping to relieve at least some of the pressure on my dreams.

Considering that he's kept the story from his wife and family for twenty years, we can assume that this is no run-of-the-mill, I-forgot-to-take-out-the-trash confession. This narrator seems thoughtful and honest, and he has a secret that has been weighing heavily on him for *twenty years*. Now, finally, he's going to come clean and reveal his secret in the hopes of unburdening himself.

That's something we'll stick around to hear.

✻ exercise: confess

> Your main character has something to confess. What is it? Write out the
> confession in his or her voice. Even if your story doesn't end up including
> the confession, you will have learned something important—and almost
> certainly useful—about your character's inner life.

START WITH A BREAK FROM ROUTINE

Imagine a story that begins like this:

> When the alarm clock went off at 6:30 a.m., Phil hit the snooze button.
> Nine minutes later, same as every weekday morning, he hit it again. Finally
> he arose from his bed and went into the bathroom to brush his teeth. He
> took a long, hot shower, got dressed in his suit and tie, and went down-
> stairs to brew a pot of his favorite coffee—hazelnut. He sat at the kitchen
> table and looked out the window. The sun was just coming up. A neigh-
> borhood kid rode his bike past the house, a stack of newspapers under his
> arm. Phil didn't receive a paper. He read all his news online. After drain-
> ing two cups of coffee, Phil put on his shoes and left the house. He arrived
> at the office eleven minutes later, same as always. He said hello to his co-
> workers and went into his office, where he began to check his email. Phil
> was an insurance broker, and he received dozens of emails a day—most,
> it seemed, from angry clients. When he looked up from his computer, his
> colleague, Sean, was standing in the doorway wearing a giraffe suit.

QUESTION: Where does this story actually begin?
CLUE: Where does Phil's story diverge from his ordinary routine?

Phil's story does not begin with the alarm clock going off. Beginning writers often confuse the beginning of a character's *day* with the beginning of a
character's *story*. They are not the same.

In the sample story opening above, Phil's morning routine is just that—
routine. It isn't news. Part of the problem is that nothing particularly distinguishes Phil's morning from that of millions of other hardworking citizens. The
bigger problem, though, is that it isn't even unusual for *him*. He awakes, he
showers, he drinks coffee, he drives to work. Does it matter that he prefers

hazelnut-flavored coffee to a basic French roast? Probably not. (If it does, we can certainly work that detail into the story later.)

Just as it's a mistake to begin this story in bed with the alarm clock going off, it would be a mistake to start it with Phil's drive to work. The drive, like the hot shower and cup of coffee, is just a preface to what really matters.

The giraffe suit? Now that's news:

> One Thursday morning, Phil looked up from his computer terminal to find his colleague, Sean, standing in the doorway wearing a giraffe suit.

Or:

> "So what do you think?" asked Sean, standing in the doorway of Phil's office dressed in a giraffe suit. Like Phil, Sean was an insurance broker. The office had a strict dress code: suit, tie. No facial hair.
> "What do I think about what?" Phil asked.

Or:

> Yesterday it was a gorilla suit. The day before, an elephant. Sean's wife had left him over the weekend, and now all week he'd been coming to the office dressed as one large mammal or another. Phil, who had always considered Sean to be one of the more boring brokers at Midwest Insurance, couldn't decide if he was more amused or annoyed. He had dozens of emails to return and calls to make. Time was money. Still, it was always interesting to see a fellow human being crack open like an egg.

The story possibilities, and the ways of telling them, are endless. But they all begin after Phil's morning routine is over, at the moment when his routine gets disrupted.

Stories, with few exceptions, are about *the day that's different*—the day that a man happens to buy God's overcoat. The day that Victor loses his job, learns about his father's death, and decides he must travel to Phoenix, Arizona. They are about the disruption from one's ordinary routine. A wise place to begin, therefore, is at the moment when this disruption first announces itself. (In *The Metamorphosis*, this difference actually does announce itself in Gregor's bed, because that's when he realizes that he has turned into a giant cockroach. In that one example, the beginning of a character's day happens to coincide with the beginning of his story. But Gregor's morning, we can safely assume, will be far from routine.)

Karen Russell's story "St. Lucy's Home for Girls Raised by Wolves" (p. 324) and ZZ Packer's story "Drinking Coffee Elsewhere" (p. 303) both take place over a large portion of a school year. Note that neither story begins at home, or on the long car ride to the academy. Instead, they both begin at their respective institutions during that first moment that reveals how uprooted the characters feel. In "Drinking Coffee Elsewhere," freshman orientation is a disorienting experience for Dina that immediately arouses her suspicion:

> Orientation games began the day I arrived at Yale from Baltimore. In my group we played heady, frustrating games for smart people. One game appeared to be charades reinterpreted by existentialists; another involved listening to rocks. Then a freshman counsellor made everyone play Trust. The idea was that if you had the faith to fall backward and wait for four scrawny former high-school geniuses to catch you, just before your head cracked on the slate sidewalk, then you might learn to trust your fellow-students. Russian roulette sounded like a better way to go.
> "No way," I said. The white boys were waiting for me to fall, holding their arms out for me, sincerely, gallantly. "No fucking way."

The opening paragraph of "St. Lucy's Home for Girls Raised by Wolves" reveals just how out-of-place the girls are upon arriving at their new school. It reveals, too, how at first the narrator considers herself one of a pack. There is no "I" perspective, but rather a "we," something that will begin to shift later in the story as the narrator, Claudette, develops her own identity apart from the pack:

> At first, our pack was all hair and snarl and floor-thumping joy. We forgot the barked cautions of our mothers and fathers, all the promises we'd made to be civilized and ladylike, couth and kempt. We tore through the austere rooms, overturning dresser drawers, pawing through the neat piles of the Stage 3 girls' starched underwear, smashing light bulbs with our bare fists. Things felt less foreign in the dark. The dim bedroom was windowless and odorless. We remedied this by spraying exuberant yellow streams all over the bunks. We jumped from bunk to bunk, spraying. We nosed each other midair, our bodies buckling in kinetic laughter. The nuns watched us from the corner of the bedroom, their tiny faces pinched with displeasure.

The place you start your story has a lot to do with what your story is ultimately about. Karen Russell could have started her story the day that Claudette first learns that there will be a dance with the boys' school—when Claudette first understands that her socialization will be put to the test. Or it could have begun even later, at the dance itself. Instead, Russell begins when the girls first arrive at their school. The story therefore covers months instead of days or hours, making it less about a single event and more about the steady erosion of Claudette's ties to her roots—her pack—as she becomes indoctrinated into "civilized" society.

Unlike Russell's story, which covers months, John Updike's story "A & P" (p. 359) begins just minutes before it ends. Maybe Updike could have begun it earlier, when Sammy first started working at the grocery store. In that version, we might see more of Sammy's transition from child to adult and might better understand how Lengel's words to Queenie were the latest in a series of uncaring actions committed by Sammy's boss, how they were the straw that broke the camel's back and led to Sammy's quitting his job.

But that isn't the story that Updike wrote. "A & P" narrates just a few minutes in the grocery story on a Thursday afternoon. It begins when the three girls enter the store and ends moments after they buy their herring snack and leave. Beginning so close to the end, the story emphasizes Sammy's sudden, nearly inexpressible flash of insight about adulthood conveyed in the story's final phrase: "and my stomach kind of fell as I felt how hard the world was going to be to me hereafter."

✳ exercise: choose the day that's different

Jot down the major events in your main character's life. Where does your main character "break from routine" for the specific story that you want to tell? Write that opening sentence, paragraph, and page.

CONSIDER STARTING *IN MEDIAS RES*

Brockmeier's and Alexie's stories both begin with the narrator providing necessary information to the reader using exposition. This is what the third example of the giraffe-suit story does, as well:

Yesterday it was a gorilla suit. The day before, an elephant. Sean's wife had left him over the weekend, and now all week he'd been coming to the office dressed as one large mammal or another.

However, a story that begins *in medias res*, a Latin phrase meaning "into the middle of things," drops us—well, into the middle of things. Here are a few stories that do just that from the first sentence:

He had been reading to her from Rilke, a poet he admired, when she fell asleep with her head on his pillow.

> ~ Raymond Carver, "The Student's Wife"

I read about it in the paper, in the subway, on my way to work.

> ~ James Baldwin, "Sonny's Blues"

I was popular in certain circles, says Aunt Rose.

> ~ Grace Paley, "Goodbye and Good Luck"

In walks these three girls in nothing but bathing suits.

> ~ John Updike, "A & P"

Look back at the first paragraph of "St. Lucy's Home for Girls Raised by Wolves." Even though that story begins at the start of the school year, Karen Russell's story begins *in medias res*, dropping us into the middle of the action. Who are the "Stage 3 girls"? What are the nuns doing there? And what, exactly, is this "pack" being referred to? These questions will all get sorted out—but not right away.

The practice of beginning a story *in medias res* isn't new: Homer did it in both the *Iliad* and the *Odyssey*. More recently, so did George Lucas in the original *Star Wars* movie—which, we're told right away, is "episode four" and therefore truly the middle of things. *Star Wars* begins with a thrilling battle scene before we have any clue who is fighting or what the battle is about. Because we haven't yet been introduced to the characters and situation, a story that begins *in medias res* often causes momentary confusion. Yet it has the benefit of urgency and, done well, can generate in the reader an oddly satisfying sensation of not quite keeping up with the story. Most action/adventure films begin *in medias res* because of a need to hook the viewer with something immediately thrilling. *Raiders of the Lost Ark* begins with Indiana Jones skillfully evading a booby-trapped cave, then stealing a huge jewel, then running like mad when a giant boulder threatens to crush him. At this point, we don't know anything about the characters or the plot, but we're intrigued because the events themselves are so gripping.

A story that begins *in medias res* eventually will need to supply the missing pieces. A reader (or viewer) will be willing to remain confused for only so long before becoming frustrated. The second scene in *Raiders of the Lost Ark* features Indiana Jones back on safer ground, at the university where he teaches anthropology. In this second scene, we learn all the necessary information that would have been supplied up front in a "once upon a time" opening.

Becky Hagenston begins her story "Midnight, Licorice, Shadow" (p. 227) *in medias res*. A "once upon a time" beginning might read:

> Donna and Jeremy, her boyfriend of three weeks, were trying to name their new cat. The cat used to belong to a woman they'd robbed and killed. Now it was theirs. They were holed up in a motel room now, and Donna was feeling an increased urgency to name the cat. That was because Jeremy had said, "If we don't have a name by tomorrow morning, it's bye-bye, Mister Kitty." He didn't like when something didn't have a name. He felt it was bad luck.

Instead, Hagenston drops us into the middle of things:

> "Midnight, Licorice, Shadow," she says. "Cocoa, Casper, Dr. Livingston."
> "Alfred Hitchcock," he says. "Dracula. Vincent Price."
> They have had the cat for nearly three days.
> "Cinderblock?" she tries. "Ice bucket?"
> It's useless. The harder they try to think of a name, the more elusive it becomes.
> "Tomorrow, then," Jeremy says. "If we don't have a name by tomorrow morning, it's bye-bye, Mr. Kitty. No offense, Cupcake," he tells the cat, and gives it a quick rub on the head.
> Donna looks at the animal, sprawled on the orange motel carpet like a black bearskin rug. One of his fangs is showing. His monkey paws are kneading at the air.

We don't learn for seven paragraphs that they're in a motel room, and we won't learn for several pages about the murder, or about Jeremy's superstition about things not having names. The story as Hagenston begins it emphasizes the oppressiveness of the relationship between Donna and Jeremy, and the urgency they feel, especially Donna. She's desperate to name that cat. Why? we wonder, and we keep reading to find out.

✳ exercise: start at the beginning — or middle

Write the first page of a story with a "once upon a time" opening, and then write the first page of the same story beginning *in medias res*. If you need a prompt, write about the time when you got into the most trouble as a child (over age ten). To help fictionalize the story, write it in the third person and change all names.

WHOSE PERSPECTIVE SHOULD YOU CHOOSE?

Knowing what you want to write about isn't the same as knowing whose perspective to tell it from. Your choice will inform just about every other aspect of your story, just as your version of the first day of school is no doubt different from your teacher's.

checklist » decide on a perspective

Chapter 4 provides an in-depth discussion of point of view; for now, here are some things to consider:

» Who has the most at stake? The most to gain or lose? Whoever is most heavily invested in the outcome of your story might well be the natural character to designate as your point-of-view character.

» On the other hand, some characters don't make especially good narrators, such as very young children and those with extremely limited perspectives or communication skills. A point-of-view character who is (1) delusional, (2) drunk, or (3) a dog presents challenges that are extremely hard to overcome. In the novel *The Great Gatsby*, Gatsby doesn't tell his own story. He is no slouch, but he can't tell his own story because he would have neither the words nor the perspective. (Plus, by the end of the novel he's dead.) Nick Carraway tells Gatsby's story because Nick possesses the narrative and interpretive skills that Gatsby lacks, as well as the capacity to change.

» Is your story less about a single character than about several people or a community? If so, then your story might best be told from several characters' perspectives, as in Jill McCorkle's story "Magic Words" (p. 262).

OTHER INFORMATION TO CONVEY SOONER RATHER THAN LATER

Early on in your story—probably within the first page or two—it's usually a good idea to provide some basic information about the characters.

checklist » establish the basics

» **Your main character's name.** Yes, some stories never name their characters, using "he" or "she" or "the man" or "the woman" throughout. Ernest Hemingway's story "Hills Like White Elephants" is a commonly cited example. However, the decision not to name your character should be just that—a decision—rather than an oversight. (The main character in Kevin Brockmeier's story "A Fable with Slips of White Paper Spilling from the Pockets" (p. 211) goes unnamed. Why do you think that is?) In general, readers like to know the names of the characters in a story, and not naming them will not make them more universal. (See "Details and Engaging the Reader" in Chapter 2.)

» **Your main character's sex.** It can be very disorienting for a reader to assume that a story's main character is female and then, on page 9, to learn that he is male.

» **The basic relationships between characters.** A story that begins

Bill kissed Brittany on the cheek and went off with Sonya to get married.

is confusing because we don't yet know Brittany's relationship to Bill or Sonya. Instead, consider something like:

> Bill kissed Brittany, his youngest sister, on the cheek and went off with Sonya to get married.

Or:

> Bill kissed Brittany, his girlfriend of eleven years, on the cheek and went off with Sonya to get married.

These are two entirely different stories. Readers deserve to know which it is so that we will create the proper picture in our minds.

ULTIMATELY, IT'S YOUR CALL

When does your character's routine get interrupted? What are your story's stakes? What key information needs to be revealed? What are the benefits of beginning either "once upon a time" or *in medias res*? Once you've given these matters some thought, you'll be well on your way to making a strong — and strongly favorable — first impression.

Whenever you work on a new story, bear in mind that the beginning might well change. As you write, your understanding of your own story grows, and that requires a rethinking of the beginning. You might change the point of view or change the tense from present to past. You might change the voice, making it more formal or less formal. Sometimes, the beginning — the first page or section — will end up staying in place all the way through to the final draft. But maybe not. You might end up using the first attempt elsewhere in the story, or maybe it will need to get cut completely once you realize that a different beginning would be better. Always, though, you'll learn something about your story from that first attempt — so the effort isn't ever wasted.

The good news about fiction writing is that you can unmake or revisit your decisions as you continue to work. Nothing is irreversible. Remember: We aren't performing surgery. We aren't defusing bombs. If we make a misstep, nobody is going to die. In fact, we *will* make missteps, guaranteed. Most of the time, they aren't actually missteps. They're necessary steps — that is, necessary parts of a creative process.

So start your story already!

✳ exercises: try a variety of openers

1. As with so many other aspects of fiction writing, our best teachers are the stories and novels we read. Seeing how other authors begin their stories, we learn to see what works and why. Read the first page (or section) of every story in the anthology. Which is your favorite? Why? Now try to write an opening of your own based on the opening that you liked (using all of your own story's content, of course).

2. Write ten different first sentences for your story-in-progress. Make them truly different from one another. Start one with dialogue, another with a character's interior thought, another with an emphasis on setting. Only after writing all ten sentences should you read them over and start to decide which you like best, and why.

3. Write the same story opening in vastly different styles. For example:

   a. Begin with a one-sentence paragraph of at least 150 words.

   b. Write the same basic paragraph using sentences of no more than 5 words each.

   c. Begin with a moderately long sentence (20–30 words); follow it with a short one (7 words or fewer), then a long one, then a short one.

   d. Begin the same story with highly formal language. (But play it straight. No satire.)

   e. Begin the same story with casual, vernacular language.

4. Begin with a claim about the world that is germane to your story—for example, "There are two kinds of drivers" or "Dogs should never, ever be let off leash." Then continue the paragraph.

5. Begin your story with a detailed description of an image—something in the physical world—that will be central to your story.

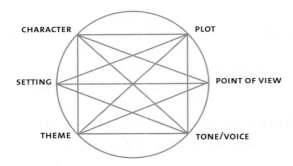

CHARACTER. PLOT. Setting. Point of view. Voice. Theme.

No book about fiction would be complete without a discussion of these fundamental concepts. Yet the reason that this book isn't organized around the elements of fiction is that nobody, as far as I know, writes fiction element by element: first character, then plot, then point of view. Or first plot, then setting, then character. Or any other order. That's because there *is* no plot without character, just as there's no setting without point of view. The elements of fiction are interdependent, even inseparable. Henry James argued this point as far back as 1884 when he wrote:

> A novel is a living thing, all one and continuous, like any other organism, and in proportion as it lives will it be found, I think, that in each of the parts there is something of each of the other parts.

To see this concept in action, try the following exercise from John Gardner's book *The Art of Fiction* (1983):

> Describe a landscape as seen by an old woman whose disgusting and detestable old husband has just died. Do not mention the husband or death.

At first glance, this might appear to be an exercise about setting. But the exercise also shows how description is colored by the consciousness of whoever is doing the describing: in other words, character and point of view. It also tests our ability to establish tone, and introduce themes, and maybe even lay the groundwork for plot.

Gardner's exercise makes us see that when we write one element of fiction, we're pretty much writing them all.

As you read this chapter, remember that no element stands alone. Henry James will be glad that you did.

CHARACTER

Unless you're doing something highly experimental, your story will have people in it. The most important person is referred to as the "main character" or "protagonist" or sometimes the "focal character." The process of establishing the people in your story is called "characterization." Here are the primary methods that writers go about it.

1. Appearance. We learn about characters from what they look like, what they wear, and what the characters themselves make of their own appearance, as in this description of Sanjeev, the focal character in Jhumpa Lahiri's story "This Blessed House" (p. 244):

> In the mirror of the medicine cabinet he inspected his long eyelashes — like a girl's, Twinkle liked to tease. Though he was of average build, his cheeks had a plumpness to them; this, along with the eyelashes, detracted, he feared, from what he hoped was a distinguished profile. He was of average height as well, and had wished ever since he had stopped growing that he were just one inch taller. For this reason it irritated him when Twinkle insisted on wearing high heels, as she had done the other night when they ate dinner in Manhattan.

Notice how this description does more than merely describe Sanjeev's physical appearance so that we can imagine what he looks like; from his outer appearance, we also learn about his inner life: He feels diminished by his wife, Twinkle.

2. Accessories. A wealthy, high-powered lawyer who drives a brand-new Porsche is a different character from one who drives a Honda Civic with 200,000 miles on it. A character who carries a photograph of his new girlfriend in his wallet is different from one who carries a picture of his ex-girlfriend who dumped him years earlier. Objects in stories have meaning, and by detailing a character's objects, you give the reader insight into the character.

3. What a character says (and how he says it).

> "Would you please pass the ketchup?"
> "Pass the damn ketchup. Now."

Two different personalities? You bet.

4. What a character does (and how he does it). Actions speak louder than words, no? The character who demands ketchup seems rude until you compare him to the character who climbs across the table, knocking plates and glasses out of his way, to reach the bottle himself.

The man who proposes to his girlfriend in a quiet park is different from the man who proposes by way of the JumboTron during the Super Bowl.

5. Personal history (backstory). Our pasts influence us. The same is true for fictional characters. In "This Blessed House," Sanjeev is confused by his feelings of irritation toward his wife, given the attributes he's been raised to value in a potential spouse:

> Now he had one, a pretty one, from a suitably high caste, who would soon have a master's degree. What was there not to love?

It's helpful when writing fiction to remember the incredibly complex relationship between past and present in real life. "B" doesn't always follow "A" when we're talking about human beings. The child of an abusive parent might grow up to become an abuser herself, or she might campaign against child abuse. She might distance herself from her past and try not to think about it, or maybe she'll become an animal person in order to avoid forming deep human connections.

In life and in fiction, our pasts influence who we are, but not in any predictable way. It all depends on the character.

6. What others say about—or to—a character. For most of Harper Lee's 1960 novel *To Kill a Mockingbird*, Scout Finch—the narrator and young protagonist—has nothing but bad things to say about her neighbor Mrs. Dubose. "Mrs. Dubose was plain hell," she claims early on. And later: "The neighborhood opinion was unanimous that Mrs. Dubose was the meanest old woman who ever lived."

The novel gives plenty of examples to back up Scout's impression. Yet after Mrs. Dubose dies, Scout's father, Atticus, claims, "She was the bravest person I ever knew."

It's a surprising pronouncement. Yet we've come to view Atticus Finch as the book's moral center, and certainly the most mature character. So when Atticus makes his character assessment of Mrs. Dubose, we, like Scout, have no choice but to reconsider our impression of her.

7. What a character thinks. Imagine Thanksgiving dinner: the extended family—three generations—seated at the dining room table, the smell of cider warming on the kitchen stove. Outside there are snow flurries, but inside is warm and cozy.

One character looks around the table and thinks:

I've waited all my life for this.

Another chews on a forkful of turkey and thinks:

I've got to get away from here.

When you reveal a character's thoughts, you reveal the character. (See "Interiority" in Chapter 5 for more about writing characters' thoughts.)

8. What the story's narrator tells us. In "This Blessed House," we're given the following information about Sanjeev:

After graduating, he moved from Boston to Connecticut, to work for a firm near Hartford, and he had recently learned that he was being considered for the position of vice president. At thirty-three he had a secretary of his own and a dozen people working under his supervision who gladly supplied him with any information he needed.

Exposition, even coming from a third-person narrator, is rarely objective. It not only relays information but also reveals somebody's feelings about the information being relayed. (See "Point of View" later in this chapter.) Sanjeev has a secretary "of his own." His subordinates "gladly" supply him with information. The depiction, in conveying facts about Sanjeev's professional life, also communicates the man's pride in his own accomplishments.

---

tip: make your characters believable

- For believability, give your likable characters flaws and your unlikable characters redeeming qualities. A character who seems perfect in every way will come across as *too* perfect to the reader and, ironically, imperfect — unrealistic, boring, or just plain annoying. And a relentlessly villainous villain will seem cartoonish and less than believable.

- For believability and complexity, give your characters some opposing or surprising traits. Maybe your fisherman is allergic to seafood. Your panhandler has the name of Francis Alexander III. Your ballet dancer's happiest memory is the winter when her leg was broken and she couldn't dance.

The challenge of characterization

As you go about developing your characters, remember that the purpose — and the challenge — of characterization is to create fictional people who seem as flesh-and-blood as the people we know in our real lives. This is no easy task, because what makes people flesh-and-blood, above all else, is that they *can't ever* be reduced to a set of characteristics. People, no matter how much we know about them, are mysterious, unpredictable, surprising creatures. To imply less in fiction is to discount the complexity of being human. In his essay "The Magic Show," Tim O'Brien writes:

> Characterization is achieved not through a "pinning down" process but rather through a process that opens up and releases mysteries of the human spirit. The object isn't to "solve" a character — to expose some hidden secret — but instead to deepen and enlarge the riddle itself. Too often, I

believe, characterization fails precisely *because* it attempts to characterize. It narrows; it pins down; it explicates; it solves. . . . The magician's credo is this: don't give away your secrets. Once a trick is explained—once a secret is divulged—the world moves from the magical to the mechanical.

As you go about creating your characters, let them surprise you from time to time. Let them befuddle you, madden you with their inconsistencies, and take your breath away—the way real people do.

✳ exercises: develop your characters

1. Write a two-page story that focuses on a single character. Use all eight methods of characterization described above.

2. Write down answers to the following questions about your main character, and ideally all the major characters in the story you're working on. Take your time with these, and make your answers as specific as possible. While not every answer will necessarily end up in your finished story, knowing the answers will help you better understand your characters.[1]

   a. What is your character's full name?

   b. What is your character's most noticeable physical characteristic?

   c. What article of clothing do you most associate with your character?

   d. What object, small enough to be held or kept in a pocket, does your character habitually carry around? What is the significance of this object?

   e. What specific smell, or smells, do you associate with your character?

   f. What does your character habitually say? Where did your character first come across this catchphrase?

   g. What is your character's happiest memory?

---

[1]This questionnaire, used and modified with permission, is adapted from one in Jesse Lee Kercheval's book *Building Fiction: How to Develop Plot and Structure* (2003).

   h. What is your character's saddest/worst memory?

   i. If your character were about to die, what would be his or her last thought?

   j. What, specifically, does your character imagine his or her life will be like five years down the road?

PLOT

Plot is what happens in a story — usually meaningful events of a causal nature.

Just as a sentence must have a verb, a story must have something happen. The reason has to do with the close relationship between character and plot: Plot is the way that characters get tested and reveal their truest, deepest selves.

When Tandolfo, the main character of Richard Bausch's story "Tandolfo the Great" (p. 198), buys a multitiered wedding cake in anticipation of asking the woman he loves to marry him, he is acting on his desires. But he can't simply go over to the young woman's house — first he must perform his magic act at a bratty kid's birthday party. The party tests him; the way Tandolfo handles himself at the party reveals his character to us and causes him to change his plans by the end of the story.

Because of plot's close relationship to story structure, a more detailed discussion of plot is found in Chapter 6, "Organizing Your Story: Form and Structure." There, we will discuss the elements of plot, including causality, conflict, and change. For now, bear in mind that when you think about plot, you're also, always, thinking about character — a point made by Henry James in "The Art of Fiction" when he wrote:

> What is character but the determination of incident? What is incident but the illustration of character?

✳ exercise: connect plot & character

Choose a story from the anthology, and write down aspects of the plot that help us better understand the main character. Then write down aspects of the main character that contribute to moving the plot forward.

SETTING

The fundamental purpose of setting is to present a believable and vivid world for the reader to imagine. But settings can, and should, do more than simply convey when and where a story takes place.

In her 1954 essay "Place in Fiction," Eudora Welty wrote, "Location is the crossroads of circumstance, the proving ground of 'What happened? Who's here? Who's coming?'—and that is the heart's field."

At the least, your story's setting(s) should do the following:

- ‣ Contribute to the story's mood
- ‣ Contribute to the story's themes
- ‣ Contribute to characterization
- ‣ Present plot possibilities

Ask yourself this question: If you changed your story's setting, how much would it change the story? If the answer is "not much," then either you should give the setting a more necessary relationship to the material, or you should change the setting to one that would better serve the story.

Anders, the main character in Tobias Wolff's story "Bullet in the Brain" (see p. 366), would behave with sarcastic nastiness just about anywhere—but the bank where the story is set serves several purposes. Most obvious is plot: It gets robbed. This setting also provides several opportunities for Anders to reveal his relentlessly critical personality, both in his dealings with the robbers and other customers and in the way he takes the time to scrutinize, and find fault with, the big ceiling mural in the middle of the robbery:

> The domed ceiling had been decorated with mythological figures whose fleshy, toga-draped ugliness Anders had taken in at a glance years earlier and afterward declined to notice. Now he had no choice but to scrutinize the painter's work. It was even worse than he remembered.

QUESTION: Why is there a mural on the bank's ceiling?
ANSWER: So that Anders can scrutinize it and find fault.

I've noticed that certain locations come up again and again in student drafts—a partial list includes kitchens, cars, restaurants, and office cubicles.

Plenty of stories have been published with these settings. Yet too often in beginners' hands these settings do little more than provide a place for the story to unfold, whereas a different setting might be more useful or relevant.

Ernest Hemingway's 1927 short story "Hills Like White Elephants" has very little plot, and the story consists almost entirely of a conversation between its two main characters. But the remote train station, with tracks leading into the distance in either direction, emphasizes the fact that the couple is at a crossroads in their relationship. On the near side of a river, where they wait, the land is described as having no shade and no trees. And the other side?

> Across, on the other side, were fields of grain and trees along the banks of the Ebro. Far away, beyond the river, were mountains. The shadow of a cloud moved across the field of grain and she saw the river through the trees.

So one side is barren, the other side fertile. The landscape thus becomes a physical representation — that is, a symbol — of the choice that the girl must make: whether or not to have an abortion.

When you go about choosing your settings, take time to consider what will most meaningfully contribute to the story.

✳ exercises: experiment with setting

1. Choose one of the anthologized stories and rewrite a scene, changing the setting to someplace significantly different. Feel free to deviate from the original story's plot as much as necessary.

2. For every scene in the story you're writing, brainstorm three alternate settings that would significantly affect each scene.

3. Choose one scene from your story-in-progress and write it with two different meteorological conditions (such as rain, snow, fog, or eclipse). If your scene takes place indoors, change the environment — for example, the lighting or temperature. Or move the scene outside.

POINT OF VIEW (POV)

Point of view (POV) is the narrative perspective and psychological distance from which a story is told.

First-person ("I") POV

In a first-person story, one of the characters, usually the main character, relates the story directly to the reader. Consequently, everything in a first-person story, both what gets told and how it gets told, comes from — and is limited to — that character's perspective. An appealing aspect of the first-person POV is exactly this close identification with a single character who narrates the story in his or her own voice.

Subjectivity and reliability

When you or I tell a story, we do so subjectively. We can't help it: We're human. First-person narrators, too, are influenced by their own experiences and per-sonalities. They can be unintentionally biased, or lack the facts necessary for objectivity, or be downright liars. But narrators nearly always have an agenda that makes them less than fully objective.

Part of understanding a story involves inferring the degree to which the narrator, intentionally or not, is distorting the truth.

For example, here's my own first-person story:

> When I was in high school, I was so popular that all the girls were too intimidated to date me. I'd say, "How about we go to a movie on Friday?" and every girl I asked would say something like "You must be joking" or "Absolutely not" or "Fat chance, weirdo." They were obviously intimidated by me. They knew how popular I was.

You might conclude that I'm trying awfully hard to convince the reader (and probably myself) of something that just isn't so.[2] In literary terms, I'm being an "unreliable narrator."

The term, however, implies that there are *reliable* (completely truthful and unbiased) narrators — and this is rarely, if ever, so. Nor are "unreliable narra-tors" always unrelentingly obtuse; our blind spots are rarely everywhere. But first-person narrators, just like living, breathing people, have reasons for telling their stories, and these reasons color the stories they tell. Often what's most

---

[2] Of course, this story is merely a fictional example. In real life, I was incredibly popular in high school. I really was. You can believe me now, since footnotes never lie.

compelling about the stories we read—and, ideally, the stories we write—is precisely this gap between the objective facts and the distorted worldview that the narrator constructs in order to live with him- or herself.

Eudora Welty's 1941 short story "Why I Live at the P.O." is narrated by Sister, who voices strong beliefs about exactly how and why she's been wronged. Here is the story's opening paragraph:

> I was getting along fine with Mama, Papa-Daddy and Uncle Rondo until my sister Stella-Rondo just separated from her husband and came back home again. Mr. Whitaker! Of course I went with Mr. Whitaker first, when he first appeared here in China Grove, taking "Pose Yourself" photos, and Stella-Rondo broke us up. Told him I was one-sided. Bigger on the one side than the other, which is a deliberate, calculated falsehood: I'm the same. Stella-Rondo is exactly twelve months to the day younger than I am and for that reason she's spoiled.

We immediately assume that there's another side to this story—very likely a more accurate side. (Was Sister *really* getting along fine with the rest of the family before Stella-Rondo returned? Is Stella-Rondo *actually* spoiled? And if so, is it for the reason that Sister gives?) Because Sister is our narrator, however, the other side of the story must be inferred from what Sister tells us.

The "double I"

A first-person story always encompasses two time periods: (1) the time when the story takes place and (2) the time when the story is being narrated. Sometimes, both times are made explicit. J. D. Salinger's 1951 novel *The Catcher in the Rye* takes place during the week when Holden Caulfield is expelled from Pencey Prep. The novel is being narrated six months later, when Holden is recuperating in a medical facility. When the novel takes place, Holden is an emotional mess. When he narrates the story, he's a little older, wiser, and more clear-headed. He's had six months to reflect on his own story and make some sense out of it.

A first-person story won't always make explicit this time lag between the events and the telling of those events, but the lag is nearly always present. This means that there's always the "I" who *experiences* the story and the "I"—the same person, but older—who *narrates* it. This older, wiser "I"—our narrator—often has thoughts and insights unavailable to the younger "I."

When you write a sentence like "I didn't know then that . . . ," you're making use of what some writers have called the "double I," giving readers access into the mind of the character both *then* and *now*.

Although the events in *To Kill a Mockingbird* begin when Scout Finch is five years old, Scout's narration immediately employs the "double I" to reveal that she is in fact an adult looking back at her childhood. The novel begins:

> When he was nearly thirteen, my brother Jem got his arm badly broken at the elbow. When it healed, and Jem's fears of never being able to play football were assuaged, he was seldom self-conscious about his injury. His left arm was somewhat shorter than his right; when he stood or walked, the back of his hand was at right angles to his body, his thumb parallel to his thigh. He couldn't have cared less, so long as he could pass and punt.
>
> When enough years had gone by to enable us to look back on them, we sometimes discussed the events leading to his accident.

The novel doesn't ever tell us exactly how old the grown Scout is when she's telling her story, but as we read, we know we're in the hands of a narrator who has had plenty of time to reflect on the formative events from her youth and the proper way in which to tell them.

✳ exercise: think about POV

For each first-person story in the anthology, what is the lag between the story's events and the telling of those events? Which stories make the most explicit use of the "double I"? Why do they use it?

Second-person ("you") POV

In the second-person point of view, *you* play the role of the story's main character. Sound strange? Of course it is—that's why it's rarely used. While there's nothing wrong with writing in the second person, this point of view usually draws attention to itself in a way that first- and third-person POVs typically don't.

Actually, there are two types of second-person POVs. One is a bit like the first-person POV, except that the pronoun has changed from "I" to "you." Jay McInerney's use of the second-person POV, along with the present tense, in his 1984 novel *Bright Lights, Big City*, creates the odd effect of dropping us—the reader—into the unfamiliar world, and body, of his protagonist:

> You are not the kind of guy who would be at a place like this at this time of the morning. But here you are, and you cannot say that the terrain is entirely unfamiliar, although the details are fuzzy. You are at a nightclub talking to a girl with a shaved head.

The other type of second-person POV is what we can call the "instructional" point of view. Lorrie Moore's 1985 story "How to Become a Writer" (p. 279) humorously parodies the step-by-step advice of the self-help book genre:

> First, try to be something, anything, else. A movie star/astronaut. A movie star/missionary. A movie star/kindergarten teacher. President of the World. Fail miserably. It is best if you fail at an early age—say, fourteen. Early, critical disillusionment is necessary so that at fifteen you can write long haiku sequences about thwarted desire.

Third-person ("he" or "she") POV

In this perspective, the separation between *narrator* and *character* is most apparent. Unlike in the first-person POV, the narrator isn't a character in the story. The author determines how much the narrator knows, which characters' thoughts the narrator will have access to, and what voice the narrator will employ to tell the story.

There are three primary varieties of third-person points of view: objective, omniscient, and limited omniscient.

Objective POV

In the objective point of view, the narrator gives readers access only to factual information (exposition) and what can be directly observed—as if by a movie camera that can film long shots and close-ups, but never a shot from inside a character's head. An objective narrator doesn't report on characters' thoughts or feelings.

"Hills Like White Elephants" is a commonly cited example of a story told in the objective POV. Here is how the story begins:

The hills across the valley of the Ebro were long and white. On this side there was no shade and no trees and the station was between two lines of rails in the sun. Close against the side of the station there was the warm shadow of the building and a curtain, made of strings of bamboo beads, hung across the open door into the bar, to keep out flies. The American and the girl with him sat at a table in the shade, outside the building. It was very hot and the express from Barcelona would come in forty minutes. It stopped at this junction for two minutes and went to Madrid.

> The story's setting, particularly the dichotomy between the two sides of the valley, comes from our objective narrator. We're to assume that the setting carries thematic meaning.

"What should we drink?" the girl asked. She had taken off her hat and put it on the table.

"It's pretty hot," the man said.

"Let's drink beer."

> We learn basic facts of the story through exposition: We're in Spain. It's hot. A couple is waiting for a train to Madrid.

> A possible power discrepancy between these two people is being implied: He's described as "the man," she as "the girl." And he's the one who chooses what they'll drink.

Before long, the couple begins to talk about the topic they've been avoiding: whether or not the girl should have an abortion, and what this operation would mean for their relationship. But because they never mention the word "abortion" and because we're denied access to the characters' thoughts, the effect is as if we're overhearing a conversation never intended for our ears:

The girl looked at the bead curtain, put her hand out and took hold of two of the strings of beads.

"And you think then we'll be all right and be happy."

"I know we will. You don't have to be afraid. I've known lots of people that have done it."

"So have I," said the girl. "And afterwards they were all so happy."

"Well," the man said, "if you don't want to you don't have to. I wouldn't have you do it if you didn't want to. But I know it's perfectly simple."

Omniscient POV

An omniscient narrator gives us access not only to the story's exterior world but also to the minds of the story's characters. The omniscient narrator is sometimes called "godlike" because it knows, and can report on, everything:

> In Alabama, a tornado touches down.
>
> Within minutes, things begin to change. Tiny green tomatoes ripen instantly. Chickens lose their feathers. Whole cotton fields spoil; their curled leaves smell like rust. The blotch on the TV map turns blue to red in three counties. Cars scatter like grass clippings.
>
> A woman in Montgomery opens her cupboard to find every dish cracked in thirds. A man in Mobile gets up from his recliner just as it bursts its seams, spews white stuffing into the living room. People all over the state report prank phone calls—hang-ups. Alarms engage for no reason.
>
> ~ KELLY MAGEE, "Not People, Not This"

Omniscient narrators can zip from character to character, telling us what they know and what they don't know. The omniscient POV rarely stays in one character's perspective for long, so it tends to be used when the story's primary concern is a group of people, or even a whole community, rather than a single character.

Limited omniscient POV (third-person limited POV)

The difference between "omniscience" and "limited omniscience" is merely one of degree. The limited omniscient story is typically told by a narrator with access to the thoughts and feelings of a single character:

> He'd thought he would put the clown outfit on, deliver the cake in person, an elaborate proposal to a girl he's never even kissed. He's a little unbalanced, and he knows it.
>
> ~ RICHARD BAUSCH, "Tandolfo the Great" (p. 198)

In some limited omniscient stories, like Jill McCorkle's "Magic Words" (p. 262), the perspective shifts, section by section, among a small number of characters. But each entire section sticks with a single character's perspective.

Narrative distance in third-person stories

A third-person story can travel into a character's mind just as in a first-person story, but it can also provide psychological distance, or an understanding of the story that is unavailable to the character himself—as in the opening sentence of Kevin Brockmeier's story "A Fable with Slips of White Paper Spilling from the Pockets" (p. 211):

> Once there was a man who happened to buy God's overcoat.

The man doesn't know that the coat he has bought belongs to God, but the narrator does. In the coat's pockets the man finds slips of paper that contain people's prayers. He tries to answer some of them, an overwhelming but enriching experience—until one day when he loses the coat. At first he misses it dearly. But then comes a sentence that makes terrific use of the separation between narrator and character:

> We are none of us so delicate as we think, though, and over the next few days, as a dozen new accounts came across his desk at work, the sharpness of his loss faded.

That first clause in particular, with its bighearted claim—*We are none of us so delicate as we think, though*—comes from the narrator's sensibility, not the character's.

In the following example from Jill McCorkle's story "Magic Words," ask yourself if these insights about Paula Blake's marriage come from Paula, or if the narrator is making insights that Paula herself couldn't make or wouldn't be able to put into words:

> They are both seeking interests outside their lackluster marriage. His are all about threat and encroachment, being on the defense, and hers are about human contact, a craving for warmth like one of the bats her husband fears might find its way into their attic.

In third-person stories, both omniscient and limited omniscient, the psychological distance—or narrative distance—between narrator and character frequently shifts throughout the story. The manipulation of narrative distance is as important a tool for fiction writers as the placement of a camera is for a photographer or a filmmaker.

In his book *The Art of Fiction*, John Gardner depicts the same action—a man leaving his house—in increasingly "close" perspectives. (Gardner's examples appear on the left, with my annotations on the right.)

It was winter of the year 1853. A large man stepped out of a doorway.	Notice how the exposition is followed by a character's formal name. The "camera" seems as though it's someplace across the street.
Henry J. Warburton had never much cared for snowstorms.	Here, the narrator gives us access to something that isn't directly observed: the man's dislike of snowstorms.
Henry hated snowstorms.	As we move "closer" to the character, he's being referred to by his first name. The language becomes less formal. This sentence seems to be less a crafted statement about his dislike of snow than a gut-level reaction to it.
God how he hated these damn snowstorms.	Here, the perspective moves even closer to Henry. Rather than the narrator interpreting Henry's feelings in the narrator's own voice, we now have language that represents Henry's own way of describing his feelings about the snow. (The narrator knows exactly what Henry is thinking, which is: "God how I hate these damn snowstorms.")
Snow. Under your collar, down inside your shoes, freezing and plugging up your miserable soul.	This is the closest perspective of all, so close that we're given Henry's feelings before even he can shape them into coherent thoughts and sentences. The use of fragments emphasizes the rawness of his sensations upon encountering the snow.

As you read fiction and write it, pay attention to shifts in narrative distance and the effect these shifts have on the story.

✳ exercise: use narrative distance

Write a brief scene set in a doctor's waiting room. In the first paragraph, describe the scene in a distant third-person POV. Then write a second paragraph, continuing the scene, from the perspective of a single character, in a much closer third-person POV.

Can third-person narrators be unreliable?

Yes. In fact, they almost always are. Especially when the narrative distance is "close" to the character, third-person narration can be every bit as unreliable as first-person narration:

Her mother had been pretty once too, if you could believe those old snapshots in the album, but now her looks were gone and that was why she was always after Connie.

~ JOYCE CAROL OATES, "Where Are You Going, Where Have You Been?"

Despite being given information in the third person *as if it were fact*, we infer that it's only Connie's opinion that (1) her mother's looks are gone and (2) jealousy accounts for her mother's unkindness toward her.

These sentences, therefore, do more than simply describe Connie's mother: They also characterize Connie as vain and naïve.

✳ exercises: practice POV

1. An airplane makes an emergency landing in which everyone survives unharmed. Describe the event in the first-person voice of three passengers: a thirteen-year-old skateboarder, a forty-year-old insurance executive, and a sixty-year-old farmer.

2. A sixteen-year-old girl gets expelled from her high school. Write this scene in the third person from the perspective of a sympathetic, mature narrator. (Imagine that your narrator is the school psychologist, a grandparent, or

another adult.) Then write it from the perspective of an unsympathetic, immature narrator (such as a sibling or a school rival). *Do not reveal who the narrator is*, but try to embody that person's voice when writing each scene.

3. Describe a Memorial Day parade from the third-person perspectives of:

   a. A soldier who has recently returned from the battlefield. Do not mention the war or that he is a soldier.

   b. The drum majorette who yesterday got accepted into her favorite university. Do not mention college.

   c. The trombonist whom the drum majorette just dumped that morning. Do not mention the drum majorette or the breakup.

tip: keep POV consistent

Whatever point of view you choose for your story, establish it quickly and remain consistent. In particular, a third-person story that for several pages stays in one character's perspective and then, mid-paragraph, suddenly changes to another's won't seem omniscient. It will seem like a mistake—a "point-of-view violation." At the very least, it will be jarring:

> Beth looked around: no customers, no employees. She slipped the earrings into her coat pocket. Piece of cake. She could sell these at school for ten bucks, easy. Then, too late, she glanced into the mirror up by the ceiling and saw some skinny teenager stocking shelves at the rear of the store. He was pretty sure he'd seen her take something, and he wondered if he should tell his boss, or maybe call the police.

If you've already established Beth as your focal character, why not keep everything in her perspective?

> Beth looked around: no customers, no employees. She slipped the earrings into her coat pocket. Piece of cake. She could sell these at school for ten bucks, easy. Then, too late, she glanced into the mirror up by the ceiling and saw some skinny teenager stocking shelves at the rear of the store. He had to have seen her. The nerd was sure to rat her out to his boss, maybe even call the cops, if it meant a ten-cent raise.

VOICE

Voice is a story's distinctive narrative presence.

The word "voice," of course, is being used figuratively. A person's voice—yours, mine—is a physical thing, an acoustical phenomenon that can be measured in decibels and pitch. A voice has timbre, a musical quality that lets you distinguish Michael Jackson from Kermit the Frog, even if they were both singing the same melody in the same register.

In literature, there are only agreed-upon symbols on a page (letters and punctuation marks) that make up words and sentences. The writer uses these non-acoustical building blocks to create a metaphorical sense of the human voice.

The principal elements that establish a voice in fiction include the following:

- **Diction** (word choice), such as the use of bigger or smaller words, the use of concreteness or abstraction, the use of standard English or vernacular.

- **Syntax** (the arrangement of words into sentences), such as whether the sentence construction is simple or complex, whether the sentences are rhythmical, lyrical, choppy, literal, or metaphorical.

- **Tone** (the attitude that the narrator has with respect to the story), such as whether the narrator is objective or invested, earnest or ironic.

- **The use of (or lack of) comparative language** (similes and metaphors).

In a first-person story, the narrative voice can't help revealing the personality of the character doing the narrating, just as we all reveal things about ourselves when we talk—whether it's our interests, our biases, or the region that gave us our particular dialect, whether we're long-winded or terse or trusting or skeptical. But every story has a narrative voice, as the following excerpts demonstrate:

I have been assured by a very knowing American of my acquaintance in London that a young healthy child well nursed is at a year old a most delicious, nourishing, and wholesome food, whether stewed, roasted, baked, or boiled; and I make no doubt that it will equally serve in a fricassee or a ragout.

~ JONATHAN SWIFT, "A Modest Proposal for Preventing the Children of Poor People in Ireland from Being a Burden to Their Parents or Country, and for Making Them Beneficial to the Public" (1729)

The cat followed me down the steep stairs, and, nearly throwing me head-long, exasperated me to madness. Uplifting an axe, and forgetting, in my wrath, the childish dread which had hitherto stayed my hand, I aimed a blow at the animal which, of course, would have proved instantly fatal had it descended as I wished. But this blow was arrested by the hand of my wife. Goaded, by interference, into a rage more than demoniacal, I with-drew my arm from her grasp and buried the axe in her brain.

~ EDGAR ALLAN POE, "The Black Cat" (1843)

This blind man, an old friend of my wife's, he was on his way to spend the night. His wife had died. So he was visiting the dead wife's relatives in Connecticut. He called my wife from his in-laws'. Arrangements were made.

~ RAYMOND CARVER, "Cathedral" (1983)

The morning of June 27th was clear and sunny, with the fresh warmth of a full-summer day; the flowers were blossoming profusely and the grass was richly green. The people of the village began to gather in the square, between the post office and the bank, around ten o'clock; in some towns there were so many people that the lottery took two days and had to be started on June 26th. But in this village, where there were only about three hundred people, the whole lottery took less than two hours, so it could begin at ten o'clock in the morning and still be through in time to allow the villagers to get home for noon dinner.

~ SHIRLEY JACKSON, "The Lottery" (1948)

I am all alone in my pad, man, my piled-up-to-the-ceiling-with-junk pad. Piled with sheet music, with piles of garbage bags bursting with rubbish and encrusted frying pans piled on the floor, embedded with unnamable flecks of putrefied wretchedness in grease. My pad, man, my own little Lower East Side Horse Badorties pad.

~ WILLIAM KOTZWINKLE, *The Fan Man* (1974)

The bullet smashed Anders' skull and ploughed through his brain and exited behind his right ear, scattering shards of bone into the cerebral cortex, the corpus callosum, back toward the basal ganglia, and down into the thalamus.

~ TOBIAS WOLFF, "Bullet in the Brain" (1996)

✳ exercises: discover voice

1. For each of the six previous excerpts, describe the narrative voice in terms of diction, syntax, and tone. How does the voice seem to contribute to the overall effect?

2. Choose a story from the anthology and rewrite the first page, sentence by sentence, in a dramatically different voice.

3. In a paragraph or two, narrate a recent event from your life (in either first- or third-person POV) using highly formal diction, but without being ironic.

THEME

Themes are the ideas and beliefs that a story embodies and communicates.

A useful way to think about theme is that it's what your story is *about* at its deepest level. John Updike's "A & P" (p. 359) tells the story of a teenager who quits his job. Thematically, one could say that the story is about the loss of innocence, a sort of initiation into an adult world where grand gestures go unappreciated and even unnoticed.

Every story in this anthology—every story for that matter—contains themes, because every story is about something (and usually more than one thing).

Ideally, your story's themes (or "about-ness") will not be neatly packaged truisms. Sometimes a beginning writer will write a story to demonstrate a belief that is already commonly accepted (driving drunk has negative consequences) or to sway the reader on some hot-button issue about which he or she has a strong opinion (the death penalty should/shouldn't be abolished). The problem with these approaches is that they put theme ahead of story, and consequently they tend to result in heavy-handed stories too easily reducible to simplistic themes.

Although stories have themes in them, stories aren't primarily a delivery system for ideas. Other kinds of writing communicate ideas more efficiently: essays, articles, manifestos, blog entries. Stories, rather, are the narratives of particular people in particular situations. Themes derive from these narratives, not the other way around. Otherwise, the story is likely to leave readers cold, because readers become emotionally invested in people and their particular conflicts, not in abstract ideas.

That doesn't mean you can ignore the themes in your own work, leaving it to future literary scholars to find them. In fact, the process of writing and revising fiction involves a continual teasing out of what the heck the story is that we're telling. "What is this story about at its deepest level?" you ask—and the answer will help you choose details and characters and settings and situations that will bring the story into sharper focus.

In "A & P," for example, Sammy's co-workers establish the story's thematic interest in the zest for life that somehow disappears, Sammy fears, with the onset of responsible adulthood. His boss, Lengel, not only introduces the story's conflict; he also represents everything that Sammy is against: He is of an older generation with no sense of humor or any aesthetic (or, apparently, sexual) appreciation for the three girls in bikinis. Lengel views their presence in his store as nothing but a rude distraction from the important business of running a grocery. The story's other male character, Stokesie, is only three years older than Sammy, yet he is already married "with two babies chalked up on his fuselage." He has succumbed, in Sammy's view, to the very pressures to conform that Sammy hopes to resist.

Note Updike's choice of setting, too: The A & P itself is situated in a town five miles from the beach, yet "people in this town haven't seen the ocean for twenty years." The story's setting highlights its thematic interest in Sammy's struggle between youthful frivolity (the beach) and adult responsibility (the A & P).

As you read, pay attention to how a story's many details contribute to its themes.

✳ exercises: identify & develop theme

1. Jot down the major themes of your favorite story in the anthology. How, specifically, does the story go about communicating its themes?

2. For the story you're currently working on, write down the major themes. When you're done, ask yourself what changes you could make to your story to better illuminate its themes.

5 creating scenes: a nuts & bolts approach

CONSIDER this sentence:

> A man worked the same job at a hardware store for thirty years.

In just thirteen words, we've traversed three decades, sailing past a man's entire working life. How long did it take you to read? A couple of seconds? That's the power of summary: It's remarkably efficient.

Now imagine going to the movie theater, paying for your popcorn and soda, taking your seat, and waiting through the previews. The movie starts. Director James Cameron looks straight into the camera and says:

> On a remote planet, a man controls his own avatar in order to infiltrate the local humanoid civilization and gain access to the planet's minerals, but then he falls in love with one of the humanoids and ends up becoming his own avatar for good. Also, the special effects are very cool. The end.

Wouldn't that be a great movie?

No? But it's so efficient—just three sentences instead of 162 minutes. Think about all the time left in your day.

Then again, my summarized version wasn't particularly thrilling. You won't be telling your friends, "You have got to watch that amazing summary of *Avatar*."

Clearly, summary—despite its efficiency—has its limitations. Most significant is that we don't watch movies or read books to hear about an experience. We want to experience the experience.

At one point or another, you've been so engrossed in a novel or story that you forgot you were reading. That's what fiction does at its best—it makes us forget we're sitting in a chair, holding a book. We don't notice that we're turning pages, or that the television is on in another room, or that somewhere outside a dog is barking. We tune out everything except for the story, which unfolds before our eyes, and we're *there*. It's the particular spell that a work of fiction is able to cast.

But in order for the spell to work—for your readers to lose themselves in the story and experience the experience—summary alone won't do. We need other tools.

Speaking of tools, think back to that man in the hardware store. In those thirty years, his life entailed more than merely selling hammers and drills. Maybe he married and raised children who grew up to be doctors or bricklayers or bank robbers. Or maybe he used to be an obese man but went on a diet, lost a lot of weight, trained hard, and ran a marathon. Or he ran ten miles and collapsed from dehydration. Maybe he put himself through business school at night and became the store manager. Thirty years of anybody's life will see innumerable triumphs and failures, both large and small, and this man—we'll name him Ben—surely experienced his share.

Let's imagine that we're writing a story about the time when Ben ran all those miles and then collapsed:

> Ben ran hard, eyes squinting with determination, but it was fiercely hot that day with no breeze, and after ten miles he found himself unable to push his body any longer.

Although that sentence includes plenty of detail, it, too, is summary, not a scene. So what exactly *is* scene? And how does it differ from summary?

One big difference between summary and scene—maybe the biggest difference—is that scenes unfold before us in something approximating real time. For instance, when characters say things to each other in a scene, we're given their actual words as dialogue.

DIALOGUE

Compare this story opening:

> A man and a woman are trying to name their cat.

with this one:

> "Midnight, Licorice, Shadow," she says. "Cocoa, Casper, Dr. Livingston."
> "Alfred Hitchcock," he says. "Dracula. Vincent Price."

The first example summarizes what the characters are doing. The second example, the actual beginning to Becky Hagenston's story "Midnight, Licorice, Shadow" (p. 227), lets us listen in on their conversation as it happens. We have entered the world of scene, and in doing so we start to learn a few things about the characters and their predicament. Subtle things. For instance, all those names in a row suggest that these two people are a little desperate to name their cat. Also, the man's suggestions seem darker and more mysterious than the woman's. Perhaps he, too, is dark and mysterious?

Now compare this line of summary:

> The man threatens to get rid of the cat if they can't choose a name by tomorrow.

with this line of dialogue:

> "Tomorrow, then," Jeremy says. "If we don't have a name by tomorrow morning, it's bye-bye, Mr. Kitty. No offense, Cupcake," he tells the cat.

Here the dialogue provides the same basic facts as the summary. But it also gives us a peek at Jeremy's personality. He uses words like "Cupcake" and "bye-bye" — but *is* he actually a sweet, innocent man? Maybe he plans to find the cat a good home. Then again, James Bond's adversaries always tell him "good-bye" just before trying to kill him. So maybe Jeremy's words — "bye-bye, Mr. Kitty" — are more sinister than we might first believe. To know for sure, we'll have to read on. So we do, because we want to know more — about him, and the woman, and why it's so important for them to name their cat.

The dialogue, in other words, has engaged us, has gotten us involved in the characters and their story, and we become curious about all the little pieces that don't quite add up. We want to understand, so we keep reading.

Dialogue is an important tool in scene-writing—in fact, it's the most *immediate* tool we have in fiction. By "immediate," I mean that through dialogue, readers gain access to characters directly, without any mediation or interpretation or judgment by the story's narrator. We hear exactly what the characters say, in their own words, and we're left to form our own judgments.

Given the immediacy of dialogue, it shouldn't surprise you that authors often use it for the most important moments in their stories. To understand why, imagine our hardware-store salesman again, running—or more accurately, failing to run—that marathon:

> By mile ten, Ben knows that it doesn't matter if the race is 26 miles or 260 miles. He isn't going to finish. He tries for one last surge, then staggers over to a table where young volunteers are handing out cups of water. A boy is watching him and frowning.
>
> He asks Ben if he's okay. Ben answers the boy's question, then goes home.

You should feel shortchanged by that last line, which is what the whole scene was driving toward. We expect—we deserve—to hear exactly what the kid asks, and what Ben says in response. Otherwise, the author is being stingy and the reader feels cheated.

So let's fix the problem:

> By mile ten, Ben knows that it doesn't matter if the race is 26 miles or 260 miles. He isn't going to finish. He tries for one last surge, then staggers over to a table where young volunteers are handing out cups of water. A boy is watching him and frowning.
>
> "You don't look so hot," the kid says.
>
> "My whole life is a waste," Ben says.

See the difference? Through dialogue, we present the scene as it unfolds. And by including Ben's actual words, we give readers a surprising glimpse into his inner life. This race, to him, is more than just a race. His failure to finish it speaks to a broader failure.

Or not. It's our story to write. Maybe Ben isn't so down on himself. After all, he has run ten miles, which is more than I could do. Maybe he believes—as I would—that ten miles is worth celebrating:

> "You don't look so hot," the kid says.
> "Oh, I haven't looked hot in forty years," Ben says. "Just give me my water and tell me 'congratulations.'"

By giving voice to our characters, we're forced to make important decisions about them. How would Ben feel about quitting the race after ten miles? And how would he express these feelings to the boy? Scene-writing requires the author to make all sorts of small and large decisions that will affect the rest of the story.

Tips for writing dialogue

1. Dialogue is not real speech. It is intended to *seem* like real speech. Think about a food magazine with a delicious dish on the cover. Most of the time, it isn't real food that's being photographed. It's fake. Delicious food, when photographed, doesn't look very delicious, while artificial food—painted plastic—looks more like delicious food than delicious food does. This sort of substitution happens all the time in any artistic medium. Paradoxically, artifice done well often seems more real than actual reality.

In the classic horror movie *Psycho*, director Alfred Hitchcock was going to use animal blood to simulate human blood, but it looked wrong on film. (The movie was shot in black and white.) Instead, he used chocolate syrup, which looked more like blood than actual blood did.

Similarly, the purpose of fictional dialogue is to represent, or seem like, real speech. Actual real speech won't work. Have you ever listened to a recorded conversation? All those hesitations, the "um's" and "you know's"—it's a real mess. We're all terribly inarticulate, and we digress like crazy. Well-written dialogue captures the feel of real speech—often right down to the hesitations, inarticulateness, and digressions—but it is a crystallized version of those things.

You'll want to avoid writing a line like this:

"Well, um, would you like to, uh, you know, go out . . . with, um . . . me . . . on a date sometime?"

Instead, you only need to hint at the character's nervousness:

"So would you like to, you know, go out on a date sometime?"

2. Unless there is very good reason, avoid having your character say too much all at once. Rarely in life do we get to pontificate for very long. Conversations are just that—people speaking back and forth, and over each other, and around each other. It doesn't seem very realistic for a character to speak uninterrupted for five or six sentences—unless, of course, he's giving a speech or lecturing somebody. But even then, it's often better to condense the dialogue to just a couple of sentences.

3. Dialogue carries meaning. It moves the story forward, or reveals character. It never does nothing. In real life, people say things all the time that don't mean much. They dial up friends to kill time. In fiction, however, dialogue should never be killing time. That's because fiction is a concentrated, highly focused version of reality, and dialogue a concentrated form of speech. If your character does digress, the digression should mean something in the context of your story. Truly idle banter does not make for compelling fiction.

Along the same lines, it's often wise to omit the routine beginnings and endings of conversations. Read the following phone call. Try not to fall asleep.

"Hello?"
"Hi, is this Alice?"
"Yes. Who's this?"
"Jack."
"Oh, hi, Jack. How's it going?"
"It's going okay. How're you?"
"Not bad," Alice said.
"Oh, that's good," Jack said. "Listen, do you still have that leaf blower? I'm doing a bunch of yard work today and wondered if I could borrow it."
"Sure. You can come over whenever."
"How's two o'clock?" Jack asked.

"Two o'clock would be fine."
"I'll see you then."
"Okay," Alice said.
"Okay. Bye."
"Bye."

Realistic? Sure. Good fiction? No. In fiction, we need only the heart of the conversation. The rest is flab.

"Any chance I can borrow your leaf blower?" Jack asked.
"Sure," Alice said. "Come over whenever."
"How's two o'clock?"

4. Often, the deeper meaning of a conversation is conveyed through subtext. Linguists tell us that we never say exactly what we mean. We couldn't even if we tried. There's always a "meta-message" going on underneath the words that get said.

Sarcasm is an obvious example:

"Gee, Bob, you look *so* handsome in that twenty-year-old sports jacket with the pit stains. Charming, really."

That's what the speaker says. However, the subtext—what she really means—is probably more like:

Bob, how could you even consider wearing that old, dirty suit? You clearly have no fashion sense at all. I can't believe I have to be seen with you.

But all dialogue, not just sarcasm, gives the writer a chance to convey more than the words themselves. In Richard Bausch's story "Tandolfo the Great" (p. 198), Tandolfo is a clown/magician with gambling debt and girl troubles. He's just arrived at a bratty kid's house to perform at a birthday party, and neither the kids nor the adults make his life any easier as he tries to set up his equipment.

Here is what he says (**text**):

"I need a table, folks. I told somebody that over the telephone."

But here is what he means (**subtext**):

My life is hard, and none of you is giving me an ounce of the respect that I deserve. Has my life really come to this?

5. When writing dialogue tags (also called "dialogue attributions"), opt for the word "said" over more colorful verbs. In not one of our examples so far has a character "chortled." Nobody "smiled" a line of dialogue or "laughed" it or "sighed" it. The reason: The word "said" functions almost like punctuation to the reader, whose eyes sail right by it. That's what you want to have happen. We want our readers to forget that they're reading.

But if you write *"I'm hungry," he whined,* the word "whined" causes us to blink. It jolts us momentarily out of the story, disrupting the reading experience. And that's something to be avoided at all costs.

This advice also holds true for adverbs and adverbial phrases. You almost never need to explain *how* something was said.

> "I'm hungry," he said ~~complainingly~~.
> "I'm hungry," he said ~~in a complaining tone~~.

In dialogue, we want the things that characters actually say—the stuff in quotes—to do the work. Readers shouldn't need to be told that a character "whined" his words. If you feel the need to write a detailed dialogue attribution, that's a good indication that the dialogue itself can be revised to more accurately convey the sentiment.

> "For the hundredth time, I'm hungry," he said.

In practice, we sometimes use words other than "said." A character might "ask" something. Maybe it's necessary to show that a character "whispers" or "shouts" something. But use even those words sparingly. Stick with "said."

Or stick with nothing. That's a good option, too. If it's clear who is doing the talking, there's no reason to use a dialogue tag at all:

> "I'm hungry," he said.
>   "There's an extra slice of pizza in the fridge," she said.
>   "Does it have meat on it? If it does, I won't eat it." [**no tag needed**]
>   "Is pepperoni meat?" [**no tag needed**]
>   "Please tell me you're joking," he said. [**Here I include the tag because it's been a while since I last used one, and I don't want the reader to become confused.**]

We've spent a good deal of time discussing dialogue because it's fundamental to scene-writing. It's fundamental because it happens in real time, is immediate, and is particularly useful in revealing the personalities of our characters.

Dialogue is so fundamental, in fact, that it is possible to write an entire scene consisting of nothing else.

✳ exercise: write a scene — just dialogue

Go ahead; give it a try. Write a scene in a page or two consisting only of dialogue between two characters. And no idle chatter — something must be at stake. Your two characters can be in disagreement, or they can be working together, as in Becky Hagenston's "Midnight, Licorice, Shadow" (p. 227), to solve a problem. But remember: only back-and-forth dialogue. And be sure to use correct punctuation and formatting (see Chapter 11).

Here is how Margaret, a student, approached this exercise. Her dialogue is between a mother and her young son.

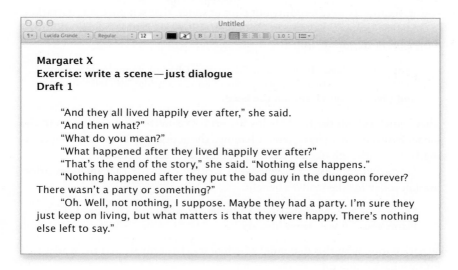

Margaret X
Exercise: write a scene — just dialogue
Draft 1

"And they all lived happily ever after," she said.
"And then what?"
"What do you mean?"
"What happened after they lived happily ever after?"
"That's the end of the story," she said. "Nothing else happens."
"Nothing happened after they put the bad guy in the dungeon forever? There wasn't a party or something?"
"Oh. Well, not nothing, I suppose. Maybe they had a party. I'm sure they just keep on living, but what matters is that they were happy. There's nothing else left to say."

> "But that's stupid," he said. "Nobody can be happy forever. The bad guy wasn't happy. He didn't get all that gold, *and* he got put in the dungeon. There's gotta be something else. Did you skip a page?"
>
> "Nope, that's the end, I promise. Want to look for yourself?"
>
> "But how do they expect me to believe that?"
>
> "Why can't someone live happily ever after?"
>
> "Because! Because grandpa died, and Blake couldn't come over and play today, and that guy from next door went to be a soldier and his mom cried, and all that makes me not happy. So people can't live happily ever after. Can they?"
>
> "You tell me. If you were writing the story, how would you have ended it?"
>
> "I don't know," he said. "But I'd make it end so people would at least believe it."

NARRATION

Think of narration as the stage directions in your story. What are your characters doing? If somebody walks across the room and opens a door, that's narration. When I wrote about my hardware salesman staggering over to a table where young volunteers were handing out cups of water, that sentence was narration.

Here is Jeremy's dialogue in "Midnight, Licorice, Shadow" again, this time with a bit of narration added:

> "Tomorrow, then," Jeremy says. "If we don't have a name by tomorrow morning, it's bye-bye, Mr. Kitty. No offense, Cupcake," he tells the cat, **and gives it a quick rub on the head**.

That "quick rub on the head" helps the reader visualize what's going on in the scene. It also further characterizes Jeremy. The action would seem loving coming from another character. Coming from him, it seems creepy.

Narration can also help you avoid writing dialogue that includes information solely for the reader's benefit:

> "Billy, you just exhaled slowly and descended that metal slide. I don't blame you—it was pretty high up."

What's wrong with this dialogue? Much of it exists only so that the reader will know what's going on.

Narration will make the scene more vivid and allow us to write natural-sounding dialogue.

> Billy peered over the edge of the slide, let out the breath he was holding, and climbed back down the ladder. [**narration**]
> "I don't blame you, pal," his dad said. [**dialogue**]

DESCRIPTION

Just like it sounds, description refers to anything that is described in a story: a house, a tree, a face, a cat. Description helps the reader to imagine the fictional world in vivid, sensory detail, a concept covered in Chapter 2. We might expand the example above by adding some description:

> Billy peered over the edge of the slide. He was higher up than the two girls on the swing-set at the top of their arc, higher even than the monkey bars that reflected the bright morning sunlight and made him squint. He let out the breath he was holding and climbed back down the long ladder.
> "I don't blame you, pal," his dad said.

In "Midnight, Licorice, Shadow," Hagenston follows Jeremy's paragraph of dialogue/narration with description:

> "Tomorrow, then," Jeremy says. "If we don't have a name by tomorrow morning, it's bye-bye, Mr. Kitty. No offense, Cupcake," he tells the cat, [**dialogue**] and gives it a quick rub on the head. [**narration**]
> Donna looks at the animal, sprawled on the orange motel carpet like a black bearskin rug. [**description**] One of his fangs is showing. [**description**]

A word about perspective

You'll notice that it's impossible to describe a scene without considering through whose eyes and ears we're experiencing the world. Unless your story is being told from an omniscient or objective point of view (see "Point of View" in Chapter 4), each scene will most likely be written from the perspective of a single character.

In Hagenston's example above, Donna—and not Jeremy—compares the sprawled cat to a bearskin rug. That's her subjective observation.

Tobias Wolff's story "Bullet in the Brain" (p. 366) describes a man named Anders who finds himself in the middle of a bank robbery. At one point, one of the robbers puts a gun to Anders's chin and tells him to look up at the ceiling. Any other person in that same situation would probably not take much notice of the mural painted on the ceiling. But Anders can't help himself. He is a book critic by profession, and a nasty one at that. Here is Wolff's complete description of the bank's ceiling as seen through Anders's hypercritical eyes:

> Anders had never paid much attention to that part of the bank, a pompous old building with marble floors and counters and pillars, and gilt scrollwork over the tellers' cages. The domed ceiling had been decorated with mythological figures whose fleshy, toga-draped ugliness Anders had taken in at a glance many years earlier and afterward declined to notice. Now he had no choice but to scrutinize the painter's work. It was even worse than he remembered, and all of it executed with the utmost gravity. The artist had a few tricks up his sleeve and used them again and again—a certain rosy blush on the underside of the clouds, a coy backwards glance on the faces of the cupids and fauns. The ceiling was crowded with various dramas, but the one that caught Anders' eye was Zeus and Europa—portrayed, in this rendition, as a bull ogling a cow from behind a haystack. To make the cow sexy, the painter had canted her hips suggestively and given her long, droopy eyelashes through which she gazed back at the bull with sultry welcome. The bull wore a smirk and his eyebrows were arched. If there'd been a bubble coming out of his mouth, it would have said, "Hubba hubba."

The thoroughness of the description and the critic's obvious disapproval heighten the scene's comedy and tell us as much about Anders as it does about the ceiling being described. Who in the world would take the time to consider all these details in the middle of a bank robbery, facing imminent death?

Anders, that's who.

What does all of this mean for your scene? Even a scene with just two people will usually focus on one of them. When you decide whose story you're telling, you're really making a decision that will affect every other aspect of your story.

✳ exercise: continue your scene—add narration & description

Your turn. In this draft, you will be expanding and revising the scene that you began. First, you'll need to select a focal character. It could be either one. Which will you choose? It's up to you. Which character seems more intriguing? Which has more at stake in the outcome of the scene? Whose story, ultimately, is it?

Work to hone the dialogue—to enhance the realism, eliminate unnecessary lines, add others, and generally sharpen the scene. Edit out any dialogue that feels as if it's solely for the reader's benefit (such as "I'm so glad you just climbed down from that slide"). You now have other tools for conveying information to the reader.

In this draft, you'll be adding *narration* and *description*. Bear in mind that narration and description are not merely tools to tell the reader what's going on. They also color the scene emotionally, making readers understand more than what is being said explicitly. So choose your details, and your way of expressing them, with care.

This draft will probably be somewhat longer than your first draft, unless you've edited down your dialogue a great deal.

Save this draft as a new file.

Here is Margaret's completed draft for this exercise.

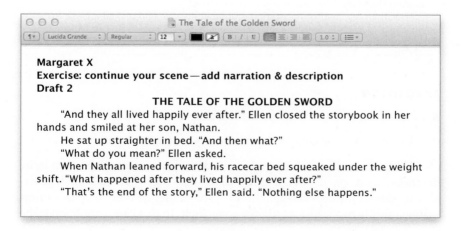

Margaret X
Exercise: continue your scene—add narration & description
Draft 2

THE TALE OF THE GOLDEN SWORD

"And they all lived happily ever after." Ellen closed the storybook in her hands and smiled at her son, Nathan.

He sat up straighter in bed. "And then what?"

"What do you mean?" Ellen asked.

When Nathan leaned forward, his racecar bed squeaked under the weight shift. "What happened after they lived happily ever after?"

"That's the end of the story," Ellen said. "Nothing else happens."

He fell back onto his sheets. "Nothing happened after they put the bad guy in the dungeon forever and ever and ever? There wasn't even a party or something?"

Ellen looked around the cluttered bedroom. Toys lay everywhere. Books, everywhere. The carpet looked clean at first glance, but it wasn't. It needed vacuuming. And the shelves needed a good dusting.

"Well, not nothing, I suppose," she said. "Maybe they did have a party. But they just keep on living. What matters is that they were happy for the rest of their lives."

When Nathan frowned, he looked much older, his expression nearly identical to that of Ellen's father after a long day presiding over family court. "But that's stupid. Nobody can be happy forever. The bad guy wasn't happy! He didn't get all that gold, and he got put in the dungeon. There's got to be something else. Did you skip a page?"

Ellen glanced down at the book and noticed, as if for the first time, the cheery riding full speed along the countryside, the princess holding on to his middle, his dark, windswept hair, her long, curly locks, his shiny boots, her shiny dress, his gleaming stallion, her silver crown, his golden sword brandished above his head.

"Why can't someone live happily ever after?" she asked him.

"Because grandpa died, and Blake couldn't come over and play yesterday, and that guy from next door went to be a soldier and it made his mom cry." He was breathing a little heavily. "Bad things always end up happening."

Ellen pushed back her hair and posed another question. "If you were writing the story, how would you have ended it?"

Nathan reached for the stuffed dragon at his side and tucked it close to his chest. "I don't know," he said. "But it needs to end so people can believe it."

EXPOSITION

Remember the sentence that opened this chapter:

A man worked the same job at a hardware store for thirty years.

Alone, this sentence of exposition is summary, not scene. Exposition is, by definition, a way of "telling," as opposed to "showing" — and telling is, generally, at odds with scene-writing. However, sometimes we need to convey information quickly to a reader within the scene itself. In that case, exposition is the ideal tool. You can include a sentence or more of exposition right in the middle of a scene. And like magic, what once was summary has now become an important component of a scene.

> Ben tries for one last surge, then staggers over to a water station. [**narration**] One of the boys behind the table studies him with squinted eyes and a slightly tilted head. The boy can't be older than twelve or thirteen, but he looks exactly like Ben's physician looked before diagnosing him with gallstones. [**two sentences of description**]
>
> "You don't look so hot," the kid says. [**dialogue**]
>
> Ben worked the same job at a hardware story for thirty years. No wife, no kids. Never even left the state of Delaware. He thought he might become a marathon runner, and now he's about to quit before his first race is even halfway through. [**a paragraph of exposition**]
>
> "My whole life is a waste," Ben says. [**dialogue**]

The paragraph of exposition situates the marathon in a broader context of Ben's entire life, a life that seems defined by monotony and lack of adventure. When he finally says, "My whole life is a waste," the exposition gives us greater appreciation for why he might say such a thing.

Here is the actual beginning to "Midnight, Licorice, Shadow." Notice the single, brief sentence of exposition, which efficiently gives the reader necessary information without disrupting the scene.

> "Midnight, Licorice, Shadow," she says. "Cocoa, Casper, Dr. Livingston."
>
> "Alfred Hitchcock," he says. "Dracula. Vincent Price."
>
> They have had the cat for nearly three days. [**exposition**]
>
> "Cinderblock?" she tries. "Ice bucket?"
>
> It's useless. The harder they try to think of a name, the more elusive it becomes.
>
> "Tomorrow, then," Jeremy says. "If we don't have a name by tomorrow morning, it's bye-bye, Mr. Kitty. No offense, Cupcake," he tells the cat, and gives it a quick rub on the head.
>
> Donna looks at the animal, sprawled on the orange motel carpet like a black bearskin rug. One of his fangs is showing. His monkey paws are kneading at the air.

When it comes to exposition in scenes, less is often more. Newer writers often overexplain. If you've already done a good job of presenting your story's physical world—coming up with precise dialogue, vivid description and narration—then there's no need to explain the same things in exposition.

In other words, if you've already "shown" it, there's no reason to then "tell" it.

"Tomorrow, then," Jeremy says. "If we don't have a name by tomorrow morning, it's bye-bye, Mr. Kitty. No offense, Cupcake," he tells the cat, and gives it a quick rub on the head. ~~Jeremy was definitely a man of great contradiction.~~

INTERIORITY

So far we've discussed four elements of scene-writing:

- ‣ Dialogue
- ‣ Narration
- ‣ Description
- ‣ Exposition

There's only one more to discuss, but it's a biggie. It also happens to be the thing that literature can do and that movies and TV can't.

Say we're shooting a movie about Ben and his marathon. Maybe we take a ride in a helicopter and film him from several hundred feet in the air. We see a pack of runners, each indistinguishable from the next except for the colors of their clothing. Zoom in closer. We set up the camera on a street corner as Ben runs by. From that distance, we see Ben's struggling gait, maybe even the sweat pouring down his face. We could mount a camera to the back of a car driving directly in front of him, filming his face.

Still closer?

We could mount a camera to his shoulder, or to the baseball cap he's wearing. During the winter Olympics, small cameras are now mounted to the skiers' helmets to give viewers glimpses of the race from the athletes' perspective. Horror movies often employ this technique, giving us the killer's perspective.

In the story "Midnight, Licorice, Shadow," the sentence "His monkey paws are kneading at the air" is "shot," if you will, from a camera that is situated on the shoulder of Donna, the story's focal character. The story could have read, simply, "His paws are kneading at the air." The phrase "monkey paws" is a cuter way to describe the paws. It's subjective. And which character in the story would have this subjective opinion about the cat's paws? Donna, the story's focal character.

What, though, if we could move the camera closer still, right inside a character's head? Movies can't do that. Neither can TV. Not without invasive surgery, which the Screen Actors Guild does not yet permit.

Film and TV can *approximate* the technique of going "inside" a character's head by using voice-over. But any movie director will tell you that is clunky moviemaking.

Literature, however, is an ideal medium for presenting the thoughts and feelings of a character, because in literature the camera is metaphorical. Thus, no surgery is required.

> Ben tries for one last surge. He imagines the crowd cheering for him at the finish line. I owe it to them to finish this race, he thinks, [**interiority**] and staggers over to a water station. [**narration**] One of the boys behind the table studies him with squinted eyes and a slightly tilted head. The boy can't be older than twelve or thirteen, but he looks exactly like Sam's physician looked before diagnosing him with gallstones. [**description**]

Let's see how Hagenston incorporates Donna's interior thoughts into her scene:

> Donna looks at the animal, sprawled on the orange motel carpet like a black bearskin rug. One of his fangs is showing. His monkey paws are kneading at the air.
>
> "Monkey Paw!" she says, but Jeremy is already headed out the door, car keys jangling. He'd invited her to go along—there's some house in Redlands he wants to check out—but she wants to stay with the cat, who now has his eyes closed in feline ecstasy and is purring louder than the air conditioner. She doesn't want to leave him (Merlin? Jasper?) all alone in a strange motel. In an hour or so she'll walk across the parking lot to the Carrows and get a chef's salad for her and a cheeseburger for Jeremy (he always comes back hungry) and maybe she'll give some of her dinner to the cat.

Notice how the line describing the cat's "monkey paws" is immediately followed by Donna's exclamation: "Monkey Paw!" The cat's cute paws are something she would notice—indeed, something she did notice, which she immediately offers up as a potential name for the animal. The longer paragraph combines moments of narration ("Jeremy is already headed out the door, car keys jangling"), description ("eyes closed in feline ecstasy"), and exposition ("He'd invited her to go along . . ."), but the overall effect of the paragraph is to convey the thoughts and feelings of Donna, the focal character. We learn what she *wants* (to stay with the cat), what she *doesn't want* (to leave the cat alone), and what she *expects* (to walk across the parking lot for dinner; maybe to share some of her dinner with the cat).

Two other points about interiority

1. When writing interior monologue, there is no need to state the obvious—especially if the dialogue has already done the work.

> "I can't believe I just won the lottery!" she said. ~~How awesome! she thought.~~

Instead, save interiority for moments when a character's thoughts *aren't* obvious, or when what a character thinks is something she has not or would not say aloud.

> "I can't believe I just won the lottery—how wonderful!" she said, smiling for the TV camera. But she knew the truth. Now every distant relative would come crawling out of the woodwork begging for money. Every neighbor, too, and her co-workers at the tire plant, and all the people from her church. Everyone. One, two, three, ready or not, here they come.

2. You almost never need to state the emotion that your character is feeling.

> Jennifer got into her car clutching her first paycheck in three months. ~~She felt so happy.~~

What's the problem with stating Jennifer's emotion? There are two. The first is that the reader is being "told" about, rather than "shown," Jennifer's happiness. Better to show her happiness with a particular action or thought:

> Jennifer got into her car clutching her first paycheck in three months. She tried to imagine what it would be like at the end of the month, sending off the rent check without the accompanying prayer that it not bounce.

The second problem is that while the emotions we feel are highly specific, the names for them are awfully general. There are many, many different shades of happiness. The excited happiness that comes from hitting a home run is different from the peaceful, contented happiness of sitting in front of a fire, reading a good book. So merely telling us that a character is feeling "happy" or "angry" or "sad" doesn't actually tell us much. Instead of naming the emotion, give a detail—a particular thought, as in the example above, or a physical action, or a bit of dialogue—that reveals to the reader exactly what this character is feeling.

SCENE-WRITING, FINAL NOTES

You now know the elements of scene-writing, which are the tools you need to write complete scenes:

- ‣ Dialogue
- ‣ Narration
- ‣ Description
- ‣ Exposition
- ‣ Interiority

Should you keep these elements in mind as you write your stories? Absolutely. Think about learning to drive a car. When you first learned, you probably ran through a series of steps in order to be sure you remembered them all. *Put on the seat belt. Adjust the mirrors. Step on the brake. Put the key in the ignition. Put the car into gear. Use the turn signal. Look in the rearview mirror. The side mirror.* In time, the actions become second nature, but until then it's extremely useful to be deliberate in what you're doing. Learning to write scenes is like learning to do anything else: It takes practice, but not just any sort of practice. You want to develop good habits now, and to repeat those good habits again and again until they become second nature.

Does this mean that every scene you write needs to include every element of scene-writing? Not necessarily. But quite likely. Could you build a house without using a basic tool, like a screwdriver? I suppose. But I'm not sure I'd want to live in it.

That said, part of what gives a story its particular style is the balance among elements. John Updike's story "A & P," for instance, has little dialogue but plenty of description because Sammy, the story's focal character and first-person narrator, is a very observant character. George Saunders's story "CivilWarLand in Bad Decline" (p. 341), on the other hand, has lots of dialogue, a source of much of the story's comedy.

No two writers will write a scene the same way because no two writers view the world—and the world of their stories—the same way. None of these elements is any more or less important than another. What matters most is that you consider the tools available to you and practice using them. If you decide to write a scene with little interiority, that's your choice to make. But you should be making that choice, rather than simply forgetting that interiority is an option. Your scene can have lots and lots of description, or almost none, but there should be a reason for either decision that stems from the story itself. What *it* demands. Everything you do as a writer must be in the best interest of your story.

✳ exercise: continue your scene — add exposition & interiority

In this draft, you will be adding *exposition* and *interiority* and revising what you've already got. By now you should know your focal character. Whether you're writing in the first-person or third-person point of view, the interior thoughts should come solely from that character.

This draft will probably be somewhat longer than your prior draft. When you are done, you'll have written a complete scene!

Remember to save this draft as a new file.

Let's take a look now at two completed scenes. The first is the entire opening scene to the story "Midnight, Licorice, Shadow." The second is Margaret's completed exercise.

As you read, ask yourself which scene-writing elements are being used, and when, and how, and why.

"Midnight, Licorice, Shadow," she says. "Cocoa, Casper, Dr. Livingston."

"Alfred Hitchcock," he says. "Dracula. Vincent Price."

They have had the cat for nearly three days.

"Cinderblock?" she tries. "Ice bucket?"

It's useless. The harder they try to think of a name, the more elusive it becomes.

"Tomorrow, then," Jeremy says. "If we don't have a name by tomorrow morning, it's bye-bye, Mr. Kitty. No offense, Cupcake," he tells the cat, and gives it a quick rub on the head.

Donna looks at the animal, sprawled on the orange motel carpet like a black bearskin rug. One of his fangs is showing. His monkey paws are kneading at the air.

"Monkey Paw!" she says, but Jeremy is already headed out the door, car keys jangling. He'd invited her to go along—there's some house in Redlands he wants to check out—but she wants to stay with the cat, who now has his eyes closed in feline ecstasy and is purring louder than the air conditioner. She doesn't want to leave him (Merlin? Jasper?) all alone in a strange motel. In an hour or so she'll walk across the parking lot to the Carrows and get a chef's salad for her and a cheeseburger for Jeremy (he always comes back hungry) and maybe she'll give some of her dinner to the cat. They've been feeding him dry food because, as Jeremy says, wet food makes a cat's shits stinkier. Donna thinks the cat's shits are stinky enough as it is. Still, she likes him. She wants the three of them to drive off together tomorrow morning, like a family on vacation. So far, they've traveled over five hundred miles together, the cat curled up on Donna's lap while Jeremy drives.

If she can just come up with his name, the way she came up with her own. She was born Lacey Love and changed her name to Donna when she left home at sixteen. She liked the wholesome, 1950s' sound of it, the name of a girl in a song. Sometimes she thinks about changing it again, to something more serious: Joan, perhaps, or Agnes. More and more, she feels like a Joan or an Agnes.

"Tango," she says to the cat. "Flower. Bambi. Mr. Jarvis."

The cat jerks his head up and fixes his yellow eyes on hers in what seems like an accusatory way, but she tells herself he must have heard something outside that startled him, something too faint for human ears.

Margaret X
Exercise: continue your scene — add exposition & interiority
Draft 3

THE TALE OF THE GOLDEN SWORD

"And they all lived happily ever after." Ellen closed the storybook in her hands and smiled at her son, Nathan.

He sat up straighter in bed. "And then what?"

"What do you mean?" Ellen asked.

Nathan leaned forward, and his racecar bed squeaked under the weight shift. "What happened after they lived happily ever after?"

A kid down the street had given Nathan a copy of *The Tale of the Golden Sword* for his birthday. For days it became his requested bedtime story. By now he knew every line.

"That's the end of the story," Ellen said. "You know that. Nothing else happens."

He fell back onto his sheets. "Nothing happened after they put the bad guy in the dungeon forever and ever and ever? There wasn't even a party or something?"

Ellen looked around the cluttered bedroom. Toys lay everywhere. Books, everywhere. The carpet looked clean at first glance, but it wasn't. It needed vacuuming. The shelves needed dusting. The day needed five or six more hours in it.

"Well, not nothing, I suppose. Maybe they did have a party," she said. "But they just keep on living. What matters is that they were happy for the rest of their lives."

When Nathan frowned, he looked much older, his expression nearly identical to that of Ellen's father after a long day presiding over family court. "But that's stupid. Nobody can be happy forever. The bad guy wasn't happy! He didn't get all that gold, and he got put in the dungeon. There's got to be something else. Did you skip a page?"

He reached forward and took the book out of her hands. He flipped to the back page and stared at it, decoding the small shapes into letters and words. Only moments before, he had been mouthing the hero's lines along with her while she read. He'd even said his favorite lines out loud. He flipped between pages as Ellen tried to explain that she had not in fact skipped anything.

Nathan let the book drop from his hands. "But how do they expect me to believe this?"

Ellen glanced down at the book that had started all the trouble and noticed, as if for the first time, the cheery cover: the prince riding full speed along the countryside, the princess holding on to his middle, his dark, windswept hair, her long, curly locks, his shiny boots, her shiny dress, his gleaming stallion, her silver crown, his golden sword brandished above his head.

"Why can't someone live happily ever after?" she asked him.

He cast his eyes around the room, as if looking for an answer among the trophies and army men and books and all those toy cars. "Because grandpa died, and Blake couldn't come over and play yesterday, and that guy from next door went to be a soldier and it made his mom cry." He was breathing a little heavily. "Bad things always end up happening."

Ellen remembered a time in the not-so-distant past when Nathan had both needed and wanted her to read him these stories. She also remembered a painful moment in the more recent past when she offered to read him a story, but he said he could do it by himself. She pushed back her hair and posed another question. "If you were writing the story, how would you have ended it?"

Nathan reached for the stuffed dragon at his side and tucked it close to his chest. "I don't know," he said. "But it needs to end so people can believe it."

He rolled over, knocking the book off the bed. It hit the floor with a thud.

✳ exercises: create scenes

1. Write a scene between two characters in which the first character tries, but fails, to get something from the second character. Use all five scene-writing elements (dialogue, narration, description, exposition, and interiority).

2. Write a scene in which a character gets what he or she wants.

3. Write a scene that occurs in a crowded place. Include a conversation between two people that gets interrupted several times by the things occurring in this crowded place.

4. Write a scene that uses mainly dialogue, description, and narration to emphasize the *external* world of your story (as opposed to your character's interior life).

5. Write the same scene using mainly interiority to emphasize your focal character's thoughts and feelings, and how he or she interprets the external world.

6. Go to a public place and listen to people talk. Try to transcribe an actual conversation. Then sharpen it into fictional dialogue that retains its realism.

7. Write a scene in which the external world has a direct effect on the scene: a couple swimming in the ocean, for instance, when a shark is spotted in the water; or a character caught in a thunderstorm.

8. Try rewriting the scene you've been crafting throughout this chapter by radically altering your use of scene-building elements. For instance, try rewriting the scene so that there are only three total lines of dialogue.

organizing your story: form & structure

A BEAUTIFUL SENTENCE, a well-written paragraph, a compelling scene: These are worthy achievements. Yet they are ultimately component parts. The end goal, after all, is to write a *story*—to shape an entire narrative from start to finish.

To some degree, a writer must figure out how to tell a story every time he or she sits down to tell one. That never changes, no matter how experienced the writer. Still, by learning the foundations of story structure, you'll increase the likelihood that all the work you put into those sentences, paragraphs, and scenes will result in a successful story.

A story without structure might intrigue us at first with its situation or characters. Before long, however, it loses focus. We're reading a scene and wondering, Why am I reading this scene? Or the plot takes a turn that feels unmotivated or strains credibility. A story without structure often becomes one-dimensional just when it should be getting more emotionally and intellectually complex, and you're likely to feel the iron hand of the writer controlling the characters.

How do you avoid these problems? Let's start by seeing what many successful stories do.

CLASSIC STORY STRUCTURE AND THE FREYTAG PYRAMID

The person usually referenced in discussions about short-story structure is Gustav Freytag (1816–1895)—even though Freytag neither wrote short stories nor wrote about them. Rather, his interest was in plays, specifically ancient Greek and Shakespearean tragedies. In his 1863 book *Technique of the Drama*, he described the form that many of these plays take:

- An *introduction* lays out the time and place of the action, introduces the characters and their relation to one another, sets the mood, and presents a complication.
- The *rising action* increasingly complicates the drama, leading to the climax.
- The *climax* depicts the rising action coming to a head, resulting in some point of no return.
- The *falling action* shows the fallout from the climactic scene.
- The *catastrophe* (remember, Freytag was interested in tragedies) amounts to the conclusion, showing life irrevocably changed.

Graphically, the Freytag Pyramid, as it became known, looks like this:

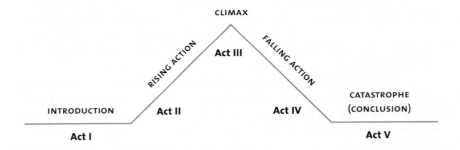

The modified pyramid

When fiction writers today talk about the Freytag Pyramid, they're usually referring to a modified pyramid. The contemporary short story, not surprisingly, differs quite a lot from Greek and Shakespearean drama. For one thing, short stories are short—shorter than three-hour plays, anyway—and often spend little time on introductions and conclusions.

In fact, it's common for the contemporary short story to start right at the beginning of the rising action, at the moment when conflict begins. Whatever would be contained in an introduction gets folded into the rising action and is revealed in smaller doses. (See Chapter 3, "Starting Your Story," for a complete discussion of story openings.)

John Updike's short story "A & P" (p. 359) is narrated by a teenager, Sammy, who works a tedious job in a grocery store. Notably, the story does not begin with Sammy talking about the repetitiveness of his days, or by describing his co-workers or the store itself. Instead, the story begins at the precise moment when an otherwise typical day at the A & P gets interrupted.

> In walk these three girls in nothing but bathing suits. I'm in the third check-out slot, with my back to the door, so I don't see them until they're over by the bread. The one that caught my eye first was the one in the plaid green two-piece. She was a chunky kid, with a good tan and a sweet broad soft-looking can with those two crescents of white just under it, where the sun never seems to hit, at the top of the backs of her legs. I stood there with my hand on a box of HiHo crackers trying to remember if I rang it up or not. I ring it up again and the customer starts giving me hell. She's one of these cash-register-watchers, a witch about fifty with rouge on her cheekbones and no eyebrows, and I know it made her day to trip me up. She'd been watching cash registers for fifty years and probably never seen a mistake before.

From this opening paragraph, we assume that most of Sammy's days do not include girls in bathing suits walking into the A & P. Yet today that's just what has happened, and the event immediately causes tension for reasons that are soon made clear.

The conflict intensifies over several points in the narrative. This intensification constitutes the story's **rising action**. Lengel, the boss, confronts the girls, telling them that "this isn't the beach." Then he tells them to be "decently dressed" the next time they come into the store. One of the girls replies, "We *are* decent." Customers stop what they're doing to watch the developing confrontation.

These moments matter because they matter to Sammy. He believes that the girls are being treated unjustly. He also sees an opportunity to look like a hero in front of them, an opportunity that leads to the story's **climax**: the confrontation between Sammy and his boss during which Sammy quits his job.

Unlike in the original Freytag diagram on page 90, the climax in "A & P" occurs close to the end of the story. After Sammy quits, there's a brief conversation between Sammy and his boss, who makes sure that Sammy understands the consequences of his actions. Then Sammy goes outside to find the girls, who are nowhere to be seen. His heroism has gone unappreciated and probably unnoticed.

The story ends with a **conclusion** that barely concludes at all—a single sentence that reveals Sammy's deepening understanding about the unpleasant world of adulthood. "A & P," like many contemporary stories, doesn't conclude in any final, absolute way. The story reveals neither Sammy's immediate nor long-term future. Rather, it ends at the place in the falling action where we get only a glimmer of the future awaiting him. (See Chapter 8, "Ending Your Story," for a complete discussion of story endings.)

Graphically, the structure of "A & P"—and many other contemporary short stories—looks more like this:

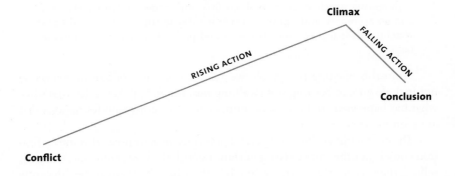

✳ exercises: plot a story

1. Think about the story you're writing. Does it begin with conflict? Does it contain complications that build to a crisis? Do you have a moment or scene in mind that will be the story's climax? Where might the story end?

2. Plot the key moments of your story on the modified Freytag Pyramid.

3. Choose a favorite short story, either from the anthology or elsewhere. Plot that story's action on the modified Freytag Pyramid pictured above.

CAUSALITY

In his 1927 book *Aspects of the Novel*, E. M. Forster famously illustrated the difference between a **story** (a series of events in chronological order) and a **plot** (a series of causal events) as follows:

> The king died, and then the queen died. [**story**]
>
> The king died, and then the queen died of grief. [**plot**]

What makes the second sentence a plot, and a heck of a lot more intriguing than the first sentence, is that the two deaths are connected—and not just by the fact that two members of the same family happen to die. Rather, the first death *causes* the second. It makes us wonder about that queen. Can one really die of grief? What are the symptoms? We wonder about the king, too, whose tie to the queen was evidently so strong that his demise leads directly to her own.

Real life versus fiction

Real life often feels random and chaotic: Robbers enter a bank, and a customer gets struck by a stray bullet. Wrong place, wrong time. Bad luck. Could've happened to anyone. In fiction, however, *any*one won't do. If a person ends up taking a bullet, he or she needs to be *some*one—the exact right someone. In Tobias Wolff's story "Bullet in the Brain" (p. 366), robbers enter a bank and shoot Anders, a professional critic, because he can't help being relentlessly critical—even to the robbers when his life is being threatened.

Or events in real life might seem completely unrelated:

1. A woman decides to go through with an extramarital affair.
2. After being assaulted, a teenage girl escapes from a young man's car and walks home in a daze.

In Jill McCorkle's short story "Magic Words" (p. 262), a woman is driving at night to a motel to commence an affair *when she sees a teenage girl walking along the road*. The girl isn't just any girl, however. She attends school with the woman's daughter. The girl is clearly distressed and begins to sob uncontrollably as soon as she's inside the woman's car. By caring for this girl and driving her home, the woman allows herself—causes herself—to end the affair before it begins.

If real life often feels random and chaotic, filled with unrelated events, then why, you might be asking, would we want the fiction we write to be otherwise?

Fiction, we need to remember, isn't real life; rather, it is an artistic representation of what real life feels like. Think for a moment about a landscape painting. Why would an oil painter use oil paint for her landscapes if she were striving for a realistic image? Why not grind up real leaves and real dirt and real bark instead and brush that onto a canvas? For that matter, why not make the canvas many miles wide to best replicate the actual landscape being painted? (The comedian Steven Wright has a joke about owning a map of his city that's "actual size.")

These are absurd propositions, but they make a point. Every art form uses artifice as a means of representing reality, and causality is a tool that fiction writers use to make a story's events seem real, relevant, and emotionally satisfying. It also happens to be an extremely useful way to navigate your story through a series of rising actions to its climax and conclusion.

Examples of causality

In "A & P," Sammy doesn't simply quit his job at the grocery store out of the blue. He feels he was provoked by the way that his boss treated the three young female customers. We might argue that Sammy's decision to quit is bold and gallant, or we might think it foolhardy. Either way, Sammy's decision is motivated—caused—by the events that preceded it. The presence of the three girls in bathing suits causes Sammy's boss, because of the sort of person he is, to speak to them in a way that causes Sammy, because of who *he* is, to quit his job.

In Tim O'Brien's story "On the Rainy River" (p. 287), the arrival of a draft notice causes the narrator, Tim, to flee to Canada. However, his fear of losing the respect of his family and community causes him to remain rooted at the US-Canadian border for several days until he can sort out what to do. The proprietor of the lodge where he is staying, a wise and quiet older man, intuits

Tim's predicament and takes him in a small motorboat right up to the Canadian shoreline. The physical reality of Canada, so close that Tim can swim to it, causes him to decide, once and for all, whether he'll live out his life forever estranged from his friends and family, or whether he'll go to Vietnam and serve despite his strong objections to the war. The story's chain of causality leads him to the exact spot where a decision can no longer be deferred.

Striking a balance

Often, stories by new writers lack sufficient causality. One event occurs, then another, then another. Each might be well written, but readers quickly lose interest in a series of sequential events (the king dying and then the queen dying) if these events lack causal connections. Lack of causality is why we're usually bored by other people's dreams. *So I was walking along this country road in my underwear, and then a turtle started to sing Beatles songs, and then my cell phone turned into a van.* Since anything can happen in a dream at any moment for any reason — or, as likely, for no reason at all — dreams don't usually make compelling narratives to anyone except maybe the psychoanalyst, whose job is to *hunt for causes* among the apparent randomness.

Or a writer might include causal connections that strain credibility. Example: *Raymond commits an armed robbery because, years earlier, his third-grade teacher once yelled at him and gave him detention.*

Call this the "billiard ball" version of causality, in which the cue ball strikes just one other ball, which moves in a perfectly predictable direction. Readers will have a hard time accepting the notion that a single lousy day in the third grade, all by itself, would result in a man's decision, years later, to commit a felony. The story doesn't jibe with what we know about the complexity of human behavior.

But what if . . .

. . . while sitting in detention that afternoon in the third grade, Raymond were to meet an older kid, a true delinquent, and fall under his spell. This older kid convinces Raymond (*causes* Raymond through charm or persuasion) to hurl bricks through his teacher's window to get back at her, an act that *causes* Raymond to get expelled from the first of many schools. And while he always feels a twinge of sorrow for the bad things he does, he can't shake the unmistakable rush of energy and power whenever he's in the midst of a destructive act. Neither evil nor immoral, he's constantly in a battle of wills with himself to stay out of trouble . . . until one day when he's depositing a paycheck in the bank for three days of labor (three days rather than the week he'd been hired for because he got into a scuffle with another employee), and he looks around at the exits and the security cameras and thinks: I'd never get away with it, not in a million years. But I'm gonna do it anyway.

So maybe there can be a causal connection between third-grade detention and armed robbery, after all—but the chain of causality requires more than two links. If you examine the stories in the anthology, and stories everywhere, you'll see just how often causality contributes to effective storytelling.

✳ exercises: make causal connections

1. Revisit the diagram you made of your story-in-progress. Are the key moments you plotted on the Freytag Pyramid causally related? If not, see if you can tighten the causal connections between them. Or consider changing the moments themselves to create a stronger sense of causality.

2. Are your causal connections believable? If not, ask yourself "What if . . ." and try adding more connective tissue, as in Raymond's story above.

CONFLICT

Imagine this story:

> A young man loves his job at the grocery store. Life gets even better when three pretty girls walk in wearing bathing suits. He flirts with them, and the one he likes best agrees to go on a date with him. His generous boss, Lengel, says, "Sammy, my boy, how about you take the rest of the day off? Catch a movie with your new friend." Sammy and the young woman go to see a matinee and have a very nice dinner together afterward. It's the start of something good.

In a word: *blech*.

Sammy's ideal day is exactly wrong for fiction. Where's the story? There is none. Unlike the actual story "A & P," nothing happens here that puts our main character to the test. We never see him under pressure. In my version, there's no actual or even implied threat to Sammy's wonderful day.

The sort of day we'd most like to experience in our actual lives—a day with only happiness and green grass and butterflies and nothing to worry about—is exactly wrong for fiction. Conversely, the kind of day we'd least like to experience in our lives—a day filled with stress and hard decisions—is exactly right for fiction.

Kurt Vonnegut put it this way:

> Be a sadist. No matter how sweet and innocent your leading characters, make awful things happen to them—in order that the reader may see what they are made of.

That last part of Vonnegut's advice is key. The purpose isn't to be mean-spirited or nihilistic, dropping pianos out of the sky onto our characters' unsuspecting heads. To do so would reveal only that our characters are squishy.

Nor must these "awful things" result in a tragic story. Not all fiction need be bleak.

But all fiction needs trouble. And the trouble that we create in a story should reveal something about our characters that the absence of that particular trouble would not reveal. To create the right sort of trouble, we have to know our characters well enough to understand what motivates them to act. The story's conflict will bump up against those motivations, moving characters away from their comfort zones and into unfamiliar, uncomfortable territory.

It might be helpful to think about conflict as having both **external** and **internal** components. The external conflict gives narrative existence to a character's internal struggle; the internal conflict gives significance to the story's external events.

Let's look again at Tim O'Brien's story "On the Rainy River." Tim, the story's narrator, is against the war in Vietnam. His being drafted—an external event—creates the story's basic conflict: Will Tim join the military? Or will he flee to Canada? Tim delays resolution to this conflict with an external action: getting into his car and driving north toward the Canadian border. Doing so only amplifies his ambivalence, his internal conflict, causing him to hole up at the Tip Top Lodge, where he can do some heavy thinking about whether he'll serve, and what kind of person he'd be if he does, and what kind of person he'd be if he doesn't. His ruminations, however, don't get him very far. What ultimately causes him to resolve his conflict is another external event: Elroy takes Tim in his motorboat, ostensibly on a fishing trip, within a few dozen yards of Canadian territory—easily close enough to jump out and swim—transforming Tim's internal conflict into a full-blown crisis with a choice that can no longer be delayed.

> For ten or fifteen minutes Elroy held a course upstream, the river choppy and silver-gray, then he turned straight north and put the engine on full throttle. I felt the bow lift beneath me. I remember the wind in my ears, the sound of the old outboard Evinrude. For a time I didn't pay attention to anything, just feeling the cold spray against my face, but then it occurred to me that at some point we must've passed into Canadian waters, across that dotted line between two different worlds, and I remember a sudden tightness in my chest as I looked up and watched the far shore come at me. This wasn't a daydream. It was tangible and real.

In this passage, Tim sees that his thoughts of flight, until now, were just daydreams. This close to Canada, however, at the precipice of a potentially new beginning, Tim feels the full force of a decision that will cause his life to fork in one of two opposing directions. Only here—on this motorboat, so close to the Canadian shore—must he reveal himself for who he is. Here we'll see what he is made of.

✳ exercises: create conflict

1. What does your main character desire, and what would be the gravest threat to that desire?

2. What would cause your character to face his or her worst fear?

3. Create a dilemma for which there are only bad solutions.

CLIMAX

In "A & P," when Sammy confronts his boss and quits his job, he is demonstrating his allegiance to the girls over his allegiance to Lengel, not just in his thoughts but in action. He knowingly alters his own fate.

You might notice how at that point in the story, the storytelling approach changes. Before then, the story had very little dialogue. But the moment when Sammy quits is full of dialogue, the effect being to underscore its importance and allow the reader to participate in the scene as it unfolds.

> "Did you say something, Sammy?"
> "I said I quit."
> "I thought you did."
> "You didn't have to embarrass them."
> "It was they who were embarrassing us."
> I started to say something that came out "Fiddle-de-doo." It's a saying of my grandmother's, and I know she would have been pleased.
> "I don't think you know what you're saying," Lengel said.
> "I know you don't," I said. "But I do." I pull the bow at the back of my apron and start shrugging it off my shoulders. A couple customers that had been heading for my slot begin to knock against each other, like scared pigs in a chute.

The reader must be able to experience this moment of high tension along with Sammy. To summarize it ("Then Sammy quit his job and left the store") would be to commit an ungenerous act upon the reader.

The climactic scene in "On the Rainy River" is prolonged for several pages as Tim, right up against the Canadian shore, is pulled harder and harder in opposing directions. In a paragraph that incrementally reveals the forces pulling at him, Tim describes how his "whole life seemed to spill out into the river." He writes:

> I saw my brother and sister, all the townsfolk, the mayor and the entire Chamber of Commerce and all my old teachers and girlfriends and high school buddies. Like some weird sporting event: everybody screaming from the sidelines, rooting me on—a loud stadium roar. Hotdogs and popcorn— stadium smells, stadium heat. A squad of cheerleaders did cartwheels along the banks of the Rainy River.

Tim's hallucination expands to include historical figures, fictional characters, his future wife and unborn daughter, and the Vietnamese soldier he would one day kill. It's a total vision of past, present, and future, real and imagined, personal and political. Crammed into a single, lengthy paragraph, the effect is overwhelming and smothering, which is exactly the effect this vision has on Tim. Were you to cut that paragraph completely out of the story, you wouldn't alter the plot one iota. All you'd be losing is *the entire story*—for that paragraph, smack in the heart of the story's climactic scene, causes us to feel, right along with Tim, the full weight bearing down on him.

Your story's conflict, whatever it is, will need to come to a climactic moment. And that moment should most likely be given its due space, dramatized rather than summarized, so that the reader can experience this crucial part of your story along with the characters.

checklist » focus on climax

» What is your story's climax? Does it have one? Will it be written (has it been written) in scene? If not, why not?

» How will the story's setting help to amplify or focus the story's climax?

CONCLUSION: WHAT HAS CHANGED?

On the Freytag Pyramid, the climax is the point at the top. After that, we change direction. We were rising; now we're falling. The story's conflict has built to the point where the pressure has to find release. The climax is where release happens, resulting in some kind of change.

In much short fiction of the nineteenth and early twentieth centuries, change came about by way of a plot twist/surprise/reversal of fortune. The stories by O. Henry exemplify this type of story. In "The Gift of the Magi," a man sells his watch to buy his wife fancy jeweled combs for her beautiful hair. Unbeknownst to him, his wife sells her hair to buy him a platinum chain for his pocket watch. Irony abounds, but love prevails.

Most contemporary literary writers, however, focus as much on changes to their characters' internal states as on changes to their external circumstances. This internal change often comes as a change in perception, or a realization or an insight that the character didn't—or couldn't—have made when the story began. James Joyce first used the term "epiphany" to describe this phenomenon in his own writing. The word "epiphany" in a Christian context describes a manifestation of the divine. Joyce's use of the term was secular; he was describing the phenomenon of a character experiencing a moment of unexpected, shimmering insight.

We can say that Sammy experiences an epiphany at the end of "A & P" when he suddenly realizes how hard the world is going to be to him hereafter. The story ends with both a change in Sammy's circumstance (he's out of a job) and a change of perception (he has begun to develop a richer understanding of adulthood).

In the story "On the Rainy River," Tim has an epiphany when he realizes, finally, that he will make what he considers to be the cowardly, rather than courageous, choice:

> I would go to the war—I would kill and maybe die—because I was embarrassed not to.

Tim's change, like Sammy's, includes both a change in circumstance (he has resolved his ambivalence and will go to Vietnam rather than to Canada) and a change in his understanding about himself (he can't, after all, summon the heroism he had always hoped lay dormant inside him).

But just as not every person is capable of surfing or performing heart surgery, not every main character is capable of insight. And an epiphany can feel every bit as forced, as imposed by the author, as a grand piano to the head. No law says that your character must grow as a human being or learn a valuable lesson about himself or anything else.

By the end of Charles Dickens's story *A Christmas Carol*, Ebenezer Scrooge has completely transformed from a nasty miser to a man of compassion and charity. Such A-to-Z change is highly unusual. Often, and especially in short fiction, a change from, say, M to P is plenty.

The main character in Kevin Brockmeier's story "A Fable with Slips of White Paper Spilling from the Pockets" (p. 211) begins with a man finding God's overcoat. In the pockets of the overcoat, the man discovers the prayers of all the people he comes in contact with. At first, he fantasizes about becoming some "benevolent stranger" who answers these prayers. But as we might expect in that situation, the man quickly becomes overwhelmed. "There were so many prayers," Brockmeier writes, "there was so much longing in the world, and in the face of it all he began to feel helpless."

One day, the man discovers that he has misplaced the coat. Without it, he loses access to the prayers of others. By now, he's gotten used to the constant barrage of prayers, and at first he feels a terrible sense of loss. Gradually, the loss fades. Yet the man doesn't return to being the same person he was at the start of the story. He has changed — but not from A to Z. His change is subtler.

> Eventually he was left with only a small ache in the back of his mind, no larger than a pebble, and a lingering sensitivity to the currents of hope and longing that flowed through the air.

His experience of wearing the coat has changed him, but no more than we might reasonably expect a person to change — no more than we might expect ourselves to change. Yet even a small, permanent change, one that leaves a man with a "lingering sensitivity" that he did not have before, can be a very big deal.

Imagine if the world were filled with people like that.

Must your main character change?

Your main character probably will, and probably should, undergo some change or development or regression, or reveal an aspect of his or her personality that had as yet gone unrevealed.

Longtime editor Rust Hills suggests that if your Scrooge is to remain a Scrooge, then the story should show how your character loses whatever potential for change might have existed when the story began — this loss of the potential for change being, itself, a kind of change.

✳ exercise: identify how your character changes

Write down, specifically, the ways in which your character changes by the end of your story. What has changed about her external circumstance? What has changed internally: about her beliefs, or the way she views herself or others? What has she learned? What *hasn't* she learned? Are these changes permanent or temporary?

FORM = MEANING

In a 1915 letter to the founding editor of *Poetry* magazine, Ezra Pound famously wrote that "rhythm must have meaning." The rhythm of a poem should never be made independently of the work's meaning, because a poem's formal attributes, like rhythm and meter, always affect meaning.

Pound's contention is no less true of fiction. There must always be a necessary relationship between a story's form and its meaning, because a story's form is part of what creates its meaning.

Jill McCorkle's story "Magic Words" is told in sections that alternate among three point-of-view characters. This technical choice suggests that "Magic Words" is less the story of any single character than the story of the interconnectedness of them all. We could even say that, thematically, the story speaks to the interconnectedness of all our seemingly disparate lives.

Sherman Alexie's story "This Is What It Means to Say Phoenix, Arizona" (p. 185) features a character, Thomas Builds-the-Fire, who is the reservation's self-appointed storyteller. But nobody wants to hear Thomas's stories, including Victor, the narrator. Still, Thomas isn't dissuaded from telling them. "Phoenix, Arizona" is peppered with brief anecdotes from Victor's and Thomas's past. In one, Victor steps on a wasp nest. In another, Thomas jumps off the school's roof in an attempt to fly. Why are these anecdotes in the story? They don't serve to move the plot forward, yet they accomplish through form what Thomas himself tries to accomplish *within* the story — to demonstrate how a community's shared stories are essential in binding that community together.

OTHER WAYS TO TELL A STORY

McCorkle's and Alexie's stories embody the successful search for meaningful form. They are also both departures, to some degree, from classic story structure.

The following forms do not usually require a wholesale disregard of the central concepts we've been discussing, such as conflict, causality, and climax. However, the following forms do draw our attention away from certain elements of the traditionally told story in order to emphasize some aspect of the particular story being told.

The out-of-sequence story

We often see this technique in movies: The films of Quentin Tarantino, including *Pulp Fiction* and *Reservoir Dogs*, are boldly out of sequence, entangling the viewer immediately in their frenetic, chaotic worlds. Jonathan Nolan's short story "Memento Mori" (and his brother Christopher Nolan's film *Memento*), in which a man has absolutely no long-term memory, is a striking example of how a work's content demands a particular sequence.

A plot need not be presented in chronological order. In fact, stories that begin *in medias res* are usually out of sequence since they must at some point fill in the skipped-over material. The first section of Becky Hagenston's story "Midnight, Licorice, Shadow" (p. 227) involves a cat-naming session. The second section fills in the backstory, depicting the moment three weeks earlier when the two characters first met.

The frame story

A frame story is a story that contains another story (or stories) within it. Geoffrey Chaucer's *The Canterbury Tales*, written in the fourteenth century, are framed as tales told by a group of pilgrims to pass the time as they travel to Canterbury. Washington Irving's *Sketch Book*, published in 1820, contains framed stories as well, including the familiar "The Legend of Sleepy Hollow" and "Rip Van Winkle."

Often the outer frame provides contextual information or encourages the reader to believe the story-within-the-story. We're familiar with these techniques from ghost stories and urban legends: *So check out this completely creepy thing that happened. It might sound unbelievable, but I swear it's true because it happened to my brother's girlfriend.*

The narrator, in providing this brief frame, is attesting that it actually happened. It isn't just some made-up story; it's something that happened to a real person: the narrator's roommate or aunt or best friend. The film *The Blair Witch Project* begins with the following statement: *In October of 1994 three student filmmakers disappeared in the woods near Burkittsville, Maryland, while shooting a documentary. . . . A year later their footage was found.*

Washington Irving's story "Sleepy Hollow" is essentially an urban legend (more accurately, a "rural legend") about an easily frightened schoolteacher who gets run out of town by the Headless Horseman (or, quite possibly, by the town's prankster). It begins with a statement that this story was "found among the papers of the late Diedrich Knickerbocker" and ends with a postscript "found in the Handwriting of Mr. Knickerbocker" that explains how and when the narrator first heard the story.

Frame stories can lack immediacy because the frame serves as a buffer between the reader and the story-within-the-story, which is often where the real drama lies. If, for example, a story begins by telling us that John is finally getting rescued from his lifeboat, then we already know that (1) a ship goes down and (2) John survives. As we read the story of the sinking ship, we'll always be one step removed from the drama because we know it isn't really unfolding before us—we're already aware of the outcome.

Beginning writers sometimes include frames at the start of their stories that unnecessarily delay the real story:

> I'm lying in bed, staring at the cracks in my ceiling, my mind reeling over the crazy thing that happened to me today.

There's no need for that sort of frame—better to start the story with the crazy thing that happened.

The question is always whether the frame is a necessary part of the whole. Here's the most basic test: Cut the frame. How does your story change? If it doesn't change very much, then you might be well served to get rid of the frame and allow your story-within-the-story to come alive.

The collage story

Rick Moody's short story "Demonology" (2002) faces the narrative challenge of presenting the sudden and untimely death of the narrator's sister. She had a seizure and then died. Earlier, I wrote that the difference between real life and fiction was that events in fiction don't happen to random people. But what if that's the *point* of your story—to present a crisis that comes out of nowhere, rather than being the logical culmination of a causal plot?

"Demonology" has two unusual features. The first is its form: It is constructed entirely of brief anecdotes about the narrator's sister. Each runs just a paragraph or two, yet collectively they form a remarkably complete collage of her life. Why does the story take this form, specifically? For one thing, the collage story is organized less by causality than by theme and pattern; each section bears a relationship to the whole, but one section doesn't lead causally to the next. The other reason has to do with the career of the narrator's sister: She worked at a photo lab. The story is therefore told in snapshots, mirroring the fragmented understanding that she had of other people's lives from looking at their photographs.

The second unusual feature is the story's final paragraph. "Demonology" ends with its narrator directly addressing the story's narrative shortcomings:

> I shouldn't clutter a narrative with fragments, with mere recollections of good times, or with regrets, I should make Meredith's death shapely and persuasive, not blunt and disjunctive.

Faulting himself for telling the story as he has, the story's narrator reveals the frustration of creating a narrative out of real life. In doing so, he's also exposing the fiction at the heart of all traditionally told narratives. The end of the story therefore reveals just why this unconventional story has taken the form that it has. The narrator, because of his intense feelings for his sister, her life, and her death, refuses to reduce her to a character, or her real life to the sort of narrative we readers have come to expect.

Metafiction

Fiction that reveals itself as fiction or that directly addresses the fictional process, as "Demonology" does, is called metafiction. Metafiction isn't itself a form, but it affects form by disrupting the reader's "vivid and continuous dream" that John Gardner explains is at the heart of much well-told fiction.

John Barth's 1963 story "Lost in the Funhouse" is a work of metafiction that narrates a thirteen-year-old boy's Independence Day at the beach while simultaneously exposing the boy's story as a work of fiction. No matter how interested you become in Ambrose's story, the running editorial commentary won't let you lose yourself in the narrative. A portion of the story's second paragraph reads:

> *En route* to Ocean City he sat in the back seat of the family car with his brother Peter, age fifteen, and Magda G____, age fourteen, a pretty girl an exquisite young lady, who lived not far from them on B____ Street in the town of D____, Maryland. Initials, blanks, or both were often substitutes for proper names in nineteenth-century fiction to enhance the illusion of reality. It is as if the author felt it necessary to delete the names for reasons of tact or legal liability. Interestingly, as with other aspects of realism, it is an *illusion* that is being enhanced, by purely artificial means.

A story like "Lost in the Funhouse" isn't for everyone, and metafiction carries inherent risks. Readers are constantly being reminded that they're reading words on a page, and that what they're reading isn't real, which are exactly the two things that a fiction writer usually tries to make readers forget. When the Wizard of Oz confesses to Dorothy that he's just an "old Kansas man" himself with nothing more than a few decent special effects, Dorothy, despite being terrified of him up to that point, feels terribly let down. Once the magic is dispelled, she gives up any hope of being transported by it. (That is, until Glinda arrives on the scene.)

Usually, we don't want readers to see the gears and wheels of our mechanisms. But if your story deals with the nature of narrative itself, then you might want to consider metafiction, which is the fiction writer's way of revealing what's behind the curtain.

Others

Of course there are others! We're talking about *writers*, who, after all, are rule-breakers and boundary-pushers by nature. Kevin Brockmeier's novel *The Illumination* follows a woman's journal that gets passed among six characters. In David Mitchell's novel *Cloud Atlas*, a character reads a book that contains a story, which itself contains a story, and so on. His novel is structured like a series of nesting dolls in which one fits inside the other, which fits inside the other and then inverts midway through.

✷ exercise: evaluate your story's form

On a sheet of paper, brainstorm the following questions: What is your story about? Are there any aspects of form that you might include to underscore your story's major thematic concerns?

SCENE AND SUMMARY

Chapter 5 explains the details of scene-writing. Most stories, however, include both scene and summary. When you write a story, you're constantly deciding which to use.

The stories in the anthology vary widely in terms of their use of scene and summary. "A & P," for example, is structured as one continuous scene, with summary information provided in bits and pieces. "This Is What It Means to Say Phoenix, Arizona" is made up of multiple scenes—the longer ones in the narrative present, the shorter ones in flashback. Where summary information is needed, Alexie typically provides it at the beginning of scenes:

> Victor didn't find much to keep in the trailer. Only a photo album and a stereo. Everything else had that smell stuck in it or was useless anyway. [**summary**]
> "I guess this is all," Victor said. "It ain't much." [**Dialogue signals the transition into scene.**]

Keep in mind that the word "dramatize" contains the word "drama." The parts of stories that we choose to dramatize (write in scene) should contribute to the story's unfolding drama.

Imagine a story in which, say, a young woman is rushing to her mother's hospital bedside. The scene includes the following dialogue:

> "Yes, I'm here to see my mother," Julie said. "Her name is Samantha Boswell. Can you tell me what room she's in?"
> "Let's see," the nurse said. "It looks like she's in room 211. It's down that hallway, the third door on the left."
> "Thank you," Julie said. "Can I see her now?"
> "Absolutely," the nurse said. "Visiting hours go on for another three hours."

Is the dialogue believable? Sure. But this fairly lengthy exchange is quite likely extraneous to the story. Unless the nurse is an important character, or this exchange truly gives valuable insight into Julie's personality or complicates the plot, we don't need it.

A simple line of summary would be more appropriate:

At the nurses' station, Julie learned that her mother was in room 211.

Or maybe we don't need this information at all, and we'd be better off jumping right into the scene once Julie has arrived at her mother's room.

Here is how Sherman Alexie gets Victor and Thomas out of a taxicab in "This Is What It Means to Say Phoenix, Arizona":

Victor paid for the taxi and the two of them stood in the hot Phoenix summer. They could smell the trailer.

There's no mention of any interaction with the cab driver, who isn't important to the story.

~~"That'll be fourteen dollars," the cabbie said.~~

~~"Do you have change for a twenty?" Victor asked.~~

That sort of chitchat would waste the reader's time and cause the story to lose focus.

✳ exercises: practice writing scene & summary

To get a feel for the different effects that scene and summary have on a story's focus and pacing, write the same section of a story two different ways.

1. Write a paragraph that summarizes an event, followed by a page-long scene that picks up right after the first event.

2. Now reverse it: Write a page-long scene that dramatizes what you'd previously summarized, followed by a paragraph that summarizes what the first version had dramatized in scene.

CASE STUDY: STRUCTURAL IMITATION

This chapter has approached form and structure in a variety of ways: with theory, examples, exercises, and close readings. We've examined classically constructed stories and interesting deviations.

Now it's time for a case study.

This imitation exercise will help you see, experientially, how one section of a particular story follows the previous one, how it leads to the next, and how all these parts contribute to the whole.

The assignment

First, you'll analyze one of the anthologized stories to uncover the function of each section. Then you'll write an original story, with your own characters, plot, voice, et cetera, in which each section of the story serves the same structural purpose as in the story you analyzed.

To see the assignment in action, let's look at the story "Water Liars" by Barry Hannah (p. 239).

This brief story is told in eight sections. Our job is to describe each section according to its function in the story, using accurate yet broad language. For instance, here is the story's entire first section:

> When I am run down and flocked around by the world, I go down to Farte Cove off the Yazoo River and take my beer to the end of the pier where the old liars are still snapping and wheezing at one another. The line-up is always different, because they're always dying out or succumbing to constipation, etc., whereupon they go back to the cabins and wait for a good day when they can come out and lie again, leaning on the rail with coats full of bran cookies. The son of the man the cove was named for is often out there. He pronounces his name Far*tay*, with a great French stress on the last syllable. Otherwise you might laugh at his history or ignore it in favor of the name as it's spelled on the sign.
>
> I'm glad it's not my name.
>
> This poor dignified man has had to explain his nobility to the semiliterate of half of America before he could even begin a decent conversation with them. On the other hand, Farte, Jr., is a great liar himself. He tells about seeing ghost people around the lake and tells big loose ones about the size of the fish those ghosts took out of Farte Cove in years past.

We might describe the function of the story's first section like this:

> Section 1 introduces the place where the story's narrator and others habitually congregate. It also overviews the sort of people who gather there, and zeroes in on one of them.

Here is the story's second section:

> Last year I turned thirty-three years old and, raised a Baptist, I had a sense of being Jesus and coming to something decided in my life—because we all know Jesus was crucified at thirty-three. It had all seemed especially important, what you do in this year, and holy with meaning.
>
> On the morning after my birthday party, during which I and my wife almost drowned in vodka cocktails, we both woke up to the making of a truth session about the lovers we'd had before we met each other. I had a mildly exciting and usual history, and she had about the same, which surprised me. For ten years she'd sworn I was the first. I could not believe her history was exactly equal with mine. It hurt me to think that in the era when there were supposed to be virgins she had allowed anyone but *me*, and so on.
>
> I was dazed and exhilarated by this information for several weeks. Finally, it drove me crazy, and I came out to Farte Cove to rest, under the pretense of a fishing week with my chum Wyatt.
>
> I'm still figuring out why I couldn't handle it.

We might describe the function of that section like this:

> Section 2 is a flashback, told in summary, that describes a conflict between the narrator and another character (in this story, his wife) that has led the narrator to go to the place described in section 1.

And so on. Remember, the purpose isn't to summarize the plot, but rather to describe the function that each section has in the story. A sentence or two for each section should suffice.

Were you to choose "Water Liars" as your model, after working through all eight sections, you would then use that same structure to write an original story. Feel free to change the point of view as well as the tense. Each section in your story can be longer or shorter than in the original. The only requirement is that your story follow the same section-by-section structure as described in your outline.

Other than its basic structure, your story shouldn't resemble "Water Liars" at all. All the details need to be completely your own.

If you're concerned that this imitation assignment is overly rigid and might inhibit your creativity, consider the Shakespearean sonnet: fourteen lines, rhyming iambic pentameter, specific rhyming pattern with a rhetorical "turn" near the end—in other words, a far more rigid structure than this assignment. Yet the sonnet is a form that poets have embraced for many hundreds of years and shows no signs of inhibiting creativity. In fact, you might well find that when you don't have to invent a structure for your story, your creativity will flourish.

I urge you not just to think about this assignment, but actually to do it. You'll be glad you did, because it will allow you to put everything discussed in this chapter into practice.

Which story should you choose as the basis for your structural imitation? Consider which story intrigues you the most. Consider which story you *like* the most.

It's up to you.

Student example. To see this exercise in action, here is a student's imitation of section 1 of "Water Liars."

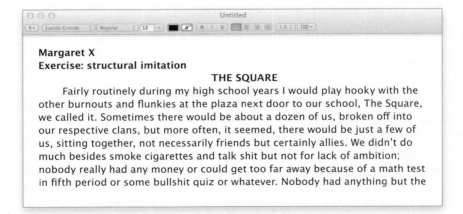

Margaret X
Exercise: structural imitation

THE SQUARE

Fairly routinely during my high school years I would play hooky with the other burnouts and flunkies at the plaza next door to our school, The Square, we called it. Sometimes there would be about a dozen of us, broken off into our respective clans, but more often, it seemed, there would be just a few of us, sitting together, not necessarily friends but certainly allies. We didn't do much besides smoke cigarettes and talk shit but not for lack of ambition; nobody really had any money or could get too far away because of a math test in fifth period or some bullshit quiz or whatever. Nobody had anything but the passing time, I suppose, and we were all stuck there in it, together. We would make plans for the weekend and exchange stories about last weekend or the weekend before that.

Despite our individual egos, we all knew our rank at The Square, and if anyone ever forgot, Ray, a senior in his fifth year, would remind them. Ray was like our president, elected by his years of service at The Square. Having been around longer than any of us, he was full of wisdom about how best to avoid school security or how not to lose credit in a course because of absences or how to get your cell phone back from the principal. He was good like that and always willing to help a fellow classmate out.

I was unduly cynical and jaded for my young years, not a favorite playmate among what my mother considered my age-appropriate peers. And so although Ray was in his fifth year when I was only starting my first, we became fast friends. It was through Ray that I learned how to talk to girls, hand-roll cigarettes, open the school windows, shoplift from Starbucks, and ride the metro for free—not the most wholesome skills, granted, but each helpful to me for one reason or another, even if it was just to relieve the bouts of boredom and dread common to my class and generation.

writing a compelling story 7

WHEN I WAS A GRADUATE student at the University of Missouri, I worked on the editorial staff of the literary journal *The Missouri Review*. Each year, the journal sponsored an Editors' Prize in fiction, poetry, and the essay. Writers from all over the world submitted their work. The winner in each genre received a cash prize and publication in the journal.

A friend and I were in charge of the fiction part of the prize. We recruited a small group of other graduate students, and together over a period of about eight weeks our job was to select ten finalists from among all the short-story entries. From those finalists, the magazine's editor would select a winner.

One year, we received 1,100 entries.

This is what we call a lot of stories. The time spent reading them was, as you'd expect, tremendous. Still, we didn't actually find it too difficult to reduce the pool of stories from 1,100 — most of which were competently written — to a group of about fifty. The process of winnowing fifty manuscripts down to ten finalists was excruciating. It's very likely that even the forty we didn't choose as finalists went on to be published anyway, in some other journal. There was no stopping those stories.

But more relevant to this chapter than the question of which ten stories made the cut is what made those fifty stories rise above the other 1,050. What made them compelling, when so many others were merely competent? What made them better?

HIGH STAKES

Here is what "high stakes" *doesn't* have to mean: a group of thieves, pretending to be terrorists, holding people hostage in an office building (as in the movie *Diehard*), or an asteroid headed for Earth that must be deflected with a perfectly timed atomic blast (as in the movie *Armageddon*).

A high-stakes story requires neither terrorists nor Earth's imminent destruction. For the stakes to be high, a story needs only for a character to care a great deal about something: a man quietly tortured by his love for a co-worker who's about to marry another man ("Tandolfo the Great"), or a young woman struggling with her identity during her first year away at college ("Drinking Coffee Elsewhere"), or a man inexplicably troubled by his wife's sexual past, which she has until now hidden from him ("Water Liars").

A story about a man stirring up trouble during a bank robbery ("Bullet in the Brain") might seem more inherently high-stakes than a man hanging out on a dock, trying to get to the root of his sour feelings ("Water Liars"). The author's job is to make whatever story is being told one that matters—a lot—to its characters and, therefore, to the reader.

As diverse as they are, the stories in this book's anthology all feature characters who experience their problems urgently. And that urgency infects the reader.

Richard Bausch's "Tandolfo the Great" (p. 198) begins comically, yet it is a comedy imbued with desperation and self-loathing:

> "Tandolfo," he says to his own image in the mirror over the bathroom sink. "She loves you not, oh, she doesn't, doesn't, doesn't."

We soon learn that time is of the essence: Tandolfo's co-worker, whom he secretly loves, is moving to Houston. He'll never see her again—unless he confesses his love to her right away. This need to act now, right now, raises the stakes by transforming his internal desires into action.

The narrator of Tim O'Brien's story "On the Rainy River" (p. 287) conveys the story's high stakes more directly: He explains them. Here is how he conveys the intense pressure he felt at the moment when he could have—but didn't—swim to Canada to avoid the Vietnam draft:

That close—twenty yards—and I could see the delicate latticework of the leaves, the texture of the soil, the browned needles beneath the pines, the configurations of geology and human history. Twenty yards. I could've done it. I could've jumped and started swimming for my life. Inside me, in my chest, I felt a terrible squeezing pressure. Even now, as I write this, I can still feel that tightness. And I want you to feel it—the wind coming off the river, the waves, the silence, the wooded frontier. You're at the bow of a boat on the Rainy River. You're twenty-one years old, you're scared, and there's a hard squeezing pressure in your chest.

What would you do?

Would you jump? Would you feel pity for yourself? Would you think about your family and your childhood and your dreams and all you're leaving behind? Would it hurt? Would it feel like dying? Would you cry, as I did?

I tried to swallow it back. I tried to smile, except I was crying.

Now, perhaps, you can understand why I've never told this story before.

✳ exercises: set the stakes

1. Write a scene in which a character finally does the thing he or she has always wanted to do, but never before had the guts.

2. Write the first two pages of a story that the narrator has kept secret for his or her entire life up until now.

CHARACTER DESIRE

Waiter: Can I get you anything else?
Customer: No, thank you. I have everything I need.

What you have just read is not compelling. Characters need to want things. Otherwise, there's no conflict, no stakes, and therefore no story.

Waiter: Can I get you anything else?
Customer: Why, yes. Please get me my wife back.
Waiter: Sir?
Customer: My wife. She left me last night. I'd like her back. Please bring her back.

Almost nothing is more fundamental to storytelling than character desire—especially strong desire, as the motivational continuum will demonstrate.

The motivational continuum

I'd been teaching this concept for a number of years before a student of mine (thanks, Jerry!) finally gave it the name that stuck. Here's how it works. Think about your own life and write down a few expectations having to do with things you care about. For example: *I expect to graduate this spring. I expect to get a new car once my junky one finally dies.*

Go ahead. Write them down.

Now think about your hopes: *I hope to get a job when I graduate. I hope that I can afford that new car when my old one inevitably dies.*

A stronger desire than a hope is a dream. What are your dreams? *I dream that after graduation I land a job reporting on international affairs for a major national newspaper. I dream that I win a car.*

Expectations lie at the center of the continuum. Hopes and dreams lie to one side. Now let's look at the other side.

What are your fears? *I fear that I won't find a job. I fear that I won't graduate. I fear that my car will die and I won't be able to afford a new one. What will I do then?*

Worse than fears are your dreads: *I dread flunking out of school. I dread my car dying on a deserted road in the middle of the night. I dread landing a great job but then one of my parents falling ill, forcing me to abandon either my dream job or my parent.*

The reason Jerry's name for this continuum of feelings fits so well is that our feelings motivate us to act. The stronger we feel about something, the more motivated we are.

Graphically, the motivational continuum looks like this:

Dreads ⟵ **Fears** ⟵ **Expectations** ⟶ **Hopes** ⟶ **Dreams**

Now here's the point: *Compelling stories (in other words, stories with high stakes) tend to dwell in the outer reaches of the motivational continuum.* They deal in the realm of characters' dreams and dreads, rather than with mere expectations. The customer in my first example expects coffee and peach cobbler. Nobody wants to read about a man who expects, and is either granted or denied, cobbler. However, the man in the second example *dreads* going home to an empty house for the first time in thirty-five years, a fact that will make even simple cobbler-eating fraught with emotion.

Dreads ⟵ **Fears** ⟵ **Expectations** ⟶ **Hopes** ⟶ **Dreams**

Tandolfo, the protagonist in Richard Bausch's story, isn't completely naïve. Certainly he can't *expect* his co-worker, who has shown him only vague signs of friendly affection, to break up with her boyfriend and reveal her love for him. What motivates him to act—to buy that giant wedding cake, profess his love for her, and presumably make a fool of himself—is that he *dreams* that the grandness of his action will stir some feeling inside of her that heretofore had been hidden even from herself. Yet what causes him to get drunk first, and to behave so badly at the kid's birthday party, is that he *dreads* confirmation of what he surely must know is the more likely truth: She does not love him and never will.

Dreams and dreads, despite being at the far reaches of the continuum, aren't opposites. The opposite of a high school student's dream of getting drafted into the NBA (a dream that includes fame, fortune, and a chance to travel the world) isn't a failure to make the NBA. Rather, his dread is to be utterly forgotten, reduced to working at his dad's garage the rest of his life while his finest moment was the night during high school when he scored thirty-six points against a weak team.

The narrator of "On the Rainy River" does not *fear* being drafted to serve in Vietnam. He *dreads* it. And having received the draft notice, he dreads the choice he has to make. The story succeeds because Tim O'Brien makes us feel the desperation that his protagonist feels, caught between two options, both of which he dreads: either risking his life in a war he is fervently against, or fleeing to Canada and disgracing himself in the eyes of everyone he loves. Another person might merely fear going to war, or hope that life in Canada might somehow turn out okay. *This* young man, however, dreads both options, and his being thrust into a problem for which there are only terrible solutions is precisely what gives the story its high stakes.

As you write, think about what, specifically, your characters dread, fear, expect, hope, and dream. Then take a close look at the outer reaches of the motivational continuum, which tend to spawn our most urgent and compelling stories.

✳ exercises: know your character's desires

1. Complete the motivational continuum for an important character in your story, listing dreads, fears, expectations, hopes, and dreams.
2. Brainstorm a list of predicaments that threaten to
   a. thwart expectations
   b. dash hopes and dreams
   c. stir fears and dreads
3. Which of these predicaments will put your character to the greatest test?
4. Based on your answers above, write the first page of the story.

ACTIVE PROTAGONISTS

Nothing can suck the energy out of a story like a passive protagonist. I don't necessarily mean a character without desire. He might want things; he just never goes after any of them. This problem occurs most commonly in first-person stories in which the narrator serves as our eyes and ears but doesn't become actively engaged in the story's events.

Certain stories might demand that a character be unable to act—an abused spouse, say, whose fear or denial might inhibit action. More often, however, a protagonist's passivity isn't a necessary aspect of the character's personality but rather is an unintended consequence of authorial timidity. Either we're protecting our characters, not wanting bad things to happen to them, or we care too much about decorum. We instinctively stop our protagonists—and often anyone else in the story—from "making a scene," when making a scene is exactly what our characters should be doing. Charles Baxter, in his 2007 book *The Art of Subtext: Beyond Plot*, explains:

> People who have practiced good manners and conflict-avoidance all their lives have to remember to leave those habits of mind at the door when they enter the theater of fiction. Stories thrive on bad behavior, bad manners, confrontations, and unpalatable characters who by wish or compulsion make their desires visible by creating scenes.

Tandolfo, in "Tandolfo the Great," could have been merely a sad sack. He's a loner with a heap of problems, and he's been quietly in love with his co-worker for a long time without ever having let her know. Surely that is a recipe for a passive protagonist. Yet in Richard Bausch's hands, Tandolfo is highly active, forcing his fate at every turn. Maybe he is usually a passive, sad sack, but today, when the story takes place, he has bought a big wedding cake that he plans to give to the woman he has until now loved only from afar. When the birthday boy, at whose house Tandolfo must perform his magic act, turns out to be a brat, Tandolfo doesn't quietly tolerate the kid's bad behavior. Rather, he grabs the kid's tongue and calls him a "little prick" in front of all the children and their parents.

Ill advised? Of course.

Active? Definitely.

Compelling? Absolutely.

If your main character isn't a key actor in all the scenes you're writing, it's worth asking yourself if you've chosen the best main character for your story. And if you have, then consider revising the scenes to give your main character a more active role.

You've probably noticed that high stakes, character desire, and active protagonists have a lot to do with one another. Characters are most inclined to be active when they face the actualization of their dreams and dreads; in other words, when they care urgently about what is happening; in other words, when the stakes are high.

✳ exercises: make your character active

1. A typically quiet character intentionally upends the table during Thanksgiving dinner. Write the scene that causes him or her to do it.

2. Write a scene in which a character interrupts an argument between two other people (such as parents or co-workers) to make a dramatic announcement that spins the scene in a new direction.

3. Write a scene in which your protagonist is caught stealing a meaningful object from someone he or she loves.

THE ATYPICAL DAY (A BREAK FROM ROUTINE)

Tandolfo has for some time quietly pined for the woman he loves. But the day when *this* story takes place is the day that's different. It's the day when the woman's imminent departure from his life, her move to Houston, causes him to act.

Compelling stories almost always depict the day (or more generally, the time period) that represents a meaningful break from routine. If I were to walk out of my campus office into the quad, typically a site of lounging and games of Frisbee, to see a military helicopter hovering low, that would be unusual. However, if I were a soldier in a war zone, my seeing the helicopter would be typical. Maybe the day that's different would be the morning when I crawled out of my army-issue sleeping bag and saw zero helicopters or tanks but did see a group of soldiers tossing around a Frisbee.

Even quiet stories about people's daily lives, so-called slice-of-life stories, usually contain some break from what's routine. A story will lack urgency, and be far less compelling, if there's nothing special about today—if the story can just as easily take place yesterday or tomorrow or next year.

✳ exercises: break from the everyday

1. Ask yourself how each story in the anthology depicts a break from the characters' usual routines. For example:

   a. "This Is What It Means to Say Phoenix, Arizona" depicts the time when Victor and Thomas leave the reservation to claim the body of Victor's father.

   b. "A & P" depicts the day when Sammy quits his job.

2. Now ask yourself how the story you're writing depicts a break from routine. (How is today different?)

3. What causes the break from routine? (Why *must* today be different?)

EXTERNAL CONFLICT

In his book *Making Shapely Fiction*, Jerome Stern advises against writing what he calls "The Bathtub Story." It's a story in which a single character is confined to a single space. In a bathtub story, Stern writes:

> [T]he character thinks, remembers, worries, plans, whatever. Before long, readers realize that the character is not going to do anything. Nothing is going to happen in terms of action. The character is not interacting with other people, but is just thinking about past interactions. Problems will not be faced but thought about. Troubles will not occur but will be remembered. That's the problem with the bathtub story: The character is never going to get out of the bathtub.

A cousin of the bathtub story is the "driving and thinking" story. The main character either is driving someplace alone and, we realize, doomed never to get out of the car or interact with anyone in the story's dramatic present, or is in some sort of public transportation (a bus, a plane). Often, a story like that is spent mainly in flashback, with the character reflecting on past events. Even if the story happens to describe a few of the other people on the bus (an elderly woman, a bratty kid), none of those characters does anything to affect the story significantly—nor does the main character do anything significant in the story's present. He sits. He thinks.

One-character stories with no external conflict are very difficult to make compelling. The external world (other people, places, events) presents opportunities to challenge your characters and move them to action. These opportunities are worth seizing, rather than avoiding (see "Active Protagonists," p. 119).

INTERNAL CONFLICT/PRESENTING CHARACTERS' INTERIOR LIVES

A story also needs to reveal something about the interior lives of its characters and the pressures weighing on them. A typical story that fails to do this depicts an athlete playing "the big game." The game might be a nail-biter, but we aren't biting our nails. Why, after all, should we care about the outcome of a fictional sporting event? A story that focuses exclusively on the external situation at the expense of its characters and what motivates them will not be compelling.

The line "this time, it's personal" is a cliché of the detective genre, but the sentiment is exactly right. The story must always be personal to the protagonist. We won't care about a story's external events unless we're made to understand why they matter to the characters in the story. (See "High Stakes," p. 115.)

George Saunders's story "CivilWarLand in Bad Decline" (p. 341) is a story with plenty of external conflict involving a man who works at an amusement park on the brink of bankruptcy. When a co-worker begins to commit atrocities against potential vandals, the protagonist becomes implicated, going so far as to bury a teenager's severed hand on park grounds to protect his deranged co-worker. Why would he do this? He is worried about the welfare of his two young sons, should he lose his job:

> I did a horrible thing. Even as I sit here I'm an accomplice and an obstructor of justice.
>
> But then I see myself in the penitentiary and the boys waking up scared in the night without me, and right then and there with my feet in the creek I decide to stay clammed up forever and take my lumps in the afterlife.

Characters expose their inner lives in many ways: They ruminate, they speak, they act out. Chapter 4 details the myriad ways that characters reveal themselves in fiction. But reveal themselves they must.

COMPRESSED TIME PERIOD

A surefire way to make your short story more compelling — specifically, more focused and tension-filled — is to *compress the story's timeline* as much as possible. Several stories in the anthology take place over part of a single day; at least one takes place over just several minutes.

In John Updike's "A & P" (p. 359), Sammy quits his job impulsively, in immediate response to the three girls being chastised by his boss. Imagine if, instead, Sammy had brooded inwardly but done nothing for a month or two before quitting. Much of the tension would have drained right out of the story.

"Tandolfo the Great" chronicles just a few hours in the life of its protagonist. He buys a wedding cake, which sits in his car while he performs magic at a bratty kid's party, and then he rushes to the home of the woman he loves. In this one emotion-filled afternoon, Tandolfo's dreams and dreads are confronted.

This is not to say that your story must take place over a single day. Maybe it will, but each story has its own demands. As you write, ask yourself if there are ways to compress the timeline. If you find yourself beginning a paragraph or section with a phrase like "The following week," ask yourself why that can't be changed to "The next morning" or even "Two hours later."

SUSPENSE (AS OPPOSED TO WITHHELD INFORMATION)

Suspense, the sort of writing that keeps us riveted to the page, requires the reader's knowledge, not ignorance. While it might be tempting to wait until the last page to reveal that your bug-eating protagonist is actually an iguana, withholding such crucial information as the species of your protagonist causes the reader to *imagine your story incorrectly*. Readers are imagining a bug-eating person. You, the writer, are imagining a reptile.

That's an extreme and rather silly example, but the point is that readers need to imagine your story accurately and know what the stakes are so that they can experience the mounting tension right along with your character. Imagine someone slowly overinflating a balloon. You know enough about the physics of air and stretched rubber to know what's going to happen. Still, it's suspenseful to watch, to wait in uncomfortable anticipation for the inevitable explosion.

Jonathan Lethem's 1999 novel *Motherless Brooklyn* depicts a private investigator, Lionel Essrog, who suffers from Tourette's syndrome, a disorder associated with vocal tics and, in some cases, the uncontrollable shouting of obscenities. In trying to crack the case, Essrog finds himself in what is surely the worst possible place for a man with a bad case of Tourette's: a Zen center where everyone has taken a vow of silence. Of all the fates that could befall a detective with this condition, surely nothing is worse than to have to sit among absolutely silent people having to be absolutely silent himself. The suspense comes from our knowing his condition, knowing him, and watching as he tries desperately to contain his uncontrollable shouts and expletives. As human beings who've come to care about this character, we don't want him to fail. And yet as readers, we do. We want that balloon to explode even as we're covering our ears.

We suspect that Essrog will not only fail, but fail spectacularly. What we don't know, and what we read to find out, is exactly how he'll fail and what the repercussions will be.

✳ exercises: build suspense

1. Write the first paragraph of a story that reveals your main character's vice or Achilles heel (something that will cause him or her trouble later in the story).

2. Write a scene in which your main character must endure a deep-seated, specific fear in order to achieve a larger goal. (For instance, a man faces his deep fear of drowning in order to hunt for his wedding ring that has fallen into the river. A child faces her fear of the dark in order to soothe her baby brother to sleep.)

ORIGINALITY

First, a caveat: Being original doesn't have to mean being completely revolutionary. Too much focus on being wholly original can lead a writer to gimmicks that (1) overshadow the story and (2) aren't actually original.

Yet originality *is* important because it means avoiding what's easy, whether that's the rehashing of stale plots, characters, and settings, or going along with conventional wisdom, or telling a story the way it's always been told.

Why must the most popular boy in school be captain of the football team? Why must the most popular girl be the head cheerleader? (And why are you writing about the "most popular" kid, anyway?) Why must the beautiful woman in the story have blond hair and blue eyes? And for her to seem beautiful, why must her hair and eyes be described, rather than her unusually erect posture, her faded Metallica T-shirt, or her skill at pinball? And why must she be beautiful? Can't a guy fall for the girl with crooked teeth or a weird blotch the shape of Florida on her neck?

In every aspect of your story, make the effort to avoid stock details. Make the reader imagine *your* particular world, not the world they could have invented themselves.

Of course, the only way for a writer to know what's actually fresh, versus what might seem fresh but is in fact a cliché, is to read and read widely.

Here's an idea that might not seem stale yet is something I see all the time in my roles as an editor and a teacher: a story in which the protagonist works a meaningless job in an office cubicle.

Problem 1: The overabundance of these stories suggests that they are not fresh.

Problem 2: Often, the corporation's actual purpose doesn't matter in terms of plot or theme. The company that sells greeting cards could just as easily sell breakfast cereal, and the story wouldn't be any different. That's because the company serves as a symbol (usually some vague commentary about the emptiness of corporate existence) rather than as an actual place of employment.

Problem 3: Often, the main character holds some undefined or unimportant position in the company. The specifics of what he or she actually does typically have no relevance in terms of characterization or plot or theme.

Problem 4: The cubicle doesn't provide much for the writer to work with in terms of setting. With few variations, a cubicle is a cubicle, except for the Meaningful Photograph attached to the cubicle wall.

There's nothing wrong with writing about a cubicle-dweller, but because it's so common, the writer needs to work extra hard to make the story original. Or maybe the character can, instead, be a marine biologist or a bereavement counselor or a minor-league mascot or a drummer in a tribute band—or hold some other job that presents refreshing opportunities for characterization, setting, conflict, and theme.

High school seniors work lots of jobs: They are salesclerks and lifeguards. They flip burgers. They park cars. But the narrator in Tim O'Brien's story "On the Rainy River," who has just been drafted into the army during the Vietnam War, does none of those things: He removes blood clots from the necks of dead pigs at a meatpacking plant, a job he describes in detail:

> As a carcass passed by, you'd lean forward and swing the gun up against the clots and squeeze the trigger, all in one motion, and the brush would whirl and water would come shooting out and you'd hear a quick splattering sound as the clots dissolved into a fine red mist.

Of all the jobs that the author could have given his teenage protagonist, he chose "pig declotter"—not because it was a job the author himself ever had as a teenager (he didn't), but because the gun and gore foreshadow the character's future as a soldier in Vietnam. And this foreshadowing isn't solely for the reader to uncover; the character, fearing what lies ahead at the end of summer, is sharp enough to make the connection himself:

> In the evenings I'd sometimes borrow my father's car and drive aimlessly around town, feeling sorry for myself, thinking about the war and the pig factory and how my life seemed to be collapsing toward slaughter.

Not only is this job thematically relevant and vividly described, but it is also unusual. How many other declotters have you read about in fiction?

The job, like the meat, is fresh.

✳ exercises: choose the unusual

1. If you've written a scene set in a common place (somebody's kitchen, a restaurant, a car), change the setting to someplace less common: a reptile zoo, a rooftop, a high diving board. Ask yourself how the new setting might influence the scene.

2. Think about all the jobs held by everyone in your extended family. Which would make the most interesting job in a story? Why?

3. Tobias Wolff's story "Bullet in the Brain" takes place amid the sort of bank robbery we're all familiar with from TV and the movies. How is this story made fresh? Choose a few favorite stories from the anthology and jot down ways that the authors made their material fresh.

ending your story

WHEN I WAS GROWING UP, every four years my family would spend hours on the living-room sofa watching the Olympics on television. The gymnastics competitions were particularly fierce, and it always struck me how much seemed to ride on that final dismount off the uneven bars or the balance beam or the rings.

When a gymnast "sticks the landing" after a seemingly impossible midair somersault, we know it. The feet plant down right where they're supposed to with no waggle, no adjustments; the athlete's weight is perfectly centered. Everything is in its place. That image of confidence and mastery over one's body lingers in the minds of millions of viewers and, more important, in the minds of the judges as they tabulate their scores.

When we read a story that "sticks the landing," we know that, too. Every word feels right. A strong ending simultaneously closes down and opens up the story. It closes the story in the sense that the main conflict has been brought to some provisional, if not final, resolution. A strong ending also opens the story up in that its world continues to live on, or resonate, in our minds even after we finish reading.

I'm no gymnast. Were you to toss me into the air and spin me around, I suppose I might get lucky and land on my feet. More likely, I'd land on my head or my back and end up in the emergency room. Likewise, it's hard to luck one's way into the right ending for a story. New writers can choose to be consoled or alarmed by the fact that experienced writers often struggle with the end of their stories. In a 1956 interview with the *Paris Review*, Ernest Hemingway said that he rewrote the ending of his novel *A Farewell to Arms* thirty-nine times before being satisfied with it.

Interviewer: Was there some technical problem there? What was it that had stumped you?

Hemingway: Getting the words right.

THE CHALLENGE

You've written several thousand words, and now it's time to wrap things up. A good ending, you've probably noticed from reading other stories, is one that is simultaneously unexpected and inevitable. It's unexpected in the sense that you didn't anticipate it playing out exactly as it does; it's inevitable in the sense that after you read it, you think, of course! Given *that* character in *that* situation, it's the only way the story could have ended.

To throw one more fairly vague requirement into the pot: A strong ending somehow *feels* like an end. To use that word again, it resonates.

Unexpectedness, inevitability, and resonance—that might sound like a tall order. Remember, though, that fiction writers have a luxury that competitive gymnasts don't: revision. We can keep working at that single landing—shaping, reshaping, reconceiving if necessary—for as long as it takes until we feel ready to impress the Russian judge.

STRATEGIES FOR ENDING YOUR STORY

Bear in mind that what follows are strategies, not tricks, and certainly not rules. Yet they demonstrate how other writers bring their stories to an emotionally and intellectually satisfying end.

For the end, look to the beginning

If you're stuck on the ending, or even if you aren't, it's worth taking a look at how your story starts. You started there for a reason, and there could be something worth returning to at the end. Repetition is satisfying to a reader, especially when, the second time around, the meaning changes or our understanding deepens.

Becky Hagenston's story "Midnight, Licorice, Shadow" (p. 227) begins with a series of names in rapid succession.

"Midnight, Licorice, Shadow," she says. "Cocoa, Casper, Dr. Livingston."
"Alfred Hitchcock," he says. "Dracula. Vincent Price."

These, we learn, are potential names for the cat that Donna and her new boyfriend, Jeremy, have recently taken in. When the story begins, we know nothing about these people or their situation, only that they seem to have an urgent need to name this animal. Midway through the story, we learn the reason for the urgency: Jeremy believes that "not knowing something's name is like having a bad spirit floating around." If they don't come up with a name for the cat in three days' time, Jeremy is going to kill it — which is exactly what he does late in the story. The trouble for Donna is that she herself is attached to no single name. She was born Lacey Love and has since changed her name whenever she feels her identity shifting. "I don't feel like a Donna anymore," she admits near the story's end. However, she doesn't know whom she *does* feel like. She is therefore in the same predicament as the cat, which Jeremy has just strangled. The implication of Donna finding herself suddenly nameless — which, given Jeremy's logic, is "like having a bad spirit floating around" — is dire. The story ends, as it began, with a desperate (and, we have to assume, fruitless) naming session:

"Linda," Jeremy says, coming toward her, and she can see it in his eyes, how badly he wants that to fit, but it doesn't. "Betty," he says, holding one of her hands in both of his own. "Amber. Millicent. Penny."
"Helen," she whispers back. "Cynthia, Regina, Anne."

At the story's beginning, the naming session in the hotel room, although urgent, seems playful, as do the names they suggest. The naming session at the end of the story is foreboding. By now we understand what happens when Jeremy can't find a name that fits. We know what is most likely about to happen to Donna — and, as her whisper implies, so does she.

Reconsider that object

In "Midnight, Licorice, Shadow," the repetition is verbal. The story ends with its two principal characters engaging in a conversation that mirrors an earlier conversation. Another sort of refrain is the return to an object of significance for which the meaning has changed in the eyes of the protagonist, implying a change or development in character.

Jhumpa Lahiri's story "This Blessed House" (p. 244) begins with a young woman, Twinkle, finding a porcelain Christ effigy in the house that she and her husband have just moved into. (They are newlyweds, and Hindu.) While she is charmed and amused by the found object, her husband, Sanjeev, the story's point-of-view character, is not. "We should call the Realtor," he suggests. "Tell him there's all this nonsense left behind. Tell him to take it away." Their disagreement over the effigies (Twinkle discovers several more scattered throughout the house) comes to a head when Sanjeev threatens to remove a statue of the Virgin Mary from their front lawn, where Twinkle has displayed it. "Don't you dare," she says, followed by "I hate you."

Of course their disagreement over the effigies is about more than just the objects themselves. Rather, the objects are the focal point for a larger disagreement about how one should behave. Sanjeev is serious, scholarly, and concerned with how others see him. Twinkle is spontaneous and free-spirited. When the couple throws a housewarming party to be attended by all of Sanjeev's acquaintances, Twinkle is the natural host, putting everybody at ease, though her actions fill Sanjeev with jealousy and anger. The guests follow her around the house on a treasure hunt for more effigies, and when she finds a solid silver bust of Christ, an object of actual beauty, he finds himself hating the object "because he knew that Twinkle loved it." Although Twinkle promises to keep this latest find in her study, Sanjeev comes to understand that "for the rest of their days together she would keep it on the center of the mantel, flanked on either side by the rest of the menagerie." The story ends with an image of Sanjeev standing with the Christ bust in his arms, following Twinkle as she and their guests continue their impromptu treasure hunt.

When the story opens, the objects are a source of curiosity that reveals the couple's differing values and personalities. By the story's end, the objects have become symbols of Twinkle's power in the relationship, of her ability to dismiss Sanjeev's piousness and civility—and, to his way of thinking, to dismiss *him*.

When you read Richard Bausch's story "Tandolfo the Great" (p. 198), it will be useful to track the evolving meaning of the wedding cake—what it means to Tandolfo upon its mention at the beginning of the story as "a big pink wedding cake, with its six tiers and scalloped edges and its miniature bride and groom on top," and what it comes to symbolize to him by the final paragraph, when he sits in his car, "gazing at the incongruous shape of the cake there in the falling dark," awaiting its destruction.

There is no shortage of classic short stories that end with a focus on a key object that represents the protagonist's evolving hopes and fears, dreams and dreads. Notable examples include Charlotte Perkins Gilman's 1892 story "The Yellow Wallpaper," Sherwood Anderson's 1920 story "The Egg," and Tim O'Brien's 1986 story "The Things They Carried."

Look to the future

Once, when I was having trouble ending a story, my professor suggested that I imagine my main character five or ten years into the future. I should imagine his life in as much detail as I could, and while I wouldn't actually be writing that future into the story, I should consider nudging the end of the story in that direction.

The "Common Pitfalls" section that follows warns against giving too much away at the end, wrapping up your story with a nice neat bow. A number of 1970s and 1980s movies, ensemble comedies like *Animal House* and *Fast Times at Ridgemont High*, contain brief "where are they now" epilogues. (At the end of *Animal House*, we learn that John Belushi's character, Bluto, becomes a US senator. In *Fast Times*, we learn that Sean Penn's character, Jeff Spicoli, saves Brooke Shields from drowning and then blows the reward money, hiring Van Halen to perform at his birthday party.) Your story should almost certainly resist this narrative device. Definitively pinning down your characters in simple terms (character 1 becomes A; character 2 becomes B) not only undercuts the complexity and mystery of character but also brings a story's narrative energy to a grinding halt.

Nevertheless, the end of a story can and often should begin to reveal what sort of challenges lie ahead for your protagonist. In Anton Chekhov's 1899 story "The Lady with the Dog," a middle-aged banker, Gurov, is content to carry on meaningless extramarital affairs until he meets the younger Anna while vacationing in Yalta. He expects his liaison with her to be just another fling, yet when his vacation ends and he returns home to his family, Gurov is shocked to discover that he can't put Anna out of his mind. He is, for the first time in his life, fully in love. This is new, frightening territory for him.

After several failed attempts to sever ties and return to their separate lives, Gurov and Anna finally decide to pursue their relationship in earnest, knowing full well that doing so will make their lives immeasurably more difficult.

> Then they discussed their situation for a long time, trying to think how they could get rid of the necessity for hiding, deception, living in different towns, being so long without meeting. How were they to shake off these intolerable fetters?
>
> "How? How?" he repeated, clutching his head. "How?"
>
> And it seemed to them that they were within an inch of arriving at a decision, and that then a new and glorious life would begin. And they both realized that the end was still far, far away, and that the hardest, the most complicated part was only just beginning.

"The Lady with the Dog" ends there, without revealing exactly what this couple will face, but with an understanding that great difficulties lie ahead, difficulties that are the price of admission into this "new and glorious life."

Karen Russell's story "St. Lucy's Home for Girls Raised by Wolves" (p. 324) depicts a group of girls, raised up until this time by their werewolf parents, who are sent to a boarding school to become socialized human beings. The parents have sent their girls away for the noblest of reasons—an education they could not themselves provide—and yet the school serves mainly to embarrass the girls about their former, animalistic lives and drive a wedge into their communal existence. At the end of the story, Claudette returns home to her family's cave for a brief visit. We can measure how much Claudette has changed by the way she views her childhood home:

> The cave looked so much smaller than I remembered it. I had to duck my head to enter. Everybody was eating when I walked in. They all looked up from the bull moose at the same time, my aunts and uncles, my sloe-eyed, lolling cousins, the parents. My uncle dropped a thighbone from his mouth.

Claudette and the other girls of St. Lucy's have been taught to eat with forks and knives. They have learned to speak politely at parties and how to dance ballroom steps. Their education seems surface-level, except for this: Their pack mentality and regard for one another has been trained out of them, making "St. Lucy's" a story about a negative side of education that is rarely talked about. The story's final sentences prove just how far Claudette's "education" has taken her away from her family:

> They stared up at me expectantly, panting in the cool gray envelope of the cave, waiting for a display of what I had learned.
> "So," I said, telling my first human lie. "I'm home."

There is nothing more human, the story suggests, than telling a lie. We are watching Claudette, in a sense, pass her final exam. What will happen to her five, ten years down the road? We don't know exactly, but we suspect she'll never be able to live in that cave again with her family. That part of her, the part that shares a communal meal with her pack, has been trained away. Rather, she'll live among the humans. Considering, however, that human existence in this story is defined by its shallowness, selfishness, and deception, we view Claudette's successful inculcation into human society as the tragic but inevitable result of her education.

Consider this: You might already have written it

In an attempt to make sure the reader understands our stories, we sometimes include more than we need to at the end—maybe even a lot more. If you find yourself at the end of a story suddenly writing a scene that takes place in a brand-new setting, or jumping ahead in time months or years, ask yourself whether those large leaps are necessary.

In an early draft of his story "A & P" (p. 359), John Updike included a scene that took place later in the day, in which Sammy went down to the beach to look for the girls who'd left him standing alone in the A & P parking lot. In revision, Updike cut that scene after coming to see that it was superfluous. (Always the productive writer, Updike later used that extra writing in another story, "Lifeguard.") We might not know all the particulars of Sammy's fate— what exactly his parents say when they learn he has quit his job, or if Sammy finds new employment, or if he ever moves away from his hometown—but we do know what matters most for *this* story. The events at the A & P awaken in him a sense of an unjust, unpleasant aspect of adulthood—and this is as much of a conclusion as "A & P" needs.

When you are first composing a story, it can be helpful to include more rather than less. That extra scene might get cut eventually, but in writing it you'll have learned something useful. When it comes time to finalizing a draft, however, take a critical look at the last part of your story.

A former teacher of mine suggests that if the ending doesn't seem to be working, try cutting the story's last line. Doing so increases the likelihood that you'll finish with a necessary part of the narrative, rather than with a commentary *about* the story or something too overtly thematic. If the ending still feels wrong, he suggests cutting the entire last paragraph. And what if that doesn't work? Maybe the entire page, or—as with Updike's "A & P"—the entire last scene, is superfluous.

COMMON PITFALLS

Tricking your reader

Chapter 3 warned against beginning a story with your character waking up in bed (specifically with the alarm clock going off). This also happens to be a problematic way to *end* your story. If you end your story with your main character waking up in bed, implying that the whole story was nothing but a dream, then your reader has every right to throw your manuscript across the room, come over to your house, and lodge a formal complaint.

Why? While you might have been aiming to surprise us, what you've really done is trick us. Unlike an unexpected ending that arises from the mysterious and often contradictory nature of character, a trick ending comes directly from the iron hand of the author, who causes us to invest our emotional energy in characters who do not exist, in a story that does not matter.

The "and then I woke up" ending is but the most infamous type of trick ending. Trick endings are all too common in the drafts of beginning writers, and these endings are nearly always unsuccessful. Jerome Stern, in his book *Making Shapely Fiction*, includes a long list of endings to avoid. Most are variations on the trick ending. He advises, for instance, to avoid writing a story that ends:

> He realized he was alone, and slowly blinked his third eye. [**Surprise! The main character is really an alien.**]
>
> I can't help it if that's all I understand. After all, I'm just a dachshund. [**Surprise! The main character is really a dog.**]
>
> The guillotine blade fell swiftly, severing my head from my body. [**Surprise! A dead narrator has been telling this story.**]

To these I would add:

> "I'll take over from here," his other personality said. [**Surprise! The narrator has multiple personalities.**]

Trick endings—or to use a kinder term, surprise endings—are most common among beginning writers who are more interested in providing a shock than in telling a story. They are nearly always a mistake. Not only do they almost never shock, but they also negate everything that preceded the ending, treating the story as an elaborate setup for a punch line. They encourage the reader to invest emotionally in a story that isn't actually the story at all.[1]

Deus ex machina

A completely understandable reason for writing the trick ending is that we can't come up with another one that works. With no clear way to end the story, we decide to have the character wake up, or be a dog or a Martian, hoping to deflect

---

[1] What about the movie *The Wizard of Oz*? you might be wondering. What about Chuck Palahniuk's novel *Fight Club*? A reasonably observant viewer will see right away that Dorothy is dreaming, since just before landing in Oz, she gets knocked unconscious and falls into her bed. So her awakening later on isn't really a surprise ending. (Furthermore, the author Salman Rushdie makes a persuasive argument that Dorothy's return to Kansas is the weakest part of the film.) As for *Fight Club*, the revelation that the narrator and Tyler Durden are one and the same happens midway through the novel (and film adaptation), not at the end.

the fact that we don't know how the story should draw to a close. A similar manifestation of our failure to find a proper ending is the *deus ex machina*. It means, in Latin, "god from the machine" and refers to the manner in which ancient Greek playwrights ended their dramas: Actors playing the gods literally descended onto the stage in a cranelike mechanism to sort out all the dilemmas created by the human characters.

Today, we use the phrase *deus ex machina* to refer to any ending in which we sense the meddling, godlike hand of the author resolving characters' predicaments for them. Lightning strikes our villain dead. Our down-and-out protagonist, on the story's last page, learns of a deceased relative who has willed him her estate.

A student of mine once turned in a first draft in which a man is on the verge of losing the family clothing store. The man has taken on a second loan and is about to default on it. To make matters worse, he hasn't been honest with his wife about the extent of their financial difficulties. This student did a fine job laying out the man's predicament. Feeling the need to "fix" his characters' problems, however, the author ended the story with the man finding a suitcase full of money, at least a million dollars, in the alley behind his store. (It's quickly explained that there had been a bank robbery earlier that day, and that the robbers, fleeing the scene, must have tossed the suitcase into the alley.)

The trouble with an ending like that, beyond the obvious logistical improbabilities and coincidences, is that it lets our protagonist off the hook far too easily. We never get to see what the man would actually do when the going gets tough, because the author has swept in, godlike, and resolved everything for him.

Many of the examples in the "Tricking Your Reader" section above are actually instances of *deus ex machina*. That is, they are ways that an author stops the story without having to deal with the story. Even death can be a form of *deus ex machina*. Although it might not seem like it, we treat our protagonists too *easily* when we kill them off. Let them stay alive and have to deal with the consequences of their actions. Now that's hard.

Everything ties up in a neat little bow

Life is complicated, and so — we hope — are our stories. At the end of "Tan-dolfo the Great," Tandolfo still has his gambling debts. We can assume he hasn't kicked the booze. He's still a second-rate clown/magician. He has, how-ever, finally accepted the fact that he won't get the girl, for she does not love him. His symbolic gesture of leaving the wedding cake in the road suggests that from now on he'll see the world a little more as it truly is. That's as much resolution as this story needs to provide. No easy solutions; no neat little bows.

Setting out to teach your characters — or, worse, the reader — a lesson

It's not that readers don't like to learn things. Sure we do. If your protagonist is a poker player or a gardener, and from reading the story we gain an increased appreciation for card-counting or beets — well, that's great.

What readers resist is a story that sets out to teach a lesson. Fiction's strength is its depiction of nuance, its admission that life is complicated. Writing a story that "teaches" a character (and, in turn, the reader) that it's wrong to drink and drive, say by having the protagonist smash into a tree and cripple his wife, reduces the art form to an after-school special or public service announcement.

If your story demands that a character drive into a tree, go ahead and write it. But let that plot decision serve the interest of the story, not the lesson.

Along those lines, readers resist stories that serve mainly to argue a particular stance on a hot-button issue. Can you write a story about a pro-life character? Of course. A pro-choice character? Sure. But the story itself isn't the forum to argue your — the author's — particular side on an issue. Like "lesson" fiction, much "issue" fiction is really thinly disguised lecturing. Nobody likes to be lectured to, even when it's disguised as a story. *Especially* when it's disguised as a story.

Solving a problem versus stating a problem

I already made the case against solving our characters' problems for them, but Anton Chekhov takes things a step further, arguing that a story's problems need not be solved at all. "The task of a writer," he asserts, "is not to solve the problem but to state the problem correctly." Certainly he followed his own advice with "The Lady with the Dog." We don't know how the problems that Gurov and Anna have gotten themselves into will be solved, yet by the end of the story we have a deep understanding of their predicament.

This is not to say that a story's plot need not come to some crisis or resolution. Gurov and Anna, after all, do come to the decision to give their relationship a shot. Their decision, however, hardly "solves" their problems, which will become increasingly messy once their relationship is out in the open. But those later concerns, and how exactly they play out, aren't the subject of *this* story.

My student who wrote the story about the clothing-store owner ultimately decided that his story could end with his protagonist still in debt. Not only did the author not need to solve his character's money troubles; those troubles didn't need to be solved at all. More important was conveying what it felt like for this man to live with the daily fear of losing the family business (handed down from his father), as well as the secrets he kept from his wife in a misguided attempt to protect her. The author was able to keep the bank robbery in the story but used it as a way for his protagonist to imagine, briefly, doing something hasty and criminal for cash. The man even enters a bank late in the story with his meager sales from the day and looks around at the tellers, the video cameras . . . but he's no bank robber. He deposits the money and leaves—but not before an unexpected and ambiguous wink at a sleepy security guard reveals either an impotent display of power or—depending on your interpretation—a genuine threat. A wink that says, "Next time, you'd better be on your toes."

GETTING THE WORDS RIGHT

Even when you know, or think you know, how to end your story, there's always the matter—as Hemingway bluntly put it—of getting the words right. We want to convey that the story is over. And yet we also want the story to linger in our readers' minds.

There's no easy trick to this; finding the right words to end a story requires a well-tuned ear and a fierce attention to the meaning, sound, and rhythm of language.

Tobias Wolff's story "Bullet in the Brain" (p. 366) concludes with a memory of the moment in which the protagonist first became a critic in the best sense—that is, the moment, during a pickup baseball game years earlier, when Anders first became attuned to the musical possibilities of language. The story ends with vivid, sensory imagery followed by a repetition of a grammatically incorrect, but strangely pleasing, phrase uttered by the kid playing shortstop in their pickup baseball game:

> [F]or now Anders can still make time. Time for the shadows to lengthen on the grass, time for the tethered dog to bark at the flying ball, time for the boy in right field to smack his sweat-blackened mitt and softly chant, *They is, they is, they is.*

Wolff is particularly adept at finding resonant language to end his stories. Another way he "gets the words right" is to write them in such a way that they apply to both the immediate and the larger predicament of the characters. In his story "Hunters in the Snow," three friends, none of them upstanding citizens, go on an ill-fated hunting trip, during which Tub shoots Kenny over a misunderstanding. Tub and Frank load Kenny, who is clearly (to the reader, anyway) dying, onto the back of their truck and set out for the hospital. However, they have misplaced the directions and don't really know where they're going.

The story's second-to-last paragraph includes images of the night sky, that ancient navigational system, that offer Kenny reason to be optimistic:

> Kenny lay with his arms folded over his stomach, moving his lips at the stars. Right overhead was the Big Dipper, and behind, hanging between Kenny's toes in the direction of the hospital, was the North Star, Pole Star, Help to Sailors. As the truck twisted through the gentle hills the star went back and forth between Kenny's boots, staying always in his sight. "I'm going to the hospital," Kenny said.

The story's final paragraph, however, shifts away from Kenny's perspective, toward a more objective truth:

But he was wrong. They had taken a different turn a long way back.

In this context, the wrong turn taken refers both to their current drive to the hospital and to the course of their lives. At some point years ago, each of these three damaged characters took a wrong turn.

Let's return for a moment to Karen Russell's story "St. Lucy's Home for Girls Raised by Wolves." Here again is that story's final paragraph:

"So," I said, telling my first human lie. "I'm home."

The last paragraph could have been written:

"So, I'm home," I said, telling my first human lie.

Ending the story as she does, however, Russell gets the words right by drawing attention to "home," something that Claudette no longer has. Saying she's "home" is a lie because she knows that she doesn't belong in her family's home anymore. Where, then, *is* her home? Back with the other humans? Not really. This is the tragedy of Claudette's experience at the boarding school: It has caused her to lose any sense of having a home.

TWO FINAL THOUGHTS ON ENDINGS

The problem might not be the ending

When you find yourself struggling to get the ending right, the problem might lie elsewhere. The ending, rather than being the problem, might merely be the symptom of the real problem, which is that you don't yet understand your own story well enough.

From time to time, sit back and consider the questions we ask when we read like a writer: What is the story about? What are its central questions? What do the characters want? What do they fear? If you aren't sure, you might need to revise parts of your story to bring these matters more to the forefront. The end of a story nearly always has thematic implications; therefore, until we know our story's thematic concerns—what, ultimately, the story is about—we won't know whether we're moving toward the right ending.

You don't need to write your story from start to finish

If an ending comes to you midway through your draft, go ahead and write it. Or maybe a final scene or image comes to you even earlier, just as you start working on the draft. Great—write it. You might change your mind about the ending once more of the story is written (always be open to revising—think of Hemingway!), but at least some of what you wrote will be useful.

Some writers, when starting out on a new story, have no idea how it might end. Others have a clear sense of how their stories will end before setting down word one. Be open to your own creative process.

✳ exercises: experiment with endings

1. Write the end of your story by referring back to the story's beginning, as in "Midnight, Licorice, Shadow."

2. Write a different ending to the same story with an emphasis on an object that appeared earlier on, as in "This Blessed House" or "Tandolfo the Great."

3. Write a different ending to the same story that provides only a glimpse of your main character's long-term future, as in "The Lady with the Dog" or "Magic Words."

4. Write a final sentence to your story that speaks simultaneously to your protagonist's immediate and more general predicaments, like the ending sentence of "Hunters in the Snow."

5. Once you have a complete draft of your story, try cutting the last line. Try cutting the last paragraph. Ask yourself how the story has changed, and whether it is weaker or stronger as a result.

6. Write the ending line to a story that doesn't yet exist. Now try to write the ending paragraph. Given that ending, where might the story begin? What might it be about?

the power of clarity

THIS CHAPTER can be summed up in two words: *Be clear.*

Whether your prose is direct and declarative or lyrical and syntactically ambitious, you should strive for clarity. Unclear writing is like a phone call with too much static. The static says nothing about the nature of the conversation. It only makes you want to end the call.

Sometimes, simple errors impede clarity—like when a writer inadvertently changes the name of a character mid-story, or begins a scene on a cloudy day and then, a few pages later, mentions the bright shadows being cast on the grass. Errors like these are common in early drafts and are easily corrected. Chapter 11 deals with a number of mechanical errors that detract from a story's clarity.

This chapter deals less with errors than with aesthetics and craft, suggesting ways to focus on clarity so that your reader will experience your story as you intend.

VAGUENESS VERSUS AMBIGUITY

First, we need to dispel the notion that there is something arty in being vague. As discussed in Chapter 2, details are the key to fiction. Vague writing creates confusion. The trouble with a sentence like "The animal stands in the yard" or, worse, "An animal is over there" is that it's imprecise. The writer has an image in her head, say an elephant standing in some character's backyard, that doesn't match what the reader imagines, maybe a dog in a field. Given the extreme vagueness of the sentence "An animal is over there," the reader might not have any image in his head at all.

Quite possibly, the writer doesn't, either. I'll ask a student who writes about a man working "a boring office job" what the man's job actually is. What does the company do? What does the man's day-to-day work consist of? The writer should know, but sometimes he doesn't. Yet how can a writer convey a particular world to the reader if he hasn't fully imagined the world himself?

A number of chapters in this book have already argued against withholding information from the reader. Vagueness is either a form of withheld information or an indication that the writer isn't yet imagining her own story in sufficient detail.

A story that states, "He did it again," and then waits for pages and pages before revealing who the "he" is or what it is that he did is being coy with the reader. A story about a man who left dirty dishes in the sink again is quite a different story from one about a man who smacked around his children again. Readers deserve to know which story it is they're reading.

Ambiguity is another matter. An ambiguous story is one that opens itself up to multiple interpretations, given the available evidence. Readers might argue over Jhumpa Lahiri's story "This Blessed House" (p. 244) — whether Twinkle's behavior is a positive antidote to Sanjeev's relentless somberness, or whether she is ultimately undermining her husband in his job and his religion. The story contains ample evidence, details about the characters and their life together, to support multiple interpretations.

In summary: An ambiguous story offers multiple ways to understand it. A vague story offers no way to understand it — not without the reader inventing details and making connections that aren't in the story, essentially doing the writer's work.

CLEAR WORDS

The ten-dollar word

As long as we're dispelling notions, let's talk about big words for a minute. Some beginning writers are drawn to them. Rather than write, *Five kittens hid in the shrubs*, she writes, *A plethora of puerile, terrestrial creatures used the lush topography to impede all knowledge of their existence*, with a belief that lofty diction is always called for and that bigger words are preferable to smaller ones.

"Five kittens hid in the shrubs," however, paints a clear picture—whereas "A plethora of puerile, terrestrial creatures used the lush topography to impede all knowledge of their existence" is less precise, pseudo-poetic, and unnecessarily wordy. It's an inferior sentence, unless the writer is going for comedy.

In fact, sometimes a writer will intentionally deploy lofty diction for comic or ironic effect. Richard Bausch's story "Tandolfo the Great" (p. 198) contains a scene in which a drunk, hostile Tandolfo is forcibly removed from the house where he was performing his magic tricks for a group of children. Sprawled on the grass, his clothes torn and his face bloody, Tandolfo tries to salvage a bit of dignity with the adults who just threw him out:

> "I would say that even though I wasn't as patient as I could've been, the adults have not comported themselves well here," he says.

Tandolfo's measured, formal address to the adults stands in ironic contrast to the near-slapstick situation that preceded it. It's a very funny moment in the story, made funnier because of Tandolfo's diction.

An expansive working vocabulary is of course extremely useful for a writer. We want to use the most precise words when we write, and we can't use words we don't know. (The philosopher Ludwig Wittgenstein wrote, "The limits of my language mean the limits of my world.") Authors from Henry James to Virginia Woolf to David Foster Wallace display enormous lexicons in their writing, deploying words with laserlike precision.

However, a sentence like "The more my neighbor praised his son's many achievements, the more disinterested I became" impedes clarity because the words *aren't* used with precision. The man is either praising *his son* or he is listing (or enumerating, or maybe cataloging) his son's *achievements*, but he probably isn't "praising" the achievements themselves. And the word "disinterested" is being used incorrectly: That word means "impartial" (like a judge), rather than "not interested." The better word, in this context, is "uninterested."

A clearer sentence would be "The more my neighbor listed his son's many achievements, the less interested I became." Or: "As my neighbor listed his son's many achievements, I became bored." Or perhaps even better: "As my neighbor listed his son's many achievements, I began to sweep leaves out of the garage and think about the errands I needed to run later that day."

With that last sentence, losing the ten-dollar words freed me up to paint the scene in greater detail. It's a more precise sentence, a clearer sentence.

Even a ten-dollar word used correctly will call undue attention to itself if it doesn't match the sentence's overall level of diction. The sentence "Jack hit the brakes and the car stopped forthwith" stops *us* forthwith. "Suddenly" would match the more casual diction ("hit the brakes") of the rest of the sentence. Or, the word can be cut entirely from the sentence: "Jack hit the brakes and the car stopped."

Or what about this one: "Jack hit the brakes."

Adjectives and adverbs

Nouns and verbs are key. *Adam swam. Tracy hiked. The dog buried its bone.* Little more needs to be said about those parts of speech, except that it's generally more vivid and economical to use active rather than passive verbs. (*The dog buried its bone*, rather than *The bone was buried by the dog.*) But this advice is nothing new—you've probably been told to avoid the passive voice all your life.

Adverbs, however—and, to a lesser degree, adjectives—are worthy of your skepticism because they're often indicators that a sentence isn't as clear as it could be. In his book *On Writing*, Stephen King puts it bluntly: "The adverb is not your friend."

Often, by choosing a more precise noun or verb, you render the adjective or adverb unnecessary and make the sentence clearer and more concise.

He lived in a gigantic house.	He lived in a mansion.
She ran quickly to the mailbox.	She raced to the mailbox.
He felt very frightened.	He felt terrified.

King goes on to explain that the goal isn't merely to edit out your adverbs, but to write in such a way that your story won't need them in the first place:

> Consider the sentence **He closed the door firmly**. It's by no means a terrible sentence (at least it's got an active verb going for it), but ask yourself if **firmly** really has to be there. You can argue that it expresses a degree of

difference between **He closed the door** and **He slammed the door**, and you'll get no argument from me . . . but what about context? What about all the enlightening (not to say emotionally moving) prose which came *before* **He closed the door firmly**? Shouldn't this tell us how he closed the door? And if the foregoing prose *does* tell us, isn't **firmly** an extra word? Isn't it redundant?

Hard-and-fast rules? No. Principles of craft and aesthetics? Yes.

Your finished story will almost certainly have some adjectives in it, and it may well contain a couple of adverbs. Your mission, however, is to be certain that these parts of speech are never being used as crutches to bolster weak or imprecise prose.

Don't be *very conscientious* in your search for the right word. Be *ruthless*.

CLEAR SENTENCES

Often, a writer doesn't set out to be imprecise or hazy. She knows what she means.

> Mother and daughter argued for over an hour until, just after midnight, she finally said, "Oh, the heck with you," and stormed out of the house.

The writer knows who is still at home and who has left. Trouble is, the reader doesn't.

Who?

Here's an example of an unnecessarily unclear opening:

> Arnie knew better than to take the threat seriously, but now Cassandra was standing by the open front door, her suitcase in hand, telling him to "have a nice life."

The sentence isn't badly written—but who are these people?

> Arnie knew better than to take the threat seriously, but now Cassandra, his five-year-old daughter, was standing by the open front door, her suitcase in hand, telling him to "have a nice life."

Ah. Now we know what we should be imagining while we read.

Readers need enough contextual information to understand the implication of what is written. A story that begins

Ralph Gwinn landed the MetroMart contract.

should fairly quickly—in the next few sentences—give us context. Or you could rewrite the opening sentence so it contains the context:

Ralph Gwinn, my mentor at the firm, landed the MetroMart contract.

Ralph Gwinn, who for the past two months had been sleeping with my wife, landed the MetroMart contract.

Ralph Gwinn, fresh out of rehab, landed the MetroMart contract.

---

tip: naming your characters (a nice trick)

Learning to write fiction is hard work, and there are very few tricks. But here's one. To avoid reader confusion, give your characters names that differ from one another. Specifically:

- Avoid using the same starting letter.
- Avoid names that rhyme with one another.
- Avoid starting all the names with either vowels or consonants.
- Vary the syllable count.

Even a careful reader might confuse characters named Rickie and Mickey, or Laura and Lauren. (Confession: My extended family includes a Laura, a Lauren, and a Lori, and at family gatherings I usually end up saying, "Hiya, cousin.")

In my example on page 147, I used the names Arnie and Cassandra, which are sufficiently different.

When?

Sentences are generally clearest when time cues are placed at the beginning. Consider the following:

I jogged down the street to the supermarket for food — past the post office, past the dry cleaners and the bank where I'd once tried to pass a bad check — at 3 a.m.

Very likely, until you read those last words, you assumed that the scene was taking place in daytime. With the time cue at the end of the sentence, I've caused you to picture the scene incorrectly. By moving it to the beginning of the sentence, I can be sure that you picture the scene correctly — a jog to the supermarket in the dead of night:

At 3 a.m., I jogged down the street to the supermarket for food — past the post office, past the dry cleaners and the bank where I'd once tried to pass a bad check.

Then and now — verb tenses

Most stories contain at least some sentences that refer to events that occurred before the story began. Stories with flashbacks contain lots of these sentences. The verb tenses to use for maximum clarity when referring to a time prior to the story's "narrative present" are the past tense and the past perfect tense.

A story written in the *present* tense usually employs the *past* tense when referring to events occurring before the story began.

Leroy has been in Kentucky for three months, and his leg is almost healed, but the accident frightened him and he does not want to drive any more long hauls. He is not sure what to do next. In the meantime, he makes things from craft kits.[1] He started by building a miniature log cabin from notched Popsicle sticks. He varnished it and placed it on the TV set,[2] where it remains. It reminds him of a rustic Nativity scene.[3]

~ Bobbie Ann Mason, "Shiloh"

[1] So far, the paragraph is told in the present tense.

[2] The story switches to the past tense to describe the time when Leroy made a miniature log cabin — an event that happened before the story's "now."

[3] We're back to the present tense; presumably, the Popsicle-stick cabin still reminds him of a Nativity scene.

A story written in the *past* tense employs the *past perfect* tense when referring to prior events.

Marian Peters came[1] back from the kitchen. She was a tall woman with worried eyes, who had once possessed a fresh American loveliness.[2] Charlie had never been sensitive to it and was always surprised when people spoke of how pretty she had been. From the first there had been an instinctive antipathy between them.[3]

~ F. Scott Fitzgerald, "Babylon Revisited"

[1] The story is being narrated in the simple past tense.

[2] Her "fresh American loveliness" ended prior to this story's beginning; thus the sentence uses the past perfect tense ("had possessed").

[3] The rest of the paragraph continues to describe events that occurred prior to this story's beginning, and therefore maintains the past perfect tense.

You might find, however, that using many past perfect verbs in a row becomes unwieldy and awkward ("Once he had eaten his sandwich, he had gone out back and had dug the garden and then had watered it"). For that reason, stories written in the past tense often signal the shift into backstory with one or two uses of the past perfect, but then continue on in the simple past tense as long as clarity isn't being sacrificed.

"You were just kidding," the dean said, "about wiping out all of mankind. That, I suppose, was a joke." She squinted at me. One of her hands curved atop the other to form a pink, freckled molehill on her desk.

"Well," I said, "maybe I meant it at the time." I quickly saw that this was not the answer she wanted. "I don't know. I think it's the architecture."[1]

Through the dimming light of the dean's-office window, I could see the fortress of the old campus. On my ride from the bus station to the campus, I'd barely glimpsed[2] New Haven—a flash of crumpled buildings here, a trio of straggly kids there. A lot like Baltimore. But everything had changed[3] when we reached[4] those streets hooded by gothic buildings. I imagined how the college must have looked when it was founded, when most of the students owned slaves. I pictured men wearing tights and knickers, smoking pipes.

"The architecture," the dean repeated.[5]

~ ZZ Packer, "Drinking Coffee Elsewhere" (p. 303)

[1] So far, the story is being told in the past tense.

[2] The shift to the past perfect ("had glimpsed") signals the transition to backstory.

[3] Continued use of the past perfect ("had changed") cements the backstory in time.

[4] Here, and for the remainder of the paragraph, the tense reverts to the simple past tense, because it's evident that we're continuing to describe this same memory of the character's ride to college.

[5] Despite the continued use of the simple past tense, we know that the memory is over, and we've returned to the story's present moment, because of (a) the paragraph break and (b) the fact that the dean is speaking again, clearly continuing the conversation she and the narrator are having.

Where?

As with time cues, location cues usually belong early in the sentence:

> Josh and I played cards for days on end—gin rummy, hearts, poker—until one morning he threw down the cards he was holding, said, "I can't stand it anymore," and leapt off the life raft into the frigid sea.

That sentence works only if we already know the characters' predicament (or if I'm aiming for comedy). Otherwise, this way of revealing their location is unnecessarily jarring. The clearer sentence reads:

> In the life raft, Josh and I played cards for days on end—gin rummy, hearts, poker—until one morning he threw down the cards he was holding, said, "I can't stand it anymore," and leapt into the frigid sea.

Here is how Richard Bausch provides a sentence of backstory in "Tandolfo the Great" (p. 198). Notice how it begins by orienting us in time and space:

> This morning at the local bakery he picked up a big pink wedding cake, with its six tiers and scalloped edges and its miniature bride and groom on top.

Sentence length

A series of short sentences might be the best way to convey a staccato scene:

> He stood at the podium. Cleared his throat. "Ladies and . . ." He looked out at the audience and felt his hands begin to sweat. "Sorry," he said, and coughed into his hand. "I'm a little nervous."

Yet short sentences might be at odds with a scene meant to convey fluidity or continuousness:

> The gulls flew overhead. They made smooth arcs over the beach. One dipped lower than the rest. It snatched a French fry from the sand. It soared away. The others chased it over the water.

The fluidity of the scene is being undercut by the choppy prose rhythm. Longer sentences might work better:

> The gulls flew overhead in wide loops over the beach. One dipped lower than the rest, snatched a French fry from the sand, and soared away, the others chasing it over the water.

Or you might find a combination of longer and shorter sentences useful. Here, a character's distress is communicated with a long sentence, which is followed by a short sentence — a fragment, really — that provides temporary closure to the character's thoughts:

> Too much to do, April thought, and too little time before the in-laws knocked on her door with their talk of how *lovely, just lovely* the house looked, while they studied the windowsills for dust, the windows for streaks, and the sofa for dog hair, which never came off the fabric no matter how diligently you vacuumed. Ah, marriage.

Here is another section from ZZ Packer's story "Drinking Coffee Elsewhere," in which the narrator recounts a session with her psychiatrist. Notice the varying sentence lengths, particularly how the shorter sentences emphasize the narrator's unwillingness to open up:

> We spent the first ten minutes discussing the *Iliad*, and whether or not the text actually states that Achilles had been dipped in the River Styx. He said it did, and I said it didn't. After we'd finished with the *Iliad*, and with my new job in what he called "the scullery," he asked questions about my parents. I told him nothing. It was none of his business. Instead, I talked about Heidi. I told him about that day in Commons, Heidi's plan to go on a date with Mr. Dick, and the invitation we'd been given to the gay party.

Writing the long sentence

In his book *The Art of Fiction*, John Gardner explains that in order to write a long sentence that has clarity and focus, it is best to expand only one or two of a sentence's components, or what Gardner calls "syntactic slots."

For example, consider the following sentence:[1]

      1   2   3
The woman drove to the theater.

To lengthen this sentence, the writer might expand only the first component:

> The woman, who had just left the babysitter with three pages of typed instructions and a promise to call her cell if *anything, anything at all,* seemed remotely out of the ordinary, drove to the theater.

Or instead of loading up component 1, the writer might add details to components 2 and 3:

> The woman drove slowly but carelessly, a constant drift into the middle lane while she texted the babysitter (dangerous, she knew, but any more dangerous than leaving her kids with that thirteen-year-old who was practically a baby herself?), to the theater—a brick, one-screen, magical place of popcorn with extra butter flavor, and soda, and sticky aisles, and, most important, a seat in the dimly lit back row, where she could close her eyes and allow herself ninety exquisite minutes of peace.

To broaden Gardner's advice a little: Long sentences are clearest when only some, rather than all, parts are expanded and modified. To expand everything is to emphasize everything, which is the same as emphasizing nothing.

CLEAR STORIES: A FEW WORDS OF ADVICE

A story written in multiple sections should generally orient the reader in time and space near the beginning of each section. That way we'll know how

---

[1] Although I borrow this concept from Gardner, the examples—for better or worse—are my own.

each section relates to the ones that came before. Simple phrases like "The next morning" and "At work later that afternoon" are enormously helpful to a reader.

A story told from multiple characters' perspectives—either in omniscient or in shifting, third-person limited omniscient points of view (see Chapter 4)—should make clear whose perspective we're reading whenever there's a switch to a new character.

Jill McCorkle's story "Magic Words" (p. 262) is told from the perspective of three characters—a married woman on the brink of having an affair, a violent teenager, and a retired schoolteacher. The story begins:

> Because Paula Blake is planning something secret, she feels she must account for her every move and action, overcompensating in her daily chores and agreeing to whatever her husband and children demand.

The second section begins:

> The kids are doing what they call creepy crawling. Their leader picked the term up from the book *Helter Skelter*.

The third section begins:

> When Agnes Hayes sees the boy bagging groceries in the market, her heart surges with pity, his complexion blotched and infected, hair long and oily.

Because the story establishes each section quickly and clearly, at no point do we wonder, "Who am I reading about right now?" Such a question would pull us out of the story.

CLARITY: SOME FINAL THOUGHTS

Remember that "clarity" and "simplicity" aren't the same. By all means, write the complex story, the difficult story, the subtle story. Just write it clearly.

Here is the opening paragraph of Toni Morrison's 1987 novel *Beloved*, for which I've provided several annotations. While Morrison's novel is complex at just about every level—emotionally, intellectually, narratively—the writing is always clear.

124 was spiteful.[1] Full of baby's venom. The women in the house knew it and so did the children.[2] For years each put up with the spite in his own way, but by 1873 Sethe and her daughter Denver were its only victims.[3] The grandmother, Baby Suggs, was dead, and the sons, Howard and Buglar, had run away by the time they were thirteen years old—as soon as merely looking in the mirror shattered it (that was the signal for Buglar); as soon as two tiny[4] hand prints appeared in the cake (that was it for Howard).[5] Neither boy waited to see more; another kettleful of chickpeas smoking in a heap on the floor; soda crackers crumbled and strewn in a line next to the doorsill. Nor did they wait for one of the relief periods: the weeks, months even, when nothing was disturbed. No.[6] Each one fled at once—the moment the house committed what was for him the one insult not to be borne or witnessed a second time. Within two months, in the dead of winter, leaving their grandmother, Baby Suggs; Sethe, their mother; and their little sister, Denver, all by themselves in the gray and white house on Bluestone Road.[7] It didn't have a number then,[8] because Cincinnati didn't stretch that far.[9] In fact, Ohio had been calling itself a state only seventy years when first one brother and then the next stuffed quilt packing into his hat, snatched up his shoes, and crept away from the lively spite the house felt for them.[10]

[1] Morrison begins with a very short sentence; we don't know what "124" means, but we trust that we'll be told before long.

[2] Okay: 124 is a house. And in it are women and children. (But no men, evidently.)

[3] This is a historical novel, taking place in 1873. The description "Sethe and her daughter Denver" implies that Sethe is the main character, since Denver is being described in relation to her.

[4] Notice how few adverbs and adjectives this paragraph contains. The word "tiny" is a rare exception. Whose "tiny" hand prints might these be? We don't yet know. It's a mystery we'll keep in the back of our minds as we keep reading the novel.

[5] Morrison introduces three more characters and explains exactly who they are. We also know that the boys ran away following events that seem supernatural. So the book's opening two sentences weren't necessarily metaphors—the house might actually be "spiteful."

[6] Notice the varying sentence lengths: Here is a one-word sentence that emphasizes the finality of the boys' decision to flee the house.

[7] More "when" — winter. More "who" — Sethe, her mother, and her daughter are left in the house. More "where" — a gray and white house on Bluestone Road.

[8] In case there was any doubt left, "124" is the house number.

[9] More "where" — we're talking about a spot in Ohio that would later become part of Cincinnati.

[10] This sentence reiterates some previous information, emphasizing the frightened urgency with which the boys fled and the fact that the house did, in fact, feel spite toward the family.

The opening paragraph of *Beloved* conveys a lot of information and establishes a mood of darkness and urgency. The paragraph, like the novel it introduces, is intricate and, at times, difficult. It is also a model of clarity.

✴ exercises: be clear

1. Write a two-page scene that has at least five characters in it. Make sure that the reader understands the character relationships and always knows what is going on and who is doing what.

2. Write a two-page story that takes place in three different locations over five different time periods. Make sure the reader never gets confused.

3. Following the advice in the section "Writing the Long Sentence," write a clear sentence of at least 80 words. (Avoid stringing together several smaller sentences with semicolons.)

4. In a paragraph, describe a place where lots of people congregate (parade, football game, wedding, funeral, accident scene, beach, or another place) in which no sentence is longer than 5 words.

5. Write a paragraph describing the same place using only sentences of 20 words or more. Use no adverbs and only active voice.

6. Choose a passage from one of the stories in the anthology (or from any favorite story or novel) and annotate it for clarity, as in the opening paragraph of Toni Morrison's *Beloved*.

10 revising your story

THE CASE FOR REVISION

Writers revise. It's a simple truth.

Writers *get* to revise—fortunately. Most people don't have multiple chances to get something right. You miss a question on an exam, you've missed it. You miss a last-second shot, the buzzer goes off, that's it. Game over. You perform surgery and remove the wrong kidney, you don't get a redo. Neither does your patient.

For writers, it's different. When we write a story, we get a second chance, and a third, and as many as we want until we're satisfied that we've said a thing the best way we know how. We talk about "writing" stories, but what we really spend much of our time doing is revising them into being.

Revision gets a bum rap. The thrill of unbridled inspiration fares better in literary lore—like how Jack Kerouac wrote his 1957 novel *On the Road* in a three-week creative frenzy, tapping out sentence after sentence of what he called "spontaneous prose" onto a single, continuous roll of typing paper. But what seldom gets mentioned is how Kerouac then spent the next four years revising his manuscript before any publisher would touch it.

This chapter contains a number of strategies to get you revising. Over time, you'll discover what works best for you. You'll refine your own process. But the most important thing is that you do it. Many authors, in fact, come to see revision as their favorite part of the writing process. Bernard Malamud went so far as to call revision "one of the exquisite pleasures of writing." When we revise, we're no longer starting from scratch, staring at a blank page or computer screen. Instead, we get to roll up our sleeves, take what's already in front of us, and shape it into art.

WHAT IS "REVISION," ANYWAY?

It's a sincere question. Before computers, writers wrote longhand or typed a first draft, marked it up, wrote a second draft, marked it up, wrote a third draft, and so on.

Some writers still work that way. Most, however, use computers, on which we continually revise our work *as* we work. That's why it always rings a little false to me when I hear talk about "drafts" as if they are discrete and countable, like nickels.

It hardly needs to be said that writers work differently from one another. Some write quickly at first, getting the basic story onto the page. In her 1994 book *Bird by Bird*, Anne Lamott talks about the "shitty first draft" that must get written in order to write "good second drafts and terrific third drafts."

Others create their initial drafts more slowly. That's how I work—slowly— revising and polishing each sentence as I go. Maybe I'll end up deleting the very paragraph I've just spent an hour writing. But maybe I'll keep it, or move it to a different part of the story. I might try adding a new scene to the beginning of a story or maybe cutting the first several pages. On the one hand, I'm meticulous when I write a first draft. On the other hand, I know that everything I write is expendable at this beginning stage, when I don't yet know my own story very well.

Becky Hagenston's compositional process for her short story "Midnight, Licorice, Shadow" (p. 227) seems to blend writing and revising into a single, ongoing activity:

> When I first started writing this story, the only conflict I had in mind was that a couple couldn't figure out what to name their cat. I knew, of course, that this was not enough, but I also didn't know anything about the couple. This is my first crack at the first scene:
>
>> "Midnight, Licorice, Shadow," she says. "Cocoa, Casper, Dr. Livingston."
>> "Alfred Hitchcock," he says. "Dracula. Vincent Price."
>> They have had the cat for four days.

"Cinderblock?" she tries. "Bedspread?"

It's useless. The harder she tries to think of his name, the more elusive it becomes.

"Tomorrow, then," James says. "If we don't have a name by tomorrow." He slices a finger across his neck. "No offense, Cupcake," he tells the cat.

Marjorie looks at the animal, sprawled on their kitchen floor like a black bearskin rug. One of his fangs is showing. His monkey paws are kneading the air. "Monkey Paw!" she says, but James is already out the door. She hears his car start in the garage. "One more day," she tells the cat.

Soon, she will leave for work and the cat, this animal purring on the kitchen floor, will spend its last day of life all alone, drinking water, crunching on chow, maybe gazing out the window at the neighbor across the street, the crazy one who's always on the porch talking to himself.

James was already creepy, but there just wasn't enough to work with. Already, I had lost momentum and the story had stalled. Then I thought: But what if they aren't a married couple in their own kitchen, with jobs to go to? What if they're in a motel, and hardly know each other, and don't have jobs? But if they don't have jobs, what do they do? Where did the cat come from? Why is James so creepy, and should his name really be James, or something else? And Marjorie's name isn't quite right, either, but maybe she knows her name doesn't fit, so she's invented another one for herself? What if they're criminals of some kind? I've never written a story about criminals; that could be fun . . . and what's a nice girl like Marjorie (or whatever her name is) doing in a place like this?

It's always a series of questions that propels a story for me. I need to find out the answers, and the only way to do that is to write the story.

WHAT IS A "FIRST DRAFT"?

As I've already alluded to, when we continually hone a story on a word processor, the definition of "draft" becomes somewhat muddy. But for the purposes of this book, *a first draft is what you get when you've taken a story as far as you can on your own.*

When you're done with a first draft, you've already addressed as best you can any problems you know about—"the ending doesn't work," or "the story's climax is rushed over." At this point, you no longer know what can be improved.

Then—and not before—is often the right time to share your work with a writing workshop. If you know on your own what needs to be improved, you don't yet need the workshop's feedback. For instance, if one of your characters works as an emergency room physician, but you haven't yet done enough research to make the hospital scene completely believable, then you're going to be told that the hospital scene isn't believable. But if you already knew that, then what's the point of the workshop?

You want the workshop members, or any trusted readers, to tell you what you *don't* know: things that will push you to explore the unexplored, to recognize how the story has opened doorways that you hadn't considered. Now, it might take you many attempts to get to this point I'm calling a first draft. You might have rewritten the beginning or ending a half-dozen times. You might have added and removed characters, changed the plot. You'll certainly have reworked many, many sentences. But to get meaningful, helpful feedback from readers, give them a draft that feels as finished to you as possible.

Then comes the hard part. Although this draft is as finished as you could make it, you need to tell yourself—and believe—that the story can, should, and will change in revision, and probably a lot. Revision, after all, isn't about correcting typos or shuffling a few words around. Rather, it's about seeing your story anew (think "re-vision"), being willing to make everything messy again and maybe take the story in an entirely new direction.

For newer writers, the thought of mucking up a perfectly decent draft triggers everything from unease to terror. Experienced writers, however, have learned that most of the good stuff happens in revision, and so it pays to be fearless.

TWELVE STRATEGIES FOR REVISION

1. Save each major revision as a new file. I put this first because I can't encourage it strongly enough: When you embark on a significant revision, save the story as a new file on your computer. Doing so will make you a braver reviser. What's the worst that can happen? You'll make some changes you don't like, or maybe cut something you later decide should've stayed. No problem: You'll still have

the old file to return to. You might never return to the older file, but just knowing it's there will keep you from being tentative in your revisions, fearing that
you'll lose something that might be precious.

And while we're on the topic of saving things — save your work often. Get
used to hitting that Save key, because at some point you'll lose power or your
word processor will quit on you, and even a lost hour of work can feel tragic.

Along those lines, *back up your work*. Do it often, at least once per writing
session. Email the file to yourself. Save it on a flash drive. Just do it. Please. Do
it for me. I'll sleep better.

2. Read your own work "like a writer." Remember those questions from Chapter
1 that are helpful to ask of the published fiction you read? Well, those same
questions will benefit your own work-in-progress.

For convenience, here they are again — with a few modifications and
references to the chapters in the book that elaborate on each point.

- Why does your story begin when it does? What would happen if you
  started earlier or later in the story's chronology? (Chapter 3)
- What is different about the day when your story takes place? (Chapter 7)
- When you close your eyes, what part of your story do you picture most
  clearly in your mind? Why might that be? (Chapters 2 and 5)
- What is the main character's underlying problem, and how does your
  story bring this problem into sharper focus? (Chapters 6 and 7)
- Why did you select this main character, as opposed to another character
  in the story? How do you want readers to feel about him or her? What
  methods of characterization do you use? (Chapters 4 and 7)
- Why is your story in the point of view that it is? (Chapter 4)
- Which parts of the story are dramatized in scene? Which parts are sum-
  marized? Why? (Chapters 5 and 6)
- How would you describe your story's voice? What does the voice do for
  the story? (Chapter 4)
- Is the writing ever less clear than it could be? (Chapter 9)
- How is your story structured? How else could it be? (Chapter 6)

- Why does your story end when it does? What would happen if you ended it earlier or later in the story's chronology? (Chapter 8)
- How is your story different from other stories you've read? (Chapter 7)
- What details can you add or change to make your story more vivid or unexpected? (Chapter 2)

3. Start with the big stuff. You wouldn't hang photographs on a wall about to be demolished in a home renovation. You'd probably wait for the new wall. Similarly, any fundamental changes to your story—like changing your narrator or point of view—are usually better made before you spend time revising, say, the narrator's description of the view from his beach house. After all, a different narrator will describe that same view differently. Or maybe he'll live in a city.

4. Break revision into small, distinct tasks. It's harder to revise a whole story than to change the setting of one scene from a restaurant to a street fair, then to do some additional research so your ice-fishing scene will be more realistic, and then to rewrite any passive-voice sentences that would be stronger in the active voice. By coming up with a plan to revise your story one step at a time, you'll avoid the vague and potentially overwhelming mission of making your story "better."

5. Ask yourself what your story is about. This is the same question we ask of the stories we read—what, at its deepest level, is the story getting at? Revision often involves finding ways to bring out the story's "about-ness"—in other words, its themes. Bear in mind, though, that in fiction you rarely want to explain your story's themes to the reader. This is delicate territory; readers don't want to feel as if you're hammering themes into their heads. So take a little time to figure out what your story is about, and then get back to the business of putting your particular characters into their particular situations, choosing details that will *evoke* the story's themes.

6. Less fact, more fiction. In a first draft, we often borrow characters, plots, and settings from real life. But once you've written a draft, with its own narrative thrust and emerging characters and thematic concerns, the "real" story elements might well need to give way to more of your imaginative creations. If a character was originally based on a family member or a friend or someone from the news, in revision you should think about ways to allow your character to become fully himself or herself, with no real-life analog. If you set a scene in a house that resembles your childhood home (which is easier than having to invent a home from scratch with its particular layout and furnishings), in revision you should ask yourself if that's the *right* home for the story you're telling.

Joyce Carol Oates described her process of revising "away from the real" when working on her 1966 story "Where Are You Going, Where Have You Been?" The story is based on an actual killer nicknamed "The Pied Piper of Tucson," whose profile in *Life* magazine first drew Oates's attention.

> An early draft of my story . . . had the rather too explicit title "Death and the Maiden." It was cast in a mode of fiction to which I am still partial—indeed, every third or fourth story of mine is probably in this mode—"realistic allegory," it might be called. . . . In subsequent drafts the story changed its tone, its focus, its language, its title. It became "Where Are You Going, Where Have You Been?" Written at a time when the author was intrigued by the music of Bob Dylan, particularly the elegiac song "It's All Over Now, Baby Blue," it was dedicated to Bob Dylan. The charismatic mass murderer drops into the background and his innocent victim, a fifteen-year-old, moves into the foreground. She becomes the true protagonist of the tale.

7. Try writing "away from the page." Suppose that the motivations of one of your characters is eluding you. Try this: Open up a new file and write a brief autobiography from that character's point of view. Have her spill her guts. You might not put all of it into the story, or maybe any of it, but you'll have figured out something important about your character. And you just *might* use some of it.

Brenda Ueland, in her 1938 book *If You Want to Write: A Book about Art, Independence, and Spirit*, wrote:

> No writing is a waste of time—no creative work where the feelings, the imagination, the intelligence must work. With every sentence you write, you have learned something. It has done you good.

That's how I like to think about revision generally, but particularly about writing "away from the page." I've found this to be an extremely helpful strategy for exploring some as yet untapped aspect of whatever I'm working on. By writing away from the page, I can dig for answers and insight without the pressure of having to figure out where, or if, my discoveries belong in the actual story.

8. Be open to changing what you set out to do. The story you set out to write probably won't end up being the same story you actually write. The journey from our brain to the page is filled with all kinds of detours and roadside attractions.

Sometimes, revision means changing what you've written to come closer to your original vision. At other times, the draft you ended up writing might be leading you to a better work of fiction than the one you originally set out to write. (See Joyce Carol Oates's statement about her process in #6 above.)

One reason to keep asking yourself what your story is about (see #5 above) is that sometimes your story's "about-ness" changes as you write, and for the better. Once you understand what has changed, you can revise in that new direction.

9. Read your story aloud. There's no better way than reading aloud to catch inconsistencies in voice, or stilted dialogue, or description that goes on too long, or any number of problems that can elude us, no matter how long we stare at the computer monitor or printed page. When we read our stories aloud, problems tend to announce themselves.

This, incidentally, is a very good reason to read your work in public, even if your "public" is a few friends who've gathered to read their work to one another. In preparing for such a reading—imagining other people hearing your words—and then from the reading itself, you'll become highly attuned to your work's strengths and weaknesses.

10. Take your trusted readers seriously . . . We all want to be told that our first drafts are beautiful works of art, surely publishable once we move a few commas around. But that just isn't the case with first drafts—and honest, informed criticism is far more valuable than any ephemeral ego boost you might get from a well-meaning friend or family member.

That's where a writing workshop comes into play.[1]

If you care at all about the work you do, then it isn't easy to listen to somebody, or a class full of somebodies, telling you what isn't working. Of course, a workshop ought to tell you, too, what *is* working. But when it comes to criticism, try to have a thick skin and distance yourself, for the moment, from your own work. *Listen. Take plenty of notes.* Ask for clarification if you need it, but don't defend your draft or tell the group that they just don't understand your subtleties. Writers don't get to explain their stories. The stories must speak for themselves.

11. . . . but remember that you can't please everyone. The last thing you want to do is take fifteen classmates' critiques of your story and incorporate every single suggestion into a revised draft. You'll end up with the story equivalent of one of Dr. Moreau's creatures—some strange hyena/puma/armadillo hybrid.

The fact is, some criticism is better than other criticism. Some readers are more careful readers than others, and even among the careful and well-meaning, some will be better readers of *your work* than others. Or maybe you'll receive two pieces of advice that are equally good but mutually exclusive. I once led a workshop in which the class was split over whether the story would be stronger with a male or a female protagonist. Both sides had valid arguments—it came down to which story the writer wanted to write. Part of the writing experience is learning how to handle readers' feedback, some of which will be contradictory, to determine what is most useful to you as you revise.

12. Resist the urge to start over too soon with a new idea. Every semester, a student who's been working diligently on his story for weeks comes up to me the day before his draft is due and says, in a kind of manic excitement, "I have a new idea. A better idea. I'm going to write it tonight and turn in that story instead."

His brand-new idea exists only as potential, while the story he's been working on all this time feels, to him, soaked with actuality. It's only natural, this

---

[1]Or, in the absence of a workshop, a few trusted readers who care more about your development as a writer than about telling you what they think you want to hear.

urge to walk away from a flawed almost-draft and start anew with some fresh idea that, being only an idea, feels as promise-laden as a dewy morning full of puppies and rainbows.

Resist this urge.

As you gain experience, you'll begin to recognize when something truly isn't working. But walking away too soon or for the wrong reason is a mistake—just as it's a mistake to think that your new story, once you actually sit down to work on it, will be any easier to write than the old one.

Sometimes what's hardest to write—technically, emotionally, intellectually—is the thing most worth writing. So resist the urge, born of panic, to ditch the story you've been working on for the last-minute story. The one you've spent time on is probably better than you think it is, and certainly better than a last-minute story will be, no matter how much adrenaline and caffeine you throw at it.

HOW DO YOU KNOW WHEN YOUR STORY IS (REALLY, TRULY) DONE?

There's always another way to say something, a new direction your story could take. And don't forget that *you* change over time—your interests, viewpoints, and artistic preferences are never static. Last year's story, the one you wrote and revised until it seemed exactly right, might seem wrong to you now that you've had new experiences and learned new things—and not just about writing. You see the world differently at different points in your life. You aren't the same writer you were last year, or even last month.

For these reasons, you could, in theory, revise the same story for the rest of your life. I would advise against this. At some point, you need to say, "There. It's done." When you've followed the strategies discussed in this chapter and believe you're done revising, give your story a final edit for conciseness, clarity, and mechanical correctness.

But then how do you know your story is done?

▸ When you've made all the changes you can make, gone through all the revision strategies you know, and find yourself adding back the same commas you just took away, it's a decent indication that you're done.

- When your creative writing instructor tells you that your story seems finished, that's a decent indication, too.
- When you submit a story to a literary journal for publication, you're telling yourself that the story is done.
- If your story is accepted for publication and appears in a print or online journal, then you know it's done.

Or do you?

The truth is that writers sometimes revise their stories yet again, after they appear in journals but before they appear in a collection of stories.

Surely, though, once a story appears in a book, then it's done. No more revising . . .

Not so fast. Raymond Carver's story "The Bath" appeared in his 1983 story collection *What We Talk About When We Talk About Love*. Two years later, he published a significantly revised version of the same story, retitled "A Small, Good Thing," in his collection *Cathedral*. In an interview, Carver explained that revising the story had to do with the fact that, two years later, he'd become a different man and writer.

> "The Bath" appeared in a magazine. It won I no longer know what prize, but the story bothered me. It didn't seem finished to me. There were still things to say, and while I was writing *Cathedral* . . . things happened for me. The story "Cathedral" seemed to me completely different from everything I'd written before. I was in a period of generosity. I looked at "The Bath" and I found the story was like an unfinished painting. So I went back and rewrote it. It's much better now.

Does this mean that a story is *never* done? Instead of looking at it like that, I'd say that you have several opportunities to call your story finished — though ultimately the story is done when you truly believe that it is.

And if later you change your mind? Well, that's your prerogative. You're the writer.

boot camp

11 the mechanics of fiction: a writer's boot camp

IF YOU'VE EVER come across an error in a published novel or story, then you know what a jarring experience it is. When we're engrossed in a work of fiction, lost in what John Gardner calls the "fictional dream," we stop being aware that we're reading words on a page. All sense of *we* disappears, and only the story's world exists.

At the moment we notice the error (factual, grammatical — it matters little), we're yanked out of the story. The fictional world disappears, and we're startled awake from the fictional dream. We notice, suddenly, the book in our hands and are reminded that we're reading. This is the last thing a writer wants.

Worse yet, once we spot the error, we start to wonder what *other* errors might be out there waiting for us. We become suspicious of the work. We lose trust in the writer.

One of the writer's most important jobs is to gain the reader's trust. Earning that trust is hard work. Losing it is easy. And one of the easiest ways to lose a reader's trust is by paying too little attention to the mechanics — things like spelling, grammar, punctuation, and usage. To quote John Gardner again: "Learning to write fiction is too serious a business to be mixed in with leftovers from freshman composition."

With that in mind, this chapter is devoted to key technical issues that fiction writers commonly come across. Will mastery of the mechanics of writing make you a better, wiser person? Will it make you more fun at parties? Will it enrich your inner life? Yes, yes, and yes.

But more to the point, you need to master the mechanics because they are some of our most basic tools. You might find, as you read this chapter, that you already know some—maybe even most—of what's contained here. The truth, however, is that you need to know all of it. After all, would you trust a carpenter who knows how to use most, but not all, of his tools, or a surgeon who's only occasionally unpredictable with her scalpel? Failure to master the mechanics of writing signals to a reader (or an editor or a teacher) that you are less than fully committed to your own work. And if you aren't committed, then why should anyone else be?

Okay, enough with the preamble. Roll up your sleeves. Or drop and give me twenty.

Anyway, welcome to boot camp.

FORMATTING AND PUNCTUATING DIALOGUE

When writing dialogue, the period or comma always goes inside the quotation marks.[1] Also, remember to capitalize only the beginning of the sentence and the beginning of the quotation.

INCORRECT

"Look at that piñata." She said.

"Look at that piñata," She said.

CORRECT

"Look at that piñata," she said.

She said, "Look at that piñata."

"I wonder," she said, "if anyone will break that piñata."

If what precedes or follows the line of dialogue is a complete sentence, then be sure to use a period, not a comma, at the end of each sentence.

---

[1]Exceptions include MLA documentation and work published in the United Kingdom and Australia. But we're talking now about creative work published in the United States.

INCORRECT

"You're a funny guy," she smiled at me.

CORRECT

"You're a funny guy." She smiled at me.

"You're a funny guy," she said, smiling at me.

The following examples are punctuated correctly:

"Look at that piñata." She pointed toward the colorful, stuffed bird hanging from a tree branch.

She tapped me on the shoulder. "Look at that piñata."

"I like you," she said. "You're a funny guy."

Compare that last example and this next one, which is also punctuated correctly:

"I like you," she said, "because you're a funny guy."

The difference? "You're a funny guy" is a complete sentence. "Because you're a funny guy" is a fragment, part of the longer sentence "I like you because you're a funny guy."

ADDRESSING A PERSON IN DIALOGUE

When a character addresses another character by name, always put a comma before and after the name.

"You need some help? Why, I'll run right over Jonathan," Sara said.

Written that way, Jonathan is about to suffer an awful fate. Let's hope that Sara is riding a bicycle, rather than driving a cement truck. What this writer probably means is:

"You need some help? Why, I'll run right over, Jonathan," Sara said.

By adding a single comma, we transform Sara from psychopathic accomplice to good pal.

All of the following sentences are correctly punctuated. Note the placement of commas before and after the character being addressed.

"Louis, please come down from the roof," Mr. Brenner said.

"Louis," Mr. Brenner said, "please come down from the roof."

"Please, Louis, come down from the roof," Mr. Brenner said.

Mr. Brenner said, "Please come down from the roof, Louis."

PARAGRAPH BREAKS IN DIALOGUE

There are no hard-and-fast rules when it comes to paragraph breaks. The best way to get a feel for when to break your paragraphs is by reading other writers and seeing what they do. The stories in this book provide many examples of how writers choose to break their paragraphs. Often, however, a change in speaker warrants a new paragraph, as in the example below from Richard Bausch's story "Tandolfo the Great" (p. 198).

"Hey, guys—it's Tandolfo the Great." The boy's hair is a bright blond color, and you can see through it to his scalp.
"Scram," Tandolfo says. "Really."
"Aw, what's your hurry, man?"
"I've just set off a nuclear device," Tandolfo says with grave seriousness. "It's on a timer. Poof."

DOUBLE QUOTATION MARKS / SINGLE QUOTATION MARKS

Unless there's a specific reason to do otherwise, always use double quotation marks (" "). Use single quotations marks (' ') when you're putting quotation marks inside another quotation. For example:

"So then," she explained, "my boss leaned over and whispered, 'You're fired.'"

She said, "You use the word 'awesome' way too often."

quick quiz: repair this sentence

Fix all that's wrong with the following:

You always use the word 'awesome', it's driving me crazy Cindy.

SCARE QUOTES

Scare quotes, sometimes called "air quotes," are the written equivalent of making quotation marks with your fingers while talking. They tend to draw unnecessary attention and are rarely needed. Instead of writing

I thought that movie was "incredible."

you probably only need to write:

I thought that movie was incredible.

Even if you are being sarcastic, trust the reader to ascertain the sarcasm from the context, rather than from using a scare quote.

When I said I was too sick to go to school, my mother said of course I should stay home. And while I was there, I could mow the lawn, vacuum the house, and clean out the gutters. What a saint my mother is.

There's no need to write:

What a "saint" my mother is.

FORMATTING AND PUNCTUATING A CHARACTER'S THOUGHTS

In contemporary fiction, it's most common not to use quotation marks when you write a character's thoughts. Usually, you don't need to use italics either.

In the following paragraph, the shaded sentences read like a line of dialogue that the character asks herself. However, because the words aren't actually said—just thought—no quotation marks are needed.

She ran out the door and drove to work, all the time thinking about her boyfriend. Why would he give me wilting roses for our anniversary? she wondered. And they'd only been together six months. What will he give me after a year, a dead puppy?

Another common way of expressing a character's thoughts is to do so indirectly, from the perspective of the third-person narrator. In the following example, notice how the pronouns change from "me" and "our" to "her" and "their," and all sentences remain in the past tense.

She ran out the door and drove to work, all the time thinking about her boyfriend. Why would he give her wilting roses for their anniversary? And they'd only been together six months. What would he give her after a year, a dead puppy?

COMMA SPLICES

Comma splices are a type of run-on sentence in which two independent clauses are connected only by a comma. They are grammatically incorrect.

INCORRECT

I ran over to the car, Bill said, "Get in."

He had a dog, it weighed eleven pounds.

CORRECT

I ran over to the car, and Bill said, "Get in."

When I ran over to the car, Bill said, "Get in."

He had a dog. It weighed eleven pounds.

He had a dog; it weighed eleven pounds.

He had a dog, and it weighed eleven pounds.

He had an eleven-pound dog.

A word about sentence fragments

If run-on sentences are a problem, shouldn't fragments also be? The short answer is not always. While run-on sentences tend to read like mistakes, fragments sometimes aid in the pacing of a story as well as in establishing a story's voice.

The second half of Tobias Wolff's story "Bullet in the Brain" (p. 366) contains a number of long sentences detailing everything that Anders, at the moment of his death, fails to remember. The story then shifts to what he *does* remember, and with this shift in focus comes a corresponding shift in the prose to short bursts of images, told in fragments:

> This is what he remembered. Heat. A baseball field. Yellow grass, the whirr of insects, himself leaning against a tree as the boys of the neighborhood gather for a pickup game.

These fragments are effective not only because they provide a counterpoint to the longer, more fluid sentences that precede them, but also because they mirror the way the images themselves come to Anders—with surprising force and clarity.

"WHO" AND "THAT"

"Who" refers to people:

> Those are the men who stole my car.

"That" refers to things:

> I'll take home any pie that you don't want.

What about animals? Doesn't anyone care about the animals? It depends on how the animal is represented in the story. A character habitually vexed by a garden-ravaging rabbit might shout:

> There's the rabbit that keeps digging up my carrots.

On the other hand, a character talking about his beloved pet might say:

> Winston is a dog who knows exactly how to enjoy a sunny afternoon.

EXCLAMATION MARKS, QUESTION MARKS, ALL CAPS

Avoid the temptation to use multiple punctuation marks for emphasis. Excessive punctuation comes across as melodramatic and suggests a deficiency in the writing that's being compensated for in the punctuation. The same holds true for all caps. If you have any friends who habitually email or text in all caps, then you'll understand immediately. For example:

> When I told my father what I'd done, he said, "What are you, crazy?!"

> When I told my father what I'd done, he said, "What are you, crazy??"

> When I told my father what I'd done, he said, "WHAT ARE YOU, CRAZY???"

You should know that I gave myself a headache just typing that last sentence. Please, let the prose itself convey the full emotion. If you feel the need to use three exclamation marks in a row, it's an indication that the scene might need to be revised to more accurately convey the intensity of the emotion being expressed.

> When I told my father what I'd done, his face turned red, then purple, then a shade I'd never seen before. "What are you, crazy?"

CONJUGATION OF "LIE" AND "LAY"

"Lie" and "lay" are two tricky verbs. Yet you need to know how to conjugate them, because they are very common and often get used in stories.

"Lie," meaning "to recline," is an intransitive verb and doesn't require a direct object.

PRESENT TENSE: *LIE*

She lies down on the sand.

PAST TENSE: *LAY*

Yesterday, she lay on the beach and read a book.

PAST PARTICIPLE: *LAIN*

She had lain on the beach all afternoon, until a thunderstorm rolled in.

PRESENT PROGRESSIVE: *LYING*

I'm lying here in bed until my headache goes away.

"Lay" is a transitive verb and requires a direct object.

PRESENT TENSE: *LAY*

She lays the towel down on the sand.

PAST TENSE: *LAID*

She laid her towel on the sand and looked up at the cloudy sky.

PAST PARTICIPLE: *LAID*

Five minutes after she had laid her towel on the sand, it started to rain.

PRESENT PROGRESSIVE: *LAYING*

She's laying her son in his crib very carefully so that he won't wake up and start to cry.

quick quiz: choose the correct sentence

Which sentence is correct? Why?

I lie myself down to take a nap.
I lay myself down to take a nap.

And now for a caveat

Let's say we're writing a story from the first-person perspective, using an informal voice. Does our narrator need to conjugate "lie" and "lay" correctly? Not at all.

So then my stupid dog lays down in the middle of the freeway and yawns.

In the context of this story, it might be fine to use the wrong verb. After all, we're trying to get the narrator's personality onto the page, and it's certainly possible that our narrator wouldn't know which verb to use, or care even if he did. But a character's ignorance should never be a reflection of the author's. The use of "lay" rather than the correct verb "lie" should be a decision made in the service of the story's voice. And to make that decision, the writer needs to know the correct verb.

SENTENCES THAT BEGIN WITH AN "-ING" WORD

If you find yourself writing a sentence that begins with an "-ing" word, take a very careful look. Often, sentences that begin either with a verb in its present-participle form or with a gerund are fraught with problems.

1. Sometimes the problem has to do with sentence logic:

> Running out the door, she drove to work.

The problem with this sentence is that it implies that the two actions occur simultaneously, which is logically impossible. You can't run out the door and drive to work at the same time. Instead, the sentence could be written, "She ran out the door and drove to work," which implies that one action follows the other. Or you could write, "She slammed the door behind her and rushed to work."

2. Other times, the sentence contains a misplaced modifier:

> Stalling out and leaking pints of oil, Ben knew it was time to trade in his old car.

Unless Ben is the one stalling out and leaking oil, the sentence should be revised:

> Ben knew it was time to trade in his old car when it began to stall out and leak pints of oil.

3. A third problem is how often sentences beginning with an "-ing" word rely on the linking verb "to be," producing a syntactically awkward result:

> Eating a big breakfast is how Sue starts her morning.

The sentence becomes a lot less tortured if we (a) change the sentence's subject to Sue, our character, rather than the "-ing" word "eating," and (b) replace the linking verb "is" with an active verb:

> Sue starts her morning with a big breakfast.

> Sue eats a big breakfast to start her morning.

Note: Karen Russell begins her story "St. Lucy's Home for Girls Raised by Wolves" (p. 324) with a vivid linking-verb sentence:

> At first, our pack was all hair and snarl and floor-thumping joy.

However, the sentence doesn't begin with an "-ing" word.

SOME FINAL ADVICE

Proofread carefully for usage errors that spell-check won't catch (for example: there/their/they're; your/you're; its/it's).

Avoid spelling mistakes of any kind whatsoever. We are well into the age of spell-check and online dictionaries, which make it easy to look up anything that needs looking up.

"A lot" is two words. But you knew that already.

"All right" is also two words.

"A while" (two words) **follows a preposition:** "I studied for a while, then took a break."

"Awhile" (one word) **is an adverb and doesn't require a preposition:** "I studied awhile, then took a break."

Avoid clichés like the plague or you'll break my heart.

Call your mother.

The Mechanics of Fiction: Practice Test

Rewrite each sentence so that it is correct. Some sentences might contain more than one error, and others might contain no errors.

1. I like her alot, she reminds me of my grandmother.
2. I lied down on the rug and petted my dog.
3. "Hey Michael". He said. "You should join our poker game".
4. "Are you kidding?!" I replied. "You guys cheat".
5. Fran thought, "Will I ever get a date for the prom?"
6. Putting on her shoes, Debra went outside and got the mail.
7. "Look at that strange map," she went over and picked it up.
8. I have laid here for hours, and I'm still not tan!!
9. "Missouri is located in the Midwest." He shut his geography book.
10. I lay my book down and lied there waiting for the movie to start.
11. Purring outside my window all night long, I felt like throwing a shoe at that cat.
12. Are you alright?
13. That's enough already David.
14. "Look Son I've had just about enough." He said.
15. Never count you're money until the dealing's done.

Extra Credit

Rewrite the following passage to correct all the errors:

While many of they're friends believe in "Santa Claus", my two children don't, they just believe in getting alot of presents. Its a good thing they're still crazy about the Easter Bunny.

anthology

12

a mini-anthology: 15 stories

Sherman Alexie

~ This Is What It Means to Say Phoenix, Arizona

Sherman Alexie was born in 1966 and grew up on the Spokane Indian Reservation in Wellpinit, Washington. He attended Gonzaga University in Spokane to prepare for a career in medicine before transferring to Washington State University, where he majored in American studies and dedicated himself to writing. His first collection of stories, *The Lone Ranger and Tonto Fistfight in Heaven*, was published in 1993 and won the PEN/Hemingway Award. He has gone on to publish numerous books of poetry and fiction, an acclaimed novel for young adults, and the screenplay for the 1998 movie *Smoke Signals*, which was based on the short story "This Is What It Means to Say Phoenix, Arizona." His many awards include a Lila Wallace–Reader's Digest Writers' Award, the Stranger Genius Award, the Pushcart Prize, the PEN/Malamud Award, the PEN/Faulkner Award, and a National Endowment for the Arts Fellowship.

> *"When you look at great writers, you're looking at people who are actually better readers. Period. So that's where you start."*
> ~ from *Jack Central*, March 5, 2009

Just after Victor lost his job at the BIA, he also found out that his father had died of a heart attack in Phoenix, Arizona. Victor hadn't seen his father in a few years, only talked to him on the telephone once or twice, but there still was a genetic pain, which was soon to be pain as real and immediate as a broken bone.

Victor didn't have any money. Who does have money on a reservation, except the cigarette and fireworks salespeople? His father had a savings account waiting to be claimed, but Victor needed to find a way to get to Phoenix. Victor's mother was just as poor as he was, and the rest of his family didn't have any use at all for him. So Victor called the Tribal Council.

"Listen," Victor said. "My father just died. I need some money to get to Phoenix to make arrangements."

"Now, Victor," the council said. "You know we're having a difficult time financially."

"But I thought the council had special funds set aside for stuff like this."

"Now, Victor, we do have some money available for the proper return of tribal members' bodies. But I don't think we have enough to bring your father all the way back from Phoenix."

"Well," Victor said. "It ain't going to cost all that much. He had to be cremated. Things were kind of ugly. He died of a heart attack in his trailer and nobody found him for a week. It was really hot, too. You get the picture."

"Now, Victor, we're sorry for your loss and the circumstances. But we can really only afford to give you one hundred dollars."

"That's not even enough for a plane ticket."

"Well, you might consider driving down to Phoenix."

"I don't have a car. Besides, I was going to drive my father's pickup back up here."

"Now, Victor," the council said. "We're sure there is somebody who could drive you to Phoenix. Or is there somebody who could lend you the rest of the money?"

"You know there ain't nobody around with that kind of money."

"Well, we're sorry, Victor, but that's the best we can do."

Victor accepted the Tribal Council's offer. What else could he do? So he signed the proper papers, picked up his check, and walked over to the Trading Post to cash it.

While Victor stood in line, he watched Thomas Builds-the-Fire standing near the magazine rack, talking to himself. Like he always did. Thomas was a storyteller that nobody wanted to listen to. That's like being a dentist in a town where everybody has false teeth.

Victor and Thomas Builds-the-Fire were the same age, had grown up and played in the dirt together. Ever since Victor could remember, it was Thomas who always had something to say.

Once, when they were seven years old, when Victor's father still lived with the family, Thomas closed his eyes and told Victor this story: "Your father's heart is weak. He is afraid of his own family. He is afraid of you. Late at night he sits in the dark. Watches the television until there's nothing but that white noise. Sometimes he feels like he wants to buy a motorcycle and ride away. He wants to run and hide. He doesn't want to be found."

Thomas Builds-the-Fire had known that Victor's father was going to leave, knew it before anyone. Now Victor stood in the Trading Post with a one-hundred-dollar check in his hand, wondering if Thomas knew that Victor's father was dead, if he knew what was going to happen next.

Just then Thomas looked at Victor, smiled, and walked over to him.

"Victor, I'm sorry about your father," Thomas said.

"How did you know about it?" Victor asked.

"I heard it on the wind. I heard it from the birds. I felt it in the sunlight. Also, your mother was just in here crying."

"Oh," Victor said and looked around the Trading Post. All the other Indians stared, surprised that Victor was even talking to Thomas. Nobody talked to Thomas anymore because he told the same damn stories over and over again. Victor was embarrassed, but he thought that Thomas might be able to help him. Victor felt a sudden need for tradition.

"I can lend you the money you need," Thomas said suddenly. "But you have to take me with you."

"I can't take your money," Victor said. "I mean, I haven't hardly talked to you in years. We're not really friends anymore."

"I didn't say we were friends. I said you had to take me with you."

"Let me think about it."

Victor went home with his one hundred dollars and sat at the kitchen table. He held his head in his hands and thought about Thomas Builds-the-Fire, remembered little details, tears and scars, the bicycle they shared for a summer, so many stories.

∞

Thomas Builds-the-Fire sat on the bicycle, waited in Victor's yard. He was ten years old and skinny. His hair was dirty because it was the Fourth of July.

"Victor," Thomas yelled. "Hurry up. We're going to miss the fireworks."

After a few minutes, Victor ran out of his house, jumped the porch railing, and landed gracefully on the sidewalk.

"And the judges award him a 9.95, the highest score of the summer," Thomas said, clapped, laughed.

"That was perfect, cousin," Victor said. "And it's my turn to ride the bike."

Thomas gave up the bike and they headed for the fairgrounds. It was nearly dark and the fireworks were about to start.

"You know," Thomas said. "It's strange how us Indians celebrate the Fourth of July. It ain't like it was *our* independence everybody was fighting for."

"You think about things too much," Victor said. "It's just supposed to be fun. Maybe Junior will be there."

"Which Junior? Everybody on this reservation is named Junior."

And they both laughed.

The fireworks were small, hardly more than a few bottle rockets and a fountain. But it was enough for two Indian boys. Years later, they would need much more.

Afterwards, sitting in the dark, fighting off mosquitoes, Victor turned to Thomas Builds-the-Fire.

"Hey," Victor said. "Tell me a story."

Thomas closed his eyes and told this story: "There were these two Indian boys who wanted to be warriors. But it was too late to be warriors in the old way. All the horses were gone. So the two Indian boys stole a car and drove to the city. They parked the stolen car in front of the police station and then hitchhiked back home to the reservation. When they got back, all their friends cheered and their parents' eyes shone with pride. *You were very brave,* everybody said to the two Indian boys. *Very brave.*"

"Ya-hey," Victor said. "That's a good one. I wish I could be a warrior."

"Me too," Thomas said.

They went home together in the dark, Thomas on the bike now, Victor on foot. They walked through shadows and light from streetlamps.

"We've come a long ways," Thomas said. "We have outdoor lighting."

"All I need is the stars," Victor said. "And besides, you still think about things too much."

They separated then, each headed for home, both laughing all the way.

∞

Victor sat at his kitchen table. He counted his one hundred dollars again and again. He knew he needed more to make it to Phoenix and back. He knew he needed Thomas Builds-the-Fire. So he put his money in his wallet and opened the front door to find Thomas on the porch.

"Ya-hey, Victor," Thomas said. "I knew you'd call me."

Thomas walked into the living room and sat down on Victor's favorite chair.

"I've got some money saved up," Thomas said. "It's enough to get us down there, but you have to get us back."

"I've got this hundred dollars," Victor said. "And my dad had a savings account I'm going to claim."

"How much in your dad's account?"

"Enough. A few hundred."

"Sounds good. When we leaving?"

∞

When they were fifteen and had long since stopped being friends, Victor and Thomas got into a fistfight. That is, Victor was really drunk and beat Thomas up for no reason at all. All the other Indian boys stood around and watched it happen. Junior was there and so were Lester, Seymour, and a lot of others. The beating might have gone on until Thomas was dead if Norma Many Horses hadn't come along and stopped it.

"Hey, you boys," Norma yelled and jumped out of her car. "Leave him alone."

If it had been someone else, even another man, the Indian boys would've just ignored the warnings. But Norma was a warrior. She was powerful. She could have picked up any two of the boys and smashed their skulls together. But worse than that, she would have dragged them all over to some tipi and made them listen to some elder tell a dusty old story.

The Indian boys scattered, and Norma walked over to Thomas and picked him up.

"Hey, little man, are you okay?" she asked.

Thomas gave her a thumbs up.

"Why they always picking on you?"

Thomas shook his head, closed his eyes, but no stories came to him, no words or music. He just wanted to go home, to lie in his bed and let his dreams tell his stories for him.

∞

Thomas Builds-the-Fire and Victor sat next to each other in the airplane, coach section. A tiny white woman had the window seat. She was busy twisting her body into pretzels. She was flexible.

"I have to ask," Thomas said, and Victor closed his eyes in embarrassment.

"Don't," Victor said.

"Excuse me, miss," Thomas asked. "Are you a gymnast or something?"

"There's no something about it," she said. "I was first alternate on the 1980 Olympic team."

"Really?" Thomas asked.

"Really."

"I mean, you used to be a world-class athlete?" Thomas asked.

"My husband still thinks I am."

Thomas Builds-the-Fire smiled. She was a mental gymnast, too. She pulled her leg straight up against her body so that she could've kissed her kneecap.

"I wish I could do that," Thomas said.

Victor was ready to jump out of the plane. Thomas, that crazy Indian storyteller with ratty old braids and broken teeth, was flirting with a beautiful Olympic gymnast. Nobody back home on the reservation would ever believe it.

"Well," the gymnast said. "It's easy. Try it."

Thomas grabbed at his leg and tried to pull it up into the same position as the gymnast. He couldn't even come close, which made Victor and the gymnast laugh.

"Hey," she asked. "You two are Indian, right?"

"Full-blood," Victor said.

"Not me," Thomas said. "I'm half magician on my mother's side and half clown on my father's."

They all laughed.

"What are your names?" she asked.

"Victor and Thomas."

"Mine is Cathy. Pleased to meet you all."

The three of them talked for the duration of the flight. Cathy the gymnast complained about the government, how they screwed the 1980 Olympic team by boycotting.

"Sounds like you all got a lot in common with Indians," Thomas said.

Nobody laughed.

After the plane landed in Phoenix and they had all found their way to the terminal, Cathy the gymnast smiled and waved good-bye.

"She was really nice," Thomas said.

"Yeah, but everybody talks to everybody on airplanes," Victor said. "It's too bad we can't always be that way."

"You always used to tell me I think too much," Thomas said. "Now it sounds like you do."

"Maybe I caught it from you."

"Yeah."

Thomas and Victor rode in a taxi to the trailer where Victor's father died.

"Listen," Victor said as they stopped in front of the trailer. "I never told you I was sorry for beating you up that time."

"Oh, it was nothing. We were just kids and you were drunk."

"Yeah, but I'm still sorry."

"That's all right."

Victor paid for the taxi and the two of them stood in the hot Phoenix summer. They could smell the trailer.

"This ain't going to be nice," Victor said. "You don't have to go in."

"You're going to need help."

Victor walked to the front door and opened it. The stink rolled out and made them both gag. Victor's father had lain in that trailer for a week in hundred-degree temperatures before anyone found him. And the only reason anyone found him was because of the smell. They needed dental records to identify him. That's exactly what the coroner said. They needed dental records.

"Oh, man," Victor said. "I don't know if I can do this."

"Well, then don't."

"But there might be something valuable in there."

"I thought his money was in the bank."

"It is. I was talking about pictures and letters and stuff like that."

"Oh," Thomas said as he held his breath and followed Victor into the trailer.

∞

When Victor was twelve, he stepped into an underground wasp nest. His foot was caught in the hole, and no matter how hard he struggled, Victor couldn't pull free. He might have died there, stung a thousand times, if Thomas Builds-the-Fire had not come by.

"Run," Thomas yelled and pulled Victor's foot from the hole. They ran then, hard as they ever had, faster than Billy Mills, faster than Jim Thorpe, faster than the wasps could fly.

Victor and Thomas ran until they couldn't breathe, ran until it was cold and dark outside, ran until they were lost and it took hours to find their way home. All the way back, Victor counted his stings.

"Seven," Victor said. "My lucky number."

∞

Victor didn't find much to keep in the trailer. Only a photo album and a stereo. Everything else had that smell stuck in it or was useless anyway.

"I guess this is all," Victor said. "It ain't much."

"Better than nothing," Thomas said.

"Yeah, and I do have the pickup."

"Yeah," Thomas said. "It's in good shape."

"Dad was good about that stuff."

"Yeah, I remember your dad."

"Really?" Victor asked. "What do you remember?"

Thomas Builds-the-Fire closed his eyes and told this story: "I remember when I had this dream that told me to go to Spokane, to stand by the Falls in the middle of the city and wait for a sign. I knew I had to go there but I didn't have a car. Didn't have a license. I was only thirteen. So I walked all the way, took me all day, and I finally made it to the Falls. I stood there for an hour waiting. Then your dad came walking up. *What the hell are you doing here?* he asked me. I said, *Waiting for a vision.* Then your father said, *All you're going to get here is mugged.* So he drove me over to Denny's, bought me dinner, and then drove me home to the reservation. For a long time I was mad because I thought my dreams had lied to me. But they didn't. Your dad was my vision. *Take care of each other* is what my dreams were saying. *Take care of each other.*"

Victor was quiet for a long time. He searched his mind for memories of his father, found the good ones, found a few bad ones, added it all up, and smiled.

"My father never told me about finding you in Spokane," Victor said.

"He said he wouldn't tell anybody. Didn't want me to get in trouble. But he said I had to watch out for you as part of the deal."

"Really?"

"Really. Your father said you would need the help. He was right."

"That's why you came down here with me, isn't it?" Victor asked.

"I came because of your father."

Victor and Thomas climbed into the pickup, drove over to the bank, and claimed the three hundred dollars in the savings account.

∾

Thomas Builds-the-Fire could fly.

Once, he jumped off the roof of the tribal school and flapped his arms like a crazy eagle. And he flew. For a second, he hovered, suspended above all the other Indian boys who were too smart or too scared to jump.

"He's flying," Junior yelled, and Seymour was busy looking for the trick wires or mirrors. But it was real. As real as the dirt when Thomas lost altitude and crashed to the ground.

He broke his arm in two places.

"He broke his wing," Victor chanted, and the other Indian boys joined in, made it a tribal song.

"He broke his wing, he broke his wing, he broke his wing," all the Indian boys chanted as they ran off, flapping their wings, wishing they could fly, too. They hated Thomas for his courage, his brief moment as a bird. Everybody has dreams about flying. Thomas flew.

One of his dreams came true for just a second, just enough to make it real.

∽

Victor's father, his ashes, fit in one wooden box with enough left over to fill a cardboard box.

"He always was a big man," Thomas said.

Victor carried part of his father and Thomas carried the rest out to the pickup. They set him down carefully behind the seats, put a cowboy hat on the wooden box and a Dodgers cap on the cardboard box. That's the way it was supposed to be.

"Ready to head back home," Victor asked.

"It's going to be a long drive."

"Yeah, take a couple days, maybe."

"We can take turns," Thomas said.

"Okay," Victor said, but they didn't take turns. Victor drove for sixteen hours straight north, made it halfway up Nevada toward home before he finally pulled over.

"Hey, Thomas," Victor said. "You got to drive for a while."

"Okay."

Thomas Builds-the Fire slid behind the wheel and started off down the road. All through Nevada, Thomas and Victor had been amazed at the lack of animal life, at the absence of water, of movement.

"Where is everything?" Victor had asked more than once.

Now when Thomas was finally driving they saw the first animal, maybe the only animal in Nevada. It was a long-eared jackrabbit.

"Look," Victor yelled. "It's alive."

Thomas and Victor were busy congratulating themselves on their discovery when the jackrabbit darted out into the road and under the wheels of the pickup.

"Stop the goddamn car," Victor yelled, and Thomas did stop, backed the pickup off the dead jackrabbit.

"Oh, man, he's dead," Victor said as he looked at the squashed animal. "Really dead."

"The only thing alive in this whole state and we just killed it."

"I don't know," Thomas said. "I think it was suicide."

Victor looked around the desert, sniffed the air, felt the emptiness and loneliness, and nodded his head.

"Yeah," Victor said. "It had to be suicide."

"I can't believe this," Thomas said. "You drive for a thousand miles and there ain't even any bugs smashed on the windshield. I drive for ten seconds and kill the only living thing in Nevada."

"Yeah," Victor said. "Maybe I should drive."

"Maybe you should."

∾

Thomas Builds-the-Fire walked through the corridors of the tribal school by himself. Nobody wanted to be anywhere near him because of all those stories. Story after story.

Thomas closed his eyes and this story came to him: "We are all given one thing by which our lives are measured, one determination. Mine are the stories which can change or not change the world. It doesn't matter which as long as I continue to tell the stories. My father, he died on Okinawa in World War II, died fighting for this country, which had tried to kill him for years. My mother, she died giving birth to me, died while I was still inside her. She pushed me out into the world with her last breath. I have no brothers or sisters. I have only my stories which came to me before I even had the words to speak. I learned a thousand stories before I took my first thousand steps. They are all I have. It's all I can do."

Thomas Builds-the-Fire told his stories to all those who would stop and listen. He kept telling them long after people had stopped listening.

∞

Victor and Thomas made it back to the reservation just as the sun was rising. It was the beginning of a new day on earth, but the same old shit on the reservation.

"Good morning," Thomas said.

"Good morning."

The tribe was waking up, ready for work, eating breakfast, reading the newspaper, just like everybody else does. Willene LeBret was out in her garden wearing a bathrobe. She waved when Thomas and Victor drove by.

"Crazy Indians made it," she said to herself and went back to her roses.

Victor stopped the pickup in front of Thomas Builds-the-Fire's HUD house. They both yawned, stretched a little, shook dust from their bodies.

"I'm tired," Victor said.

"Of everything," Thomas added.

They both searched for words to end the journey. Victor needed to thank Thomas for his help, for the money, and make the promise to pay it all back.

"Don't worry about the money," Thomas said. "It don't make any difference anyhow."

"Probably not, enit?"

"Nope."

Victor knew that Thomas would remain the crazy storyteller who talked to dogs and cars, who listened to the wind and pine trees. Victor knew that he couldn't really be friends with Thomas, even after all that had happened. It was cruel but it was real. As real as the ashes, as Victor's father, sitting behind the seats.

"I know how it is," Thomas said. "I know you ain't going to treat me any better than you did before. I know your friends would give you too much shit about it."

Victor was ashamed of himself. Whatever happened to the tribal ties, the sense of community? The only real thing he shared with anybody was a bottle and broken dreams. He owed Thomas something, anything.

"Listen," Victor said and handed Thomas the cardboard box which contained half of his father. "I want you to have this."

Thomas took the ashes and smiled, closed his eyes, and told this story: "I'm going to travel to Spokane Falls one last time and toss these ashes into the water. And your father will rise like a salmon, leap over the bridge, over me, and find his way home. It will be beautiful. His teeth will shine like silver, like a rainbow. He will rise, Victor, he will rise."

Victor smiled.

"I was planning on doing the same thing with my half," Victor said. "But I didn't imagine my father looking anything like a salmon. I thought it'd be like cleaning the attic or something. Like letting things go after they've stopped having any use."

"Nothing stops, cousin," Thomas said. "Nothing stops."

Thomas Builds-the-Fire got out of the pickup and walked up his driveway. Victor started the pickup and began the drive home.

"Wait," Thomas yelled suddenly from his porch. "I just got to ask one favor."

Victor stopped the pickup, leaned out the window, and shouted back. "What do you want?"

"Just one time when I'm telling a story somewhere, why don't you stop and listen?" Thomas asked.

"Just once?"

"Just once."

Victor waved his arms to let Thomas know that the deal was good. It was a fair trade, and that was all Victor had ever wanted from his whole life. So Victor drove his father's pickup toward home while Thomas went into his house, closed the door behind him, and heard a new story come to him in the silence afterwards.

~ 1993

Richard Bausch

∾ Tandolfo the Great

"I start writing with an image or a voice, but I don't know anything when I start. The only thing I know is that I'm starting. And learn it as I go. That's why it's so hard, you have to learn all over again, because each one is different. I've written sixteen books, and I had to learn how to write each one of them."

~ from *The Washington Post*,
November 20, 2003

Richard Bausch was born in 1945 in Georgia and grew up in the Washington, D.C., area. He served in the Air Force and later attended George Mason University and the Iowa Writers' Workshop. He is the author of eleven novels and eight story collections. His stories have appeared in periodicals such as *The New Yorker*, *Harper's*, and *The Southern Review* and have been selected for *The O. Henry Prize Stories*, *Best American Short Stories*, and *New Stories from the South*. He has won two National Magazine Awards, a Guggenheim Fellowship, a Lila Wallace–Reader's Digest Writers' Award, the Award of the American Academy of Arts and Letters, and the PEN/Malamud Award for Excellence in the Short Story. Bausch currently holds the Moss Chair of Excellence in English at the University of Memphis.

for Stephen & Karen & Nicholas Goodwin

"Tandolfo," he says to his own image in the mirror over the bathroom sink. "She loves you not, oh, she doesn't, doesn't, doesn't."

He's put the makeup on, packed the bag of tricks—including the rabbit that he calls Chi-Chi, and the bird, the attention getter, Witch. He's to do a birthday party for some five-year-old on the other side of the river. A crowd of babies, and the adults waiting around for him to screw up—this is going to be one of those tough ones.

He has fortified himself, and he feels ready. He isn't particularly worried about it. But there's a little something else he has to do first. Something on the order of the embarrassingly ridiculous: he has to make a delivery.

This morning at the local bakery he picked up a big pink wedding cake, with its six tiers and scalloped edges and its miniature bride and groom on top. He'd ordered it on his own; he'd taken the initiative, planning to offer it to a young woman he works with. He managed somehow to set the thing on the back seat of the car, and when he got home he found a note from her announcing, excited and happy, that she's engaged. The man she'd had such difficulty with has had a change of heart; he wants to get married after all. She's going off to Houston to live. She loves her dear old Tandolfo with a big kiss and a hug always, and she knows he'll have every happiness. She's so thankful for his friendship. Her magic man. Her sweet clown. She actually drove over here and, finding him gone, left the note for him, folded under the door knocker—her notepaper with the tangle of flowers at the top. She wants him to call her, come by as soon as he can, to help celebrate. *Please*, she says. *I want to give you a big hug.* He read this and then walked out to stand on the sidewalk and look at the cake in its place on the back seat of the car.

"Good God," he said.

He'd thought he would put the clown outfit on, deliver the cake in person, an elaborate proposal to a girl he's never even kissed. He's a little unbalanced, and he knows it. Over the months of their working together at Bailey & Brecht department store, he's built up tremendous feelings of loyalty and yearning toward her. He thought she felt it, too. He interpreted gestures—her hand lingering on his shoulder when he made her laugh; her endearments, tinged as they seemed to be with a kind of sadness, as if she were afraid for what the world might do to someone so romantic.

"You sweet clown," she said. She said it a lot. And she talked to him about her ongoing sorrows, the man she'd been in love with who kept waffling about getting married, wanting no commitments. Tandolfo, a.k.a. Rodney Wilbury, told her that he hated men who weren't willing to run the risks of love. Why, he personally was the type who'd always believed in marriage and children, life-long commitments. It was true that he had caused difficulties for himself, and life was a disappointment so far, but he believed in falling in love and starting a family. She didn't hear him. It all went right through her, like white noise on the radio. For weeks he had come around to visit her, had invited her to watch him perform. She confided in him, and he thought of movies where the friend stays loyal and is a good listener, and eventually gets the girl: they fall in love. He put his hope in that. He was optimistic; he'd ordered and bought the cake, and apparently the whole time, all through the listening and being noble with her, she thought of it as nothing more than friendship, accepting it from him because she was accustomed to being offered friendship.

Now he leans close to the mirror to look at his own eyes through the makeup. They look clear enough. "Loves you absolutely not. You must be crazy. You must be the Great Tandolfo."

Yes.

Twenty-six years old, out-of-luck Tandolfo. In love. With a great over-sized cake in the back seat of his car. It's Sunday, a cool April day. He's a little inebriated. That's the word he prefers. It's polite; it suggests something faintly silly. Nothing could be sillier than to be dressed like this in broad daylight and to go driving across the bridge into Virginia to put on a magic show. Nothing could be sillier than to have spent all that money on a completely useless purchase—a cake six tiers high. Maybe fifteen pounds of sugar.

When he has made his last inspection of the clown face in the mirror, and checked the bag of tricks and props, he goes to his front door and looks through the screen at the architectural shadow of the cake in the back seat. The inside of the car will smell like icing for days. He'll have to keep the windows open even if it rains; he'll go to work smelling like confectionery delights. The whole thing makes him laugh. A wedding cake. He steps out of the house and makes his way in the late afternoon sun down the sidewalk to the car. As if they have been waiting for him, three boys come skating down from the top of the hill. He has the feeling that if he tried to sneak out like this at two in the morning, someone would come by and see him anyway. "Hey, Rodney," one boy says. "I mean, Tandolfo."

Tandolfo recognizes him. A neighborhood boy, a tough. Just the kind to make trouble, just the kind with no sensitivity to the suffering of others. "Leave me alone or I'll turn you into spaghetti," he says.

"Hey guys, it's Tandolfo the Great." The boy's hair is a bright blond color, and you can see through it to his scalp.

"Scram," Tandolfo says. "Really."

"Aw, what's your hurry, man?"

"I've just set off a nuclear device," Tandolfo says with grave seriousness. "It's on a timer. Poof."

"Do a trick for us," the blond one says. "Where's the scurvy rabbit of yours?"

"I gave it the week off." Someone, last winter, poisoned the first Chi-Chi. He keeps the cage indoors now. "I'm in a hurry. No rabbit to help with the driving."

But they're interested in the cake now. "Hey, what's that? Jesus, is that real?"

"Just stay back." Tandolfo gets his cases into the trunk and hurries to the driver's side door. The three boys are peering into the back seat. To the blond boy he says, "You're going to go bald, aren't you?"

"Hey man, a cake. Can we have a piece of it?" one of them says.

"Back off," Tandolfo says.

Another says, "Come on, Tandolfo."

"Hey, Tandolfo, I saw some guys looking for you, man. They said you owed them money."

He gets in, ignoring them, and starts the car.

"Sucker," the blond one says.

"Hey man, who's the cake for?"

He drives away, thinks of himself leaving them in a cloud of exhaust. Riding through the green shade, he glances in the rear-view mirror and sees the clown face, the painted smile. It makes him want to laugh. He tells himself he's his own cliché—a clown with a broken heart. Looming behind him is the cake, like a passenger in the back seat. The people in the cake store had offered it to him in a box; he had made them give it to him like this, on a cardboard slab. It looks like it might melt.

He drives slow, worried that it might sag, or even fall over. He has always believed viscerally that gestures mean everything. When he moves his hands and brings about the effects that amaze little children, he feels larger than life, unforgettable. He learned the magic while in high school, as a way of making friends, and though it didn't really make him any friends, he's been practicing it ever since. It's an extra source of income, and lately income has had a way of disappearing too quickly. He has been in some travail, betting the horses, betting the sports events. He's hung over all the time. There have been several polite warnings at work. He has managed so far to tease everyone out of the serious looks, the cool study of his face. The fact is, people like him in an abstract way, the way they like distant clownish figures: the comedian whose name they can't remember. He can see it in their eyes. Even the rough characters after his loose change have a certain sense of humor about it.

He's a phenomenon, a subject of conversation.

There's traffic on Key Bridge, and he's stuck for a while. It becomes clear that he'll have to go straight to the birthday party. Sitting behind the wheel of the car with his cake behind him, he becomes aware of people in other cars noticing him. In the car to his left, a girl stares, chewing gum. She waves, rolls her window down. Two others are with her, one in the back seat. "Hey," she says. He nods, smiles inside what he knows is the clown smile. His teeth will look dark against the makeup.

"Where's the party?" she says.

But the traffic moves again. He concentrates. The snarl is on the other side of the bridge, construction of some kind. He can see the cars in a line, waiting to go up the hill into Roslyn and beyond. Time is beginning to be a consideration. In his glove box he has a flask of bourbon. More fortification. He reaches over and takes it out, looks around himself. No police anywhere. Just the idling cars and people tuning their radios or arguing or simply staring out as if at some distressing event. The smell of the cake is making him woozy. He takes a swallow of the bourbon, then puts it away. The car with the girls in it goes by in the left lane, and they are not looking at him. He watches them go on ahead. He's in the wrong lane again; he can't remember a time when *his* lane was the only one moving. He told her once that he considered himself of the race of people who gravitate to the non-moving lanes of highways, and who cause green lights to turn yellow merely by approaching them. She took the idea and ran with it, saying she was of the race of people who emit enzymes which instill a sense of impending doom in marriageable young men.

"No," Tandolfo/Rodney said. "I'm living proof that isn't so. I have no such fear, and I'm with you."

"But you're of the race of people who make mine relax all the enzymes."

"You're not emitting the enzymes now, I see."

"No," she said. "It's only with marriageable young men."

"I emit enzymes that prevent people like you from seeing that I'm a marriageable young man."

"I'm too relaxed to tell," she said, and touched his shoulder. A plain affectionate moment that gave him tossing nights and fever.

Because of the traffic, he's late to the birthday party. He gets out of the car and two men come down to greet him. He keeps his face turned away, remembering too late the breath mints in his pocket.

"Jesus," one of the men says, "look at this. Hey, who ordered the cake? I'm not paying for the cake."

"The cake stays," Tandolfo says.

"What does he mean, it stays? Is that a trick?"

They're both looking at him. The one spoken to must be the birthday boy's father—he's wearing a party cap that says DAD. He has long, dirty-looking strands of brown hair jutting out from the cap, and there are streaks of sweaty grit on the sides of his face. "So you're the Great Tandolfo," he says, extending a meaty red hand. "Isn't it hot in that makeup?"

"No, sir."

"We've been playing volleyball."

"You've exerted yourselves."

They look at him. "What do you do with the cake?" the one in the DAD cap asks.

"Cake's not part of the show, actually."

"You just carry it around with you?"

The other man laughs. He's wearing a T-shirt with a smiley face on the chest. "This ought to be some show," he says.

They all make their way across the lawn, to the porch of the house. It's a big party, bunting everywhere and children gathering quickly to see the clown.

"Ladies and gentlemen," says the man in the DAD cap. "I give you Tandolfo the Great."

Tandolfo isn't ready yet. He's got his cases open, but he needs a table to put everything on. The first trick is where he releases the bird; he'll finish with the best trick, in which the rabbit appears as if from a pan of flames. This always draws a gasp, even from the adults: the fire blooms in the pan, down goes the "lid"—it's the rabbit's tight container—the latch is tripped, and the skin of the lid lifts off. Voilà! Rabbit. The fire is put out by the fireproof cage bottom. He's gotten pretty good at making the switch, and if the crowd isn't too attentive—as children often are not—he can perform certain sleight-of-hand tricks with some style. But he needs a table, and he needs time to set up.

The whole crowd of children is seated in front of their parents, on either side of the doorway into the house. Tandolfo is standing on the porch, his back to the stairs, and he's been introduced.

"Hello boys and girls," he says, and bows. "Tandolfo needs a table."

"A table," one of the women says. The adults simply regard him. He sees light sweaters, shapely hips, and wild hair; he sees beer cans in tight fists, heavy jowls, bright ice-blue eyes. A little row of faces, and one elderly face. He feels more inebriated than he likes, and tries to concentrate.

"Mommy, I want to touch him," one child says.

"Look at the cake," says another, who gets up and moves to the railing on Tandolfo's right and trains a new pair of shiny binoculars on the car. "Do we get some cake?"

"There's cake," says the man in the DAD cap. "But not that cake. Get down, Ethan."

"I want that cake."

"Get down. This is Teddy's birthday."

"Mommy, I want to touch him."

"I need a table, folks. I told somebody that over the telephone."

"He did say he needed a table. I'm sorry," says a woman who is probably the birthday boy's mother. She's quite pretty, leaning in the door frame with a sweater tied to her waist.

"A table," says still another woman. Tandolfo sees the birthmark on her mouth, which looks like a stain. He thinks of this woman as a child in school, with this difference from other children, and his heart goes out to her.

"I need a table," he says to her, his voice as gentle as he can make it.

"What's he going to do, perform an operation?" says DAD.

It amazes Tandolfo how easily people fall into talking about him as though he were an inanimate object or something on a television screen. "The Great Tandolfo can do nothing until he gets a table," he says with as much mysteriousness and drama as he can muster under the circumstances.

"I want that cake out there," says Ethan, still at the porch railing. The other children start talking about cake and ice cream, and the big cake Ethan has spotted; there's a lot of confusion and restlessness. One of the smaller children, a girl in a blue dress, approaches Tandolfo. "What's your name?" she says, swaying slightly, her hands behind her back.

"Go sit down," he says to her. "We have to sit down or Tandolfo can't do his magic."

In the doorway, two of the men are struggling with a folding card table. It's one of those rickety ones with the skinny legs, and it probably won't do.

"That's kind of shaky, isn't it?" says the woman with the birthmark.

"I said, Tandolfo needs a sturdy table, boys and girls."

There's more confusion. The little girl has come forward and taken hold of his pant leg. She's just standing there holding it, looking up at him. "We have to go sit down," he says, bending to her, speaking sweetly, clownlike. "We have to do what Tandolfo wants."

Her small mouth opens wide, as if she's trying to yawn, and with pale eyes quite calm and staring she emits a screech, an ear-piercing, non-human shriek that brings everything to a stop. Tandolfo/Rodney steps back, with his amazement and his inebriate heart. Everyone gathers around the girl, who continues to scream, less piercing now, her hands fisted at her sides, those pale eyes closed tight.

"What happened?" the man in the DAD cap wants to know. "Where the hell's the magic tricks?"

"I told you, all I needed is a *table*."

"What'd you say to her to make her cry?" DAD indicates the little girl, who is giving forth a series of broken, grief-stricken howls.

"I want magic tricks," the birthday boy says, loud. "Where's the magic tricks?"

"Perhaps if we moved the whole thing inside," the woman with the birthmark says, fingering her left ear and making a face.

The card table has somehow made its way to Tandolfo, through the confusion and grief. The man in the DAD cap sets it down and opens it.

"There," he says, as if his point has been made.

In the next moment, Tandolfo realizes that someone's removed the little girl. Everything's relatively quiet again, though her cries are coming through the walls of one of the rooms inside the house. There are perhaps fifteen children, mostly seated before him, and five or six men and women behind them, or kneeling with them. "Okay, now," DAD says. "Tandolfo the Great."

"Hello, little boys and girls," Tandolfo says, deciding that the table will have to suffice. "I'm happy to be here. Are you glad to see me?" A general uproar commences. "Well, good," he says. "Because just look what I have in my magic bag." And with a flourish he brings out the hat that he will release Witch from. The bird is encased in a fold of shiny cloth, pulsing there. He can feel it. He rambles on, talking fast, or trying to, and when the time comes to reveal the bird, he almost flubs it. But Witch flaps his wings and makes enough of a commotion to distract even the adults, who applaud and urge the stunned children to follow suit. "Isn't that wonderful," Tandolfo hears. "Out of nowhere."

"He had it hidden away," says the birthday boy, managing to temper his astonishment. He's clearly the type who heaps scorn on those things he can't understand, or own.

"Now," Tandolfo says, "for my next spell, I need a helper from the audience." He looks right at the birthday boy—round face, short nose, freckles. Bright red hair. Little green eyes. The whole countenance speaks of glutted appetites and sloth. This kid could be on Roman coins, an emperor. He's not used to being compelled to do anything, but he seems eager for a chance to get into the act. "How about you," Tandolfo says to him.

The others, led by their parents, cheer.

The birthday boy gets to his feet and makes his way over the bodies of the other children to stand with Tandolfo. In order for the trick to work, Tandolfo must get everyone watching the birthday boy, and there's a funny hat he keeps in the bag for this purpose. "Now," he says to the boy, "since you're part of the show, you have to wear a costume." He produces the hat as if from behind the boy's ear. Another cheer goes up. He puts the hat on the boy's head and adjusts it, crouching down. The green eyes stare impassively at him; there's no hint of awe or fascination in them. "There we are," he says. "What a handsome fellow."

But the birthday boy takes the hat off.

"We have to wear the hat to be onstage."

"Ain't a stage," the boy says.

"Well, but hey," Tandolfo says for the benefit of the adults. "Didn't you know that all the world's a stage?" He tries to put the hat on him again, but the boy moves from under his reach and slaps his hand away. "We have to wear the hat," Tandolfo says, trying to control his anger. "We can't do the magic without our magic hats." He tries once more, and the boy waits until the hat is on, then simply removes it and holds it behind him, shying away when Tandolfo tries to retrieve it. The noise of the others now sounds like the crowd at a prizefight; there's a contest going on, and they're enjoying it. "Give Tandolfo the hat. We want magic, don't we?"

"Do the magic," the boy demands.

"I'll do the magic if you give me the hat."

"I won't."

Nothing. No support from the adults. Perhaps if he weren't a little tipsy; perhaps if he didn't feel ridiculous and sick at heart and forlorn, with his wedding cake and his odd mistaken romance, his loneliness, which he has always borne gracefully and with humor, and his general dismay; perhaps if he were to find it in himself to deny the sudden, overwhelming sense of the unearned affection given this lumpish, slovenly version of stupid complacent spoiled satiation standing before him—he might've simply gone on to the next trick.

Instead, at precisely that moment when everyone seems to pause, he leans down and says, "Give me the hat, you little prick."

The green eyes widen.

The quiet is heavy with disbelief. Even the small children can tell that something's happened to change everything.

"Tandolfo has another trick," Rodney says, loud, "where he makes the birthday boy pop like a balloon. Especially if he's a fat birthday boy."

A stirring among the adults.

"Especially if he's an ugly slab of gross flesh like this one here."

"Now just a minute," says DAD.

"*Pop*," Rodney says to the birthday boy, who drops the hat and then, seeming to remember that defiance is expected, makes a face. Sticks out his tongue. Rodney/Tandolfo is quick with his hands by training, and he grabs the tongue.

"Awk," the boy says. "Aw-aw-aw."

"Abracadabra!" Rodney lets go and the boy falls backward onto the lap of one of the other children. More cries. "Whoops, time to sit down," says Rodney. "Sorry you had to leave so soon."

Very quickly, he's being forcibly removed. They're rougher than gangsters. They lift him, punch him, tear at his costume—even the women. Someone hits him with a spoon. The whole scene boils over onto the lawn, where some-one has released Chi-Chi from her case. Chi-Chi moves about wide-eyed, hopping between running children, evading them, as Tandolfo the Great can-not evade the adults. He's being pummeled, because he keeps trying to return for his rabbit. And the adults won't let him off the curb. "Okay," he says finally, collecting himself. He wants to let them know he's not like this all the time; wants to say it's circumstances, grief, personal pain hidden inside seeming brightness and cleverness. He's a man in love, humiliated, wrong about every-thing. He wants to tell them, but he can't speak for a moment, can't even quite catch his breath. He stands in the middle of the street, his funny clothes torn, his face bleeding, all his magic strewn everywhere. "I would at least like to collect my rabbit," he says, and is appalled at the absurd sound of it—its huge difference from what he intended to say. He straightens, pushes the grime from his face, adjusts the clown nose, and looks at them. "I would say that even though I wasn't as patient as I could've been, the adults have not comported themselves well here," he says.

"Drunk," one of the women says.

Almost everyone's chasing Chi-Chi now. One of the older boys approaches, carrying Witch's case. Witch looks out the air hole, impervious, quiet as an idea. And now one of the men, someone Rodney hasn't noticed before, an older man clearly wearing a hairpiece, brings Chi-Chi to him. "Bless you," Rodney says, staring into the man's sleepy, deploring eyes.

"I don't think we'll pay you," the man says. The others are filing back into the house, herding the children before them.

Rodney speaks to the man. "The rabbit appears out of fire."

The man nods. "Go home and sleep it off, kid."

"Right. Thank you."

He puts Chi-Chi in his compartment, stuffs everything in its place in the trunk. Then he gets in the car and drives away. Around the corner he stops, wipes off what he can of the makeup; it's as if he's trying to remove the stain of bad opinion and disapproval. Nothing feels any different. He drives to the suburban street where she lives with her parents, and by the time he gets there it's almost dark.

The houses are set back in the trees. He sees lighted windows, hears music, the sound of children playing in the yards. He parks the car and gets out. A breezy April dusk. "I am Tandolfo the soft-hearted," he says. "Hearken to me." Then he sobs. He can't believe it. "Jeez," he says. "Lord." He opens the back door of the car, leans in to get the cake. He'd forgot how heavy it is. Staggering with it, making his way along the sidewalk, intending to leave it on her door-step, he has an inspiration. Hesitating only for the moment it takes to make sure there are no cars coming, he goes out and sets it down in the middle of the street. Part of the top sags from having bumped his shoulder as he pulled it off the back seat. The bride and groom are almost supine, one on top of the other. He straightens them, steps back and looks at it. In the dusky light it looks blue. It sags just right, with just the right angle expressing disappoint-ment and sorrow. Yes, he thinks. This is the place for it. The aptness of it, sitting out like this, where anyone might come by and splatter it all over creation, makes him feel a faint sense of release, as if he were at the end of a story. Everything will be all right if he can think of it that way. He's wiping his eyes, thinking of moving to another town. Failures are beginning to catch up to him, and he's still aching in love. He thinks how he has suffered the pangs of failure and misadventure, but in this painful instance there's symmetry, and he will make the one eloquent gesture—leaving a wedding cake in the middle of the road, like a sugar-icinged pylon. Yes.

He walks back to the car, gets in, pulls around, and backs into the driveway of the house across the street from hers. Leaving the engine idling, he rolls the window down and rests his arm on the sill, gazing at the incongruous shape of the cake there in the falling dark. He feels almost glad, almost, in some strange inexpressible way, vindicated. He imagines what she might do if she saw him here, imagines that she comes running from her house, calling his name, looking at the cake and admiring it. He conjures a picture of her, attacking the tiers of pink sugar, and the muscles of his abdomen tighten. But then this all gives way to something else: images of destruction, of flying dollops of icing. He's surprised to find that he wants her to stay where she is, doing whatever she's doing. He realizes that what he wants—and for the moment all he really wants—is what he now has: a perfect vantage point from which to watch oncoming cars. Turning the engine off, he waits, concentrating on the one thing. He's a man imbued with interest, almost peaceful with it—almost, in fact, happy with it—sitting there in the quiet car and patiently awaiting the results of his labor.

~ 2004

Kevin Brockmeier

∽ A Fable with Slips of White Paper
    Spilling from the Pockets

Born in 1972, Kevin Brockmeier grew up in Little Rock, Arkansas, and graduated from Missouri State University with an interdisciplinary major in creative writing, philosophy, and theater. He received his M.F.A. from the Iowa Writers' Workshop and has gone on to publish three novels, two story collections, and two novels for children. His stories have appeared several times in *The O. Henry Prize Stories* and *Best American Short Stories* anthologies, and in 2007 he was named one of *Granta* Magazine's Best Young American Novelists. He has received the Chicago Tribune's Nelson Algren Award for Short Fiction, the Italo Calvino Short Fiction Award, and a National Endowment for the Arts Fellowship.

"I try to keep faith with the idea that each sentence's inflections will help determine the one that follows and that gradually, if I pay close attention, all those sentences will add up to a coherent and meaningful story—and also, somehow, mysteriously, with an expression of my own personality."

~ from an interview with
Michael Kardos, May 2012

Once there was a man who happened to buy God's overcoat. He was rummaging through a thrift store when he found it hanging on a rack by the fire exit, nestled between a birch-colored fisherman's sweater and a cotton blazer with a suede patch on one of the elbows. Though the sleeves were a bit too long for him and one of the buttons was cracked, the coat fit him well across the chest and shoulders, lending him a regal look that brought a pleased yet diffident smile to his face, so the man took it to the register and paid for it. He was walking home when he discovered a slip of paper in one of the pockets.

An old receipt, he thought, or maybe a to-do list forgotten by the coat's previous owner. But when he took it out, he found a curious note typed across the front: *Please help me figure out what to do about Albert.*

The man wondered who had written the note, and whether, in fact, that person had figured out what to do about Albert—but not, it must be said, for very long. After he got home, he folded the slip of paper into quarters and dropped it in the ceramic dish where he kept his breath mints and his car keys.

It might never have crossed his mind again had his fingers not fallen upon two more slips of paper in the coat's pocket while he was riding the elevator up to his office the next morning. One read, *Don't let my nerves get the better of me this afternoon,* and the other, *I'm asking you with all humility to keep that boy away from my daughter.*

The man shut himself in his office and went through the coat pocket by pocket. It had five compartments altogether: two front flap pockets, each of which lay over an angled hand-warmer pocket with the fleece almost completely worn away, as well as a small inside pocket above the left breast. He rooted through them one by one until he was sure they were completely empty, uncovering seven more slips of paper. The messages typed across the front of the slips all seemed to be wishes or requests of one sort or another. *Please let my mom know I love her. I'll never touch another cigarette as long as I live if you'll just make the lump go away. Give me back the joy I used to know.*

There was a tone of quiet intimacy to the notes, a starkness, an openhearted pleading that seemed familiar to the man from somewhere.

Prayers, he realized.

That's what they were—prayers.

But where on earth did they come from?

He was lining them up along the edge of his desk when Eiseley from technical support rapped on the door to remind him about the ten o'clock meeting. "Half an hour of coffee and spreadsheet displays," he said. "Should be relatively painless," and he winked, firing an imaginary pistol at his head. As soon as Eiseley left, the man felt the prickle of an obscure instinct and checked the pockets of his coat again. He found a slip of paper reading, *The only thing I'm asking is that you give my Cindy another few years.* Cindy was Eiseley's cat, familiar to everyone in the office from his Christmas cards and his online photo diary. A simple coincidence? Somehow he didn't think so.

For the rest of the day the man kept the coat close at hand, draping it over his arm when he was inside and wearing it buttoned to the collar when he was out. By the time he locked his office for the night, he believed he had come to understand how it worked. The coat was — or seemed to be — a repository for prayers. Not unerringly, but often enough, when the man passed somebody on the street or stepped into a crowded room, he would tuck his hands into the coat's pockets and feel the thin flexed form of a slip of paper brushing his fingers. He took a meeting with one of the interns from the marketing division and afterward discovered a note that read, *Please, oh please, keep me from embarrassing myself.* He grazed the arm of a man who was muttering obscenities, his feet planted flat on the sidewalk, and a few seconds later found a note that read, *Why do you do it? Why can't you stop torturing me?*

That afternoon, on his way out, he was standing by the bank of elevators next to the waiting room when he came upon yet another prayer: *All I want — just this once — is for somebody to tell me how pretty I look today.* He glanced around. The only person he could see was Jenna, the receptionist, who was sitting behind the front desk with her purse in her lap and her fingers covering her lips. He stepped up to her and said, "By the way, that new girl from supplies was right."

"Right about what?"

"I heard her talking about you in the break room. She was saying how pretty you look today. She was right. That's a beautiful dress you're wearing."

The brightness in her face was like the reflection of the sun in a pool of water — you could toss a stone in and watch it fracture into a thousand pieces, throwing off sparks as it gathered itself back together.

So that was one prayer, and the man could answer it, but what was he to do with all the others?

In the weeks that followed, he found thousands upon thousands more. Prayers for comfort and prayers for wealth. Prayers for love and prayers for good fortune. It seemed that at any one time half the people in the city were likely to be praying. Some of them were praying for things he could understand, even if he could not provide them, like the waitress who wanted some graceful way to back out of her wedding or the UPS driver who asked for a single night of unbroken sleep, while some were praying for things he could not even understand: *Let the voice choose lunch this time. Either Amy Sussen or Amy Goodale. Nothing less than 30 percent.* He walked past a ring of elementary school students playing Duck, Duck, Goose and collected a dozen notes reading, *Pick me, pick me,* along with one that read, *I wish you would kill Matthew Brantman.* He went to a one-man show at the repertory theater, sitting directly next to the stage, and afterward found a handful of notes that contained nothing but the lines the actor had spoken. He made the mistake of wearing the coat to a baseball game and had to leave at the top of the second inning when slips of white paper began spilling from his pockets like confetti.

Soon the man realized that he was able to detect the pressure of an incoming prayer before it even arrived. The space around him would take on a certain elasticity, as though thousands of tiny sinews were being summoned up out of the emptiness and drawn tight, and he would know, suddenly and without question, that someone was offering his yearning up to the air. It was like the invisible resistance he remembered feeling when he tried to bring the common poles of two magnets together. The sensation was unmistakable. And it seemed that the stronger the force of the prayer, the greater the distance it was able to travel. There were prayers that he received only when he skimmed directly up against another person, but there were others that had the power to find him even when he was walking alone through the empty soccer field in the middle of the park, his footsteps setting little riffles of birds into motion. He wondered whether the prayers were something he had always subconsciously felt, he and everyone else in the world, stirring around between their bodies like invisible eddies, but which none of them had ever had the acuity to recognize for what they were, or whether he was able to perceive them only because he had happened to find the overcoat in the thrift store. He just didn't know.

At first, when the man had realized what the coat could do, he had indulged in the kind of fantasies that used to fill his daydreams as a child. He would turn himself into the benevolent stranger, answering people's wishes without ever revealing himself to them. Or he would use the pockets to read people's fortunes somehow (he hadn't yet figured out the details). Or he would be the mysterious, slightly menacing figure who would take people by the shoulder, lock gazes with them, and say, "I can tell what you've been thinking." But it was not long before he gave up on those ideas.

There were so many prayers, there was so much longing in the world, and in the face of it all he began to feel helpless.

One night the man had a dream that he was walking by a hotel swimming pool, beneath a sky the same lambent blue as the water, when he recognized God spread out like a convalescent in one of the hotel's deck chairs. "You!" the man said. "What are you doing here? I have your coat. Don't you want it back?"

God set his magazine down on his lap, folding one of the corners over, and shook his head. "It's yours now. They're all yours now. I don't want the responsibility anymore."

"But don't you understand?" the man said to him. "We need you down here. How could you just abandon us?"

And God answered, "I came to understand the limitations of my character."

It was shortly after two in the morning when the man woke up. In the moonlight he could see the laundry hamper, the clay bowl, and the dozens of cardboard boxes that covered the floor of his bedroom, all of them filled with slips of white paper he could not bear to throw away.

The next day he decided to place an ad in the classified pages: "Purchased at thrift store. One overcoat, sable brown with chestnut buttons. Pockets worn. Possibly of sentimental value. Wish to return to original owner." He allowed the ad to run for a full two weeks, going so far as to pin copies of it to the bulletin boards of several nearby churches, but he did not receive an answer. Nor, it must be said, had he honestly expected to. The coat belonged to him now. It had changed him into someone he had never expected to be. He found it hard to imagine turning back to the life he used to know, a life in which he saw people everywhere he went, in which he looked into their faces and even spoke to them, but was only able to guess at what lay in their souls.

One Saturday he took a train to the city's pedestrian mall. It was a mild day, the first gleam of spring after a long and frigid winter, and though he did not really need the coat, he had grown so used to wearing it that he put it on without a second thought. The pedestrian mall was not far from the airport, and as he arrived he watched a low plane passing overhead, dipping through the lee waves above the river. A handful of notes appeared in his pockets: *Please don't let us fall. Please keep us from going down. Let this be the one that makes the pain go away.*

The shops, restaurants, and street cafés along the pavement were quiet at first, but as the afternoon took hold, more and more people arrived. The man was walking down a set of steps toward the center of the square when he discovered a prayer that read, *Let someone speak to me this time—anyone, anyone at all—or else . . .* The prayer was a powerful one, as taut as a steel cord in the air. It appeared to be coming from the woman sitting on the edge of the dry fountain, her feet raking two straight lines in the leaves. The man sat down beside her and asked, "Or else what?"

She did not seem surprised to hear him raise the question. "Or else . . ." she said quietly.

He could tell by the soreness in her voice that she was about to cry.

"Or else . . ."

He took her by the hand. "Come on. Why don't I buy you some coffee?" He led her to the coffeehouse, hanging his coat over the back of a chair and listening to her talk, and before long he had little question what the "or else" was. She seemed so disconsolate, so terribly isolated. He insisted she spend the rest of the afternoon with him. He took her to see the wooden boxes that were on display at a small art gallery and then the Victorian lamps in the front room of an antique store. A movie was playing at the bargain theater, a comedy, and he bought a pair of tickets for it, and after it was finished, the two of them settled down to dinner at a Chinese restaurant. Finally they picked up a bag of freshly roasted pecans from a pushcart down by the river. By then the sun was falling, and the woman seemed in better spirits. He made her promise to call him the next time she needed someone to talk to.

"I will," she said, tucking her chin into the collar of her shirt like a little girl. Though he wanted to believe her, he wondered as he rode the train home if he would ever hear from her again.

It was the next morning before he realized his overcoat was missing. He went to the lost-and-found counter at the train station and, when he was told that no one had turned it in, traveled back to the pedestrian mall to retrace his steps. He remembered draping the coat over his chair at the coffeehouse, but none of the baristas there had seen it. Nor had the manager of the movie theater. Nor had the owner of the art gallery. The man searched for it in every shop along the square, but without success. That evening, as he unlocked the door of his house, he knew that the coat had fallen out of his hands for good. It was already plain to him how much he was going to miss it. It had brought him little ease — that was true — but it had made his life incomparably richer, and he was not sure what he was going to do without it.

We are none of us so delicate as we think, though, and over the next few days, as a dozen new accounts came across his desk at work, the sharpness of his loss faded. He no longer experienced the compulsion to hunt through his pockets all the time. He stopped feeling as though he had made some terrible mistake. Eventually he was left with only a small ache in the back of his mind, no larger than a pebble, and a lingering sensitivity to the currents of hope and longing that flowed through the air.

And at Pang Lin's Chinese Restaurant a new sign soon appeared in the window: CUSTOM FORTUNE COOKIES MADE NIGHTLY AND ON THE PREMISES. The diners at the restaurant found the fortune cookies brittle and tasteless, but the messages inside were unlike any they had ever seen, and before long they developed a reputation for their peculiarity and their singular wisdom. Crack open one of the cookies at Pang Lin's, it was said, and you never knew what fortune you might find inside.

Please let the test be canceled.
Thy will be done, but I could really use a woman right about now.
Why would you do something like this to me? Why?
Oh make me happy.

~ 2008

Percival Everett

∼ The Appropriation of Cultures

"I learn a lot writing. And with every book I learn more about how little I know. So by now at the end of fifteen books I know a lot less than almost anybody."

∼ from *Identity Theory*, May 6, 2003

Poet, novelist, and short-fiction writer Percival Everett was born in 1956 and grew up in South Carolina. He attended undergraduate programs at the University of Miami and the University of Oregon and received an M.F.A. in creative writing from Brown University. Author of numerous books of fiction and poetry, Everett has received awards including the PEN Center USA Award for Fiction, the Academy Award in Literature from the American Academy of Arts and Letters, the Believer Book Award, and the New American Writing Award. His work has been selected for *The Pushcart Prize Anthology* and *Best American Short Stories*. Everett is currently Distinguished Professor of English at the University of Southern California.

Daniel Barkley had money left to him by his mother. He had a house that had been left to him by his mother. He had a degree in American Studies from Brown University that he had in some way earned, but that had not yet earned anything for him. He played a 1940 Martin guitar with a Barkus-Berry pickup and drove a 1976 Jensen Interceptor, which he had purchased after his mother's sister had died and left him her money because she had no children of her own. Daniel Barkley didn't work and didn't pretend to need to, spending most of his time reading. Some nights he went to a joint near the campus of the University of South Carolina and played jazz with some old guys who all worked very hard during the day, but didn't hold Daniel's condition against him.

Daniel played standards with the old guys, but what he loved to play were old-time slide tunes. One night, some white boys from a fraternity yelled forward to the stage at the black man holding the acoustic guitar and began to shout, "Play 'Dixie' for us! Play 'Dixie' for us!"

Daniel gave them a long look, studied their big-toothed grins and the beer-shiny eyes stuck into puffy, pale faces, hovering over golf shirts and chinos. He looked from them to the uncomfortable expressions on the faces of the old guys with whom he was playing and then to the embarrassed faces of the other college kids in the club.

And then he started to play. He felt his way slowly through the chords of the song once and listened to the deadened hush as it fell over the room. He used the slide to squeeze out the melody of the song he had grown up hating, the song the whites had always pulled out to remind themselves and those other people just where they were. Daniel sang the song. He sang it slowly. He sang it, feeling the lyrics, deciding that the lyrics were his, deciding that the song was his. *Old times there are not forgotten . . .* He sang the song and listened to the silence around him. He resisted the urge to let satire ring through his voice. He meant what he sang. *Look away, look away, look away, Dixieland.*

When he was finished, he looked up to see the roomful of eyes on him. One person clapped. Then another. And soon the tavern was filled with applause and hoots. He found the frat boys in the back and watched as they stormed out, a couple of people near the door chuckling at them as they passed.

Roger, the old guy who played tenor sax, slapped Daniel on the back and said something like, "Right on" or "Cool." Roger then played the first few notes of "Take the A Train" and they were off. When the set was done, all the college kids slapped Daniel on the back as he walked toward the bar where he found a beer waiting.

Daniel didn't much care for the slaps on the back, but he didn't focus too much energy on that. He was busy trying to sort out his feelings about what he had just played. The irony of his playing the song straight and from the heart was made more ironic by the fact that as he played it, it came straight and from his heart, as he was claiming Southern soil, or at least recognizing his blood in it. His was the land of cotton and hell no, it was not forgotten. At twenty-three, his anger was fresh and typical, and so was his ease with it, the way it could be forgotten for chunks of time, until something like that night with the white frat boys or simply a flashing blue light in the rearview mirror brought it all back. He liked the song, wanted to play it again, knew that he would.

He drove home from the bar on Green Street and back to his house where he made tea and read about Pickett's charge at Gettysburg while he sat in the big leather chair that had been his father's. He fell asleep and had a dream in which he stopped Pickett's men on the Emmitsburg Road on their way to the field and said, "Give me back my flag."

∾

Daniel's friend Sarah was a very large woman with a very large Afro hairdo. They were sitting on the porch of Daniel's house having tea. The late fall afternoon was mild and slightly overcast. Daniel sat in the wicker rocker while Sarah curled her feet under her on the glider.

"I wish I could have heard it," Sarah said.

"Yeah, me too."

"Personally, I can't even stand to go in that place. All that drinking. Those white kids love to drink." Sarah studied her fingernails.

"I guess. The place is harmless. They seem to like the music."

"Do you think I should paint my nails?"

Daniel frowned at her. "If you want to."

"I mean really paint them. You know, black, or with red, white, and blue stripes. Something like that." She held her hand out, appearing to imagine the colors. "I'd have to grow them long."

"What are you talking about?"

"Just bullshitting."

Daniel and Sarah went to a grocery market to buy food for lunch and Daniel's dinner. Daniel pushed the cart through the Piggly Wiggly while Sarah walked ahead of him. He watched her large movements and her confident stride. At the checkout, he added a bulletin full of pictures of local cars and trucks for sale to his items on the conveyer.

"What's that for?" Sarah asked.

"I think I want to buy a truck."

"Buy a truck?"

"So I can drive you around when you paint your nails."

∾

Later, after lunch and after Sarah had left him alone, Daniel sat in his living room and picked up the car-sale magazine. As he suspected, there were several trucks he liked and one in particular, a 1968 Ford three-quarter ton with the one thing it shared with the other possibilities, a full rear cab window decal of the Confederate flag. He called the number the following morning and arranged with Barb, Travis's wife, to stop by and see the truck.

∾

Travis and Barb lived across the river in the town of Irmo, a name that Daniel had always thought suited a disease for cattle. He drove around the maze of tract homes until he found the right street and number. A woman in a housecoat across the street watched from her porch, safe inside the chain-link fence around her yard. From down the street a man and a teenager, who were covered with grease and apparently engaged in work on a torn-apart Dodge Charger, mindlessly wiped their hands and studied him.

Daniel walked across the front yard, through a maze of plastic toys, and knocked on the front door. Travis opened the door and asked in a surly voice, "What is it?"

"I called about the truck," Daniel said.

"Oh, you're Dan?"

Daniel nodded.

"The truck's in the backyard. Let me get the keys." He pushed the door to, but it didn't catch. Daniel heard the quality of the exchange between Travis and Barb, but not the words. He did hear Barb say, as Travis pulled open the door. "I couldn't tell over the phone."

"Got 'em." Travis. said. "Come on with me." He looked at Daniel's Jensen as they walked through the yard. "What kind of car is that?"

"It's a Jensen."

"Nice looking. Is it fast?"

"I guess."

The truck looked a little rough, a pale blue with a bleached-out hood and a crack across the top of the windshield. Travis opened the driver's side door and pushed the key into the ignition. "It's a strong runner," he said. Daniel put his hand on the faded hood and felt the warmth, knew that Travis had already warmed up the motor. Travis turned the key and the engine kicked over. He nodded to Daniel. Daniel nodded back. He looked up to see a blond woman looking on from behind the screen door of the back porch.

"The clutch and the alternator are new this year." Travis stepped backward to the wall of the bed and looked in. "There's some rust back here, but the bottom's pretty solid."

Daniel attended to the sound of the engine. "Misses just a little," he said.

"A tune-up will fix that."

Daniel regarded the rebel-flag decal covering the rear window of the cab, touched it with his finger.

"That thing will peel right off," Travis said.

"No, I like it." Daniel sat down in the truck behind the steering wheel. "Mind if I take it for a spin?"

"Sure thing." Travis looked toward the house, then back to Daniel. "The brakes are good, but you got to press hard."

Daniel nodded.

Travis shut the door, his long fingers wrapped over the edge of the half-lowered glass. Daniel noticed that one of the man's fingernails was blackened.

"I'll just take it around a block or two."

The blond woman was now standing outside the door on the concrete steps. Daniel put the truck in gear and drove out of the yard, past his car and down the street by the man and teenager who were still at work on the Charger. They stared at him, were still watching him as he turned right at the corner. The truck handled decently, but that really wasn't important.

Back at Travis's house Daniel left the keys in the truck and got out to observe the bald tires while Travis looked on. "The ad in the magazine said two thousand."

"Yeah, but I'm willing to work with you."

"Tell you what, I'll give you twenty-two hundred if you deliver it to my house."

Travis was lost, scratching his head and looking back at the house for his wife, who was no longer standing there. "Whereabouts do you live?"

"I live over near the university. Near Five Points."

"Twenty-two hundred?" Travis said more to himself than to Daniel. "Sure I can get it to your house."

"Here's two hundred." Daniel counted out the money and handed it to the man. "I'll have the rest for you in cash when you deliver the truck." He watched Travis feel the bills with his skinny fingers. "Can you have it there at about four?"

"I can do that."

~

"What in the world do you need a truck for?" Sarah asked. She stepped over to the counter and poured herself another cup of coffee, then sat back down at the table with Daniel.

"I'm not buying the truck. Well, I am buying a truck, but only because I need the truck for the decal. I'm buying the decal."

"Decal?"

"Yes. This truck has a Confederate flag in the back window."

"What?"

"I've decided that the rebel flag is my flag. My blood is Southern blood, right? Well, it's my flag."

Sarah put down her cup and saucer and picked up a cookie from the plate in the middle of the table. "You've flipped. I knew this would happen to you if you didn't work. A person needs to work."

"I don't need money."

"That's not the point. You don't have to work for money." She stood and walked to the edge of the porch and looked up and down the street.

"I've got my books and my music."

"You need a job so you can be around people you don't care about, doing stuff you don't care about. You need a job to occupy that part of your brain. I suppose it's too late now, though."

"Nonetheless," Daniel said. "You should have seen those redneck boys when I took 'Dixie' from them. They didn't know what to do. So, the goddamn flag is flying over the State Capitol. Don't take it down, just take it. That's what I say."

"That's all you have to do? That's all there is to it?"

"Yep." Daniel leaned back in his rocker. "You watch ol' Travis when he gets here."

∾

Travis arrived with the pickup a little before four, his wife pulling up behind him in a yellow TransAm. Barb got out of the car and walked up to the porch with Travis. She gave the house a careful look.

"Hey, Travis," Daniel said. "This is my friend, Sarah."

Travis nodded hello.

"You must be Barb," Daniel said.

Barb smiled weakly.

Travis looked at Sarah, then back at the truck, and then to Daniel. "You sure you don't want me to peel that thing off the window?"

"I'm positive."

"Okay."

Daniel gave Sarah a glance, to be sure she was watching Travis's face. "Here's the balance," he said, handing over the money. He took the truck keys from the skinny fingers.

Barb sighed and asked, as if the question were burning right through her. "Why do you want that flag on the truck?"

"Why shouldn't I want it?" Daniel asked.

Barb didn't know what to say. She studied her feet for a second, then regarded the house again. "I mean, you live in a nice house and drive that sports car. What do you need a truck like that for?"

"You don't want the money?"

"Yes, we want the money," Travis said, trying to silence Barb with a look.

"I need the truck for hauling stuff," Daniel said. "You know like groceries and—" he looked to Sarah for help.

"Books," Sarah said.

"Books. Things like that." Daniel held Barb's eyes until she looked away. He watched Travis sign his name to the the back of the title and hand it to him and as he took it, he said. "I was just lucky enough to find a truck with the black-power flag already on it."

"What?" Travis screwed up his face, trying to understand.

"The black-power flag on the window. You mean, you didn't know?"

Travis and Barb looked at each other.

"Well, anyway," Daniel said, "I'm glad we could do business." He turned to Sarah. "Let me take you for a ride in my new truck." He and Sarah walked across the yard, got into the pickup, and waved to Travis and Barb who were still standing in Daniel's yard as they drove away.

Sarah was on the verge of hysterics by the time they were out of sight. "That was beautiful," she said.

"No," Daniel said, softly. "That was true."

∾

Over the next weeks, sightings of Daniel and his truck proved problematic for some. He was accosted by two big white men in a '72 Monte Carlo in the parking lot of a 7-Eleven on Two Notch Road.

"What are you doing with that on your truck, boy?" the bigger of the two asked.

"Flying it proudly," Daniel said, noticing the rebel front plate on the Chevrolet. "Just like you, brothers."

The confused second man took a step toward Daniel. "What did you call us?"

"Brothers."

The second man pushed Daniel in the chest with two extended fists, but not terribly hard.

"I don't want any trouble," Daniel told them.

Then a Volkswagen with four black teenagers parked in the slot beside Daniel's truck and they jumped out, staring and looking serious. "What's going on?" the driver and largest of the teenagers asked.

"They were admiring our flag," Daniel said, pointing to his truck.

The teenagers were confused.

"We fly the flag proudly, don't we, young brothers?" Daniel gave a bent-arm, black-power, closed-fist salute. "Don't we?" he repeated. "Don't we?"

"Yeah," the young men said.

The white men had backed away to their car. They slipped into it and drove away.

Daniel looked at the teenagers and, with as serious a face as he could manage, he said, "Get a flag and fly it proudly."

∾

At a gas station, a lawyer named Ahmad Wilson stood filling the tank of his BMW and staring at the back window of Daniel's truck. He then looked at Daniel. "Your truck?" he asked.

Daniel stopped cleaning the windshield and nodded.

Wilson didn't ask a question, just pointed at the rear window of Daniel's pickup.

"Power to the people," Daniel said and laughed.

∾

Daniel played "Dixie" in another bar in town, this time with a R&B dance band at a banquet of the black medical association. The strange looks and expressions of outrage changed to bemused laughter and finally to open joking and acceptance as the song was played fast enough for dancing. Then the song was sung, slowly, to the profound surprise of those singing the song. *I wish I was in the land of cotton, old times there are not forgotten . . . Look away, look away, look away . . .*

∾

Soon, there were several, then many cars and trucks in Columbia, South Carolina, sporting Confederate flags and being driven by black people. Black businessmen and ministers wore rebel-flag buttons on their lapels and clips on their ties. The marching band of South Carolina State College, a predominantly black land-grant institution in Orangeburg, paraded with the flag during homecoming. Black people all over the state flew the Confederate flag. The symbol began to disappear from the fronts of big rigs and the back windows of jacked-up four-wheelers. And after the emblem was used to dress the yards and mark picnic sites of black family reunions the following Fourth of July, the piece of cloth was quietly dismissed from its station with the U.S. and State flags atop the State Capitol. There was no ceremony, no notice. One day, it was not there.

Look away, look away, look away . . .

~ 2004

Becky Hagenston

~ Midnight, Licorice, Shadow

Born in 1967, Becky Hagenston grew up in Maryland and received graduate degrees from New Mexico State University and the University of Arizona. She is the author of two story collections, *A Gram of Mars* (1998) and *Strange Weather* (2010). Her stories have appeared in periodicals including *The Gettysburg Review*, *The Southern Review*, and *The Mid-American Review*, and her awards include the Mary McCarthy Prize in Short Fiction, the Spokane Prize for Short Fiction, and an O. Henry award. Her story "Midnight, Licorice, Shadow," first published in the fall 2008 issue of *Crazyhorse*, was later selected for that journal's fiftieth anniversary issue. Hagenston is currently an associate professor of English at Mississippi State University.

> *"I think it's really important not to be discouraged when your stories aren't working—or when they outright fail. I have written so many failed stories that will never be published (and never should be), but they were all necessary in some way."*
>
> ~ from an interview with
> Michael Kardos, May 2012

"Midnight, Licorice, Shadow," she says. "Cocoa, Casper, Dr. Livingston."
"Alfred Hitchcock," he says. "Dracula. Vincent Price."

They have had the cat for nearly three days.

"Cinderblock?" she tries. "Ice bucket?"

It's useless. The harder they try to think of a name, the more elusive it becomes.

"Tomorrow, then," Jeremy says. "If we don't have a name by tomorrow morning, it's bye-bye, Mr. Kitty. No offense, Cupcake," he tells the cat, and gives it a quick rub on the head.

Donna looks at the animal, sprawled on the orange motel carpet like a black bearskin rug. One of his fangs is showing. His monkey paws are kneading at the air.

"Monkey Paw!" she says, but Jeremy is already headed out the door, car keys jangling. He'd invited her to go along—there's some house in Redlands he wants to check out—but she wants to stay with the cat, who now has his eyes closed in feline ecstasy and is purring louder than the air conditioner. She doesn't want to leave him (Merlin? Jasper?) all alone in a strange motel. In an hour or so she'll walk across the parking lot to the Carrows and get a chef's salad for her and a cheeseburger for Jeremy (he always comes back hungry) and maybe she'll give some of her dinner to the cat. They've been feeding him dry food because, as Jeremy says, wet food makes a cat's shits stinkier. Donna thinks the cat's shits are stinky enough as it is. Still, she likes him. She wants the three of them to drive off together tomorrow morning, like a family on vacation. So far, they've traveled over five hundred miles together, the cat curled up on Donna's lap while Jeremy drives.

If she can just come up with his name, the way she came up with her own. She was born Lacey Love and changed her name to Donna when she left home at sixteen. She liked the wholesome, 1950s sound of it, the name of a girl in a song. Sometimes she thinks about changing it again, to something more serious: Joan, perhaps, or Agnes. More and more, she feels like a Joan or an Agnes.

"Tango," she says to the cat. "Flower. Bambi. Mr. Jarvis."

The cat jerks his head up and fixes his yellow eyes on hers in what seems like an accusatory way, but she tells herself he must have heard something outside that startled him, something too faint for human ears.

∾

When they first met, she had almost told Jeremy that her name was Sunshine—partly as a joke but partly because she *felt* like a Sunshine right then, surrounded by wildflowers by the side of I-10, halfway between Tucson and Phoenix.

"I would have believed you," he told her later. "Because you are my sunshine. My *only* sunshine," he added, in a low growl. He was prone to saying cheesy things, but he said them in a way that seemed mean and dangerous, and therefore struck her as truthful. For instance, the first time he called her his soul mate, he had his right hand around her neck, and he squeezed just enough to let her know he meant business. "I *know* things about you," he said to her, staring her in the eyes, and she knew those things had nothing to do with any part of her past—certainly not the Lacey Love part of her past—but with who she was at that moment, Donna with Jeremy's hand on her neck.

The things Jeremy knows about her are more mysterious and important than the things he doesn't know. He doesn't know, for instance, that she'd been married and divorced at eighteen, though she would certainly have told him if he asked. He's never asked about her family or her childhood, which she finds refreshing. Why did men always pretend they cared about that? If they could get you to spill one childhood memory, they figured they could get you into bed.

And she always lied about the childhood memory anyway, making something up about her dog being smashed by her father's Oldsmobile when she was seven, right before her eyes. She'd told a man she met at a skanky bar outside of Alamagordo that her uncle had diddled her for three years, from the time she was seven (a lie), and the man had taken her back to his foul-smelling motel room and laid her down on the bed and said, "Now tell old Terry how your uncle did you."

Sometimes it makes her smile, thinking about old Terry waking up the next morning with a concussion and his car and wallet stolen.

She told Jeremy she was twenty-three, which was the truth, and he told her he was twenty-four, though he seems much older. Still, she has no reason not to believe him. And what do ages matter anyway?

If Jeremy had asked her what she was doing there on the side of I-10 in the middle of a field of yellow wildflowers, she would have told him the truth: she'd been driving for seven hours and needed to pee so badly her vision was blurring. But he didn't ask. He pulled over and jogged toward her and then stopped and said, "There you are."

"Here I am," she said. It didn't hurt that he was handsome, and that the sun was going down in a particularly spectacular way, and that she wasn't headed anyplace in particular, and that she hadn't eaten in almost twenty-four hours. The mountains in the distance were prehistoric creatures that could rise up and stomp them both. She had no problem leaving old Terry's crappy Datsun on the side of the road and getting into Jeremy's white pickup truck. He took her to a truck stop and bought her a BLT and then to K-Mart for shoes and underwear and a bathing suit.

That was three weeks ago.

"Sink Drip," she says to the cat, which is still sprawled on the floor, eyes closed. She wishes he would be a little bit more attentive. "Moldy Shower," she says, and sighs. It's getting old, living in crappy motel rooms. Soon, they'll have enough money to buy someplace nice, maybe in the mountains. "Which mountains?" she'd asked, and Jeremy said, "Any of them. All of them."

She turns on the television. "Stone Phillips," she says. The cat's toes and whiskers twitch, in some kind of cat-dream. She leans down next to his ear. "Get it," she whispers. "Catch that mouse. Good boy."

∞

The first car she'd ever stolen, when she was eighteen, belonged to her landlord— hers and Tim's. Tim was her husband, a thirty-eight-year-old slightly retarded janitor she'd met at the Catty Shack Catfish House in Tupelo, Mississippi. He was so charming that at first you didn't realize he was retarded. She'd married him because she was tired of living in a trailer with Ilene, a community college student who shot up heroin with her Western Civ book propped on her knees.

But after a couple of months of married life, she realized she'd had enough; she'd gotten fired at Catty Shack for slapping Tim's face in front of customers and calling him a fucking retard. The worst part of all that was that then Tim had started to cry. He threw his mop on the floor and ran out the door, got in his truck, and a day later he still hadn't come back.

She was standing at the kitchen window, eating a peanut butter and butter sandwich and staring across the yard at Mr. Harvey, the landlord, when she got the idea. Mr. Harvey kept trying to save her and Tim, coming to the door with pamphlets and tiny green New Testaments. His car, a Chevy Malibu, was parked as usual in the driveway, coated yellow with the pollen that blew all through northern Mississippi that time of year. He was out on his front porch, setting for a spell (as he called it; he was always trying to get Donna to set for a spell with him) with an old black lady who was nearly as crazy as he was. Donna had taken him for a racist, an ex-Klan member perhaps (he reminded her of her daddy), and so this friendship surprised and confused her. She liked to have people figured out.

Then Mr. Harvey and the old black lady stood up and started heading down the street, chatting intently. Even he had a friend. And there she was, eighteen years old, married to a retard, fired from a catfish restaurant, and there didn't seem to be a good reason *not* to walk up onto Mr. Harvey's back porch — it smelled like boiled vegetables and grease and tobacco — and take the car keys from his kitchen table.

She left a note: *I need this to do the Lord's work, will return it to you in 2 days, please do not call the police. GOD BLESS YOU.*

Then she found some money, too — in a sock in his underwear drawer (just like her daddy, after all) — and took off for the West, where anything could happen.

∾

It was a hundred and six degrees today, according to the Weather Channel, and even at seven in the evening the heat comes off the asphalt in waves. "Why is it so smoggy and suffocating here?" she'd asked Jeremy. "I thought California was supposed to be sunny and beachy and fun, with celebrities all over the place."

"This here's the Inland Empire," he said. Whatever that meant; it sounded like something out of *Star Wars.* They'd driven past charred hillsides, palm trees burnt up like match heads. And yet people live here; they even come here on vacation. The Carrows across the parking lot is full of families: weary-looking mothers; stern, sunburned fathers; cranky children. They take up all the benches and fill up the vestibule.

Her pickup order isn't ready yet, so she stands at the brochure stand and flips through the Area Attractions: Joshua Tree National Park, Death Valley, the Hollywood Walk of Fame, Disneyland. Donna didn't tell Jeremy this, but she actually wouldn't mind going to Disneyland; she might actually enjoy it. But Jeremy has a low tolerance for people — except for her, of course. Yesterday, when they first arrived and checked in, they'd come here for lunch and Jeremy had been so annoyed that he'd handed her a twenty and told her to get something to bring back to the room.

"Excuse me," says someone. "Ma'am?" A large man in khaki shorts and a Van Halen tour T-shirt is standing up, pointing to a place on a bench. "Why don't you have a seat?"

"Thank you!" she says. "I appreciate that."

People could be so kind; that's one thing she's just beginning to understand about the world since she met Jeremy. Even the sweaty, tired-looking families around her seem like they get along; nobody's crying or smacking anyone; no one's kneeled down whispering threats in anybody's ear.

When she picks up her order finally, she looks back at the khaki-pants man on the way out the door; he's telling a little girl something that's making her laugh. Yes, people aren't so bad after all, and they don't expect you to be bad, either.

That's the thing. They don't expect you to be bad. It's amazing, she thinks — walking across the parking lot, pocketknife clutched between her knuckles — that in this day and age, people will just let you into their houses, that they will look out their peepholes and see two complete strangers standing there, and then pull the door open.

That's what Mrs. Jarvis had done. She had greeted them with an expression of confusion and expectation, as if they had been standing there holding gift-wrapped boxes. "Yes?" she had said, and that's when Jeremy (who had gotten her name from the mailbox) said, "I'm sorry to bother you, but is Mr. Jarvis home?"

"No?" the woman answered, as if this were a quiz show and she wasn't certain what she'd won but knew — knew — that she'd won something. "Is this about the boat?" she said then (and Donna nearly laughed out loud — a boat!), and Jeremy said, without missing a beat, "Yes, it is."

"I'm sorry, but we already sold that," Mrs. Jarvis said, smiling. "Thanks for coming by, though."

The plan wasn't to go inside; the plan was to get a sense of the place, see if there was anything worth stealing and come back for it later.

"Can I use your bathroom?" Donna said then. She could practically feel Jeremy's heart beating harder; the heat radiating from him almost made her dizzy.

The truth was, she had briefly forgotten about the plan. She suddenly wanted to see inside the house; she wanted to know if it was full of votive candles and Hummels, and if there was a room where everything—the furniture, the carpet—was covered in clear plastic like there was in her grandmother's home—the entire living room forbidden entry by anyone other than "company," whom she never saw.

She wanted to see if there was a bathroom cabinet full of pill bottles and if there were razor blades under the sink, and if the whole house smelled of disinfectant and Bengay.

And Mrs. Jarvis had just kept smiling. "Please," she said, "won't you come in?"

∞

Jeremy's truck isn't there yet, but that's fine. "Here I am, Kitty-Kitty," she announces, opening the door. "Did you miss me?"

And the cat did miss her, because he comes leaping up on the bed like a dog to meow at her, welcoming her back.

She'd left the television on to keep him company. Donna loves cable TV, but Jeremy thinks it's dangerous. Last night, they had fallen asleep watching *Law and Order*, the cat curled up at the foot of their bed, and had woken up to some espionage movie.

Jeremy had jumped out of bed, saying, "Shit! Shit! We shouldn't have done that!"

"Done what?"

"Left the TV on all night. Fuck." Then he told her that all the stuff that had been on all night long had seeped into their subconscious, and they had no idea what it might have done to them, what kind of bad ideas and thoughts might have gotten into their brains. He grabbed the TV guide and they saw it had been a *Law and Order* marathon and he was even more pissed off.

"Better than *Golden Girls*," she'd said. "We might've woken up thinking we were horny old ladies." He didn't think that was funny.

Jeremy likes watching nature programs and documentaries about haunted houses. He told her that when he was a little boy, he'd seen a ghost appear to him in his bedroom mirror and tell him that his grandfather was about to die. "And three days later, he did. He wasn't even sick!"

And after that he'd had "the gift"—he didn't specify exactly what the gift was, just that it made him realize when something was right (like when he saw her by the side of the road with the wildflowers) or wrong (like not having a name for the cat).

She knows Jeremy wants to keep the cat, because on the way home after they found him, Jeremy had stopped at Wal-Mart—leaving her and the kitty (Biscuit? Muffin?) in the car with the air conditioner running—and came back with a litter box, litter, a ball full of catnip, and a bag of expensive, veterinarian-recommended chow made with salmon and spinach. "Nothing but the best for Whoosits," he said.

"Maybe we should call him Bluebell," she suggested. "Because of the blue bell around his neck. It's kind of obvious, but it's cute."

Then Jeremy frowned and didn't say anything until they got back to their motel room. They set the cat on the floor and he immediately lay down and began purring.

"Bluebell likes us," she said.

"His name isn't Bluebell," Jeremy said. "I think you know that. It doesn't fit."

And he was right; it didn't. This cat was stronger and bigger than a Bluebell. He was more of a . . . what?

"I don't like not knowing his name," Jeremy said, later that evening when they were eating Chinese takeout and watching a special on the Roman ghosts of Yorkshire. "It's bad luck. Not knowing something's name is like having a bad spirit floating around. Until we know what to call him, we won't be safe." He took a bite of egg roll. "Three days, and if we don't have a name for him, he's history."

Then he closed his eyes and sniffed the air, which he did sometimes, as if he could sense things coming from miles, days, even weeks away. Once he'd done this—after a job in Sedona—and said, "Trouble. We've gotta get the hell out of here." They'd packed up that night and driven up to Utah, and they hadn't had any trouble at all.

"Three days," Jeremy repeated. "And that's pushing it."

∞

At nine-thirty, when Jeremy hasn't come back yet, Donna eats her chef's salad and gives all the ham to the cat, who rubs his head against her hand again and again even when there's nothing left. He knows that if she had more, she would give it to him. "You're a smart cat," she tells him. (Einstein?) Then she thinks: Maybe he doesn't want anything. Maybe he's just being nice.

Outside her window, there's the sound of a family walking down the pavement toward their room, a little boy whining about his sunburn, a mother telling him she warned him, didn't she? The voices get fainter, then a door opens and slams shut.

Before her daddy ran off and her mother went crazy and Donna (Lacey Love) went to live with her grandmother in Jackson—in the house with all the plastic on the furniture—they had all gone on a family trip to Vicksburg. "This field was running with blood," her daddy said. "Right where we're standing." Her mother had sighed and trembled. Her grandmother had refused to get out of the car. She had wanted to go to Dollywood.

Donna peeks out the window. The parking lot is nearly half empty; the fortunate families are staying down the street at the Holiday Inn or the Ramada. She steps out into the hot desert air, the pavement warm beneath her bare feet.

"You have a real knack for this kind of thing," Jeremy had told her—the way she's able to scan an entire parking lot and know which car is unlocked, or which trunk is not latched. "I'm good at guessing," she told him. "I'm lucky."

And she's lucky again tonight, locating a red Honda Civic with a piece of fabric—a beach blanket—sticking out of the trunk. The laptop is right on top—asking to be stolen, really—and she digs around a little more and finds some backpacks that don't interest her, and some AAA tour books, and some sun visors. She closes the trunk carefully and quietly. Before she met Jeremy, she would have taken the car and driven away, just because she could, but she hasn't wanted to do that in weeks. She's not sure she even could anymore.

"We're not bad people," Jeremy had told her. "We're just getting by in a world that's fucked us over."

When she asked him how the world had fucked him over, he'd sighed and his eyes had gotten damp, and he'd held her and stroked her hair—as if to say all that didn't matter, now that he'd found her.

She takes the laptop inside and places it on the nightstand. Inside the nightstand, she knows, is the ubiquitous Bible; it's as if it's the same one, following them from town to town, wanting something. She thinks of Mr. Harvey, can almost imagine him sneaking into the rooms and placing them furtively in drawers, convinced that he's saving the world. But she knows it's more complicated than that. Her mother thought she was saved, even when she was taking her clothes off in the middle of Wal-Mart, even when the doctor was giving her a shot in the arm to keep her from pulling out all her hair.

Donna has Jeremy, and that's better than salvation.

∾

"Good old Mrs. Jarvis," Jeremy had said, in a playful, affectionate way, when they were standing in her living room. He was tapping his gun against his palm, thoughtfully, though there was nothing really to think about.

"I'm not old," Mrs. Jarvis said. "I'm only forty-seven. I have a daughter at Bryn Mawr. My husband is dead. I'm the only person she has left."

Donna had drifted through the house, which was bright and sunny and smelled nothing at all like disinfectant. It smelled like flowers. There was no fancy "company" room. The bathroom was green and pink, with a shower curtain of plastic pink flowers. The tub was empty, of course—no old lady lying there with a razor blade beside her, her eyes closed under the red water.

There was a lime tree growing in black dirt. The limes were hard and small but she took two of them anyway and put them in her pocket. She wondered if the daughter at Bryn Mawr had played in this garden as a little girl, if she'd had tea parties and cut up little limes for her dolls. Donna—back when she was Lacey Love—had made dolls out of her mother's stockings, had set them around the card table and given them Dixie cups of cold Sanka.

Later, when her grandmother took her to the hospital for a visit, her mother would hold her on her lap—even though she was getting too big for that—and sing a song from her own childhood: *Donna, Donna, where have you gone? Where have you gone?*

The gunshot came as if from far away—a distant *pop*, like a toy, and she wondered vaguely if the Bryn Mawr girl would come back here and pack up her own toys, and where she would go, and if she had someone who loved her the way Jeremy loved Donna.

Jeremy stuck his head out the screen door. "Let's hit the road," he said. "Maybe get some Wendy's on the way."

That's when the black cat dashed out the door, blue collar jingling. One of his paws had blood on it.

"There you are," Jeremy said, and scooped him up.

"Cutie," said Donna. "Let's take him with us."

"He's ours," said Jeremy.

∾

She must have fallen asleep. When she hears the door open, the cat (Rex? Blossom?) is curled up next to her, on Jeremy's pillow.

"Aww," says Jeremy. "So, what'd you come up with?"

"Where were you?"

"I had a hard time finding a place. Damn guard dogs everywhere, and alarms and shit like that. I couldn't get a break. It was like an omen or something. Bad luck." He looks at the cat. "That's how I know you didn't come up with a name for him."

"Noodle," she tells him, sitting up and rubbing her eyes. Jeremy gives her a long look.

"I think you know that his name isn't Noodle."

"He looks like a noodle! Sort of. Doesn't he?"

But Jeremy is right. Noodle is wrong.

"Maybe the name of a famous person," she suggests. "Or a movie character. Like Clyde, of Bonnie and Clyde. Or maybe Billy the Kid. Or Sundance."

Jeremy is shaking his head. Daylight is leaking under the thick orange curtains, staining the carpet with smears of brightness.

"Potsie!" she says, and laughs. "Or maybe Cousin Oliver."

"Nope," says Jeremy, and moves closer to the bed, where the cat is sprawled blissfully on the pillow, one yellow eye barely visible. He rubs the cat on its stomach, and the cat stretches even further, his back legs twitching.

"Let's just keep him," Donna whispers, but Jeremy already has the cat by the neck, is squeezing with both hands while the cat (Inky! Frodo!) flails and twists and opens his poor little mouth and waves his paws in the air, his back legs frantically clawing at Jeremy's hands, until finally Donna looks away, sobbing, and there's a *crack*, and when she looks again, Jeremy is holding the limp cat on his lap, petting it. The tops of his hands are bleeding.

She watches as Jeremy picks up the animal and carries it outside; she hears something thud into the dumpster outside their room, and then Jeremy reappears and heads into the bathroom to wash his hands.

"Are you going to get ready?" he asks her.

She doesn't answer.

"Donna?"

"I don't feel like a Donna anymore," she admits, and something in Jeremy's eyes goes dark and bright and dark again. "I think I feel like a Joan," she tells him quickly, but as soon as she says it she knows it's wrong; she's not a Joan, any more than she's a Lacey Love or a Sunshine or a Donna.

Donna, where did you go?

"Agnes?" she says, but that's not right, either.

"Linda," Jeremy says, coming toward her, and she can see it in his eyes, how badly he wants that to fit, but it doesn't. "Betty," he says, holding one of her hands in both of his own. "Amber. Millicent. Penny."

"Helen," she whispers back. "Cynthia, Regina, Anne."

~ 2010

Barry Hannah

ᔋ Water Liars

Barry Hannah was born in Meridian, Mississippi, in 1942 and earned his bachelor's degree at the University of Mississippi. He received an M.A. and M.F.A. from the University of Arkansas. Over the course of his career, Hannah published eight novels and five story collections. His many awards include the William Faulkner Prize, a Guggenheim Fellowship, the Arnold Gingrich Short Fiction Award, the Award for Literature from the American Academy and Institute of Arts and Letters, and a PEN/Malamud Award for Excellence in the Short Story. Hannah died in 2010 at the age of sixty-seven.

"I only heard by secondhand that my sister said that my mother was very disturbed by my first novel. But on the other hand, she went and gave a book report about that novel to her study club, bless her heart."

~ from *Oxford American*,
March 2, 2012

When I am run down and flocked around by the world, I go down to Farte Cove off the Yazoo River and take my beer to the end of the pier where the old liars are still snapping and wheezing at one another. The line-up is always different, because they're always dying out or succumbing to constipation, etc., whereupon they go back to the cabins and wait for a good day when they can come out and lie again, leaning on the rail with coats full of bran cookies. The son of the man the cove was named for is often out there. He pronounces his name Far*tay*, with a great French stress on the last syllable. Otherwise you might laugh at his history or ignore it in favor of the name as it's spelled on the sign.

I'm glad it's not my name.

This poor dignified man has had to explain his nobility to the semiliterate of half of America before he could even begin a decent conversation with them. On the other hand, Farte, Jr., is a great liar himself. He tells about seeing ghost people around the lake and tells big loose ones about the size of the fish those ghosts took out of Farte Cove in years past.

∞

Last year I turned thirty-three years old and, raised a Baptist, I had a sense of being Jesus and coming to something decided in my life — because we all know Jesus was crucified at thirty-three. It had all seemed especially important, what you do in this year, and holy with meaning.

On the morning after my birthday party, during which I and my wife almost drowned in vodka cocktails, we both woke up to the making of a truth session about the lovers we'd had before we met each other. I had a mildly exciting and usual history, and she had about the same, which surprised me. For ten years she'd sworn I was the first. I could not believe her history was exactly equal with mine. It hurt me to think that in the era when there were supposed to be virgins she had allowed anyone but *me*, and so on.

I was dazed and exhilarated by this information for several weeks. Finally, it drove me crazy, and I came out to Farte Cove to rest, under the pretense of a fishing week with my chum Wyatt.

I'm still figuring out why I couldn't handle it.

∞

My sense of the past is vivid and slow. I hear every sign and see every shadow. The movement of every limb in every passionate event occupies my mind. I have a prurience on the grand scale. It makes no sense that I should be angry about happenings before she and I ever saw each other. Yet I feel an impotent homicidal urge in the matter of her lovers. She has excused my episodes as the course of things, though she has a vivid memory too. But there is a blurred nostalgia women have that men don't.

You could not believe how handsome and delicate my wife is naked.

I was driven wild by the bodies that had trespassed her twelve and thirteen years ago.

∞

My vacation at Farte Cove wasn't like that easy little bit you get as a rich New Yorker. My finances weren't in great shape; to be true, they were about in ruin, and I left the house knowing my wife would have to answer the phone to hold off, for instance, the phone company itself. Everybody wanted money and I didn't have any.

I was going to take the next week in the house while she went away, watch our three kids and all the rest. When you both teach part-time in the high schools, the income can be slow in summer.

No poor-mouthing here. I don't want anybody's pity. I just want to explain. I've got good hopes of a job over at Alabama next year. Then I'll get myself among higher-paid liars, that's all.

∞

Sidney Farte was out there prevaricating away at the end of the pier when Wyatt and I got there Friday evening. The old faces I recognized; a few new harkening idlers I didn't.

"Now, Doctor Mooney, he not only saw the ghost of Lily, he says he had intercourse with her. Said it was involuntary. Before he knew what he was doing, he was on her making cadence and all their clothes blown away off in the trees around the shore. She turned into a wax candle right under him."

"Intercourse," said an old-timer, breathing heavy. He sat up on the rail. It was a word of high danger to his old mind. He said it with a long disgust, glad, I guess, he was not involved.

"MacIntire, a Presbyterian preacher, I seen him come out here with his son-and-law, anchor near the bridge, and pull up fifty or more white perch big as small pumpkins. You know what they was using for bait?"

"What?" asked another geezer.

"*Nuthin.* Caught on the bare hook. It was Gawd made them fish bite," said Sidney Farte, going at it good.

"Naw. There be a season they bite a bare hook. Gawd didn't have to've done that," said another old guy, with a fringe of red hair and a racy Florida shirt.

"Nother night," said Sidney Farte, "I saw the ghost of Yazoo hisself with my pa, who's dead. A Indian king with four deer around him."

The old boys seemed to be used to this one. Nobody said anything. They ignored Sidney.

"Tell you what," said a well-built small old boy. "That was somethin when we come down here and had to chase that whole high-school party off the end of this pier, them drunken children. They was smokin dope and two-thirds a them nekid swimmin in the water. Good hunnerd of em. From your so-called *good* high school. What you think's happnin at the bad ones?"

∾

I dropped my beer and grew suddenly sick. Wyatt asked me what was wrong. I could see my wife in 1960 in the group of high-schoolers she must have had. My jealousy went out into the stars of the night above me. I could not bear the roving carelessness of teen-agers, their judgeless tangling of wanting and bodies. But I was the worst back then. In the mad days back then, I dragged the panties off girls I hated and talked badly about them once the sun came up.

∾

"Worst time in my life," said a new, younger man, maybe sixty but with the face of a man who had surrendered, "me and Woody was fishing. Had a lantern. It was about eleven. We was catching a few fish but rowed on into that little cove over there near town. We heard all these sounds, like they was ghosts. We was scared. We thought it might be the Yazoo hisself. We known of some fellows the Yazoo had killed to death just from fright. It was the over the sounds of what was normal human sighin and amoanin. It was big unhuman sounds. We just stood still in the boat. Ain't nuthin else us to do. For thirty minutes."

"An what was it?" said the old geezer, letting himself off the rail.

"We had a big flashlight. There came up this rustlin in the brush and I beamed it over there. The two of em makin the sounds get up with half they clothes on. It was my own daughter Charlotte and an older guy I didn't even know with a mustache. My *own* daughter, and them sounds over the water scarin us like ghosts."

"My Gawd, that's awful," said the old geezer by the rail. "Is that the truth? I wouldn't've told that. That's terrible."

Sidney Farte was really upset.

"This ain't the place!" he said. "Tell your kind of story somewhere else."

∞

The old man who'd told his story was calm and fixed to his place. He'd told the truth. The crowd on the pier was outraged and discomfited. He wasn't one of them. But he stood his place. He had a distressed pride. You could see he had never recovered from the thing he'd told about.

I told Wyatt to bring the old man back to the cabin. He was out here away from his wife the same as me and Wyatt. Just an older guy with a big hurting bosom. He wore a suit and the only way you'd know he was on vacation was he'd removed his tie. He didn't know where the bait house was. He didn't know what to do on vacation at all. But he got drunk with us and I can tell you he and I went out the next morning with our poles, Wyatt driving the motorboat, fishing for white perch in the cove near the town. And we were kindred.

We were both crucified by the truth.

~ 1978

Jhumpa Lahiri

∽ This Blessed House

"There's form and there's function and I have never been a fan of just form. My husband and I always have this argument because we go shopping for furniture and he always looks at chairs that are spectacular and beautiful and unusual, and I never want to get a chair if it isn't comfortable."

∼ from *The Atlantic*, March 2008

Born in London to Bengali immigrants, Jhumpa Lahiri came to the United States in 1970 at the age of three. She was raised in Rhode Island and attended Barnard College, where she received a B.A. in English literature. She continued her education at Boston University, earning an M.A. in English and an M.F.A in creative writing, as well as an M.A. in comparative literature and a Ph.D. in Renaissance studies. Lahiri's debut collection of stories, *Interpreter of Maladies* (1999), won the Pulitzer Prize for Fiction in 2000 as well as the PEN/Hemingway Award, and it was chosen as the New Yorker Debut of the Year. She has published a novel, *The Namesake* (2003), and a second story collection, *Unaccustomed Earth* (2008). Lahiri is currently a vice president of the PEN American Center and a member of the Committee on the Arts and Humanities.

They discovered the first one in a cupboard above the stove, beside an unopened bottle of malt vinegar. "Guess what I found." Twinkle walked into the living room, lined from end to end with taped-up packing boxes, waving the vinegar in one hand and a white porcelain effigy of Christ, roughly the same size as the vinegar bottle, in the other.

Sanjeev looked up. He was kneeling on the floor, marking, with ripped bits of a Post-it, patches on the baseboard that needed to be retouched with paint. "Throw it away."

"Which?"

"Both."

"But I can cook something with the vinegar. It's brand-new."

"You've never cooked anything with vinegar."

"I'll look something up. In one of those books we got for our wedding."

Sanjeev turned back to the baseboard, to replace a Post-it scrap that had fallen to the floor. "Check the expiration. And at the very least get rid of that idiotic statue."

"But it could be worth something. Who knows?" She turned it upside down, then stroked, with her index finger, the minuscule frozen folds of its robes. "It's pretty."

"We're not Christian," Sanjeev said. Lately he had begun noticing the need to state the obvious to Twinkle. The day before he had to tell her that if she dragged her end of the bureau instead of lifting it, the parquet floor would scratch.

She shrugged. "No, we're not Christian. We're good little Hindus." She planted a kiss on top of Christ's head, then placed the statue on top of the fireplace mantel, which needed, Sanjeev observed, to be dusted.

∾

By the end of the week the mantel had still not been dusted; it had, however, come to serve as the display shelf for a sizable collection of Christian paraphernalia. There was a 3-D postcard of Saint Francis done in four colors, which Twinkle had found taped to the back of the medicine cabinet, and a wooden cross key chain, which Sanjeev had stepped on with bare feet as he was installing extra shelving in Twinkle's study. There was a framed paint-by-number of the three wise men, against a black velvet background, tucked in the linen closet. There was also a tile trivet depicting a blond, unbearded Jesus, delivering a sermon on a mountaintop, left in one of the drawers of the built-in china cabinet in the dining room.

"Do you think the previous owners were born-agains?" asked Twinkle, making room the next day for a small plastic snow-filled dome containing a miniature Nativity scene, found behind the pipes of the kitchen sink.

Sanjeev was organizing his engineering texts from MIT in alphabetical order on a bookshelf, though it had been several years since he had needed to consult any of them. After graduating, he moved from Boston to Connecticut, to work for a firm near Hartford, and he had recently learned that he was being considered for the position of vice president. At thirty-three he had a secretary of his own and a dozen people working under his supervision who gladly supplied him with any information he needed. Still, the presence of his college books in the room reminded him of a time in his life he recalled with fondness, when he would walk each evening across the Mass. Avenue bridge to order Mughlai chicken with spinach from his favorite Indian restaurant on the other side of the Charles, and return to his dorm to write out clean copies of his problem sets.

"Or perhaps it's an attempt to convert people," Twinkle mused.

"Clearly the scheme has succeeded in your case."

She disregarded him, shaking the little plastic dome so that the snow swirled over the manger.

He studied the items on the mantel. It puzzled him that each was in its own way so silly. Clearly they lacked a sense of sacredness. He was further puzzled that Twinkle, who normally displayed good taste, was so charmed. These objects meant something to Twinkle, but they meant nothing to him. They irritated him. "We should call the Realtor. Tell him there's all this nonsense left behind. Tell him to take it away."

"Oh, Sanj." Twinkle groaned. "Please. I would feel terrible throwing them away. Obviously they were important to the people who used to live here. It would feel, I don't know, sacrilegious or something."

"If they're so precious, then why are they hidden all over the house? Why didn't they take them with them?"

"There must be others," Twinkle said. Her eyes roamed the bare off-white walls of the room, as if there were other things concealed behind the plaster. "What else do you think we'll find?"

But as they unpacked their boxes and hung up their winter clothes and the silk paintings of elephant processions bought on their honeymoon in Jaipur, Twinkle, much to her dismay, could not find a thing. Nearly a week had passed before they discovered, one Saturday afternoon, a larger-than-life-sized watercolor poster of Christ, weeping translucent tears the size of peanut shells and sporting a crown of thorns, rolled up behind a radiator in the guest bedroom. Sanjeev had mistaken it for a window shade.

"Oh, we must, we simply must put it up. It's too spectacular." Twinkle lit a cigarette and began to smoke it with relish, waving it around Sanjeev's head as if it were a conductor's baton as Mahler's Fifth Symphony roared from the stereo downstairs.

"Now, look. I will tolerate, for now, your little biblical menagerie in the living room. But I refuse to have this," he said, flicking at one of the painted peanut-tears, "displayed in our home."

Twinkle stared at him, placidly exhaling, the smoke emerging in two thin blue streams from her nostrils. She rolled up the poster slowly, securing it with one of the elastic bands she always wore around her wrist for tying back her thick, unruly hair, streaked here and there with henna. "I'm going to put it in my study," she informed him. "That way you don't have to look at it."

"What about the housewarming? They'll want to see all the rooms. I've invited people from the office."

She rolled her eyes. Sanjeev noted that the symphony, now in its third movement, had reached a crescendo, for it pulsed with the telltale clashing of cymbals.

"I'll put it behind the door," she offered. "That way, when they peek in, they won't see. Happy?"

He stood watching her as she left the room, with her poster and her cigarette; a few ashes had fallen to the floor where she'd been standing. He bent down, pinched them between his fingers, and deposited them in his cupped palm. The tender fourth movement, the *adagietto*, began. During breakfast, Sanjeev had read in the liner notes that Mahler had proposed to his wife by sending her the manuscript of this portion of the score. Although there were elements of tragedy and struggle in the Fifth Symphony, he had read, it was principally music of love and happiness.

He heard the toilet flush. "By the way," Twinkle hollered, "if you want to impress people, I wouldn't play this music. It's putting me to sleep."

Sanjeev went to the bathroom to throw away the ashes. The cigarette butt still bobbed in the toilet bowl, but the tank was refilling, so he had to wait a moment before he could flush it again. In the mirror of the medicine cabinet he inspected his long eyelashes—like a girl's, Twinkle liked to tease. Though he was of average build, his cheeks had a plumpness to them; this, along with the eyelashes, detracted, he feared, from what he hoped was a distinguished profile. He was of average height as well, and had wished ever since he had stopped growing that he were just one inch taller. For this reason it irritated him when Twinkle insisted on wearing high heels, as she had done the other night when they ate dinner in Manhattan. This was the first weekend after they'd moved into the house; by then the mantel had already filled up considerably, and they had bickered about it in the car on the way down. But then Twinkle had drunk four glasses of whiskey in a nameless bar in Alphabet City, and forgot all about it. She dragged him to a tiny bookshop on St. Mark's Place, where she browsed for nearly an hour, and when they left she insisted that they dance a tango on the sidewalk in front of strangers.

Afterward, she tottered on his arm, rising faintly over his line of vision, in a pair of suede three-inch leopard-print pumps. In this manner they walked the endless blocks back to a parking garage on Washington Square, for Sanjeev had heard far too many stories about the terrible things that happened to cars in Manhattan. "But I do nothing all day except sit at my desk," she fretted when they were driving home, after he had mentioned that her shoes looked uncomfortable and suggested that perhaps she should not wear them. "I can't exactly wear heels when I'm typing." Though he abandoned the argument, he knew for a fact that she didn't spend all day at her desk; just that afternoon, when he got back from a run, he found her inexplicably in bed, reading. When he asked why she was in bed in the middle of the day she told him she was bored. He had wanted to say to her then, You could unpack some boxes. You could sweep the attic. You could retouch the paint on the bathroom windowsill, and after you do it you could warn me so that I don't put my watch on it. They didn't bother her, these scattered, unsettled matters. She seemed content with whatever clothes she found at the front of the closet, with whatever magazine was lying around, with whatever song was on the radio—content yet curious. And now all of her curiosity centered around discovering the next treasure.

A few days later when Sanjeev returned from the office, he found Twinkle on the telephone, smoking and talking to one of her girlfriends in California even though it was before five o'clock and the long-distance rates were at their peak. "Highly devout people," she was saying, pausing every now and then to exhale. "Each day is like a treasure hunt. I'm serious. This you won't believe. The switch plates in the bedrooms were decorated with scenes from the Bible. You know, Noah's Ark and all that. Three bedrooms, but one is my study. Sanjeev went to the hardware store right away and replaced them, can you imagine, he replaced every single one."

Now it was the friend's turn to talk. Twinkle nodded, slouched on the floor in front of the fridge, wearing black stirrup pants and a yellow chenille sweater, groping for her lighter. Sanjeev could smell something aromatic on the stove, and he picked his way carefully across the extra-long phone cord tangled on the Mexican terra-cotta tiles. He opened the lid of a pot with some sort of reddish brown sauce dripping over the sides, boiling furiously.

"It's a stew made with fish. I put the vinegar in it," she said to him, interrupting her friend, crossing her fingers. "Sorry, you were saying?" She was like that, excited and delighted by little things, crossing her fingers before any remotely unpredictable event, like tasting a new flavor of ice cream, or dropping a letter in a mailbox. It was a quality he did not understand. It made him feel stupid, as if the world contained hidden wonders he could not anticipate, or see. He looked at her face, which, it occurred to him, had not grown out of its girlhood, the eyes untroubled, the pleasing features unfirm, as if they still had to settle into some sort of permanent expression. Nicknamed after a nursery rhyme, she had yet to shed a childhood endearment. Now, in the second month of their marriage, certain things nettled him — the way she sometimes spat a little when she spoke, or left her undergarments after removing them at night at the foot of their bed rather than depositing them in the laundry hamper.

They had met only four months before. Her parents, who lived in California, and his, who still lived in Calcutta, were old friends, and across continents they had arranged the occasion at which Twinkle and Sanjeev were introduced — a sixteenth birthday party for a daughter in their circle — when Sanjeev was in Palo Alto on business. At the restaurant they were seated side by side at a round table with a revolving platter of spareribs and egg rolls and chicken wings, which, they concurred, all tasted the same. They had concurred too on their adolescent but still persistent fondness for Wodehouse novels, and their dislike for the sitar, and later Twinkle confessed that she was charmed by the way Sanjeev had dutifully refilled her teacup during their conversation.

And so the phone calls began, and grew longer, and then the visits, first he to Stanford, then she to Connecticut, after which Sanjeev would save in an ashtray left on the balcony the crushed cigarettes she had smoked during the weekend—saved them, that is, until the next time she came to visit him, and then he vacuumed the apartment, washed the sheets, even dusted the plant leaves in her honor. She was twenty-seven and recently abandoned, he had gathered, by an American who had tried and failed to be an actor; Sanjeev was lonely, with an excessively generous income for a single man, and had never been in love. At the urging of their matchmakers, they married in India, amid hundreds of well-wishers whom he barely remembered from his childhood, in incessant August rains, under a red and orange tent strung with Christmas tree lights on Mandeville Road.

∾

"Did you sweep the attic?" he asked Twinkle later as she was folding paper napkins and wedging them by their plates. The attic was the only part of the house they had not yet given an initial cleaning.

"Not yet. I will, I promise. I hope this tastes good," she said, planting the steaming pot on top of the Jesus trivet. There was a loaf of Italian bread in a little basket, and iceberg lettuce and grated carrots tossed with bottled dressing and croutons, and glasses of red wine. She was not terribly ambitious in the kitchen. She bought preroasted chickens from the supermarket and served them with potato salad prepared who knew when, sold in little plastic containers. Indian food, she complained, was a bother; she detested chopping garlic, and peeling ginger, and could not operate a blender, and so it was Sanjeev who, on weekends, seasoned mustard oil with cinnamon sticks and cloves in order to produce a proper curry.

He had to admit, though, that whatever it was that she had cooked today, it was unusually tasty, attractive even, with bright white cubes of fish, and flecks of parsley, and fresh tomatoes gleaming in the dark brown-red broth.

"How did you make it?"

"I made it up."

"What did you do?"

"I just put some things into the pot and added the malt vinegar at the end."

"How much vinegar?"

She shrugged, ripping off some bread and plunging it into her bowl.

"What do you mean you don't know? You should write it down. What if you need to make it again, for a party or something?"

"I'll remember," she said. She covered the bread basket with a dishtowel that had, he suddenly noticed, the Ten Commandments printed on it. She flashed him a smile, giving his knee a little squeeze under the table. "Face it. This house is blessed."

∞

The housewarming party was scheduled for the last Saturday in October, and they had invited about thirty people. All were Sanjeev's acquaintances, people from the office, and a number of Indian couples in the Connecticut area, many of whom he barely knew, but who had regularly invited him, in his bachelor days, to supper on Saturdays. He often wondered why they included him in their circle. He had little in common with any of them, but he always attended their gatherings, to eat spiced chickpeas and shrimp cutlets, and gossip and discuss politics, for he seldom had other plans. So far, no one had met Twinkle; back when they were still dating, Sanjeev didn't want to waste their brief weekends together with people he associated with being alone. Other than Sanjeev and an ex-boyfriend who she believed worked in a pottery studio in Brookfield, she knew no one in the state of Connecticut. She was completing her master's thesis at Stanford, a study of an Irish poet whom Sanjeev had never heard of.

Sanjeev had found the house on his own before leaving for the wedding, for a good price, in a neighborhood with a fine school system. He was impressed by the elegant curved staircase with its wrought-iron banister, and the dark wooden wainscoting, and the solarium overlooking rhododendron bushes, and the solid brass 22, which also happened to be the date of his birth, nailed impressively to the vaguely Tudor facade. There were two working fireplaces, a two-car garage, and an attic suitable for converting into extra bedrooms if, the Realtor mentioned, the need should arise. By then Sanjeev had already made up his mind, was determined that he and Twinkle should live there to-gether, forever, and so he had not bothered to notice the switch plates covered with biblical stickers, or the transparent decal of the Virgin on the half shell, as Twinkle liked to call it, adhered to the window in the master bedroom. When, after moving in, he tried to scrape it off, he scratched the glass.

∾

The weekend before the party they were raking the lawn when he heard Twinkle shriek. He ran to her, clutching his rake, worried that she had discov-ered a dead animal, or a snake. A brisk October breeze stung the tops of his ears as his sneakers crunched over brown and yellow leaves. When he reached her, she had collapsed on the grass, dissolved in nearly silent laughter. Behind an overgrown forsythia bush was a plaster Virgin Mary as tall as their waists, with a blue painted hood draped over her head in the manner of an Indian bride. Twinkle grabbed the hem of her T-shirt and began wiping away the dirt staining the statue's brow.

"I suppose you want to put her by the foot of our bed," Sanjeev said.

She looked at him, astonished. Her belly was exposed, and he saw that there were goose bumps around her navel. "What do you think? Of course we can't put this in our bedroom."

"We can't?"

"No, silly Sanj. This is meant for outside. For the lawn."

"Oh God, no. Twinkle, no."

"But we must. It would be bad luck not to."

"All the neighbors will see. They'll think we're insane."

"Why, for having a statue of the Virgin Mary on our lawn? Every other person in this neighborhood has a statue of Mary on the lawn. We'll fit right in."

"We're not Christian."

"So you keep reminding me." She spat onto the tip of her finger and started to rub intently at a particularly stubborn stain on Mary's chin. "Do you think this is dirt, or some kind of fungus?"

He was getting nowhere with her, with this woman whom he had known for only four months and whom he had married, this woman with whom he now shared his life. He thought with a flicker of regret of the snapshots his mother used to send him from Calcutta, of prospective brides who could sing and sew and season lentils without consulting a cookbook. Sanjeev had considered these women, had even ranked them in order of preference, but then he had met Twinkle. "Twinkle, I can't have the people I work with see this statue on my lawn."

"They can't fire you for being a believer. It would be discrimination."

"That's not the point."

"Why does it matter to you so much what other people think?"

"Twinkle, please." He was tired. He let his weight rest against his rake as she began dragging the statue toward an oval bed of myrtle, beside the lamppost that flanked the brick pathway. "Look, Sanj. She's so lovely."

He returned to his pile of leaves and began to deposit them by handfuls into a plastic garbage bag. Over his head the blue sky was cloudless. One tree on the lawn was still full of leaves, red and orange, like the tent in which he had married Twinkle.

He did not know if he loved her. He said he did when she had first asked him, one afternoon in Palo Alto as they sat side by side in a darkened, nearly empty movie theater. Before the film, one of her favorites, something in German that he found extremely depressing, she had pressed the tip of her nose to his so that he could feel the flutter of her mascara-coated eyelashes. That afternoon he had replied, yes, he loved her, and she was delighted, and fed him a piece of popcorn, letting her finger linger an instant between his lips, as if it were his reward for coming up with the right answer.

Though she did not say it herself, he assumed then that she loved him too, but now he was no longer sure. In truth, Sanjeev did not know what love was, only what he thought it was not. It was not, he had decided, returning to an empty carpeted condominium each night, and using only the top fork in his cutlery drawer, and turning away politely at those weekend dinner parties when the other men eventually put their arms around the waists of their wives and girlfriends, leaning over every now and again to kiss their shoulders or necks. It was not sending away for classical music CDs by mail, working his way methodically through the major composers that the catalogue recommended, and always sending his payments in on time. In the months before meeting Twinkle, Sanjeev had begun to realize this. "You have enough money in the bank to raise three families," his mother reminded him when they spoke at the start of each month on the phone. "You need a wife to look after and love." Now he had one, a pretty one, from a suitably high caste, who would soon have a master's degree. What was there not to love?

∾

That evening Sanjeev poured himself a gin and tonic, drank it and most of another during one segment of the news, and then approached Twinkle, who was taking a bubble bath, for she announced that her limbs ached from raking the lawn, something she had never done before. He didn't knock. She had applied a bright blue mask to her face, was smoking and sipping some bourbon with ice and leafing through a fat paperback book whose pages had buckled and turned gray from the water. He glanced at the cover; the only thing written on it was the word "Sonnets" in dark red letters. He took a breath, and then he informed her very calmly that after finishing his drink he was going to put on his shoes and go outside and remove the Virgin from the front lawn.

"Where are you going to put it?" she asked him dreamily, her eyes closed. One of her legs emerged, unfolding gracefully, from the layer of suds. She flexed and pointed her toes.

"For now I am going to put it in the garage. Then tomorrow morning on my way to work I am going to take it to the dump."

"Don't you dare." She stood up, letting the book fall into the water, bubbles dripping down her thighs. "I hate you," she informed him, her eyes narrowing at the word "hate." She reached for her bathrobe, tied it tightly about her waist, and padded down the winding staircase, leaving sloppy wet footprints along the parquet floor. When she reached the foyer, Sanjeev said, "Are you planning on leaving the house that way?" He felt a throbbing in his temples, and his voice revealed an unfamiliar snarl when he spoke.

"Who cares? Who cares what way I leave this house?"

"Where are you planning on going at this hour?"

"You can't throw away that statue. I won't let you." Her mask, now dry, had assumed an ashen quality, and water from her hair dripped onto the caked contours of her face.

"Yes I can. I will."

"No," Twinkle said, her voice suddenly small. "This is our house. We own it together. The statue is a part of our property." She had begun to shiver. A small pool of bathwater had collected around her ankles. He went to shut a window, fearing that she would catch cold. Then he noticed that some of the water dripping down her hard blue face was tears.

"Oh God, Twinkle, please, I didn't mean it." He had never seen her cry before, had never seen such sadness in her eyes. She didn't turn away or try to stop the tears; instead she looked strangely at peace. For a moment she closed her lids, pale and unprotected compared to the blue that caked the rest of her face. Sanjeev felt ill, as if he had eaten either too much or too little.

She went to him, placing her damp toweled arms about his neck, sobbing into his chest, soaking his shirt. The mask flaked onto his shoulders.

In the end they settled on a compromise: the statue would be placed in a recess at the side of the house, so that it wasn't obvious to passersby, but was still clearly visible to all who came.

∾

The menu for the party was fairly simple: there would be a case of champagne, and samosas from an Indian restaurant in Hartford, and big trays of rice with chicken and almonds and orange peels, which Sanjeev had spent the greater part of the morning and afternoon preparing. He had never entertained on such a large scale before and, worried that there would not be enough to drink, ran out at one point to buy another case of champagne just in case. For this reason he burned one of the rice trays and had to start it over again. Twinkle swept the floors and volunteered to pick up the samosas; she had an appointment for a manicure and a pedicure in that direction, anyway. Sanjeev had planned to ask if she would consider clearing the menagerie off the mantel, if only for the party, but she left while he was in the shower. She was gone for a good three hours, and so it was Sanjeev who did the rest of the cleaning. By five-thirty the entire house sparkled, with scented candles that Twinkle had picked up in Hartford illuminating the items on the mantel, and slender stalks of burning incense planted into the soil of potted plants. Each time he passed the mantel he winced, dreading the raised eyebrows of his guests as they viewed the flickering ceramic saints, the salt and pepper shakers designed to resemble

Mary and Joseph. Still, they would be impressed, he hoped, by the lovely bay windows, the shining parquet floors, the impressive winding staircase, the wooden wainscoting, as they sipped champagne and dipped samosas in chutney.

Douglas, one of the new consultants at the firm, and his girlfriend Nora were the first to arrive. Both were tall and blond, wearing matching wire-rimmed glasses and long black overcoats. Nora wore a black hat full of sharp thin feathers that corresponded to the sharp thin angles of her face. Her left hand was joined with Douglas's. In her right hand was a bottle of cognac with a red ribbon wrapped around its neck, which she gave to Twinkle.

"Great lawn, Sanjeev," Douglas remarked. "We've got to get that rake out ourselves, sweetie. And this must be . . ."

"My wife. Tanima."

"Call me Twinkle."

"What an unusual name," Nora remarked.

Twinkle shrugged. "Not really. There's an actress in Bombay named Dimple Kapadia. She even has a sister named Simple."

Douglas and Nora raised their eyebrows simultaneously, nodding slowly, as if to let the absurdity of the names settle in. "Pleased to meet you, Twinkle."

"Help yourself to champagne. There's gallons."

"I hope you don't mind my asking," Douglas said, "but I noticed the statue outside, and are you guys Christian? I thought you were Indian."

"There are Christians in India," Sanjeev replied, "but we're not."

"I love your outfit," Nora told Twinkle.

"And I adore your hat. Would you like the grand tour?"

The bell rang again, and again and again. Within minutes, it seemed, the house had filled with bodies and conversations and unfamiliar fragrances. The women wore heels and sheer stockings, and short black dresses made of crepe and chiffon. They handed their wraps and coats to Sanjeev, who draped them carefully on hangers in the spacious coat closet, though Twinkle told people to throw their things on the ottomans in the solarium. Some of the Indian women wore their finest saris, made with gold filigree that draped in elegant pleats over their shoulders. The men wore jackets and ties and citrus-scented aftershaves. As people filtered from one room to the next, presents piled onto the long cherry-wood table that ran from one end of the downstairs hall to the other.

It bewildered Sanjeev that it was for him, and his house, and his wife, that they had all gone to so much care. The only other time in his life that something similar had happened was his wedding day, but somehow this was different, for these were not his family, but people who knew him only casually, and in a sense owed him nothing. Everyone congratulated him. Lester, another coworker, predicted that Sanjeev would be promoted to vice president in two months maximum. People devoured the samosas, and dutifully admired the freshly painted ceilings and walls, the hanging plants, the bay windows, the silk paintings from Jaipur. But most of all they admired Twinkle, and her brocaded *salwar-kameez*, which was the shade of a persimmon with a low scoop in the back, and the little string of white rose petals she had coiled cleverly around her head, and the pearl choker with a sapphire at its center that adorned her throat. Over hectic jazz records, played under Twinkle's supervision, they laughed at her anecdotes and observations, forming a widening circle around her, while Sanjeev replenished the samosas that he kept warming evenly in the oven, and getting ice for people's drinks, and opening more bottles of champagne with some difficulty, and explaining for the fortieth time that he wasn't Christian. It was Twinkle who led them in separate groups up and down the winding stairs, to gaze at the back lawn, to peer down the cellar steps. "Your friends adore the poster in my study," she mentioned to him triumphantly, placing her hand on the small of his back as they, at one point, brushed past each other.

Sanjeev went to the kitchen, which was empty, and ate a piece of chicken out of the tray on the counter with his fingers because he thought no one was looking. He ate a second piece, then washed it down with a gulp of gin straight from the bottle.

"Great house. Great rice." Sunil, an anesthesiologist, walked in, spooning food from his paper plate into his mouth. "Do you have more champagne?"

"Your wife's wow," added Prabal, following behind. He was an unmarried professor of physics at Yale. For a moment Sanjeev stared at him blankly, then blushed; once at a dinner party Prabal had pronounced that Sophia Loren was wow, as was Audrey Hepburn. "Does she have a sister?"

Sunil picked a raisin out of the rice tray. "Is her last name Little Star?"

The two men laughed and started eating more rice from the tray, plowing through it with their plastic spoons. Sanjeev went down to the cellar for more liquor. For a few minutes he paused on the steps, in the damp, cool silence, hugging the second crate of champagne to his chest as the party drifted above the rafters. Then he set the reinforcements on the dining table.

"Yes, everything, we found them all in the house, in the most unusual places," he heard Twinkle saying in the living room, "In fact we keep finding them."

"No!"

"Yes! Every day is like a treasure hunt. It's too good. God only knows what else we'll find, no pun intended."

That was what started it. As if by some unspoken pact, the whole party joined forces and began combing through each of the rooms, opening closets on their own, peering under chairs and cushions, feeling behind curtains, removing books from bookcases. Groups scampered, giggling and swaying, up and down the winding staircase.

"We've never explored the attic," Twinkle announced suddenly, and so everybody followed.

"How do we get up there?"

"There's a ladder in the hallway, somewhere in the ceiling."

Wearily Sanjeev followed at the back of the crowd, to point out the location of the ladder, but Twinkle had already found it on her own. "Eureka!" she hollered.

Douglas pulled the chain that released the steps. His face was flushed and he was wearing Nora's feather hat on his head. One by one the guests disappeared, men helping women as they placed their strappy high heels on the narrow slats of the ladder, the Indian women wrapping the free ends of their expensive saris into their waistbands. The men followed behind, all quickly disappearing, until Sanjeev alone remained at the top of the winding staircase. Footsteps thundered over his head. He had no desire to join them. He wondered if the ceiling would collapse, imagined, for a split second, the sight of all the tumbling drunk perfumed bodies crashing, tangled, around him. He heard a shriek, and then rising, spreading waves of laughter in discordant tones. Something fell, something else shattered. He could hear them babbling about a trunk. They seemed to be struggling to get it open, banging feverishly on its surface.

He thought perhaps Twinkle would call for his assistance, but he was not summoned. He looked about the hallway and to the landing below, at the champagne glasses and half-eaten samosas and napkins smeared with lipstick abandoned in every corner, on every available surface. Then he noticed that Twinkle, in her haste, had discarded her shoes altogether, for they lay by the foot of the ladder, black patent-leather mules with heels like golf tees, open toes, and slightly soiled silk labels on the instep where her soles had rested. He placed them in the doorway of the master bedroom so that no one would trip when they descended.

He heard something creaking open slowly. The strident voices had subsided to an even murmur. It occurred to Sanjeev that he had the house all to himself. The music had ended and he could hear, if he concentrated, the hum of the refrigerator, and the rustle of the last leaves on the trees outside, and the tapping of their branches against the windowpanes. With one flick of his hand he could snap the ladder back on its spring into the ceiling, and they would have no way of getting down unless he were to pull the chain and let them. He thought of all the things he could do, undisturbed. He could sweep Twinkle's menagerie into a garbage bag and get in the car and drive it all to the dump, and tear down the poster of weeping Jesus, and take a hammer to the Virgin Mary while he was at it. Then he would return to the empty house; he could easily clear up the cups and plates in an hour's time, and pour himself a gin and tonic, and eat a plate of warmed rice and listen to his new Bach CD while reading the liner notes so as to understand it properly. He nudged the ladder slightly, but it was sturdily planted against the floor. Budging it would require some effort.

"My God, I need a cigarette," Twinkle exclaimed from above.

Sanjeev felt knots forming at the back of his neck. He felt dizzy. He needed to lie down. He walked toward the bedroom, but stopped short when he saw Twinkle's shoes facing him in the doorway. He thought of her slipping them on her feet. But instead of feeling irritated, as he had ever since they'd moved into the house together, he felt a pang of anticipation at the thought of her rushing unsteadily down the winding staircase in them, scratching the floor a bit in her path. The pang intensified as he thought of her rushing to the bathroom to brighten her lipstick, and eventually rushing to get people their coats, and finally rushing to the cherry-wood table when the last guest had left, to begin opening their housewarming presents. It was the same pang he used to feel before they were married, when he would hang up the phone after one of their conversations, or when he would drive back from the airport, wondering which ascending plane in the sky was hers.

"Sanj, you won't believe this."

She emerged with her back to him, her hands over her head, the tops of her bare shoulder blades perspiring, supporting something still hidden from view.

"You got it, Twinkle?" someone asked.

"Yes, you can let go."

Now he saw that her hands were wrapped around it: a solid silver bust of Christ, the head easily three times the size of his own. It had a patrician bump on its nose, magnificent curly hair that rested atop a pronounced collarbone, and a broad forehead that reflected in miniature the walls and doors and lampshades around them. Its expression was confident, as if assured of its devotees, the unyielding lips sensuous and full. It was also sporting Nora's feather hat. As Twinkle descended, Sanjeev put his hands around her waist to balance her, and he relieved her of the bust when she had reached the ground. It weighed a good thirty pounds. The others began lowering themselves slowly, exhausted from the hunt. Some trickled downstairs in search of a fresh drink.

She took a breath, raised her eyebrows, crossed her fingers. "Would you mind terribly if we displayed it on the mantel? Just for tonight? I know you hate it."

He did hate it. He hated its immensity, and its flawless, polished surface, and its undeniable value. He hated that it was in his house, and that he owned it. Unlike the other things they'd found, this contained dignity, solemnity, beauty even. But to his surprise these qualities made him hate it all the more. Most of all he hated it because he knew that Twinkle loved it.

"I'll keep it in my study from tomorrow," Twinkle added. "I promise."

She would never put it in her study, he knew. For the rest of their days together she would keep it on the center of the mantel, flanked on either side by the rest of the menagerie. Each time they had guests Twinkle would explain how she had found it, and they would admire her as they listened. He gazed at the crushed rose petals in her hair, at the pearl and sapphire choker at her throat, at the sparkly crimson polish on her toes. He decided these were among the things that made Prabal think she was wow. His head ached from gin and his arms ached from the weight of the statue. He said, "I put your shoes in the bedroom."

"Thanks. But my feet are killing me." Twinkle gave his elbow a little squeeze and headed for the living room.

Sanjeev pressed the massive silver face to his ribs, careful not to let the feather hat slip, and followed her.

~ 1999

Jill McCorkle

∾ Magic Words

"I would say that the first draft for me, especially with stories, is like a skeleton and then each run of revision is like transparencies in an anatomy book, you're adding the muscles and the tissues and the organs, and you begin to see how they all connect and work together."

~ from *Agni* Online, 2003

A North Carolina native, Jill McCorkle saw her first two novels published on the same day in 1984, when she was twenty-six. Since then, she has published three more novels and four collections of stories. Her stories have appeared in *The Atlantic, Ploughshares*, and *Oxford American* and have been selected for *Best American Short Stories* and *New Stories from the South*. McCorkle is a member of the Fellowship of Southern Writers, and her awards include the New England Book Award, the John Dos Passos Prize for Excellence in Literature, and the North Carolina Award for Literature. She is currently a professor in the M.F.A. program at North Carolina State University.

Because Paula Blake is planning something secret, she feels she must account for her every move and action, overcompensating in her daily chores and agreeing to whatever her husband and children demand. *Of course I'll pick up the dry cleaning, drive the kids, swing by the drugstore.* This is where the murderer always screws up in a movie, way too accommodating, too much information. The guilty one always has trouble maintaining direct eye contact.

"Of course I will take you and your friends to the movies," she tells Erin late one afternoon. "But do you think her mom can drive you home? I'm taking your brother to a sleepover too." She is doing it again, talking too much.

"Where are *you* going?" Erin asks, mouth sullen and sarcastic as it has been since her thirteenth birthday two years ago.

"Out with a friend," Paula says, forcing herself to make eye contact, the rest of the story she has practiced for days ready to roll. She's someone I work with, someone going through a really hard time, someone brand-new to the area, knows no one, really needs a friend.

But her daughter never looks up from the glossy magazine spread before her, engrossed in yet another drama about a teen star lost to drugs and wild nights. Her husband doesn't even ask her new friend's name or where she moved from, yet the answer is poised and waiting on her tongue. Tonya Matthews from Phoenix, Arizona. He is glued to the latest issue of *Our Domestic Wildlife*—his own newsletter to the neighborhood about various sightings of wild and possibly dangerous creatures, coyotes, raccoons, bats. Their message box is regularly filled with detailed sightings of raccoons acting funny in daylight or reports of missing cats. Then there's the occasional giggling kid faking a deep voice to report a kangaroo or rhino. She married a reserved and responsible banker who now fancies himself a kind of watchdog Crocodile Dundee. They are both seeking interests outside their lackluster marriage. His are all about threat and encroachment, being on the defense, and hers are about human contact, a craving for warmth like one of the bats her husband fears might find its way into their attic.

Her silky legs burn as if shamed where she has slathered lavender body lotion whipped as light as something you might eat. And the new silk panties, bought earlier in the day, feel heavy around her hips. But it is not enough to thwart the thought of what lies ahead, the consummation of all those notes and looks exchanged with the sales rep on the second floor during weeks at work, that one time in the stairwell—hard thrust of a kiss interrupted by the heavy door and footsteps two floors up—when the fantasy became enough of a reality to lead to this date. They have been careful, and the paper trail is slight—unsigned suggestive notes with penciled times and places—all neatly rolled like tiny scrolls and saved in the toe of the heavy wool ski socks in the far corner of her underwear drawer, where heavier, far more substantial pairs of underwear than what she is wearing cover the surface. It all feels as safe as it can be because he has a family too. He has just as much to lose as she does.

And now she looks around to see the table filled with cartons of Chinese food from last night and cereal boxes from the morning, and the television blares from the other room. Her son is anxious to get to his sleepover; her daughter has painted her toenails, and the fumes of the purple enamel fill the air. Her husband is studying a map showing the progression of killer bees up the coast. He speaks of them like hated relatives who are determined to drop in, whether you want them to or not. Their arrival is as inevitable as all the other predicted disasters that will wreak havoc on human life.

"Where did you say you've got to go?" her husband asks, and she immediately jumps to her creation. Tonya Matthews, Phoenix, Arizona, new to the area, just divorced. Her palms are sweating, and she is glad she is wearing a turtleneck to hide the nervous splotches on her chest. She won't be wearing it later. She will slip it off in the darkness of the car after she takes Gregory to the sleepover and Erin and her friend to the cinema. Under the turtleneck she is wearing a thin silk camisole, also purchased that afternoon at a pricey boutique she had never been in before, a place the size of a closet where individual lingerie items hang separately on the wall like art. A young girl, sleek, pierced, and polished, gave a cool nod of approval when she leaned in to look at the camisole. Paula finally chose the black one after debating between it and the peacock blue. Maybe she will get the blue next time, already hoping that this new part of her life will remain. Instead of the turtleneck, she will wear a loose cashmere cardigan that slides from one shoulder when she inclines her head inquisitively. It will come off easily, leaving only the camisole between them in those first awkward seconds. She tilts her head as she has practiced, and with that thought all others disappear, and now she doesn't know what has even been asked of her. Her heart beats a little too fast. She once failed a polygraph test for this reason. She had never — would never — shoot heroin, but her pulse had raced with the memory of someone she knew who had. Did she do drugs? Her answer was no, but her mind had taken her elsewhere, panicked when she remembered the boy who gave her a ride home from a high school party with his head thrown back and teeth gritted, arm tied off with a large rubber band while a friend loomed overhead to inject him, one bloody needle already on the littered floor.

You can't afford to let your mind wander in a polygraph test — or in life, as now, when once again she finds herself looking at her husband with no idea of what he has just said. Her ability to hold eye contact is waning, the light out the window waning, but the desire that has built all these weeks is determined to linger, flickering like a candle under labored breath. Somewhere, her husband says, between their house and the interstate, are several packs of coyotes, their little dens tucked away in brush and fallen trees. The coyote is a creature that often remains monogamous. The big bumbling mouthful of a word lingers there, a pause that lasts too long before he continues with his report. He heard the coyotes last night, so this is a good time to get the newsletter out, a good time to remind people to bring their pets indoors. Dusk is when they come out, same as the bats, most likely rabid.

∾

The kids are doing what they call creepy crawling. Their leader picked the term up from the book *Helter Skelter*. They slip in and out behind trees and bushes, surveying houses, peeping in windows, finding windows and doors ajar or unlocked. Their leader is a badly wounded boy in need of wounding others, and so he frightens them, holds them enthralled with his stories of violence or murder. They might not believe all he says, but they believe enough to know he is capable of bad things. As frightening as it is to be with him, it is more frightening not to be — to be on the outside and thus a potential victim.

To the kids he looks tough with his tongue ring and tattoos, his mouth tight and drawn by a bitterness rarely seen on such a young face, some vicious word always coiled on his tongue and ready to strike those who least expect it — though he has to be careful when bagging groceries at Food Lion; he has been reprimanded twice for making sarcastic remarks to elderly shoppers, things like *You sure you need these cookies, fat granny?* He has been told he will be fired the next time he is disrespectful, which is fine with him. He doesn't give a shit what any of them says. Dirt cakes the soles of his feet, like calloused hooves, as he stands on the asphalt in front of the bowling alley, smoking, guzzling, or ingesting whatever gifts his flock of disciples brings to him. He likes to make and hold eye contact until people grow nervous.

∾

When Agnes Hayes sees the boy bagging groceries in the market, her heart surges with pity, his complexion blotched and infected, hair long and oily.

"Don't I know you?" she asks, but he doesn't even look up, his arms all inked with reptiles and knives and what looks like a religious symbol. Now she has spent the day trying to place him. She taught so many of them, but their names and faces run together. In the three years since retirement, she has missed them more than she ever dreamed. Some days she even drives her car and parks near the high school to watch them, to catch a glimpse of all that energy and to once again feel it in her own pulse. She still drives Edwin's copper-colored Electra and has since he died almost two years ago. She would never have retired had she seen his death coming, and with it an end to all their plans about where they would go and what they would do. One day she was complaining about plastic golf balls strewn all over the living room, and the next she was calling 911, knowing even as she dialed and begged for someone to *please help* that it was too late.

The school is built on the same land where she went to school. She once practiced there, her clarinet held in young hands while she stepped high with the marching band. Edwin's cigar is there in the ashtray, stinking as always, only now she loves the stink, can't get enough of it, wishes that she had never complained and made him go out to the garage or down to the basement to smoke. She wishes he were sitting there beside her, ringed in smoke. Their son, Preston, is clear across the country, barely in touch.

∾

Sometimes creepy crawling involves only the car, cruising slowly through a driveway, headlights turned off, gravel crunching. There are lots of dogs. Lots of sensor lights. Lots of security systems, or at least signs *saying* there are systems. The boy trusts nothing and no one. He believes in jiggling knobs and trying windows. When asked one time, by a guidance counselor feigning compassion and concern, what he believed in, he said, "Not a goddamn thing," but of course he did. Anyone drawing breath believes in something, even if it is only that life sucks and there's no reason to live. Tonight he has announced that it is Lauren's turn to prove herself. She is a pretty girl behind the wall of heavy black makeup and black studded clothing. She wants out of the car, but she owes him fifty dollars. He makes it sound like if she doesn't pay it back soon he'll take it out in sex. She is only here to get back at the boy she loved enough to do everything he asked. She wants him to worry about her, to want her, to think about that night at the campground the way she does.

The leader reminds her often that he was there for her when no one else was. He listened to her story about the squeaky-clean asshole boyfriend, feeding her sips of cheap wine and stroking her dyed black hair the whole time she cried and talked and later reeled and heaved on all fours in a roadside ditch.

"He's an asswipe," the boy had said. "He used you." And then later when she woke just before dawn with her head pounding and her body filled with the sick knowledge that she had to go home and face her parents, he reminded her again how much she needed him, couldn't survive without him. "I didn't leave you," he said. "Could've easily fucked you and didn't."

And now she is here, and the boy who broke her heart is out with someone else or maybe just eating dinner with his parents and talking about where he might choose to go to school. He is a boy who always smells clean, even right off the track where he runs long-distance, his thigh muscles like hard ropes, his lungs healthy and strong. He might be at the movies, and she wishes she were there too—the darkness, the popcorn. She wishes she were anywhere else. She had wanted her parents to restrict her after that night, to say she couldn't go anywhere for weeks and weeks, but they did something so much worse; they said how disappointed they were, that they had given up, how she would have to work really hard to regain their trust, and by *trust* it seems they meant love.

The leader is talking about how he hates their old math teacher. "And I know where she lives too." He circles the block, drives slowly past a neat gray colonial with a bright red door, the big Electra parked in the drive. "What's the magic word?" he mimics in a high Southern voice and reaches over to grab Lauren's thigh, then inches up, gripping harder as if daring her to move. He motions for her to unzip her jeans, wanting her to just sit there that way, silver chain from her navel grazing the thin strip of nylon that covers her. Lower, he says, even though there is a boy in the backseat hearing every word. She feels cold but doesn't say a word. Her shoes and jacket and purse are locked in the trunk of his car. "For safekeeping," he said. She is about to readjust the V of denim when he swings the car off the side of the road behind a tall hedge of lagustrum, where they are partially hidden but can still see the house. "Like this," he says and tugs, a seam ripping, and then he slides across the seat toward her, his mouth hard on hers as he forces her hand to his own zipper. The boy in the backseat lights a cigarette, and she focuses on that, the sound, the smell; she can hear the paper burn.

∽

Erin and her friend, Tina, sit in the backseat, and Gregory is in front with his Power Ranger sleeping bag rolled up at his feet. Paula will drop him off at the party and then go to the cinema, and then she will still have time to sit and collect herself before driving seven miles down the interstate to the Days Inn, where he will be waiting. The children have said that this car—their dad's— smells like old farts and jelly beans. They say he saves up all day at the bank and then rips all the way home. Gregory acts this out, and with each "Ewww" and laugh from the girls, he gets a little more confident and louder. He says their grandmother smells like diarrhea dipped in peppermint and their grand- father is chocolate vomick. They are having a wonderful time, mainly because it's daring, the way he is testing Paula, the way they all are waiting for her to intervene and reprimand, but she is so distracted she forgets to be a good mother. When he turns and scrutinizes her with a mischievous look, she snaps back.

"Not acceptable, young man, and you know it," she says, but really she is worried that they are right and that *she* will smell like old farts and jelly beans when she arrives at the motel. Her cell phone buzzes against her hip, and she knows that he is calling to see if they are on schedule, calling to make sure that she doesn't stand him up again.

"Aren't you going to answer that?" Erin says. "Who is it, Dad looking for underwear? Some lame friend in need of a heart-to-heart?" The laughing contin- ues as Paula turns onto the street where a crowd of eight-year-olds and sleeping bags is gathered in the front yard of a small brick ranch.

"One of my lame friends, I'm sure," she answers but with the words pic- tures him there in the room, maybe already undressed, a glass of wine poured. They have already said so much in their little notes that it feels not only like they have already made love but like they have done so for so long that they are already needing to think up new things to do. Her pulse races, and she slams on the brakes when Gregory screams, "Stop!"

"Pay attention, Mom," Gregory says. "See, they're everywhere," and she thinks he means her lame friends, or kids at the party, but he picks up one of those little gourmet jelly beans, tosses it at his sister, and then jumps from the car. "Thanks, Mom," he says, and Paula waves to the already frazzled-looking mother who has taken this on. Thank you, Ronald Reagan. That's when the jelly bean frenzy started, and then after her husband said something cute and trite about sharing the desires of the president since he was now a vice president at the bank, all his workers gave him jelly beans because what else can you give someone you don't know at all who has power and authority over you? He got all kinds of jelly beans. And now if people hear about the neighborhood wildlife, it means many more years of useless presents—coyote and raccoon and bat figurines and mugs and mugs and more mugs. She will write and send all those thank-you notes. She will take all the crap to Goodwill.

∾

Sometimes Agnes watches television in the dark. She likes a lot of these new shows that are all about humiliating people until they confess that they are fat and need to lose weight or that they are inept workers who need to be fired or bad members of a team who need to be rejected and banished from the island. Her pug, Oliver, died not long after Edwin did, and she misses the way he used to paw and tug and make a little nest at the foot of her bed. She misses the sounds of his little snorts in the night. How could there have been a moment in life when she wished for this—the quiet, the lack of activity and noise? The clock ticks, the refrigerator hums. She could call Preston. She could give him an apology, whether or not she owes it. What she could say is that she is so sorry they misunderstood each other. Or she could call him and pretend nothing ever happened. She keeps thinking of the boy at the grocery, trying to place what year she taught him. Who were his parents? What is his name? Some children she gave things to over the years—her son's outgrown clothes and shoes—but then she stopped, dumping it all at the church instead, because the children never acted the same afterward, and that bothered her. They never said thank you, and they never looked her in the eye, as if she had never made a difference in their lives, and that was what hurt so much when she thought of Preston, how easily he had let a few things make him forget all that she had done for him in his life. She stated the truth, is all. When Preston planned to marry Amy, she told him how people might talk about them, might call their children names.

Right after Edwin's funeral, he called her Miss Christian Ethics, Miss Righteous Soul. He told her he wished he could stay and dig into all that ham and Jell-O but that Amy was at the Holiday Inn waiting for him. "They let dogs stay there too," he said and lingered over the prize rod and reel of his father's she had handed to him, only to put it back and leave. She hasn't seen him since. Now her chest is heavy with the memory, and her head and arm and side ache.

∞

The parking lot stretches for miles, it seems, kids everywhere in packs, snuggly couples, the occasional middle-aged, settled-looking couple Paula envies more than all the others. The Cinema Fourteen Plex looms up ahead like Oz, like a big bright fake city offering anything and everything, a smorgasbord of action and emotion as varied as the jelly bean connoisseur basket her husband's secretary sent at Christmas, a woman Paula has so often wished would become something more. Wouldn't that be easier?

"He's here," Tina says and points to where a tall skinny kid in a letter jacket is pacing along the curb. "Oh, my God. Oh, my God."

"Puhleeze," Erin says, sounding way too old. "Chill out. He's *just* a *boy*." And then they collapse in another round of laughter and are out of the car and gone. Paula's hip is buzzing again. Buzzing and buzzing. What if it's Gregory and the sleepover is canceled? Or he fell on the skate ramp and broke something or needs stitches and her husband can't be found because he's out in the woods with a flashlight looking for wildlife? Or maybe her husband really does need her. He just got a call that his mother died. Does she know where he put the Havahart trap? And when is the last time she saw *their* cat?

∞

Lauren is feeling frightened. The other boy, the one from the backseat who is always quiet and refuses to talk about the bruises on his face and arms, has announced he's leaving. He can't do this anymore. The leader slams on the brakes and calls him a pussy. The leader says that if he leaves that's it, no more rides, no more pot, no more anything except he'll catch him some dark night and beat the shit out of him. "I'll beat you worse than whatever goes on in that trash house of yours," he says, but the boy keeps walking, and Lauren feels herself wanting to yell out for him to wait for her. She has always found him scary and disgusting, but now she admires his ability to put one foot in front of the other. He says he's bored with it all — lame amateur shit — but she sees a fear in him as recognizable as her own. "Let him go," she whispers. She is watching the flicker of television light in the teacher's upstairs window. "Please. Can't we just ride around or something?"

"Afraid you won't get any more tonight?" he asks and leans in so close she can smell his breath, oddly sweet with Dentyne. The lost possibility of his features makes her sad, eyes you might otherwise think a beautiful shade of blue, dimple in the left cheek. He pulls a coiled rope from under the seat. "You gonna stay put, or do I need to tie you up?" She forces herself to laugh, assure him that she will stay put, but she makes the mistake of glancing at the key in the ignition, and he reaches and takes it.

She cautions herself to keep breathing, to act like she's with him. "Next one," she says. "I need to collect myself."

"Well, you just collect," he says. "I'll be back to deal with you in a minute." She doesn't ask what he plans to do. His outlines of all the ways such an event might go are lengthy and varied, some of them tame and pointless and others not pretty at all. He has already said he wants to scare the hell out of the old woman, let *her* know what it feels like to have someone make you say *please* and *thank you* every goddamn day. The girl watches him move into the darkness, numb fingers struggling to finally zip her pants back up, to pretend that his rough fingertips never touched her there. She will get out and run. She will leave the door open and crawl through the hedge until she reaches the main road. She will call her parents, beg for their forgiveness. There is no way now to get her shoes or phone, but she moves and keeps moving. She thinks of her bed and how good it will feel to crawl between clean sheets, to stare at the faces of all the dolls collected before everything in her life seemed to go so bad. Now all the things she has been so upset about mean nothing. So what if she let the handsome, clean-smelling track star do everything he wanted to do? She liked it too, didn't she? Not making the soccer team last year, being told on college day that she had no prayer of getting into any of the schools she had listed, most of them ones he was considering if he could run track. But losing or getting rejected—that happens to a lot of people, doesn't it? She can still find something she's good at, go *somewhere*. Right now she just wants to get home, to shower herself clean with the hottest water she can stand, to soap and scrub and wrap up in a flannel robe. She once watched her uncle skin a catfish, tearing the tight skin from the meat like an elastic suit, and she keeps thinking of the sound it made, a sound that made her want to pull her jacket close, to hide and protect her own skin. She feels that way now, only there's nothing to pull around her, the night air much cooler than she'd thought—and she keeps thinking she hears him behind her, so she moves faster. She is almost to the main road, the busy intersection, the rows of cars heading toward the cinema. Her foot is bleeding, a sliver of glass, and she is pinned at a corner, lines upon lines of cars waiting for the light to change.

∾

Paula's cell phone buzzes again, and she takes a deep breath and answers. "Where are you?" he asks. She can hear the impatience, perhaps a twinge of anger, and his voice does not match the way she remembers him sounding in the stairwell. When she pictures his face or reads his tiny penciled scrawl, it's a different voice, like it's been dubbed.

"Almost there," she says and tries to sound flirtatious, leaving him a promise of making up for lost time. Then she glances out her window and sees a girl she thinks she recognizes. Shirt torn and barefooted. They certainly won't let her in the theater that way. The girl is so familiar, and then she remembers— her daughter's school, story time in the library. But that was years ago when the girl's hair was light brown and pulled up in a high ponytail. She knows exactly who she is. This is a girl parents caution their *good* girls against. She is rumored to be bulimic. She locks herself in the school bathroom and cuts her arms. She once tried to overdose on vodka and aspirin and had to have her stomach pumped. She gives blow jobs in the stairwell of the high school in exchange for drugs. She has blackened ghoulish eyes and jet black hair, silver safety pins through her eyebrows and lip. Paula has heard parents whispering about her at various school functions. They say, "Last year she was perfectly normal, and now this. She was a B student with some artistic talent and a pretty face, and now this." She is the "Don't" poster child of this town, the local object lesson in how quickly a child can go bad.

∽

Agnes is trying to remember what exactly it was she said to anger Preston so. She had tried to make it complimentary, something about skin like café au lait. She had often seen black people described that way in stories, coffee and chocolates, conjuring delicious smells instead of those like the bus station or fish market across the river, which is what a lot of people might associate with black people. Her maid once used a pomade so powerful smelling Agnes had to ask that she please stop wearing it, but certainly Agnes never held that against the woman; she couldn't help being born into a culture that thought that was the thing to do.

"Sometimes it's not even *what* stupid thing you say," Preston shouted, the vein in his forehead throbbing like it might burst. "It's *how* you say it. So, so goddamned *godlike*." He spit the word and shook all over, hands clenched into fists. But now she wants him to come back and be with her. She didn't know coffee would be insulting. She is going through her phone numbers, she has it somewhere. That same day she reminded him that even the president of the United States said things like that. The president had once referred to his grandchildren as "the little brown ones," and why is that okay and chocolate and coffee are not?

It's your mom, she practices now. *Please talk to me, Preston.* She is dialing when she hears something down on her front porch. The wind? Her cat? There was a flyer in her mailbox just this evening saying how she should not leave the cat outside.

∽

Lauren shivers as she stands there on the corner. She expects to hear his car roar up any second and wonders what she will do when that happens. She will have to tell her parents that she lost her purse, that it got stolen, and her shoes and jacket. She shudders with the thought of the boy pawing through her personal things, a picture of the track star cut from the school newspaper, a poem she was writing about the ocean, a pale pink rabbit's foot she has carried since sixth grade when she won the school math bee with it in her pocket. The light is about to change, and she concentrates on that instead of imagining her parents' reaction. Just once she wishes one of them would pull her close and say, "Please, tell me what's wrong," and then she would. She would start talking and not stop, like a dam breaking; she would tell them so many things if there were really such a thing as unconditional love. But instead they will say, "What is wrong with you? Why are you doing this to us? Do you know what people are saying about you?"

"Do you need a ride?" A woman in an old black Audi leans out the window and motions her to hurry. "I know you from school."

She does know the woman, the mother of a girl in her class, a girl who makes good grades and doesn't get into trouble. Not a popular girl, just a normal girl. A nice girl who smiles shyly and will let you copy her notes if you get behind. Erin from Algebra I freshman year. This is Erin's mother.

She hears a car slowing in the lane beside her and runs to get in with the woman just as the light changes. "Thank you."

"My daughter goes to your school," the woman says. She is wearing a low-cut camisole with a pretty silver necklace. Her black sweater is soft and loose around her shoulders. The car smells like crayons and the woman's cologne. "I'm sorry my car is so messy. My husband's car, that is." Her cell phone buzzes in the cup holder, but she ignores it. "Where are you going, sweetheart?" she asks. "It's too chilly to be out without shoes and long sleeves." Something in her voice brings tears to the girl's eyes, and then her crying is uncontrollable. The woman just keeps driving, circling first the cinema and then many of the neighborhoods around the area. The girl sinks low in her seat when they pass the teacher's house, that old Pontiac still parked behind the hedge. She can't allow herself to imagine what he is doing, what he will do when he finds her gone. They drive out to the interstate and make a big loop, the woman patting her shoulder from time to time, telling her it's okay, that nothing can be that bad. Every third or fourth time the woman asks for her address, but for now the girl just wants to be here in this car riding. The woman's cell phone keeps buzzing and buzzing. Once she answers it to the loud voice of her daughter from the movie lobby saying she will need a ride home after all. "Are you mad, Mom?" the girl screams. "Is that okay?" And the woman assures her that it is okay. It is fine. She will be there. Then she answers to say she saw their cat early this morning. And then, apologizing when it rings again, she answers and says little at all, except that so much has happened, she just might not get there at all. "In fact," she whispers, "I know I can't get there." And Lauren knows there is a good chance that she is part of what has happened, but the heat is blowing on her cold feet and the woman has the radio turned down low with classical music, and her eyelids are so heavy she can barely keep them open. When she was little and couldn't sleep, her parents would sometimes put her in a warm car and drive her around. Her dad called it a "get lost" drive, and he let her make all the choices, turn here, turn there, turn there again, and then she would relax while he untangled the route and led them back home, by which time she would be nearly or already asleep. There was never any doubt that he could find the way home and that she would wake to find herself already tucked in her bed or in his arms being taken there.

∾

Preston's answering machine comes on, and Agnes is about to speak, but then she hears the noise again and puts down the phone. She wishes she would find Preston there—Preston and Amy, waiting to embrace her and start all over again. Preston in his letter jacket like he was all those nights she waited up for him and said, "Where have you been, young man?" And Edwin would be in the basement smoking, and Oliver would be rooting around at the foot of her bed.

Her chest is tight with the worry of it all. She swallows and opens the door. Nothing.

"Here, kitty," she calls in a faint voice. She steps out on the stoop into the chilly air. The sky is clear overhead, a sliver of a moon. There is a car parked way down at the end of her drive, just the front bumper showing beyond the hedge. It wasn't there when she came home. Perhaps someone had a flat or ran out of gas. She calls the cat again and hears leaves crunching around the side of the house. She waits, expecting to see it slink around the corner, but then nothing. There is more noise beyond the darkness, where she can't see. And it is coming closer, short quick sounds, footsteps in the leaves. She is backing into the house when she thinks she sees something much larger than the cat slip around the corner near her kitchen door. She pulls her sweater close and pushes the door to, turns the dead bolt. The flyer talked about coyotes and how they have been spotted all over town.

∽

The girl finally tells Paula where she lives, a neighborhood out of town and in the opposite direction from the motel. Paula's cell phone beeps with yet another message, but now she ignores it. She doesn't want to hear what he has to say now that he has had time to shape an answer to her standing him up yet again. She parks in front of a small brick ranch. The front porch is lit with a yellow bulb, all the drapes pulled closed.

"I'm happy to walk you up," Paula says, but the girl shakes her head. She says thank you without making eye contact and then gets out, making her way across the yard in slow, careful steps. Paula waits to see if a parent comes out, but the girl slips in and recloses the door without a trace.

Paula sits there in the dark as if expecting something to happen. And then she slips off the cardigan and pulls her turtleneck over her head. The message is waiting. He might be saying this is the last time he will do this, he has wasted too much time on her already. "Why are you fucking with me?" he might ask. Or, "Who do you think you are?" The chances of him saying he understands completely and they will try again some other, better time are slim. She imagines him there in the room, bare chested and waiting, already thinking about his other options, his better options. And she imagines her own house and her return, sink full of dirty dishes, purple nail polish and Power Ranger figures everywhere. A litter box that needs scooping and clothes that need washing and an empty pantry that would have been filled had she not been out buying lingerie all day.

She saw a coyote just last week, but she didn't report it. She was standing at the kitchen window and glanced out to see a tall, skinny shepherd mix—except just as her mind was shaping the thought about someone letting a dog run loose in the neighborhood, it came to her that this was not a dog. It was wild and fearful looking, thin and hungry, and she felt a kinship as they stood frozen, staring at each other. Everyone wants something.

∞

The leader can see her in there, old bat, holding her chest and shaking. She looks like a puppet, her old bitch of a body jerking in time with his jiggling the knob. "I wore your fucking boy's shirt," he will say. "Thank you so much. That little polo fucker really helped turn my life around." She lifts the phone and pulls the cord around the corner where he can't see her, so he jiggles harder, leans the weight of his body against the door. "Loafers! Neckties! *F* in fucking math." He creeps around and climbs high enough on a trellis to see that she is slumped down in a chair with the receiver clutched against her chest. "Say the magic word," he says and covers his fist with his shirt before punching out the window. "Say it."

∞

When Paula pulls up to the theater, Erin and Tina are waiting. A tall, thin boy in a letter jacket trails alongside Tina, his hand in her hip pocket in a familiar way, and then they kiss before the girls get in the car. Paula is about to mention the girl she picked up but then thinks better of it. She wants to say things like, "Don't you ever . . ." but the sound of her daughter's laughter makes her think better of it.

"I can't believe you, like, ate face in front of my mom," Erin says, and Tina blushes and grins. She is a girl with cleavage and braces, betwixt and between.

"Jesus, Mom, let some air in this stinkhole car," Erin laughs, and then the two girls talk over the movie and everyone they saw there as if Paula were not even present. Paula can't stop thinking about the girl and how she came to be on that busy corner with no shoes, how she looks so different from that clean-faced little girl in a library chair, and yet she is one and the same. And what will she write and slip to her co-worker on Monday, or will she avoid him altogether and pretend nothing ever happened, that she never ventured from her own darkened den in search of excitement? She imagines the coyotes living as her husband has described, little nests under piles of brush, helpless cubs curled there waiting for the return of their mother.

"I'm sorry if I messed up your time with your lame friend," Erin says sarcastically and then leans in close. "Really, Momsy, I am." She air-kisses Paula and smiles a sincere thanks before turning back to her friend with a shriek of something she can't believe she forgot to tell, something about cheating, someone getting caught with a teacher's grade book. She has licorice twists braided and tied around her throat like a necklace, and her breath is sweet with Milk Duds.

∞

The old woman is dead or acting dead, the recorded voice from the receiver on her chest telling her to please hang up and try her call again. It's one of those houses where everything is in place, little useless bullshit glass things nobody wants. She looks as miserable dead as she did alive. It makes him want to trash the place, but why bother now? He didn't kill her. He didn't do a thing but pop out a pane of glass. He searches around and then carefully, using his shirt so as not to leave a print, takes a golf ball from the basket beside the fireplace and places it down in the broken glass. Television is too big to lift, no purse in sight, not even a liquor cabinet. She gives him the creeps, and so do all the people looking out from portraits and photographs. He'll tell the girl that he just scared the old bitch, threatened to tie her up and put a bullet in her head until she cried and begged for his mercy and forgiveness. He'll say he left her alive and grateful.

The moon is high in the bright clear sky when Paula ventures outside to look for their cat. She pulls her sweater close and steps away from the light of the house, the woods around her spreading into darkness. Her husband is sleeping, and Erin is on the phone. There were no messages other than the one on her cell phone, still trapped there and waiting. She hears a distant siren, the wind in the trees, the bass beat from a passing car. *Please*, she thinks. *Please*. She is about to go inside for a flashlight when she hears the familiar bell and then sees the cat slinking up from the dark woods, her manner cool and unaffected.

~ 2008

Lorrie Moore

∽ How to Become a Writer

Lorrie Moore was born in 1957 and raised in eastern New York State. After graduating from St. Lawrence University, Moore enrolled in Cornell's M.F.A program and published her first collection of short stories, *Self-Help* (1985), shortly after graduating. She has published three other story collections and three novels, as well as a children's novel. Her work has been selected for *The O. Henry Prize Stories* and *Best American Short Stories*, and her awards include a National Endowment for the Arts Fellowship, a Guggenheim Fellowship, the Irish Times International Fiction Prize, and the Rea Award for the Short Story. She is currently the Delmore Schwartz Professor in the Humanities at the University of Wisconsin–Madison.

> *"I'm a little harsh. When people say, 'I have writer's block. What do you suggest?' I say, 'If you can't write, don't write. No one needs your writing. Don't torture yourself.'"*
>
> ~from *The Telegraph*, October 7, 2009

First, try to be something, anything, else. A movie star/astronaut. A movie star/missionary. A movie star/kindergarten teacher. President of the World. Fail miserably. It is best if you fail at an early age—say, fourteen. Early, critical disillusionment is necessary so that at fifteen you can write long haiku sequences about thwarted desire. It is a pond, a cherry blossom, a wind brushing against sparrow wing leaving for mountain. Count the syllables. Show it to your mom. She is tough and practical. She has a son in Vietnam and a husband who may be having an affair. She believes in wearing brown because it hides spots. She'll look briefly at your writing, then back up at you with a face blank as a donut. She'll say: "How about emptying the dishwasher?" Look away. Shove the forks in the fork drawer. Accidentally break one of the freebie gas station glasses. This is the required pain and suffering. This is only for starters.

In your high school English class look only at Mr. Killian's face. Decide faces are important. Write a villanelle about pores. Struggle. Write a sonnet. Count the syllables: nine, ten, eleven, thirteen. Decide to experiment with fiction. Here you don't have to count syllables. Write a short story about an elderly man and woman who accidentally shoot each other in the head, the result of an inexplicable malfunction of a shotgun which appears mysteriously in their living room one night. Give it to Mr. Killian as your final project. When you get it back, he has written on it: "Some of your images are quite nice, but you have no sense of plot." When you are home, in the privacy of your own room, faintly scrawl in pencil beneath his black-inked comments: "Plots are for dead people, pore-face."

∽

Take all the babysitting jobs you can get. You are great with kids. They love you. You tell them stories about old people who die idiot deaths. You sing them songs like "Blue Bells of Scotland," which is their favorite. And when they are in their pajamas and have finally stopped pinching each other, when they are fast asleep, you read every sex manual in the house, and wonder how on earth anyone could ever do those things with someone they truly loved. Fall asleep in a chair reading Mr. McMurphy's *Playboy*. When the McMurphys come home, they will tap you on the shoulder, look at the magazine in your lap, and grin. You will want to die. They will ask you if Tracey took her medicine all right. Explain, yes, she did, that you promised her a story if she would take it like a big girl and that seemed to work out just fine. "Oh, marvelous," they will exclaim.

Try to smile proudly.

Apply to college as a child psychology major.

∽

As a child psychology major, you have some electives. You've always liked birds. Sign up for something called "The Ornithological Field Trip." It meets Tuesdays and Thursdays at two. When you arrive at Room 134 on the first day of class, everyone is sitting around a seminar table talking about metaphors. You've heard of these. After a short, excruciating while, raise your hand and say diffidently, "Excuse me, isn't this Birdwatching One-oh-one?" The class stops and turns to look at you. They seem to all have one face—giant and blank as a vandalized clock. Someone with a beard booms out, "No, this is Creative Writing." Say: "Oh—right," as if perhaps you knew all along. Look down at your schedule. Wonder how the hell you ended up here. The computer, apparently, has made an error. You start to get up to leave and then don't. The lines at the registrar this week are huge. Perhaps you should stick with this mistake. Perhaps your creative writing isn't all that bad. Perhaps it is fate. Perhaps this is what your dad meant when he said, "It's the age of computers, Francie, it's the age of computers."

∽

Decide that you like college life. In your dorm you meet many nice people. Some are smarter than you. And some, you notice, are dumber than you. You will continue, unfortunately, to view the world in exactly these terms for the rest of your life.

∽

The assignment this week in creative writing is to narrate a violent happening. Turn in a story about driving with your Uncle Gordon and another one about two old people who are accidentally electrocuted when they go to turn on a badly wired desk lamp. The teacher will hand them back to you with comments: "Much of your writing is smooth and energetic. You have, however, a ludicrous notion of plot." Write another story about a man and a woman who, in the very first paragraph, have their lower torsos accidentally blitzed away by dynamite. In the second paragraph, with the insurance money, they buy a frozen yogurt stand together. There are six more paragraphs. You read the whole thing out loud in class. No one likes it. They say your sense of plot is outrageous and incompetent. After class someone asks you if you are crazy.

∽

Decide that perhaps you should stick to comedies. Start dating someone who is funny, someone who has what in high school you called a "really great sense of humor" and what now your creative writing class calls "self-contempt giving rise to comic form." Write down all of his jokes, but don't tell him you are doing this. Make up anagrams of his old girlfriend's name and name all of your socially handicapped characters with them. Tell him his old girlfriend is in all of your stories and then watch how funny he can be, see what a really great sense of humor he can have.

∞

Your child psychology advisor tells you you are neglecting courses in your major. What you spend the most time on should be what you're majoring in. Say yes, you understand.

∞

In creative writing seminars over the next two years, everyone continues to smoke cigarettes and ask the same things: "But does it work?" "Why should we care about this character?" "Have you earned this cliché?" These seem like important questions.

On days when it is your turn, you look at the class hopefully as they scour your mimeographs for a plot. They look back up at you, drag deeply, and then smile in a sweet sort of way.

∞

You spend too much time slouched and demoralized. Your boyfriend suggests bicycling. Your roommate suggests a new boyfriend. You are said to be self-mutilating and losing weight, but you continue writing. The only happiness you have is writing something new, in the middle of the night, armpits damp, heart pounding, something no one has yet seen. You have only those brief, fragile, untested moments of exhilaration when you know: you are a genius. Understand what you must do. Switch majors. The kids in your nursery project will be disappointed, but you have a calling, an urge, a delusion, an unfortunate habit. You have, as your mother would say, fallen in with a bad crowd.

∞

Why write? Where does writing come from? These are questions to ask your-self. They are like: Where does dust come from? Or: Why is there war? Or: If there's a God, then why is my brother now a cripple?

These are questions that you keep in your wallet, like calling cards. These are questions, your creative writing teacher says, that are good to address in your journals but rarely in your fiction.

The writing professor this fall is stressing the Power of the Imagination. Which means he doesn't want long descriptive stories about your camping trip last July. He wants you to start in a realistic context but then to alter it. Like recombinant DNA. He wants you to let your imagination sail, to let it grow big-bellied in the wind. This is a quote from Shakespeare.

∽

Tell your roommate your great idea, your great exercise of imaginative power: a transformation of Melville to contemporary life. It will be about monomania and the fish-eat-fish world of life insurance in Rochester, New York. The first line will be "Call me Fishmeal," and it will feature a menopausal suburban husband named Richard, who because he is so depressed all the time is called "Mopey Dick" by his witty wife Elaine. Say to your roommate: "Mopey Dick, get it?" Your roommate looks at you, her face blank as a large Kleenex. She comes up to you, like a buddy, and puts an arm around your burdened shoulders. "Listen, Francie," she says, slow as speech therapy. "Let's go out and get a big beer."

∽

The seminar doesn't like this one either. You suspect they are beginning to feel sorry for you. They say: "You have to think about what is happening. Where is the story here?"

∽

The next semester the writing professor is obsessed with writing from personal experience. You must write from what you know, from what has happened to you. He wants death, he wants camping trips. Think about what has happened to you. In three years there have been three things: you lost your virginity; your parents got divorced; and your brother came home from a forest ten miles from the Cambodian border with only half a thigh, a permanent smirk nestled into one corner of his mouth.

About the first you write: "It created a new space, which hurt and cried in a voice that wasn't mine, 'I'm not the same anymore, but I'll be okay.'"

About the second you write an elaborate story of an old married couple who stumble upon an unknown land mine in their kitchen and accidentally blow themselves up. You call it: "For Better or for Liverwurst."

About the last you write nothing. There are no words for this. Your typewriter hums. You can find no words.

∾

At undergraduate cocktail parties, people say, "Oh, you write? What do you write about?" Your roommate, who has consumed too much wine, too little cheese, and no crackers at all, blurts: "Oh, my god, she always writes about her dumb boyfriend."

Later on in life you will learn that writers are merely open, helpless texts with no real understanding of what they have written and therefore must half-believe anything and everything that is said of them. You, however, have not yet reached this stage of literary criticism. You stiffen and say, "I do not," the same way you said it when someone in the fourth grade accused you of really liking oboe lessons and your parents really weren't just making you take them.

Insist you are not very interested in any one subject at all, that you are interested in the music of language, that you are interested in — in — syllables, because they are the atoms of poetry, the cells of the mind, the breath of the soul. Begin to feel woozy. Stare into your plastic wine cup.

"Syllables?" you will hear someone ask, voice trailing off, as they glide slowly toward the reassuring white of the dip.

∾

Begin to wonder what you do write about. Or if you have anything to say. Or if there even is such a thing as a thing to say. Limit these thoughts to no more than ten minutes a day; like sit-ups, they can make you thin.

You will read somewhere that all writing has to do with one's genitals. Don't dwell on this. It will make you nervous.

∾

Your mother will come visit you. She will look at the circles under your eyes and hand you a brown book with a brown briefcase on the cover. It is entitled:

How to Become a Business Executive. She has also brought the *Names for Baby* encyclopedia you asked for; one of your characters, the aging clown-schoolteacher, needs a new name. Your mother will shake her head and say: "Francie, Francie, remember when you were going to be a child psychology major?"

Say: "Mom, I like to write."

She'll say: "Sure you like to write. Of course. Sure you like to write."

∾

Write a story about a confused music student and title it: "Schubert Was the One with the Glasses, Right?" It's not a big hit, although your roommate likes the part where the two violinists accidentally blow themselves up in a recital room. "I went out with a violinist once," she says, snapping her gum.

∾

Thank god you are taking other courses. You can find sanctuary in nineteenth-century ontological snags and invertebrate courting rituals. Certain globular mollusks have what is called "Sex by the Arm." The male octopus, for instance, loses the end of one arm when placing it inside the female body during intercourse. Marine biologists call it "Seven Heaven." Be glad you know these things. Be glad you are not just a writer. Apply to law school.

∾

From here on in, many things can happen. But the main one will be this: you decide not to go to law school after all, and, instead, you spend a good, big chunk of your adult life telling people how you decided not to go to law school after all. Somehow you end up writing again. Perhaps you go to graduate school. Perhaps you work odd jobs and take writing courses at night. Perhaps you are working on a novel and writing down all the clever remarks and intimate personal confessions you hear during the day. Perhaps you are losing your pals, your acquaintances, your balance.

You have broken up with your boyfriend. You now go out with men who, instead of whispering "I love you," shout: "Do it to me, baby." This is good for your writing.

Sooner or later you have a finished manuscript more or less. People look at it in a vaguely troubled sort of way and say, "I'll bet becoming a writer was always a fantasy of yours, wasn't it?" Your lips dry to salt. Say that of all the fantasies possible in the world, you can't imagine being a writer even making the top twenty. Tell them you were going to be a child psychology major. "I bet," they always sigh, "you'd be great with kids." Scowl fiercely. Tell them you're a walking blade.

∾

Quit classes. Quit jobs. Cash in old savings bonds. Now you have time like warts on your hands. Slowly copy all of your friends' addresses into a new address book.

Vacuum. Chew cough drops. Keep a folder full of fragments.

An eyelid darkening sideways.

World as conspiracy.

Possible plot? A woman gets on a bus.

Suppose you threw a love affair and nobody came?

At home drink a lot of coffee. At Howard Johnson's order the cole slaw. Consider how it looks like the soggy confetti of a map: where you've been, where you're going— "You Are Here," says the red star on the back of the menu.

Occasionally a date with a face blank as a sheet of paper asks you whether writers often become discouraged. Say that sometimes they do and sometimes they do. Say it's a lot like having polio.

"Interesting," smiles your date, and then he looks down at his arm hairs and starts to smooth them, all, always, in the same direction.

~ 1985

Tim O'Brien

∼ On the Rainy River

Tim O'Brien is the author of eight books, including story collections, novels, and a memoir. Born in 1946, he grew up in Minnesota and studied political science at Macalester University. After graduation, he was drafted into the Army and served in Vietnam from 1969 to 1970. Upon his return, he enrolled in graduate school in government at Harvard Uni-

"To revisit tragedy in a way that's imaginative and challenging is not the same as lying in bed picking at the scabs of memory. It's trying to salvage something from memory and make something beautiful out of it."

∼ from *The New York Times*,
January 31, 2010

versity but left to work as a national affairs reporter for *The Washington Post*. His first published book was a memoir of his time in Vietnam, *If I Die in a Combat Zone, Box Me Up and Ship Me Home* (1973). His novel *Going After Cacciato* (1978) won the National Book Award, and his collection *The Things They Carried* (1990) won the French Prix du Meilleur Livre Étranger and was a finalist for the Pulitzer Prize and the National Book Critics Circle Award. Additional awards have come from the Guggenheim Foundation and the National Endowment for the Arts. He is currently a visiting professor and holds an endowed chair at Southwest Texas State University.

This is one story I've never told before. Not to anyone. Not to my parents, not to my brother or sister, not even to my wife. To go into it, I've always thought, would only cause embarrassment for all of us, a sudden need to be elsewhere, which is the natural response to a confession. Even now, I'll admit, the story makes me squirm. For more than twenty years I've had to live with it, feeling the shame, trying to push it away, and so by this act of remembrance, by putting the facts down on paper, I'm hoping to relieve at least some of the pressure on my dreams. Still, it's a hard story to tell. All of us, I suppose, like to believe that in a moral emergency we will behave like the heroes of our youth, bravely and forthrightly, without thought of personal loss or discredit. Certainly that was my conviction back in the summer of 1968. Tim O'Brien: a secret hero. The Lone Ranger. If the stakes ever became high enough — if the evil were evil enough, if the good were good enough — I would simply tap a secret reservoir of courage that had been accumulating inside me over the years. Courage, I seemed to think, comes to us in finite quantities, like an inheritance, and by being frugal and stashing it away and letting it earn interest, we steadily increase our moral capital in preparation for that day when the account must be drawn down. It was a comforting theory. It dispensed with all those bothersome little acts of daily courage; it offered hope and grace to the repetitive coward; it justified the past while amortizing the future.

In June of 1968, a month after graduating from Macalester College, I was drafted to fight a war I hated. I was twenty-one years old. Young, yes, and politically naive, but even so the American war in Vietnam seemed to me wrong. Certain blood was being shed for uncertain reasons. I saw no unity of purpose, no consensus on matters of philosophy or history or law. The very facts were shrouded in uncertainty: Was it a civil war? A war of national liberation or simple aggression? Who started it, and when, and why? What really happened to the USS *Maddox* on that dark night in the Gulf of Tonkin? Was Ho Chi Minh a Communist stooge, or a nationalist savior, or both, or neither? What about the Geneva Accords? What about SEATO and the Cold War? What about dominoes? America was divided on these and a thousand other issues, and the debate had spilled out across the floor of the United States Senate and into the streets, and smart men in pinstripes could not agree on even the most fundamental matters of public policy. The only certainty that summer was moral confusion. It was my view then, and still is, that you don't make war without knowing why. Knowledge, of course, is always imperfect, but it seemed to me that when a nation goes to war it must have reasonable confidence in the justice and imperative of its cause. You can't fix your mistakes. Once people are dead, you can't make them undead.

In any case those were my convictions, and back in college I had taken a modest stand against the war. Nothing radical, no hothead stuff, just ringing a few doorbells for Gene McCarthy, composing a few tedious, uninspired editorials for the campus newspaper. Oddly, though, it was almost entirely an intellectual activity. I brought some energy to it, of course, but it was the energy that accompanies almost any abstract endeavor; I felt no personal danger; I felt no sense of an impending crisis in my life. Stupidly, with a kind of smug removal that I can't begin to fathom, I assumed that the problems of killing and dying did not fall within my special province.

The draft notice arrived on June 17, 1968. It was a humid afternoon, I remember, cloudy and very quiet, and I'd just come in from a round of golf. My mother and father were having lunch out in the kitchen. I remember opening up the letter, scanning the first few lines, feeling the blood go thick behind my eyes. I remember a sound in my head. It wasn't thinking, it was just a silent howl. A million things all at once—I was too *good* for this war. Too smart, too compassionate, too everything. It couldn't happen. I was above it. I had the world dicked—Phi Beta Kappa and summa cum laude and president of the student body and a full-ride scholarship for grad studies at Harvard. A mistake, maybe—a foul-up in the paperwork. I was no soldier. I hated Boy Scouts. I hated camping out. I hated dirt and tents and mosquitoes. The sight of blood made me queasy, and I couldn't tolerate authority, and I didn't know a rifle from a slingshot. I was a *liberal*, for Christ sake: If they needed fresh bodies, why not draft some back-to-the-stone-age hawk? Or some dumb jingo in his hard hat and Bomb Hanoi button? Or one of LBJ's pretty daughters? Or Westmoreland's whole family—nephews and nieces and baby grandson? There should be a law, I thought. If you support a war, if you think it's worth the price, that's fine, but you have to put your own life on the line. You have to head for the front and hook up with an infantry unit and help spill the blood. And you have to bring along your wife, or your kids, or your lover. A *law*, I thought.

I remember the rage in my stomach. Later it burned down to a smoldering self-pity, then to numbness. At dinner that night my father asked what my plans were.

"Nothing," I said. "Wait."

∞

I spent the summer of 1968 working in an Armour meatpacking plant in my hometown of Worthington, Minnesota. The plant specialized in pork products, and for eight hours a day I stood on a quarter-mile assembly line—more properly, a disassembly line — removing blood clots from the necks of dead pigs. My job title, I believe, was Declotter. After slaughter, the hogs were decapitated, split down the length of the belly, pried open, eviscerated, and strung up by the hind hocks on a high conveyer belt. Then gravity took over. By the time a carcass reached my spot on the line, the fluids had mostly drained out, everything except for thick clots of blood in the neck and upper chest cavity. To remove the stuff, I used a kind of water gun. The machine was heavy, maybe eighty pounds, and was suspended from the ceiling by a heavy rubber cord. There was some bounce to it, an elastic up-and-down give, and the trick was to maneuver the gun with your whole body, not lifting with the arms, just letting the rubber cord do the work for you. At one end was a trigger; at the muzzle end was a small nozzle and a steel roller brush. As a carcass passed by, you'd lean forward and swing the gun up against the clots and squeeze the trigger, all in one motion, and the brush would whirl and water would come shooting out and you'd hear a quick splattering sound as the clots dissolved into a fine red mist. It was not pleasant work. Goggles were a necessity, and a rubber apron, but even so it was like standing for eight hours a day under a lukewarm blood-shower. At night I'd go home smelling of pig. I couldn't wash it out. Even after a hot bath, scrubbing hard, the stink was always there — like old bacon, or sausage, a dense greasy pig-stink that soaked deep into my skin and hair. Among other things, I remember, it was tough getting dates that summer. I felt isolated; I spent a lot of time alone. And there was also that draft notice tucked away in my wallet.

In the evenings I'd sometimes borrow my father's car and drive aimlessly around town, feeling sorry for myself, thinking about the war and the pig factory and how my life seemed to be collapsing toward slaughter. I felt paralyzed. All around me the options seemed to be narrowing, as if I were hurtling down a huge black funnel, the whole world squeezing in tight. There was no happy way out. The government had ended most graduate school deferments; the waiting lists for the National Guard and Reserves were impossibly long; my health was solid; I didn't qualify for CO status — no religious grounds, no history as a pacifist. Moreover, I could not claim to be opposed to war as a matter of general principle. There were occasions, I believed, when a nation was justified in using military force to achieve its ends, to stop a Hitler or some comparable evil, and I told myself that in such circumstances I would've willingly marched off to the battle. The problem, though, was that a draft board did not let you choose your war.

Beyond all this, or at the very center, was the raw fact of terror. I did not want to die. Not ever. But certainly not then, not there, not in a wrong war. Driving up Main Street, past the courthouse and the Ben Franklin store, I sometimes felt the fear spreading inside me like weeds. I imagined myself dead. I imagined myself doing things I could not do — charging an enemy position, taking aim at another human being.

At some point in mid-July I began thinking seriously about Canada. The border lay a few hundred miles north, an eight-hour drive. Both my conscience and my instincts were telling me to make a break for it, just take off and run like hell and never stop. In the beginning the idea seemed purely abstract, the word Canada printing itself out in my head; but after a time I could see particular shapes and images, the sorry details of my own future — a hotel room in Winnipeg, a battered old suitcase, my father's eyes as I tried to explain myself over the telephone. I could almost hear his voice, and my mother's. Run, I'd think. Then I'd think, Impossible. Then a second later I'd think, *Run.*

It was a kind of schizophrenia. A moral split. I couldn't make up my mind. I feared the war, yes, but I also feared exile. I was afraid of walking away from my own life, my friends and my family, my whole history, everything that mattered to me. I feared losing the respect of my parents. I feared the law. I feared ridicule and censure. My hometown was a conservative little spot on the prairie, a place where tradition counted, and it was easy to imagine people sitting around a table down at the old Gobbler Café on Main Street, coffee cups poised, the conversation slowly zeroing in on the young O'Brien kid, how the damned sissy had taken off for Canada. At night, when I couldn't sleep, I'd sometimes carry on fierce arguments with those people. I'd be screaming at them, telling them how much I detested their blind, thoughtless, automatic acquiescence to it all, their simpleminded patriotism, their prideful ignorance, their love-it-or-leave-it platitudes, how they were sending me off to fight a war they didn't understand and didn't want to understand. I held them responsible. By God, yes, I *did.* All of them — I held them personally and individually responsible — the polyestered Kiwanis boys, the merchants and farmers, the pious churchgoers, the chatty housewives, the PTA and the Lions club and the Veterans of Foreign Wars and the fine upstanding gentry out at the country club. They didn't know Bao Dai from the man in the moon. They didn't know history. They didn't know the first thing about Diem's tyranny, or the nature of Vietnamese nationalism, or the long colonialism of the French — this was all too damned complicated, it required some reading — but no matter, it was a war to stop the Communists, plain and simple, which was how they liked things, and you were a treasonous pussy if you had second thoughts about killing or dying for plain and simple reasons.

I was bitter, sure. But it was so much more than that. The emotions went from outrage to terror to bewilderment to guilt to sorrow and then back again to outrage. I felt a sickness inside me. Real disease.

Most of this I've told before, or at least hinted at, but what I have never told is the full truth. How I cracked. How at work one morning, standing on the pig line, I felt something break open in my chest. I don't know what it was. I'll never know. But it was real, I know that much, it was a physical rupture — a cracking-leaking-popping feeling. I remember dropping my water gun. Quickly, almost without thought, I took off my apron and walked out of the plant and drove home. It was midmorning, I remember, and the house was empty. Down in my chest there was still that leaking sensation, something very warm and precious spilling out, and I was covered with blood and hog-stink, and for a long while I just concentrated on holding myself together. I remember taking a hot shower. I remember packing a suitcase and carrying it out to the kitchen, standing very still for a few minutes, looking carefully at the familiar objects all around me. The old chrome toaster, the telephone, the pink and white Formica on the kitchen counters. The room was full of bright sunshine. Everything sparkled. My house, I thought. My life. I'm not sure how long I stood there, but later I scribbled out a short note to my parents.

What it said, exactly, I don't recall now. Something vague. Taking off, will call, love Tim.

∾

I drove north.

It's a blur now, as it was then, and all I remember is a sense of high velocity and the feel of the steering wheel in my hands. I was riding on adrenaline. A giddy feeling, in a way, except there was the dreamy edge of impossibility to it—like running a dead-end maze—no way out—it couldn't come to a happy conclusion and yet I was doing it anyway because it was all I could think of to do. It was pure flight, fast and mindless. I had no plan. Just hit the border at high speed and crash through and keep on running. Near dusk I passed through Bemidji, then turned northeast toward International Falls. I spent the night in the car behind a closed-down gas station a half mile from the border. In the morning, after gassing up, I headed straight west along the Rainy River, which separates Minnesota from Canada, and which for me separated one life from another. The land was mostly wilderness. Here and there I passed a motel or bait shop, but otherwise the country unfolded in great sweeps of pine and birch and sumac. Though it was still August, the air already had the smell of October, football season, piles of yellow-red leaves, everything crisp and clean. I remember a huge blue sky. Off to my right was the Rainy River, wide as a lake in places, and beyond the Rainy River was Canada.

For a while I just drove, not aiming at anything, then in the late morning I began looking for a place to lie low for a day or two. I was exhausted, and scared sick, and around noon I pulled into an old fishing resort called the Tip Top Lodge. Actually it was not a lodge at all, just eight or nine tiny yellow cabins clustered on a peninsula that jutted northward into the Rainy River. The place was in sorry shape. There was a dangerous wooden dock, an old minnow tank, a flimsy tar paper boathouse along the shore. The main building, which stood in a cluster of pines on high ground, seemed to lean heavily to one side, like a cripple, the roof sagging toward Canada. Briefly, I thought about turning around, just giving up, but then I got out of the car and walked up to the front porch.

The man who opened the door that day is the hero of my life. How do I say this without sounding sappy? Blurt it out—the man saved me. He offered exactly what I needed, without questions, without any words at all. He took me in. He was there at the critical time—a silent, watchful presence. Six days later, when it ended, I was unable to find a proper way to thank him, and I never have, and so, if nothing else, this story represents a small gesture of gratitude twenty years overdue.

Even after two decades I can close my eyes and return to that porch at the Tip Top Lodge. I can see the old guy staring at me. Elroy Berdahl: eighty-one years old, skinny and shrunken and mostly bald. He wore a flannel shirt and brown work pants. In one hand, I remember, he carried a green apple, a small paring knife in the other. His eyes had the bluish gray color of a razor blade, the same polished shine, and as he peered up at me I felt a strange sharpness, almost painful, a cutting sensation, as if his gaze were somehow slicing me open. In part, no doubt, it was my own sense of guilt, but even so I'm absolutely certain that the old man took one look and went right to the heart of things—a kid in trouble. When I asked for a room, Elroy made a little clicking sound with his tongue. He nodded, led me out to one of the cabins, and dropped a key in my hand. I remember smiling at him. I also remember wishing I hadn't. The old man shook his head as if to tell me it wasn't worth the bother.

"Dinner at five-thirty," he said. "You eat fish?"

"Anything," I said.

Elroy grunted and said, "I'll bet."

∾

We spent six days together at the Tip Top Lodge. Just the two of us. Tourist season was over, and there were no boats on the river, and the wilderness seemed to withdraw into a great permanent stillness. Over those six days Elroy Berdahl and I took most of our meals together. In the mornings we sometimes went out on long hikes into the woods, and at night we played Scrabble or listened to records or sat reading in front of his big stone fireplace. At times I felt the awkwardness of an intruder, but Elroy accepted me into his quiet routine without fuss or ceremony. He took my presence for granted, the same way he might've sheltered a stray cat—no wasted sighs or pity—and there was never any talk about it. Just the opposite. What I remember more than anything is the man's willful, almost ferocious silence. In all that time together, all those hours, he never asked the obvious questions: Why was I there? Why alone? Why so preoccupied? If Elroy was curious about any of this, he was careful never to put it into words.

My hunch, though, is that he already knew. At least the basics. After all, it was 1968, and guys were burning draft cards, and Canada was just a boat ride away. Elroy Berdahl was no hick. His bedroom, I remember, was cluttered with books and newspapers. He killed me at the Scrabble board, barely concentrating, and on those occasions when speech was necessary he had a way of compressing large thoughts into small, cryptic packets of language. One evening, just at sunset, he pointed up at an owl circling over the violet-lighted forest to the west.

"Hey, O'Brien," he said. "There's Jesus."

The man was sharp—he didn't miss much. Those razor eyes. Now and then he'd catch me staring out at the river, at the far shore, and I could almost hear the tumblers clicking in his head. Maybe I'm wrong, but I doubt it.

One thing for certain, he knew I was in desperate trouble. And he knew I couldn't talk about it. The wrong word—or even the right word—and I would've disappeared. I was wired and jittery. My skin felt too tight. After supper one evening I vomited and went back to my cabin and lay down for a few moments and then vomited again; another time, in the middle of the afternoon, I began sweating and couldn't shut it off. I went through whole days feeling dizzy with sorrow. I couldn't sleep; I couldn't lie still. At night I'd toss around in bed, half awake, half dreaming, imagining how I'd sneak down to the beach and quietly push one of the old man's boats out into the river and start paddling my way toward Canada. There were times when I thought I'd gone off the psychic edge. I couldn't tell up from down, I was just falling, and late in the night I'd lie there watching weird pictures spin through my head. Getting chased by the Border Patrol—helicopters and searchlights and barking dogs—I'd be crashing through the woods, I'd be down on my hands and knees—people shouting out my name—the law closing in on all sides—my hometown draft board and the FBI and the Royal Canadian Mounted Police. It all seemed crazy and impossible. Twenty-one years old, an ordinary kid with all the ordinary dreams and ambitions, and all I wanted was to live the life I was born to—a mainstream life—I loved baseball and hamburgers and cherry Cokes—and now I was off on the margins of exile, leaving my country forever, and it seemed so impossible and terrible and sad.

I'm not sure how I made it through those six days. Most of it I can't remember. On two or three afternoons, to pass some time, I helped Elroy get the place ready for winter, sweeping down the cabins and hauling in the boats, little chores that kept my body moving. The days were cool and bright. The nights were very dark. One morning the old man showed me how to split and stack firewood, and for several hours we just worked in silence out behind his house. At one point, I remember, Elroy put down his maul and looked at me for a long time, his lips drawn as if framing a difficult question, but then he shook his head and went back to work. The man's self-control was amazing. He never pried. He never put me in a position that required lies or denials. To an extent, I suppose, his reticence was typical of that part of Minnesota, where privacy still held value, and even if I'd been walking around with some horrible deformity—four arms and three heads—I'm sure the old man would've talked about everything except those extra arms and heads. Simple politeness was part of it. But even more than that, I think, the man understood that words were insufficient. The problem had gone beyond discussion. During that long summer I'd been over and over the various arguments, all the pros and cons, and it was no longer a question that could be decided by an act of pure reason. Intellect had come up against emotion. My conscience told me to run, but some irrational and powerful force was resisting, like a weight pushing me toward the war. What it came down to, stupidly, was a sense of shame. Hot, stupid shame. I did not want people to think badly of me. Not my parents, not my brother and sister, not even the folks down at the Gobbler Café. I was ashamed to be there at the Tip Top Lodge. I was ashamed of my conscience, ashamed to be doing the right thing.

Some of this Elroy must've understood. Not the details, of course, but the plain fact of crisis.

Although the old man never confronted me about it, there was one occasion when he came close to forcing the whole thing out into the open. It was early evening, and we'd just finished supper, and over coffee and dessert I asked him about my bill, how much I owed so far. For a long while the old man squinted down at the tablecloth.

"Well, the basic rate," he said, "is fifty bucks a night. Not counting meals. This makes four nights, right?"

I nodded. I had three hundred and twelve dollars in my wallet.

Elroy kept his eyes on the tablecloth. "Now that's an on-season price. To be fair, I suppose we should knock it down a peg or two." He leaned back in his chair. "What's a reasonable number, you figure?"

"I don't know," I said. "Forty?"

"Forty's good. Forty a night. Then we tack on food—say another hundred? Two hundred sixty total?"

"I guess."

He raised his eyebrows. "Too much?"

"No, that's fair. It's fine. Tomorrow, though . . . I think I'd better take off tomorrow."

Elroy shrugged and began clearing the table. For a time he fussed with the dishes, whistling to himself as if the subject had been settled. After a second he slapped his hands together.

"You know what we forgot?" he said. "We forgot wages. Those odd jobs you done. What we have to do, we have to figure out what your time's worth. Your last job—how much did you pull in an hour?"

"Not enough," I said.

"A bad one?"

"Yes. Pretty bad."

Slowly then, without intending any long sermon, I told him about my days at the pig plant. It began as a straight recitation of the facts, but before I could stop myself I was talking about the blood clots and the water gun and how the smell had soaked into my skin and how I couldn't wash it away. I went on for a long time. I told him about wild hogs squealing in my dreams, the sounds of butchery, slaughterhouse sounds, and how I'd sometimes wake up with that greasy pig-stink in my throat.

When I was finished, Elroy nodded at me.

"Well, to be honest," he said, "when you first showed up here, I wondered about all that. The aroma, I mean. Smelled like you was awful damned fond of pork chops." The old man almost smiled. He made a snuffling sound, then sat down with a pencil and a piece of paper. "So what'd this crud job pay? Ten bucks an hour? Fifteen?"

"Less."

Elroy shook his head. "Let's make it fifteen. You put in twenty-five hours here, easy. That's three hundred seventy-five bucks total wages. We subtract the two hundred sixty for food and lodging, I still owe you a hundred and fifteen."

He took four fifties out of his shirt pocket and laid them on the table.

"Call it even," he said.

"No."

"Pick it up. Get yourself a haircut."

The money lay on the table for the rest of the evening. It was still there when I went back to my cabin. In the morning, though, I found an envelope tacked to my door. Inside were the four fifties and a two-word note that said EMERGENCY FUND.

The man knew.

∞

Looking back after twenty years, I sometimes wonder if the events of that summer didn't happen in some other dimension, a place where your life exists before you've lived it, and where it goes afterward. None of it ever seemed real. During my time at the Tip Top Lodge I had the feeling that I'd slipped out of my own skin, hovering a few feet away while some poor yo-yo with my name and face tried to make his way toward a future he didn't understand and didn't want. Even now I can see myself as I was then. It's like watching an old home movie: I'm young and tan and fit. I've got hair—lots of it. I don't smoke or drink. I'm wearing faded blue jeans and a white polo shirt. I can see myself sitting on Elroy Berdahl's dock near dusk one evening, the sky a bright shimmering pink, and I'm finishing up a letter to my parents that tells what I'm about to do and why I'm doing it and how sorry I am that I'd never found the courage to talk to them about it. I ask them not to be angry. I try to explain some of my feelings, but there aren't enough words, and so I just say that it's a thing that has to be done. At the end of the letter I talk about the vacations we used to take up in this north country, at a place called Whitefish Lake, and how the scenery here reminds me of those good times. I tell them I'm fine. I tell them I'll write again from Winnipeg or Montreal or wherever I end up.

∞

On my last full day, the sixth day, the old man took me out fishing on the Rainy River. The afternoon was sunny and cold. A stiff breeze came in from the north, and I remember how the little fourteen-foot boat made sharp rocking motions as we pushed off from the dock. The current was fast. All around us, I remember, there was a vastness to the world, an unpeopled rawness, just the trees and the sky and the water reaching out toward nowhere. The air had the brittle scent of October.

For ten or fifteen minutes Elroy held a course upstream, the river choppy and silver-gray, then he turned straight north and put the engine on full throttle. I felt the bow lift beneath me. I remember the wind in my ears, the sound of the old outboard Evinrude. For a time I didn't pay attention to anything, just feeling the cold spray against my face, but then it occurred to me that at some point we must've passed into Canadian waters, across that dotted line between two different worlds, and I remember a sudden tightness in my chest as I looked up and watched the far shore come at me. This wasn't a daydream. It was tangible and real. As we came in toward land, Elroy cut the engine, letting the boat fishtail lightly about twenty yards off shore. The old man didn't look at me or speak. Bending down, he opened up his tackle box and busied himself with a bobber and a piece of wire leader, humming to himself, his eyes down.

It struck me then that he must've planned it. I'll never be certain, of course, but I think he meant to bring me up against the realities, to guide me across the river and to take me to the edge and to stand a kind of vigil as I chose a life for myself.

I remember staring at the old man, then at my hands, then at Canada. The shoreline was dense with brush and timber. I could see tiny red berries on the bushes. I could see a squirrel up in one of the birch trees, a big crow looking at me from a boulder along the river. That close—twenty yards—and I could see the delicate latticework of the leaves, the texture of the soil, the browned needles beneath the pines, the configurations of geology and human history. Twenty yards. I could've done it. I could've jumped and started swimming for my life. Inside me, in my chest, I felt a terrible squeezing pressure. Even now, as I write this, I can still feel that tightness. And I want you to feel it—the wind coming off the river, the waves, the silence, the wooded frontier. You're at the bow of a boat on the Rainy River. You're twenty-one years old, you're scared, and there's a hard squeezing pressure in your chest.

What would you do?

Would you jump? Would you feel pity for yourself? Would you think about your family and your childhood and your dreams and all you're leaving behind? Would it hurt? Would it feel like dying? Would you cry, as I did?

I tried to swallow it back. I tried to smile, except I was crying.

Now, perhaps, you can understand why I've never told this story before. It's not just the embarrassment of tears. That's part of it, no doubt, but what embarrasses me much more, and always will, is the paralysis that took my heart. A moral freeze: I couldn't decide, I couldn't act, I couldn't comport myself with even a pretense of modest human dignity.

All I could do was cry. Quietly, not bawling, just the chest-chokes.

At the rear of the boat Elroy Berdahl pretended not to notice. He held a fishing rod in his hands, his head bowed to hide his eyes. He kept humming a soft, monotonous little tune. Everywhere, it seemed, in the trees and water and sky, a great worldwide sadness came pressing down on me, a crushing sorrow, sorrow like I had never known it before. And what was so sad, I realized, was that Canada had become a pitiful fantasy. Silly and hopeless. It was no longer a possibility. Right then, with the shore so close, I understood that I would not do what I should do. I would not swim away from my hometown and my country and my life. I would not be brave. That old image of myself as a hero, as a man of conscience and courage, all that was just a threadbare pipe dream. Bobbing there on the Rainy River, looking back at the Minnesota shore, I felt a sudden swell of helplessness come over me, a drowning sensation, as if I had toppled overboard and was being swept away by the silver waves. Chunks of my own history flashed by. I saw a seven-year-old boy in a white cowboy hat and a Lone Ranger mask and a pair of holstered six-shooters; I saw a twelve-year-old Little League shortstop pivoting to turn a double play; I saw a sixteen-year-old kid decked out for his first prom, looking spiffy in a white tux and a black bow tie, his hair cut short and flat, his shoes freshly polished. My whole life seemed to spill out into the river, swirling away from me, everything I had ever been or ever wanted to be. I couldn't get my breath; I couldn't stay afloat; I couldn't tell which way to swim. A hallucination, I suppose, but it was as real as anything I would ever feel. I saw my parents calling to me from the far shoreline. I saw my brother and sister, all the townsfolk, the mayor and the entire Chamber of Commerce and all my old teachers and girlfriends and high school buddies. Like some weird sporting event: everybody screaming from the sidelines, rooting me on—a loud stadium roar. Hotdogs and popcorn—stadium smells, stadium heat. A squad of cheerleaders did cartwheels along the banks of the Rainy River; they had megaphones and pompoms and smooth brown thighs. The crowd swayed left and right. A marching band played fight songs. All my aunts and uncles were there, and Abraham Lincoln, and Saint George, and a nine-year-old girl named Linda who had died of a brain tumor back in fifth grade, and several members of the United States Senate, and a blind poet scribbling notes, and LBJ, and Huck Finn, and Abbie Hoffman, and all the dead soldiers back from the grave, and the many thousands who were later to die—villagers with terrible burns, little kids without arms or legs—yes, and the Joint Chiefs of Staff were there, and a couple of popes, and a first lieutenant named Jimmy Cross, and the last surviving veteran of the American Civil War, and Jane Fonda dressed up as Barbarella, and an old man sprawled beside a pigpen, and my grandfather, and Gary Cooper, and a kind-faced woman carrying an umbrella and a copy of Plato's *Republic*, and a million ferocious citizens waving flags of all shapes and colors—people in hard hats, people in headbands—they were all whooping and chanting and urging me toward one shore or the other. I saw faces from my distant past and distant future. My wife was there. My unborn daughter waved at me, and my two sons hopped up and down, and a drill sergeant named Blyton sneered and shot up a finger and shook his head. There was a choir in bright purple robes. There was a cabbie from the Bronx. There was a slim young man I would one day kill with a hand grenade along a red clay trail outside the village of My Khe.

The little aluminum boat rocked softly beneath me. There was the wind and the sky.

I tried to will myself overboard.

I gripped the edge of the boat and leaned forward and thought, *Now.*

I did try. It just wasn't possible.

All those eyes on me—the town, the whole universe—and I couldn't risk the embarrassment. It was as if there were an audience to my life, that swirl of faces along the river, and in my head I could hear people screaming at me. Traitor! they yelled. Turncoat! Pussy! I felt myself blush. I couldn't tolerate it. I couldn't endure the mockery, or the disgrace, or the patriotic ridicule. Even in my imagination, the shore just twenty yards away, I couldn't make myself be brave. It had nothing to do with morality. Embarrassment, that's all it was.

And right then I submitted.

I would go to the war—I would kill and maybe die—because I was embarrassed not to.

That was the sad thing. And so I sat in the bow of the boat and cried.

It was loud now. Loud, hard crying.

Elroy Berdahl remained quiet. He kept fishing. He worked his line with the tips of his fingers, patiently, squinting out at his red and white bobber on the Rainy River. His eyes were flat and impassive. He didn't speak. He was simply there, like the river and the late-summer sun. And yet by his presence, his mute watchfulness, he made it real. He was the true audience. He was a witness, like God, or like the gods, who look on in absolute silence as we live our lives, as we make our choices or fail to make them.

"Ain't biting," he said.

Then after a time the old man pulled in his line and turned the boat back toward Minnesota.

∾

I don't remember saying goodbye. That last night we had dinner together, and I went to bed early, and in the morning Elroy fixed breakfast for me. When I told him I'd be leaving, the old man nodded as if he already knew. He looked down at the table and smiled.

At some point later in the morning it's possible that we shook hands—I just don't remember—but I do know that by the time I'd finished packing the old man had disappeared. Around noon, when I took my suitcase out to the car, I noticed that his old black pickup truck was no longer parked in front of the house. I went inside and waited for a while, but I felt a bone certainty that he wouldn't be back. In a way, I thought, it was appropriate. I washed up the breakfast dishes, left his two hundred dollars on the kitchen counter, got into the car, and drove south toward home.

The day was cloudy. I passed through towns with familiar names, through the pine forests and down to the prairie, and then to Vietnam, where I was a soldier, and then home again. I survived, but it's not a happy ending. I was a coward. I went to the war.

~ 1990

ZZ Packer

∿ Drinking Coffee Elsewhere

ZZ Packer was born in Chicago in 1973 and grew up in Atlanta, Georgia, and Louisville, Kentucky. She received a B.A. from Yale University, an M.A. from Johns Hopkins University, and an M.F.A. from the Iowa Writers' Workshop. She subsequently attended Stanford University, where she was awarded a Wallace Stegner

> *"I assumed that becoming a professional writer was out of my hands, but writing every day (or nearly every day) is something one does, rather than something one becomes."*
>
> ~ from *The New Yorker*, June 14, 2010

Fellowship in creative writing. Her short story "Drinking Coffee Elsewhere" first appeared in a Debut Fiction issue of *The New Yorker* and became the title story of her first book, which was a New York Times Notable Book and a finalist for the PEN/Faulkner Award. Packer's stories have twice appeared in *Best American Short Stories*, and she has been awarded a Guggenheim Fellowship and was named one of *Granta* Magazine's Best Young American Novelists.

Orientation games began the day I arrived at Yale from Baltimore. In my group we played heady, frustrating games for smart people. One game appeared to be charades reinterpreted by existentialists; another involved listening to rocks. Then a freshman counsellor made everyone play Trust. The idea was that if you had the faith to fall backward and wait for four scrawny former high school geniuses to catch you, just before your head cracked on the slate sidewalk, then you might learn to trust your fellow students. Russian roulette sounded like a better way to go.

"No way," I said. The white boys were waiting for me to fall, holding their arms out for me, sincerely, gallantly. "No fucking way."

"It's all cool, it's all cool," the counselor said. Her hair was a shade of blond I'd seen only on *Playboy* covers, and she raised her hands as though backing away from a growling dog. "Sister," she said, in an I'm-down-with-the-struggle voice, "you don't have to play this game. As a person of color, you shouldn't have to fit into any white, patriarchal system."

I said, "It's a bit too late for that."

In the next game, all I had to do was wait in a circle until it was my turn to say what inanimate object I wanted to be. One guy said he'd like to be a gadfly, like Socrates. "Stop me if I wax Platonic," he said. I didn't bother mentioning that gadflies weren't inanimate—it didn't seem to make a difference. The girl next to him was eating a rice cake. She wanted to be the Earth, she said. Earth with a capital E.

There was one other black person in the circle. He wore an Exeter T-shirt and his overly elastic expressions resembled a series of facial exercises. At the end of each person's turn, he smiled and bobbed his head with unfettered enthusiasm. "Oh, that was good," he said, as if the game were an experiment he'd set up and the results were turning out better than he'd expected. "Good, good, good!"

When it was my turn I said, "My name is Dina, and if I had to be any object, I guess I'd be a revolver." The sunlight dulled as if on cue. Clouds passed rapidly overhead, presaging rain. I don't know why I said it. Until that moment I'd been good in all the ways that were meant to matter. I was an honor roll student—though I'd learned long ago not to mention it in the part of Baltimore where I lived. Suddenly I was hard-bitten and recalcitrant, the kind of kid who took pleasure in sticking pins into cats; the kind who chased down smart kids to spray them with Mace.

"A revolver," a counselor said, stroking his chin, as if it had grown a rabbinical beard. "Could you please elaborate?"

The black guy cocked his head and frowned, as if the beakers and Erlenmeyer flasks of his experiment had grown legs and scurried off.

$$\infty$$

"You were just kidding," the dean said, "about wiping out all of mankind. That, I suppose, was a joke." She squinted at me. One of her hands curved atop the other to form a pink, freckled molehill on her desk.

"Well," I said, "maybe I meant it at the time." I quickly saw that this was not the answer she wanted. "I don't know. I think it's the architecture."

Through the dimming light of the dean's office window, I could see the fortress of the old campus. On my ride from the bus station to the campus, I'd barely glimpsed New Haven—a flash of crumpled building here, a trio of straggly kids there. A lot like Baltimore. But everything had changed when we reached those streets hooded by gothic buildings. I imagined how the college must have looked when it was founded, when most of the students owned slaves. I pictured men wearing tights and knickers, smoking pipes.

"The architecture," the dean repeated. She bit her lip and seemed to be making a calculation of some sort. I noticed that she blinked less often than most people. I sat there, intrigued, waiting to see how long it would be before she blinked again.

∾

My revolver comment won me a year's worth of psychiatric counseling, weekly meetings with Dean Guest, and—since the parents of the roommate I'd never met weren't too hip on the idea of their Amy sharing a bunk bed with a budding homicidal loony—my very own room.

Shortly after getting my first C ever, I also received the first knock on my door. The female counselors never knocked. The dean had spoken to them; I was a priority. Every other day, right before dinnertime, they'd look in on me, unannounced. "Just checking up," a counselor would say. It was the voice of a suburban mother in training. By the second week, I had made a point of sitting in a chair in front of the door, just when I expected a counselor to pop her head around. This was intended to startle them. I also made a point of being naked. The unannounced visits ended.

The knocking persisted. Through the peephole I saw a white face, distorted and balloonish.

"Let me in." The person looked like a boy but sounded like a girl. "Let me in," the voice repeated.

"Not a chance," I said. I had a suicide single, and I wanted to keep it that way. No roommates, no visitors.

Then the person began to sob, and I heard a back slump against the door. If I hadn't known the person was white from the peephole, I'd have known it from a display like this. Black people didn't knock on strangers' doors, crying. Not that I understood the black people at Yale. Most of them were from New York and tried hard to pretend that they hadn't gone to prep schools. And there was something pitiful in how cool they were. Occasionally one would reach out to me with missionary zeal, but I'd rebuff the person with haughty silence.

"I don't have anyone to talk to!" the person on the other side of the door cried.

"That is correct."

"When I was a child," the person said, "I played by myself in a corner of the schoolyard all alone. I hated dolls and I hated games, animals were not friendly and birds flew away. If anyone was looking for me I hid behind a tree and cried out 'I am an orphan—'"

I opened the door. It was a she.

"Plagiarist!" I yelled. She had just recited a Frank O'Hara poem as though she'd thought it up herself. I knew the poem because it was one of the few things I'd been forced to read that I wished I'd written myself.

The girl turned to face me, smiling weakly, as though her triumph was not in getting me to open the door but in the fact that she was able to smile at all when she was so accustomed to crying. She was large but not obese, and crying had turned her face the color of raw chicken. She blew her nose into the waist end of her T-shirt, revealing a pale belly.

"How do you know that poem?"

She sniffed. "I'm in your Contemporary Poetry class."

She said she was Canadian and her name was Heidi, although she said she wanted people to call her Henrik. "That's a guy's name," I said. "What do you want? A sex change?"

She looked at me with so little surprise that I suspected she hadn't discounted this as an option. Then her story came out in teary, hiccup-like bursts. She had sucked some "cute guy's dick" and he'd told everybody and now people thought she was "a slut."

"Why'd you suck his dick? Aren't you a lesbian?"

She fit the bill. Short hair, hard, roach-stomping shoes. Dressed like an aspiring plumber. And then there was the name Henrik. The lesbians I'd seen on TV were wiry, thin strips of muscle, but Heidi was round and soft and had a moonlike face. Drab henna-colored hair. And lesbians had cats. "Do you have a cat?" I asked.

Her eyes turned glossy with new tears. "No," she said, her voice wavering, "and I'm not a lesbian. Are you?"

"Do I look like one?" I said.

She didn't answer.

"O.K." I said. "I could suck a guy's dick, too, if I wanted. But I don't. The human penis is one of the most germ-ridden objects there is." Heidi looked at me, unconvinced. "What I meant to say," I began again, "is that I don't like anybody. Period. Guys or girls. I'm a misanthrope."

"I am, too."

"No," I said, guiding her back through my door and out into the hallway. "You're not."

"Have you had dinner?" she asked. "Let's go to Commons."

I pointed to a pyramid of ramen noodle packages on my windowsill. "See that? That means I never have to go to Commons. Aside from class, I have contact with no one."

"I hate it here, too," she said. "I should have gone to McGill, eh."

"The way to feel better," I said, "is to get some ramen and lock yourself in your room. Everyone will forget about you and that guy's dick and you won't have to see anyone ever again. If anyone looks for you—"

"I'll hide behind a tree."

∞

"A revolver?" Dr. Raeburn said, flipping through a manila folder. He looked up at me as if to ask another question, but he didn't.

Dr. Raeburn was the psychiatrist. He had the gray hair and whiskers of a Civil War general. He was also a chain smoker with beige teeth and a navy wool jacket smeared with ash. He asked about the revolver at the beginning of my first visit. When I was unable to explain myself, he smiled, as if this were perfectly reasonable.

"Tell me about your parents."

I wondered what he already had on file. The folder was thick, though I hadn't said a thing of significance since Day One.

"My father was a dick and my mother seemed to like him."

He patted his pockets for his cigarettes. "That's some heavy stuff," he said. "How do you feel about Dad?" The man couldn't say the word "father." "Is Dad someone you see often?"

"I hate my father almost as much as I hate the word 'Dad.' "

He started tapping his cigarette.

"You can't smoke in here."

"That's right," he said, and slipped the cigarette back into the packet. He smiled, widening his eyes brightly. "Don't ever start."

∾

I thought that that first encounter would be the last of Heidi or Henrik, or whatever, but then her head appeared in a window of Linsly-Chit during my Chaucer class. A few days later, she swooped down a flight of stairs in Harkness, following me. She hailed me from across Elm Street and found me in the Sterling Library stacks. After one of my meetings with Dr. Raeburn, she was waiting for me outside Health Services, legs crossed, cleaning her fingernails.

"You know," she said, as we walked through Old Campus, "you've got to stop eating ramen. Not only does it lack a single nutrient but it's full of MSG."

I wondered why she even bothered, and was vaguely flattered she cared, but I said, "I like eating chemicals. It keeps the skin radiant."

"There's also hepatitis." She knew how to get my attention — mention a disease.

"You get hepatitis from unwashed lettuce," I said. "If there's anything safe from the perils of the food chain, it's ramen."

"But do you refrigerate what you don't eat? Each time you reheat it, you're killing good bacteria, which then can't keep the bad bacteria in check. A guy got sick from reheating Chinese noodles, and his son died from it. I read it in the *Times.*" With this, she put a jovial arm around my neck. I continued walking, a little stunned. Then, just as quickly, she dropped her arm and stopped walking. I stopped, too.

"Did you notice that I put my arm around you?"

"Yes," I said. "Next time, I'll have to chop it off."

"I don't want you to get sick," she said. "Let's eat at Commons."

In the cold air, her arm had felt good.

∞

The problem with Commons was that it was too big; its ceiling was as high as a cathedral's, but below it there were no awestruck worshippers, only eighteen-year-olds at heavy wooden tables, chatting over veal patties and Jell-O.

We got our food, tacos stuffed with meat substitute, and made our way through the maze of tables. The Koreans had a table. Each singing group had a table. The crew team sat at a long table of its own. We passed the black table. Heidi was so plump and moonfaced that the sheer quantity of her flesh accentuated just how white she was. The black students gave me a long, hard stare.

"How you doing, sista?" a guy asked, his voice full of accusation, eyeballing me as though I were clad in a Klansman's sheet and hood. "I guess we won't see you till graduation."

"If," I said, "you graduate."

The remark was not well received. As I walked past, I heard protests, angry and loud, as if they'd discovered a cheat at their poker game. Heidi and I found an unoccupied table along the periphery, which was isolated and dark. We sat down. Heidi prayed over her tacos.

"I thought you didn't believe in God," I said.

"Not in the God depicted in the Judeo-Christian Bible, but I do believe that nature's essence is a spirit that—"

"All right," I said. I had begun to eat, and cubes of diced tomato fell from my mouth when I spoke. "Stop right there. Tacos and spirits don't mix."

"You've always got to be so flip," she said. "I'm going to apply for another friend."

"There's always Mr. Dick," I said. "Slurp, slurp."

"You are so lame. So unbelievably lame. I'm going out with Mr. Dick. Thursday night at Atticus. His name is Keith."

Heidi hadn't mentioned Mr. Dick since the day I'd met her. That was more than a month ago and we'd spent a lot of that time together. I checked for signs that she was lying; her habit of smiling too much, her eyes bright and cheeks full so that she looked like a chipmunk. But she looked normal. Pleased, even, to see me so flustered.

"You're insane! What are you going to do this time?" I asked. "Sleep with him? Then when he makes fun of you, what? Come pound your head on my door reciting the collected poems of Sylvia Plath?"

"He's going to apologize for before. And don't call me insane. You're the one going to the psychiatrist."

"Well, I'm not going to suck his dick, that's for sure."

She put her arm around me in mock comfort, but I pushed it off, and ignored her. She touched my shoulder again, and I turned, annoyed, but it wasn't Heidi after all; a sepia-toned boy dressed in khakis and a crisp plaid shirt was standing behind me. He thrust a hot-pink square of paper toward me without a word, then briskly made his way toward the other end of Commons, where the crowds blossomed. Heidi leaned over and read it: "Wear Black Leather — the Less, the Better."

"It's a gay party," I said, crumpling the card. "He thinks we're fucking gay."

∾

Heidi and I signed on to work at the Saybrook dining hall as dishwashers. The job consisted of dumping food from plates and trays into a vat of rushing water. It seemed straightforward, but then I learned better. You wouldn't believe what people could do with food until you worked in a dish room. Lettuce and crackers and soup would be bullied into a pulp in the bowl of some bored anorexic; ziti would be mixed with honey and granola; trays would appear heaped with mashed potato snow women with melted chocolate ice cream for hair. Frat boys arrived at the dish-room window, en masse. They liked to fill glasses with food, then seal them, airtight, onto their trays. If you tried to prize them off, milk, Worcestershire sauce, peas, chunks of bread vomited onto your dish-room uniform.

When this happened one day in the middle of the lunch rush, for what seemed like the hundredth time, I tipped the tray toward one of the frat boys as he turned to walk away, popping the glasses off so that the mess spurted onto his Shetland sweater.

He looked down at his sweater. "Lesbo bitch!"

"No," I said, "that would be your mother."

Heidi, next to me, clenched my arm in support, but I remained motion-less, waiting to see what the frat boy would do. He glared at me for a minute, then walked away.

"Let's take a smoke break," Heidi said.

I didn't smoke, but Heidi had begun to, because she thought it would help her lose weight. As I hefted a stack of glasses through the steamer, she lit up.

"Soft packs remind me of you," she said. "Just when you've smoked them all and you think there's none left, there's always one more, hiding in that little crushed corner." Before I could respond she said, "Oh, God. Not another mouse. You know whose job that is."

By the end of the rush, the floor mats got full and slippery with food. This was when mice tended to appear, scurrying over our shoes; more often than not, a mouse got caught in the grating that covered the drains in the floor. Some-times the mouse was already dead by the time we noticed it. This one was alive.

"No way," I said. "This time you're going to help. Get some gloves and a trash bag."

"That's all I'm getting. I'm not getting that mouse out of there."

"Put on the gloves," I ordered. She winced, but put them on. "Reach down," I said. "At an angle, so you get at its middle. Otherwise, if you try to get it by its tail, the tail will break off."

"This is filthy, eh."

"That's why we're here," I said. "To clean up filth. Eh."

She reached down, but would not touch the mouse. I put my hand around her arm and pushed it till her hand made contact. The cries from the mouse were soft, songlike. "Oh, my God," she said. "Oh, my God, ohmigod." She wrestled it out of the grating and turned her head away.

"Don't you let it go," I said.

"Where's the food bag? It'll smother itself if I drop it in the food bag. Quick," she said, her head still turned away, her eyes closed. "Lead me to it."

"No. We are not going to smother this mouse. We've got to break its neck."

"You're one heartless bitch."

I wondered how to explain that if death is unavoidable it should be quick and painless. My mother had died slowly. At the hospital, they'd said it was kidney failure, but I knew that, in the end, it was my father. He made her so scared to live in her own home that she was finally driven away from it in an ambulance.

"Breaking its neck will save it the pain of smothering," I said. "Breaking its neck is more humane. Take the trash bag and cover it so you won't get any blood on you, then crush."

The loud jets of the steamer had shut off automatically and the dish room grew quiet. Heidi breathed in deeply, then crushed the mouse. She shuddered, disgusted. "Now what?"

"What do you mean, 'now what?' Throw the little bastard in the trash."

∾

At our third session, I told Dr. Raeburn I didn't mind if he smoked. He sat on the sill of his open window, smoking behind a jungle screen of office plants.

We spent the first ten minutes discussing the *Iliad*, and whether or not the text actually states that Achilles had been dipped in the River Styx. He said it did, and I said it didn't. After we'd finished with the *Iliad*, and with my new job in what he called "the scullery," he asked questions about my parents. I told him nothing. It was none of his business. Instead, I talked about Heidi. I told him about that day in Commons, Heidi's plan to go on a date with Mr. Dick, and the invitation we'd been given to the gay party.

"You seem preoccupied by this soirée." He arched his eyebrows at the word "soirée."

"Wouldn't you be?"

"Dina," he said slowly, in a way that made my name seem like a song title, "have you ever had a romantic interest?"

"You want to know if I've ever had a boyfriend?" I said. "Just go ahead and ask if I've ever fucked anybody."

This appeared to surprise him. "I think that you are having a crisis of identity," he said.

"Oh, is that what this is?"

His profession had taught him not to roll his eyes. Instead, his exasperation revealed itself in a tiny pursing of his lips, as though he'd just tasted something awful and was trying very hard not to offend the cook.

"It doesn't have to be, as you say, someone you've fucked, it doesn't have to be a boyfriend," he said.

"Well, what are you trying to say? If it's not a boy, then you're saying it's a girl—"

"Calm down. It could be a crush, Dina." He lit one cigarette off another. "A crush on a male teacher, a crush on a dog, for heaven's sake. An interest. Not necessarily a relationship."

It was sacrifice time. If I could spend the next half hour talking about some boy, then I'd have given him what he wanted.

So I told him about the boy with the nice shoes.

I was sixteen and had spent the last few coins in my pocket on bus fare to buy groceries. I didn't like going to the Super Fresh two blocks away from my house, plunking government food stamps into the hands of the cashiers.

"There she go reading," one of them once said, even though I was only carrying a book. "Don't your eyes get tired?"

On Greenmount Avenue you could read schoolbooks—that was understandable. The government and your teachers forced you to read them. But anything else was antisocial. It meant you'd rather submit to the words of some white dude than shoot the breeze with your neighbors.

I hated those cashiers, and I hated them seeing me with food stamps, so I took the bus and shopped elsewhere. That day, I got off the bus at Govans, and though the neighborhood was black like my own—hair salon after hair salon of airbrushed signs promising arabesque hair styles and inch-long fingernails—the houses were neat and orderly, nothing at all like Greenmount, where every other house had at least one shattered window. The store was well swept, and people quietly checked long grocery lists—no screaming kids, no loud cashier-customer altercations. I got the groceries and left the store.

I decided to walk back. It was a fall day, and I walked for blocks. Then I sensed someone following me. I walked more quickly, my arms around the sack, the leafy lettuce tickling my nose. I didn't want to hold the sack so close that it would break the eggs or squash the hamburger buns, but it was slipping, and as I looked behind a boy my age, maybe older, rushed toward me.

"Let me help you," he said.

"That's all right." I set the bag on the sidewalk. Maybe I saw his face, maybe it was handsome enough, but what I noticed first, splayed on either side of the bag, were his shoes. They were nice shoes, real leather, a stitched design like a widow's peak on each one, or like birds' wings, and for the first time in my life I understood what people meant when they said "wing-tip shoes."

"I watched you carry them groceries out that store, then you look around, like you're lost, but like you liked being lost, then you walk down the sidewalk for blocks and blocks. Rearranging that bag, it almost gone to slip, then hefting it back up again."

"Uh-huh," I said.

"And then I passed my own house and was still following you. And then your bag really look like it was gone crash and everything. So I just thought I'd help." He sucked in his bottom lip, as if to keep it from making a smile. "What's your name?" When I told him, he said, "Dina, my name is Cecil." Then he said, "D comes right after C."

"Yes," I said, "it does, doesn't it."

Then, half question, half statement, he said, "I could carry your groceries for you? And walk you home?"

I stopped the story there. Dr. Raeburn kept looking at me. "Then what happened?"

I couldn't tell him the rest: that I had not wanted the boy to walk me home, that I didn't want someone with such nice shoes to see where I lived.

Dr. Raeburn would only have pitied me if I'd told him that I ran down the sidewalk after I told the boy no, that I fell, the bag slipped, and the eggs cracked, their yolks running all over the lettuce. Clear amniotic fluid coated the can of cinnamon rolls. I left the bag there on the sidewalk, the groceries spilled out randomly like cards loosed from a deck. When I returned home, I told my mother that I'd lost the food stamps.

"Lost?" she said. I'd expected her to get angry, I'd wanted her to get angry, but she hadn't. "Lost?" she repeated. Why had I been so clumsy and nervous around a harmless boy? I could have brought the groceries home and washed off the egg yolk, but instead I'd just left them there. "Come on," Mama said, snuffing her tears, pulling my arm, trying to get me to join her and start yanking cushions off the couch. "We'll find enough change here. We got to get something for dinner before your father gets back."

We'd already searched the couch for money the previous week, and I knew there'd be nothing now, but I began to push my fingers into the couch's boniest corners, pretending that it was only a matter of time before I'd find some change or a lost watch or an earring. Something pawnable, perhaps.

"What happened next?" Dr. Raeburn asked again. "Did you let the boy walk you home?"

"My house was far, so we went to his house instead." Though I was sure Dr. Raeburn knew that I was making this part up, I continued. "We made out on his sofa. He kissed me."

Dr. Raeburn lit his next cigarette like a detective. Cool, suspicious. "How did it feel?"

"You know," I said. "Like a kiss feels. It felt nice. The kiss felt very, very nice."

Raeburn smiled gently, though he seemed unconvinced. When he called time on our session his cigarette had become one long pole of ash. I left his office, walking quickly down the corridor, afraid to look back. It would be like him to trot after me, his navy blazer flapping, just to get the truth out of me. *You never kissed anyone.* The words slid from my brain, and knotted in my stomach.

When I reached my dorm, I found an old record player blocking my door and a Charles Mingus LP propped beside it. I carried them inside and then, lying on the floor, I played the Mingus over and over again until I fell asleep. I slept feeling as though Dr. Raeburn had attached electrodes to my head, willing into my mind a dream about my mother. I saw the lemon meringue of her skin, the long bone of her arm as she reached down to clip her toenails. I'd come home from a school trip to an aquarium, and I was explaining the differences between baleen and sperm whales according to the size of their heads, the range of their habitats, their feeding patterns.

I awoke remembering the expression on her face after I'd finished my dizzying whale lecture. She looked like a tourist who'd asked for directions to a place she thought was simple enough to get to only to hear a series of hypothetical turns, alleys, one-way streets. Her response was to nod politely at the perilous elaborateness of it all; to nod and save herself from the knowledge that she would never be able to get where she wanted to go.

∾

The dishwashers always closed down the dining hall. One night, after everyone else had punched out, Heidi and I took a break, and though I wasn't a smoker, we set two milk crates upside down on the floor and smoked cigarettes.

The dishwashing machines were off, but steam still rose from them like a jungle mist. Outside in the winter air, students were singing carols in their groomed and tailored singing-group voices. The Whiffenpoofs were back in New Haven after a tour around the world, and I guess their return was a huge deal. Heidi and I craned our necks to watch the year's first snow through an open window.

"What are you going to do when you're finished?" Heidi asked. Sexy question marks of smoke drifted up to the windows before vanishing.

"Take a bath."

She swatted me with her free hand. "No, silly. Three years from now. When you leave Yale."

"I don't know. Open up a library. Somewhere where no one comes in for books. A library in a desert."

She looked at me as though she'd expected this sort of answer and didn't know why she'd asked in the first place.

"What are you going to do?" I asked her.

"Open up a psych clinic. In a desert. And my only patient will be some wacko who runs a library."

"Ha," I said. "Whatever you do, don't work in a dish room ever again. You're no good." I got up from the crate. "C'mon. Let's hose the place down."

We put out our cigarettes on the floor, since it was our job to clean it anyway. We held squirt guns in one hand and used the other to douse the floors with the standard-issue, eye-burning cleaning solution. We hosed the dish room, the kitchen, the serving line, sending the water and crud and suds into the drains. Then we hosed them again so the solution wouldn't eat holes in our shoes as we left. Then I had an idea. I unbuckled my belt.

"What the hell are you doing?" Heidi said.

"Listen, it's too cold to go outside with our uniforms all wet. We could just take a shower right here. There's nobody but us."

"What the fuck, eh?"

I let my pants drop, then took off my shirt and panties. I didn't wear a bra, since I didn't have much to fill one. I took off my shoes and hung my clothes on the stepladder.

"You've flipped," Heidi said. "I mean, really, psych-ward flipped."

I soaped up with the liquid hand soap until I felt as glazed as a ham. "Stand back and spray me."

"Oh, my God," she said. I didn't know whether she was confused or delighted, but she picked up the squirt gun and sprayed me. She was laughing. Then she got too close and the water started to sting.

"God damn it!" I said. "That hurt!"

"I was wondering what it would take to make you say that."

When all the soap had been rinsed off, I put on my regular clothes and said, "O.K. You're up next."

"No way," she said.

"Yes way."

She started to take off her uniform shirt, then stopped.

"What?"

"I'm too fat."

"You goddam right." She always said she was fat. One time, I'd told her that she should shut up about it, that large black women wore their fat like mink coats. "You're big as a house," I said now. "Frozen yogurt may be low in calories but not if you eat five tubs of it. Take your clothes off. I want to get out of here."

She began taking off her uniform, then stood there, hands cupped over her breasts, crouching at the pubic bone.

"Open up," I said, "or we'll never get done."

Her hands remained where they were. I threw the bottle of liquid soap at her, and she had to catch it, revealing herself as she did.

I turned on the squirt gun, and she stood there, stiff, arms at her sides, eyes closed, as though awaiting mummification. I began with the water on low, and she turned around in a full circle, hesitantly, letting the droplets from the spray fall on her as if she were submitting to a death by stoning.

When I increased the water pressure, she slipped and fell on the sudsy floor. She stood up and then slipped again. This time she laughed and remained on the floor, rolling around on it as I sprayed.

I think I began to love Heidi that night in the dish room, but who is to say that I hadn't begun to love her the first time I met her? I sprayed her and sprayed her, and she turned over and over like a large beautiful dolphin, lolling about in the sun.

∾

Heidi started sleeping at my place. Sometimes she slept on the floor; sometimes we slept sardinelike, my feet at her head, until she complained that my feet were "taunting" her. When we finally slept head to head, she said, "Much better." She was so close I could smell her toothpaste. "I like your hair," she told me, touching it through the darkness. "You should wear it out more often."

"White people always say that about black people's hair. The worse it looks, the more they say they like it."

I'd expected her to disagree, but she kept touching my hair, her hands passing through it till my scalp tingled. When she began to touch the hair around the edge of my face, I felt myself quake. Her fingertips stopped for a moment, as if checking my pulse, then resumed.

"I like how it feels right here. See, mine just starts with the same old texture as the rest of my hair." She found my hand under the blanket and brought it to her hairline. "See," she said.

It was dark. As I touched her hair, it seemed as though I could smell it, too. Not a shampoo smell. Something richer, murkier. A bit dead, but sweet, like the decaying wood of a ship. She guided my hand.

"I see," I said. The record she'd given me was playing in my mind, and I kept trying to shut it off. I could also hear my mother saying that this is what happens when you've been around white people: things get weird. So weird I could hear the stylus etching its way into the flat vinyl of the record. "Listen," I said finally, when the bass and saxes started up. I heard Heidi breathe deeply, but she said nothing.

∞

We spent the winter and some of the spring in my room — never hers — missing tests, listening to music, looking out my window to comment on people who wouldn't have given us a second thought. We read books related to none of our classes. I got riled up by *The Autobiography of Malcolm X* and *The Chomsky Reader*; Heidi read aloud passages from *The Anxiety of Influence*. We guiltily read mysteries and *Clan of the Cave Bear*, then immediately threw them away. Once we looked up from our books at exactly the same moment, as though trapped at a dinner table with nothing to say. A pleasant trap of silence.

∞

Then one weekend I went back to Baltimore and stayed with my father. He asked me how school was going, but besides that, we didn't talk much. He knew what I thought of him. I stopped by the Enoch Pratt Library, where my favorite librarian, Mrs. Ardelia, cornered me into giving a little talk to the after-school kids, telling them to stay in school. They just looked at me like I was crazy; they were only nine or ten, and it hadn't even occurred to them to bail.

When I returned to Yale — to a sleepy, tree-scented spring — a group of students were holding what was called "Coming Out Day." I watched it from my room.

The emcee was the sepia boy who'd given us the invitation months back. His speech was strident but still smooth and peppered with jokes. There was a speech about AIDS, with lots of statistics: nothing that seemed to make "coming out" worth it. Then the women spoke. One girl pronounced herself "out" as casually as if she'd announced the time. Another said nothing at all: she came to the microphone with a woman who began cutting off her waist-length, bleached-blond hair. The woman doing the cutting tossed the shorn hair in every direction as she cut. People were clapping and cheering and catching the locks of hair.

And then there was Heidi. She was proud that she liked girls, she said when she reached the microphone. She loved them, wanted to sleep with them. She was a dyke, she said repeatedly, stabbing her finger to her chest in case anyone was unsure to whom she was referring. She could not have seen me. I was across the street, three stories up. And yet, when everyone clapped for her, she seemed to be looking straight at me.

∞

Heidi knocked. "Let me in."

It was like the first time I met her. The tears, the raw pink of her face.

We hadn't spoken in weeks. Outside, pink-and-white blossoms hung from the Old Campus trees. Students played Hacky Sack in T-shirts and shorts. Though I was the one who'd broken away after she went up to that podium, I still half expected her to poke her head out a window in Linsly-Chit, or tap on my back in Harkness, or even join me in the Commons dining hall, where I'd asked for my dish-room shift to be transferred. She did none of these.

"Well," I said, "what is it?"

She looked at me. "My mother," she said.

She continued to cry, but seemed to have grown so silent in my room I wondered if I could hear the numbers change on my digital clock.

"When my parents were getting divorced," she said, "my mother bought a car. A used one. An El Dorado. It was filthy. It looked like a huge crushed can coming up the street. She kept trying to clean it out. I mean—"

I nodded and tried to think what to say in the pause she left behind. Finally I said, "We had one of those," though I was sure ours was an Impala.

She looked at me, eyes steely from trying not to cry. "Anyway, she'd drive me around in it and although she didn't like me to eat in it, I always did. One day, I was eating cantaloupe slices, spitting the seeds on the floor. Maybe a month later, I saw this little sprout, growing right up from the car floor. I just started laughing and she kept saying what, what? I was laughing and then I saw she was so—"

She didn't finish. So what? So sad? So awful? Heidi looked at me with what seemed to be a renewed vigor. "We could have gotten a better car, eh?"

"It's all right. It's not a big deal," I said.

Of course, that was the wrong thing to say. And I really didn't mean it to sound the way it had come out.

∞

I told Dr. Raeburn about Heidi's mother having cancer and how I'd said it wasn't a big deal, though I'd wanted to say the opposite. I told Dr. Raeburn how I meant to tell Heidi that my mother had died, that I knew how one eventually accustoms oneself to the physical world's lack of sympathy: the buses that are still running late, the kids who still play in the street, the clocks that won't stop ticking for the person who's gone.

"You're pretending," Dr. Raeburn said, not sage or professional, but a little shocked by the discovery, as if I'd been trying to hide a pack of his cigarettes behind my back.

"I'm pretending?" I shook my head. "All those years of psych grad," I said. "And to tell me *that?*"

"What I mean is that you construct stories about yourself and dish them out—one for you, one for you—" Here he reenacted this process, showing me handing out lies as if they were apples.

"Pretending. I believe the professional name for it might be denial," I said. "Are you calling me gay?"

He pursed his lips noncommittally, then finally said, "No, Dina. I don't think you're gay."

I checked his eyes. I couldn't read them.

"No. Not at all," he said, sounding as if he were telling a subtle joke. "But maybe you'll finally understand."

"Understand what?"

"Oh, just that constantly saying what one doesn't mean accustoms the mouth to meaningless phrases." His eyes narrowed. "Maybe you'll understand that when you finally need to express something truly significant your mouth will revert to the insignificant nonsense it knows so well." He looked at me, his hands sputtering in the air in a gesture of defeat. "Who knows?" he asked with a glib, psychiatric smile I'd never seen before. "Maybe it's your survival mechanism. Black living in a white world."

I heard him, but only vaguely. I'd hooked on to that one word, pretending. Dr. Raeburn would never realize that "pretending" was what had got me this far. I remembered the morning of my mother's funeral. I'd been given milk to settle my stomach; I'd pretended it was coffee. I imagined I was drinking coffee elsewhere. Some Arabic-speaking country where the thick coffee served in little cups was so strong it could keep you awake for days.

∞

Heidi wanted me to go with her to the funeral. She'd sent this message through the dean. "We'll pay for your ticket to Vancouver," the dean said.

These people wanted you to owe them for everything. "What about my return ticket?" I asked the dean. "Maybe the shrink will chip in for that."

The dean looked at me as though I were an insect she'd like to squash. "We'll pay for the whole thing. We might even pay for some lessons in manners."

So I packed my suitcase and walked from my suicide single dorm to Heidi's room. A thin wispy girl in ragged cutoffs and a shirt that read "LSBN!" answered the door. A group of short-haired girls in thick black leather jackets, bundled up despite the summer heat, encircled Heidi in a protective fairy ring. They looked at me critically, clearly wondering if Heidi was too fragile for my company.

"You've got our numbers," one said, holding onto Heidi's shoulder. "And Vancouver's got a great gay community."

"Oh, God," I said. "She's going to a funeral, not a Save the Dykes rally."

One of the girls stepped in front of me.

"It's O.K., Cynthia," Heidi said. Then she ushered me into her bedroom and closed the door. A suitcase was on her bed, half packed.

"I could just uninvite you," Heidi said. "How about that? You want that?" She folded a polka-dotted T-shirt that was wrong for any occasion and put it in her suitcase. "Why haven't you talked to me?" she said, looking at the shirt instead of me. "Why haven't you talked to me in two months?"

"I don't know," I said.

"You don't know," she said, each syllable steeped in sarcasm. "You don't know. Well, *I* know. You thought I was going to try to sleep with you."

"Try to? We slept together all winter!"

"If you call smelling your feet sleeping together, you've got a lot to learn." She seemed thinner and meaner; every line of her body held me at bay.

"So tell me," I said. "What can you show me that I need to learn?" But as soon as I said it I somehow knew that she still hadn't slept with anyone. "Am

I supposed to come over there and sweep your enraged self into my arms?" I said. "Like in the movies? Is this the part where we're both so mad we kiss each other?"

She shook her head and smiled weakly. "You don't get it," she said. "My mother is dead." She closed her suitcase, clicking shut the old-fashioned locks. "My mother is dead," she said again, this time reminding herself. She set her suitcase upright on the floor and sat on it. She looked like someone waiting for a train.

"Fine," I said. "And she's going to be dead for a long time." Though it sounded stupid, I felt good saying it. As though I had my own locks to click shut.

∞

Heidi went to Vancouver for her mother's funeral. I didn't go. Instead, I went back to Baltimore and moved in with an aunt I barely knew. Every day was the same: I read and smoked outside my aunt's apartment, studying the row of hair salons across the street, where girls in denim cutoffs and tank tops would troop in and come out hours later, a flash of neon nails, coifs the color and sheen of patent leather. And every day I imagined Heidi's house in Vancouver. Her place would not be large, but it would be clean. Flowery shrubs would line the walks. The Canadian wind would whip us about like pennants. I'd be visiting her in some vague time in the future, deliberately vague, for people like me, who realign past events to suit themselves. In that future time, you always have a chance to catch the groceries before they fall; your words can always be rewound and erased, rewritten and revised.

Then I'd imagine Heidi visiting me. There are no psychiatrists or deans, no boys with nice shoes or flip cashiers. Just me in my single room. She knocks on the door and says, "Open up."

~ 2000

Karen Russell

∾ St. Lucy's Home for Girls Raised by Wolves

"One reason I think I like to write from adolescent points of view is because of that kid-elasticity—at that age you can really straddle two worlds, a childhood realm that's colored by games and fairy tales and an adult reality."

~ from *Granta*, November 11, 2011

Originally from Florida, Karen Russell received a B.A. from Northwestern University in 2003 and went on to earn an M.F.A. from Columbia University. Her short fiction has appeared in *Granta, Zoetrope, Oxford American*, and *The New Yorker*. Her short story "St. Lucy's Home for Girls Raised by Wolves" was selected for *Best American Short Stories* and became the title story of her first collection. Russell has won the Bard Fiction Prize and a National Magazine Award. She was named one of *Granta* Magazine's Best Young American Novelists, and her debut novel, *Swamplandia!*, was a finalist for the 2012 Pulitzer Prize.

Stage 1: The initial period is one in which everything is new, exciting, and interesting for your students. It is fun for your students to explore their new environment.

~ from *The Jesuit Handbook on Lycanthropic Culture Shock*

At first, our pack was all hair and snarl and floor-thumping joy. We forgot the barked cautions of our mothers and fathers, all the promises we'd made to be civilized and ladylike, couth and kempt. We tore through the austere rooms, overturning dresser drawers, pawing through the neat piles of the Stage 3 girls' starched underwear, smashing light bulbs with our bare fists. Things felt less foreign in the dark. The dim bedroom was windowless and odorless. We remedied this by spraying exuberant yellow streams all over the bunks. We jumped from bunk to bunk, spraying. We nosed each other midair, our bodies buckling in kinetic laughter. The nuns watched us from the corner of the bedroom, their tiny faces pinched with displeasure.

"*Ay caramba*," Sister Maria de la Guardia sighed. "*Que barbaridad!*" She made the Sign of the Cross. Sister Maria came to St. Lucy's from a Halfway House in Copacabana. In Copacabana, the girls are fat and languid and eat pink slivers of guava right out of your hand. Even at Stage 1, their pelts are silky, sun-bleached to near invisibility. Our pack was hirsute and sinewy and mostly brunette. We had terrible posture. We went knuckling along the wooden floor on the callused pads of our fists, baring row after row of tiny, wood-rotted teeth. Sister Josephine sucked in her breath. She removed a yellow wheel of floss from under her robes, looping it like a miniature lasso.

"The girls at our facility are *backwoods*," Sister Josephine whispered to Sister Maria de la Guardia with a beatific smile. "You must be patient with them." I clamped down on her ankle, straining to close my jaws around the woolly XXL sock. Sister Josephine tasted like sweat and freckles. She smelled easy to kill.

We'd arrived at St. Lucy's that morning, part of a pack fifteen-strong. We were accompanied by a mousy, nervous-smelling social worker; the baby-faced deacon; Bartholomew the blue wolfhound; and four burly woodsmen. The deacon handed out some stale cupcakes and said a quick prayer. Then he led us through the woods. We ran past the wild apiary, past the felled oaks, until we could see the white steeple of St. Lucy's rising out of the forest. We stopped short at the edge of a muddy lake. Then the deacon took our brothers. Bartholomew helped him to herd the boys up the ramp of a small ferry. We girls ran along the shore, tearing at our new jumpers in a plaid agitation. Our brothers stood on the deck, looking small and confused.

Our mothers and fathers were werewolves. They lived an outsider's existence in caves at the edge of the forest, threatened by frost and pitchforks. They had been ostracized by the local farmers for eating their silled fruit pies and terrorizing the heifers. They had ostracized the local wolves by having sometimes-thumbs, and regrets, and human children. (Their condition skips a generation.) Our pack grew up in a green purgatory. We couldn't keep up with the purebred wolves, but we never stopped crawling. We spoke a slab-tongued pidgin in the cave, inflected with frequent howls. Our parents wanted something better for us; they wanted us to get braces, use towels, be fully bilingual. When the nuns showed up, our parents couldn't refuse their offer. The nuns, they said, would make us naturalized citizens of human society. We would go to St. Lucy's to study a better culture. We didn't know at the time that our parents were sending us away for good. Neither did they.

That first afternoon, the nuns gave us free rein of the grounds. Everything was new, exciting, and interesting. A low granite wall surrounded St. Lucy's, the blue woods humming for miles behind it. There was a stone fountain full of delectable birds. There was a statue of St. Lucy. Her marble skin was colder than our mother's nose, her pupilless eyes rolled heavenward. Doomed squirrels gamboled around her stony toes. Our diminished pack threw back our heads in a celebratory howl—an exultant and terrible noise, even without a chorus of wolf-brothers in the background. There were holes everywhere!

We supplemented these holes by digging some of our own. We interred sticks, and our itchy new jumpers, and the bones of the friendly, unfortunate squirrels. Our noses ached beneath an invisible assault. Everything was smudged with a human odor: baking bread, petrol, the nun's faint woman-smell sweating out beneath a dark perfume of tallow and incense. We smelled one another, too, with the same astounded fascination. Our own scent had become foreign in this strange place.

We had just sprawled out in the sun for an afternoon nap, yawning into the warm dirt, when the nuns reappeared. They conferred in the shadow of the juniper tree, whispering and pointing. Then they started toward us. The oldest sister had spent the past hour twitching in her sleep, dreaming of fatty and infirm elk. (The pack used to dream the same dreams back then, as naturally as we drank the same water and slept on the same red scree.) When our oldest sister saw the nuns approaching, she instinctively bristled. It was an improvised bristle, given her new, human limitations. She took clumps of her scraggly, nut-brown hair and held it straight out from her head.

Sister Maria gave her a brave smile.

"And what is your name?" she asked.

The oldest sister howled something awful and inarticulate, a distillate of hurt and panic, half-forgotten hunts and eclipsed moons. Sister Maria nodded and scribbled on a yellow legal pad. She slapped on a nametag: HELLO, MY NAME IS _____! "Jeanette it is."

The rest of the pack ran in a loose, uncertain circle, torn between our instinct to help her and our new fear. We sensed some subtler danger afoot, written in a language we didn't understand.

Our littlest sister had the quickest reflexes. She used her hands to flatten her ears to the side of her head. She backed toward the far corner of the garden, snarling in the most menacing register that an eight-year-old wolf-girl can muster. Then she ran. It took them two hours to pin her down and tag her: HELLO, MY NAME IS MIRABELLA!

"Stage 1," Sister Maria sighed, taking careful aim with her tranquilizer dart. "It can be a little overstimulating."

∾

Stage 2: After a time, your students realize that they must work to adjust to the new culture. This work may be stressful and students may experience a strong sense of dislocation. They may miss certain foods. They may spend a lot of time daydreaming during this period. Many students feel isolated, irritated, bewildered, depressed, or generally uncomfortable.

Those were the days when we dreamed of rivers and meat. The full-moon nights were the worst! Worse than cold toilet seats and boiled tomatoes, worse than trying to will our tongues to curl around our false new names. We would snarl at one another for no reason. I remember how disorienting it was to look down and see two square-toed shoes instead of my own four feet. Keep your mouth shut, I repeated during our walking drills, staring straight ahead. Keep your shoes on your feet. Mouth shut, shoes on feet. Do not chew on your new penny loafers. Do not. I stumbled around in a daze, my mouth black with shoe polish. The whole pack was irritated, bewildered, depressed. We were all uncomfortable, and between languages. We had never wanted to run away so badly in our lives; but who did we have to run back to? Only the curled black grimace of the mother. Only the father, holding his tawny head between his paws. Could we betray our parents by going back to them? After they'd given us the choicest part of the woodchuck, loved us at our hairless worst, nosed us across the ice floes, and abandoned us at the Halfway House for our own betterment?

Physically, we were all easily capable of clearing the low stone walls. Sister Josephine left the wooden gates wide open. They unslatted the windows at night, so that long fingers of moonlight beckoned us from the woods. But we knew we couldn't return to the woods; not till we were civilized, not if we didn't want to break the mother's heart. It all felt like a sly, human taunt.

It was impossible to make the blank, chilly bedroom feel like home. In the beginning, we drank gallons of bathwater as part of a collaborative effort to mark our territory. We puddled up the yellow carpet of old newspapers. But later, when we returned to the bedroom, we were dismayed to find all trace of the pack musk had vanished. Someone was coming in and erasing us. We sprayed and sprayed every morning; and every night, we returned to the same ammonium eradication. We couldn't make our scent stick here; it made us feel invisible. Eventually we gave up. Still, the pack seemed to be adjusting on the same timetable. The advanced girls could already alternate between two speeds, "slouch" and "amble." Almost everybody was fully bipedal.

Almost.

The pack was worried about Mirabella.

Mirabella would rip foamy chunks out of the church pews and replace them with ham bones and girl dander. She loved to roam the grounds wagging her invisible tail. (We all had a hard time giving that up. When we got excited, we would fall to the ground and start pumping our backsides. Back in those days we could pump at rabbity velocities. *Que horror!* Sister Maria frowned, looking more than a little jealous.) We'd give her scolding pinches. "Mirabella," we hissed, imitating the nuns. "No." Mirabella cocked her ears at us, hurt and confused.

Still, some things remained the same. The main commandment of wolf life is Know Your Place, and that translated perfectly. Being around other humans had awakened a slavish-dog affection in us. An abasing, belly-to-the-ground desire to please. As soon as we realized that others higher up in the food chain were watching us, we wanted only to be pleasing in their sight. Mouth shut, I repeated, shoes on feet. But if Mirabella had this latent instinct, the nuns couldn't figure out how to activate it. She'd go bounding around, gleefully spraying on their gilded statue of St. Lucy, mad-scratching at the virulent fleas that survived all of their powders and baths. At Sister Maria's tearful insistence, she'd stand upright for roll call, her knobby, oddly muscled legs quivering from the effort. Then she'd collapse right back to the ground with an ecstatic *oomph!* She was still loping around on all fours (which the nuns had taught us to see looked unnatural and ridiculous—we could barely believe it now, the shame of it, that we used to locomote like that!), her fists blue-white from the strain. As if she were holding a secret tight to the ground. Sister Maria de la Guardia would sigh every time she saw her. *"Caramba!"* She'd sit down with Mirabella and pry her fingers apart. "You see?" she'd say softly, again and again. "What are you holding on to? Nothing, little one. Nothing."

Then she would sing out the standard chorus, "Why can't you be more like your sister Jeanette?"

The pack hated Jeanette. She was the most successful of us, the one furthest removed from her origins. Her real name was GWARR! but she wouldn't respond to this anymore. Jeanette spiffed her penny loafers until her very shoes seemed to gloat. (Linguists have since traced the colloquial origins of "goody two-shoes" back to our facilities.) She could even growl out a demonic-sounding precursor to "Pleased to meet you." She'd delicately extend her former paws to visitors, wearing white kid gloves.

"Our little wolf, disguised in sheep's clothing!" Sister Ignatius liked to joke with the visiting deacons, and Jeanette would surprise everyone by laughing along with them, a harsh, inhuman, barking sound. Her hearing was still twig-snap sharp. Jeanette was the first among us to apologize; to drink apple juice out of a sippy cup; to quit eyeballing the cleric's jugular in a disconcerting fashion. She curled her lips back into a cousin of a smile as the traveling barber cut her pelt into bangs. Then she swept her coarse black curls under the rug. When we entered a room, our nostrils flared beneath the new odors: onion and bleach, candle wax, the turnipy smell of unwashed bodies. Not Jeanette. Jeanette smiled and pretended she couldn't smell a thing.

I was one of the good girls. Not great and not terrible, solidly middle-of-the-pack. But I had an ear for languages, and I could read before I could adequately wash myself. I probably could have vied with Jeanette for the number one spot; but I'd seen what happened if you gave in to your natural aptitudes. This wasn't like the woods, where you had to be your fastest and your strongest and your bravest self. Different sorts of calculations were required to survive at the Home.

The pack hated Jeanette, but we hated Mirabella more. We began to avoid her, but sometimes she'd surprise us, curled up beneath the beds or gnawing on a scapula in the garden. It was scary to be ambushed by your sister. I'd bristle and growl, the way that I'd begun to snarl at my own reflection as if it were a stranger.

"Whatever will become of Mirabella?" we asked, gulping back our own fear. We'd heard rumors about former wolf-girls who never adapted to their new culture. It was assumed that they were returned to our native country, the vanishing woods. We liked to speculate about this before bedtime, scaring ourselves with stories of catastrophic bliss. It was the disgrace, the failure that we all guiltily hoped for in our hard beds. Twitching with the shadow question: *Whatever will become of me?*

We spent a lot of time daydreaming during this period. Even Jeanette. Sometimes I'd see her looking out at the woods in a vacant way. If you interrupted her in the midst of one of these reveries, she would lunge at you with an elder-sister ferocity, momentarily forgetting her human catechism. We liked her better then, startled back into being foamy old Jeanette.

In school, they showed us the St. Francis of Assisi slide show, again and again. Then the nuns would give us bags of bread. They never announced these things as a test; it was only much later that I realized that we were under constant examination. "Go feed the ducks," they urged us. "Go practice compassion for all God's creatures." *Don't pair me with Mirabella,* I prayed, *anybody but Mirabella.* "Claudette," Sister Josephine beamed, "why don't you and Mirabella take some pumpernickel down to the ducks?"

"Ohhkaaythankyou," I said. (It took me a long time to say anything; first I had to translate it in my head from the Wolf.) It wasn't fair. They knew Mirabella couldn't make bread balls yet. She couldn't even undo the twist tie of the bag. She was sure to eat the birds; Mirabella didn't even try to curb her desire to kill things—and then who would get blamed for the dark spots of duck blood on our Peter Pan collars? Who would get penalized with negative Skill Points? Exactly.

As soon as we were beyond the wooden gates, I snatched the bread away from Mirabella and ran off to the duck pond on my own. Mirabella gave chase, nipping at my heels. She thought it was a game. "Stop it," I growled. I ran faster, but it was Stage 2 and I was still unsteady on my two feet. I fell sideways into a leaf pile, and then all I could see was my sister's blurry form, bounding toward me. In a moment, she was on top of me, barking the old word for tug-of-war. When she tried to steal the bread out of my hands, I whirled around and snarled at her, pushing my ears back from my head. I bit her shoulder, once, twice, the only language she would respond to, I used my new motor skills. I threw dirt, I threw stones. "Get away!" I screamed, long after she had made a cringing retreat into the shadows of the purple saplings. "Get away, get away!"

Much later, they found Mirabella wading in the shallows of a distant river, trying to strangle a mallard with her rosary beads. I was at the lake; I'd been sitting there for hours. Hunched in the long cattails, my yellow eyes flashing, shoving ragged hunks of bread into my mouth.

I don't know what they did to Mirabella. Me they separated from my sisters. They made me watch another slide show. This one showed images of former wolf-girls, the ones who had failed to be rehabilitated. Longhaired, sad-eyed women, limping after their former wolf packs in white tennis shoes and pleated culottes. A wolf-girl bank teller, her makeup smeared in oily rainbows, eating a raw steak on the deposit slips while her colleagues looked on in disgust. Our parents. The final slide was a bolded sentence in St. Lucy's prim script:

DO YOU WANT TO END UP SHUNNED BY BOTH SPECIES?

After that, I spent less time with Mirabella. One night she came to me, holding her hand out. She was covered with splinters, keening a high, whining noise through her nostrils. Of course I understood what she wanted; I wasn't that far removed from our language (even though I was reading at a fifth-grade level, halfway into Jack London's *The Son of the Wolf*).

"Lick your own wounds," I said, not unkindly. It was what the nuns had instructed us to say; wound licking was not something you did in polite company. Etiquette was so confounding in this country. Still, looking at Mirabella — her fists balled together like small white porcupines, her brows knitted in animal confusion — I felt a throb of compassion. How can people live like they do? I wondered. Then I congratulated myself. This was a Stage 3 thought.

∾

Stage 3: It is common that students who start living in a new and different culture come to a point where they reject the host culture and withdraw into themselves. During this period, they make generalizations about the host culture and wonder how the people can live like they do. Your students may feel that their own culture's lifestyle and customs are far superior to those of the host country.

The nuns were worried about Mirabella too. To correct a failing, you must first be aware of it as a failing. And there was Mirabella, shucking her plaid jumper in full view of the visiting cardinal. Mirabella, battling a raccoon under the dinner table while the rest of us took dainty bites of peas and borscht. Mirabella, doing belly flops into compost.

"You have to pull your weight around here," we overheard Sister Josephine saying one night. We paused below the vestry window and peered inside.

"Does Mirabella try to earn Skill Points by shelling walnuts and polishing Saint-in-the-Box? No. Does Mirabella even know how to say the word *walnut*? Has she learned how to say anything besides a sinful 'HraaaHA!' as she commits frottage against the organ pipes? No."

There was a long silence.

"Something must be done," Sister Ignatius said firmly. The other nuns nodded, a sea of thin, colorless lips and kettle-black brows. "Something must be done," they intoned. That ominously passive construction; a something so awful that nobody wanted to assume responsibility for it.

I could have warned her. If we were back home, and Mirabella had come under attack by territorial beavers or snow-blind bears, I would have warned her. But the truth is that by Stage 3 I wanted her gone. Mirabella's inability to adapt was taking a visible toll. Her teeth were ground down to nubbins; her hair was falling out. She hated the spongy, long-dead foods we were served, and it showed—her ribs were poking through her uniform. Her bright eyes had dulled to a sour whiskey color. But you couldn't show Mirabella the slightest kindness anymore—she'd never leave you alone! You'd have to sit across from her at meals, shoving her away as she begged for your scraps. I slept fitfully during that period, unable to forget that Mirabella was living under my bed, gnawing on my loafers.

It was during Stage 3 that we met our first purebred girls. These were girls raised in captivity, volunteers from St. Lucy's School for Girls. The apple-cheeked fourth-grade class came to tutor us in playing. They had long golden braids or short, severe bobs. They had frilly-duvet names like Felicity and Beulah; and pert, bunny noses; and terrified smiles. We grinned back at them with genuine ferocity. It made us nervous to meet new humans. There were so many things that we could do wrong! And the rules here were different depending on which humans we were with: dancing or no dancing, checkers playing or no checkers playing, pumping or no pumping.

The purebred girls played checkers with us.

"These girl-girls sure is dumb," my sister Lavash panted to me between games. "I win it again! Five to none."

She was right. The purebred girls were making mistakes on purpose, in order to give us an advantage. "King me," I growled, out of turn. "I SAY KING ME!" and Felicity meekly complied. Beulah pretended not to mind when we got frustrated with the oblique, fussy movement from square to square and shredded the board to ribbons. I felt sorry for them. I wondered what it would be like to be bred in captivity and always homesick for a dimly sensed forest, the trees you've never seen.

Jeanette was learning how to dance. On Holy Thursday, she mastered a rudimentary form of the Charleston. "Brava!" the nuns clapped. "Brava!"

Every Friday, the girls who had learned how to ride a bicycle celebrated by going on chaperoned trips into town. The purebred girls sold seven hundred rolls of gift-wrap paper and used the proceeds to buy us a yellow fleet of bicycles built for two. We'd ride the bicycles uphill, a sanctioned pumping, a grim-faced nun pedaling behind each one of us. "Congratulations!" the nuns would huff. "Being human is like riding this bicycle. Once you've learned how, you'll never forget." Mirabella would run after the bicycles, growling out our old names. "Hwraa! Gwarr! Trrrrrrr!" We pedaled faster.

At this point, we'd had six weeks of lessons, and still nobody could do the Sausalito but Jeanette. The nuns decided we needed an inducement to dance. They announced that we would celebrate our successful rehabilitations with a Debutante Ball. There would be brothers, ferried over from the Home for Man-Boys Raised by Wolves. There would be a photographer from the *Gazette Sophisticate*. There would be a three-piece jazz band from West Toowoomba, and root beer in tiny plastic cups. The brothers! We'd almost forgotten about them. Our invisible tails went limp. I should have been excited; instead I felt a low mad anger at the nuns. They knew we weren't ready to dance with the brothers; we weren't even ready to talk to them. Things had been so much simpler in the woods. That night I waited until my sisters were asleep. Then I slunk into the closet and practiced the Sausalito two-step in secret, a private mass of twitch and foam. Mouth shut—shoes on feet! Mouth shut—shoes on feet! Mouthshutmouthshut . . .

One night I came back early from the closet and stumbled on Jeanette. She was sitting in a patch of moonlight on the windowsill, reading from one of her library books. (She was the first of us to sign for her library card too.) Her cheeks looked dewy.

"Why you cry?" I asked her, instinctively reaching over to lick Jeanette's cheek and catching myself in the nick of time.

Jeanette blew her nose into a nearby curtain. (Even her mistakes annoyed us—they were always so well intentioned.) She sniffled and pointed to a line in her book: "The lake water was reinventing the forest and the white moon above it, and wolves lapped up the cold reflection of the sky." But none of the pack besides me could read yet; and I wasn't ready to claim a common language with Jeanette.

The following day, Jeanette golfed. The nuns set up a miniature put-put course in the garden. Sister Maria dug four sand traps and got Clyde the grounds-keeper to make a windmill out of a lawnmower engine. The eighteenth hole was what they called a "doozy," a minuscule crack in St. Lucy's marble dress. Jeanette got a hole in one.

On Sundays, the pretending felt almost as natural as nature. The chapel was our favorite place. Long before we could understand what the priest was saying, the music instructed us in how to feel. The choir director—aggressively perfumed Mrs. Valuchi, gold necklaces like pineapple rings around her neck— taught us more than the nuns ever did. She showed us how to pattern the old hunger into arias. Clouds moved behind the frosted oculus of the nave, glass shadows that reminded me of my mother. The mother, I'd think, struggling to conjure up a picture. A black shadow, running behind the watery screen of pines.

We sang at the chapel annexed to the Halfway House every morning. We understood that this was the human's moon, the place for howling beyond purpose. Not for mating, not for hunting, not for fighting, not for anything but the sound itself. And we'd howl along with the choir, hurling every pitted thing within us at the stained glass. "Sotto voce." The nuns would frown. But you could tell that they were pleased.

∾

Stage 4: As a more thorough understanding of the host culture is acquired, your students will begin to feel more comfortable in their new environment. Your students feel more at home and their self-confidence grows. Everything begins to make sense.

"Hey, Claudette," Jeanette growled to me on the day before the ball. "Have you noticed that everything's beginning to make sense?"

Before I could answer, Mirabella sprang out of the hall closet and snapped through Jeanette's homework binder. Pages and pages of words swirled around the stone corridor, like dead leaves off trees.

"What about you, Mirabella?" Jeanette asked politely, stooping to pick up her erasers. She was the only one of us who would still talk to Mirabella; she was high enough in the rankings that she could afford to talk to the scrugliest wolf-girl. "Has everything begun to make more sense, Mirabella?"

Mirabella let out a whimper. She scratched at us and scratched at us, raking her nails along our shins, so hard that she drew blood. Then she rolled belly-up on the cold stone floor, squirming on a bed of spelling-bee worksheets. Above us, small pearls of light dotted the high tinted window.

Jeanette frowned. "You are a late bloomer, Mirabella! Usually, everything's begun to make more sense by Month Twelve at the latest." I noticed that she stumbled on the word *bloomer*. HraaaHA! Jeanette could never fully shake our accent. She'd talk like that her whole life, I thought with a gloomy satisfaction, each word winced out like an apology for itself.

"Claudette, help me," she yelped. Mirabella had closed her jaws around Jeanette's bald ankle and was dragging her toward the closet. "Please. Help me to mop up Mirabella's mess."

I ignored her and continued down the hall. I only had four more hours to perfect the Sausalito. I was worried only about myself. By that stage, I was no longer certain of how the pack felt about anything.

At seven o'clock on the dot, Sister Ignatius blew her whistle and frog-marched us into the ball. The nuns had transformed the rectory into a very scary place. Purple and silver balloons started popping all around us. Black streamers swooped down from the eaves and got stuck in our hair like bats. A full yellow moon smirked outside the window. We were greeted by blasts of a saxophone, and fizzy pink drinks, and the brothers.

The brothers didn't smell like our brothers anymore. They smelled like pomade and cold, sterile sweat. They looked like little boys. Someone had washed behind their ears and made them wear suspendered dungarees. Kyle used to be the blustery alpha male BTWWWR!, chewing through rattle-snakes, spooking badgers, snatching a live trout out of a grizzly's mouth. He stood by the punch bowl, looking pained and out of place.

"My stars!" I growled. "What lovely weather we've been having!"

"Yeees," Kyle growled back, "It is beginning to look a lot like Christmas." All around the room, boys and girls raised by wolves were having the same conversation. Actually, it had been an unseasonably warm and brown winter, and just that morning a freak hailstorm had sent Sister Josephine to an early grave. But we had only gotten up to Unit 7: Party Dialogue; we hadn't yet learned the vocabulary for Unit 12: How to Tactfully Acknowledge Disaster.

Instead, we wore pink party hats and sucked olives on little sticks, inured to our own strangeness.

The sisters swept our hair back into high, bouffant hairstyles. This made us look more girlish and less inclined to eat people, the way that squirrels are saved from looking like rodents by their poofy tails. I was wearing a white organdy dress with orange polka dots. Jeanette was wearing a mauve organdy dress with blue polka dots. Linette was wearing a red organdy dress with white polka dots. Mirabella was in a dark corner, wearing a muzzle. Her party culottes were duct-taped to her knees. The nuns had tied little bows on the muzzle to make it more festive. Even so, the jazz band from West Toowoomba kept glancing nervously her way.

"You smell astooooounding!" Kyle was saying, accidentally stretching the diphthong into a howl and then blushing. "I mean . . ."

"Yes, I know what it is that you mean," I snapped. (That's probably a little narrative embellishment on my part; it must have been months before I could really "snap" out words.) I didn't smell astounding. I had rubbed a pumpkin muffin all over my body earlier that morning to mask my natural, feral scent. Now I smelled like a purebred girl, easy to kill. I narrowed my eyes at Kyle and flattened my ears, something I hadn't done for months. Kyle looked panicked, trying to remember the words that would make me act like a girl again. I felt hot, oily tears squeezing out of the red corners of my eyes. Shoesonfeet! I barked at myself. I tried again. "My! What lovely weather . . ."

The jazz band struck up a tune.

"The time has come to do the Sausalito," Sister Maria announced, beaming into the microphone. "Every sister grab a brother!" She switched on Clyde's industrial flashlight, struggling beneath its weight, and aimed the beam in the center of the room.

Uh-oh. I tried to skulk off into Mirabella's corner, but Kyle pushed me into the spotlight. "No," I moaned through my teeth, "noooooo." All of a sudden the only thing my body could remember how to do was pump and pump. In a flash of white-hot light, my months at St. Lucy's had vanished, and I was just a terrified animal again. As if of their own accord, my feet started to wiggle out of my shoes. *Mouth shut*, I gasped, staring down at my naked toes, *mouthshutmouthshut.*

"Ahem. The time has come," Sister Maria coughed, "to do the Sausalito." She paused. "The Sausalito," she added helpfully, "does not in any way resemble the thing that you are doing."

Beads of sweat stood out on my forehead. I could feel my jaws gaping open, my tongue lolling out of the left side of my mouth. What were the steps? I looked frantically for Jeanette; she would help me, she would tell me what to do.

Jeanette was sitting in the corner, sipping punch through a long straw and watching me with uninterest. I locked eyes with her, pleading with the mute intensity that I had used to beg her for weasel bones in the forest. "What are the steps?" I mouthed. "The steps!"

"The steps?" Then Jeanette gave me a wide, true wolf smile. For an instant, she looked just like our mother. "Not for you," she mouthed back.

I threw my head back, a howl clawing its way up my throat. I was about to lose all my Skill Points, I was about to fail my Adaptive Dancing test. But before the air could burst from my lungs, the wind got knocked out of me. *Oomph!* I fell to the ground, my skirt falling softly over my head. Mirabella had intercepted my eye-cry for help. She'd chewed through her restraints and tackled me from behind, barking at unseen cougars, trying to shield me with her tiny body. "*Caramba!*" Sister Maria squealed, dropping the flashlight. The music ground to a halt. And I have never loved someone so much, before or since, as I loved my littlest sister at that moment. I wanted to roll over and lick her ears; I wanted to kill a dozen spotted fawns and let her eat first.

But everybody was watching; everybody was waiting to see what I would do. "I wasn't talking to you," I grunted from underneath her. "I didn't want your help. Now you have ruined the Sausalito! You have ruined the ball!" I said more loudly, hoping the nuns would hear how much my enunciation had improved.

"You have ruined it!" my sisters panted, circling around us, eager to close ranks. "Mirabella has ruined it!" Every girl was wild-eyed and itching under her polka dots, punch froth dribbling down her chin. The pack had been waiting for this moment for some time. "Mirabella cannot adapt! Back to the woods, back to the woods!"

The band from West Toowoomba had quietly packed their instruments into black suitcases and were sneaking out the back. The boys had fled back toward the lake, bow ties spinning, suspenders snapping in their haste. Mirabella was still snarling in the center of it all, trying to figure out where the danger was so that she could defend me against it. The nuns exchanged glances.

In the morning, Mirabella was gone. We checked under all the beds. I pretended to be surprised. I'd known she would have to be expelled the minute I felt her weight on my back. Clyde had come and told me this in secret after the ball, "So you can say yer goodbyes." I didn't want to face Mirabella. Instead, I packed a tin lunch pail for her: two jelly sandwiches on saltine crackers, a chloroformed squirrel, a gilt-edged placard of St. Bolio. I left it for her with Sister Ignatius, with a little note: *Best wishes!* I told myself I'd done everything I could.

"Hooray!" the pack crowed. "Something has been done!"

We raced outside into the bright sunlight, knowing full well that our sister had been turned loose, that we'd never find her. A low roar rippled through us and surged up and up, disappearing into the trees. I listened for an answering howl from Mirabella, heart thumping—what if she heard us and came back? But there was nothing.

We graduated from St. Lucy's shortly thereafter. As far as I can recollect, that was our last communal howl.

∾

Stage 5: At this point your students are able to interact effectively in the new cultural environment. They find it easy to move between the two cultures.

One Sunday, near the end of my time at St. Lucy's, the sisters gave me a special pass to go visit the parents. The woodsman had to accompany me; I couldn't remember how to find the way back on my own. I wore my best dress and brought along some prosciutto and dill pickles in a picnic basket. We crunched through the fall leaves in silence, and every step made me sadder. "I'll wait out here," the woodsman said, leaning on a blue elm and lighting a cigarette.

The cave looked so much smaller than I remembered it. I had to duck my head to enter. Everybody was eating when I walked in. They all looked up from the bull moose at the same time, my aunts and uncles, my sloe-eyed, lolling cousins, the parents. My uncle dropped a thighbone from his mouth. My littlest brother, a cross-eyed wolf-boy who has since been successfully rehabilitated and is now a dour, balding children's book author, started whining in terror. My mother recoiled from me, as if I were a stranger. TRRR? She sniffed me for a long moment. Then she sank her teeth into my ankle, looking proud and sad. After all the tail wagging and perfunctory barking had died down, the parents sat back on their hind legs. They stared up at me expectantly, panting in the cool gray envelope of the cave, waiting for a display of what I had learned.

"So," I said, telling my first human lie. "I'm home."

~ 2007

George Saunders

~ CivilWarLand in Bad Decline

Born in Texas in 1958 and raised in Chicago, George Saunders received a B.S. in geophysical engineering from the Colorado School of Mines in Golden, Colorado. After working as a technical writer and geophysical engineer and holding a number of odd jobs, he enrolled in the creative writing program at Syracuse University, receiving an M.A. in 1988. His first book, the story collection *CivilWarLand in Bad Decline*, was a finalist for the PEN/Hemingway Award. His other works include stories, novellas, and a book of essays. His work often appears in periodicals, including *The New Yorker*, *Harper's*, and *McSweeney's*, and has been included in *Best American Short Stories* and *The O. Henry Prize Stories*. His awards include the National Magazine Award for Fiction, a Guggenheim Fellowship, and a MacArthur Fellowship. Saunders is currently on the creative writing faculty at Syracuse University.

> *"[While writing* CivilWarLand in Bad Decline*] the tech writing I was doing influenced both style and subject. And any claim I might make to 'originality' in my fiction is really just the result of this odd background: basically, just me working inefficiently, with flawed tools, in a mode I don't have sufficient background to really understand. Like if you put a welder to designing dresses."*
>
> ~from *The Wag*, July 1, 2000

Whenever a potential big investor comes for the tour the first thing I do is take him out to the transplanted Erie Canal Lock. We've got a good ninety feet of actual Canal out there and a well-researched dioramic of a coolie campsite. Were our faces ever red when we found out it was actually the Irish who built the Canal. We've got no budget to correct, so every fifteen minutes or so a device in the bunkhouse gives off the approximate aroma of an Oriental meal.

Today my possible Historical Reconstruction Associate is Mr. Haberstrom, founder of Burn'n'Learn. Burn'n'Learn is national. Their gimmick is a fully stocked library on the premises and as you tan you call out the name of any book you want to these high-school girls on roller skates. As we walk up the trail he's wearing a sweatsuit and smoking a cigar and I tell him I admire his acumen. I tell him some men are dreamers and others are doers. He asks which am I and I say let's face it, I'm basically the guy who leads the dreamers up the trail to view the Canal Segment. He likes that. He says I have a good head on my shoulders. He touches my arm and says he's hot to spend some reflective moments at the Canal because his great-grandfather was a barge guider way back when who got killed by a donkey. When we reach the clearing he gets all emotional and bolts off through the gambling plaster Chinese. Not to be crass but I sense an impending sizable contribution.

When I come up behind him however I see that once again the gangs have been at it with their spray cans, all over my Lock. Haberstrom takes a nice long look. Then he pokes me with the spiny end of his cigar and says not with his money I don't, and storms back down the trail.

I stand there alone a few minutes. The last thing I need is some fat guy's spit on my tie. I think about quitting. Then I think about my last degrading batch of résumés. Two hundred send-outs and no nibbles. My feeling is that prospective employers are put off by the fact that I was a lowly Verisimilitude Inspector for nine years with no promotions. I think of my car payment. I think of how much Marcus and Howie love the little playhouse I'm still paying off. Once again I decide to eat my pride and sit tight.

So I wipe off my tie with a leaf and start down to break the Haberstrom news to Mr. Alsuga.

Mr. A's another self-made man. He cashed in on his love of history by conceptualizing CivilWarLand in his spare time. He started out with just a settler's shack and one Union costume and now has considerable influence in Rotary.

His office is in City Hall. He agrees that the gangs are getting out of hand. Last month they wounded three Visitors and killed a dray horse. Several of them encircled and made fun of Mrs. Dugan in her settler outfit as she was taking her fresh-baked bread over to the simulated Towne Meeting. No way they're paying admission, so they're either tunneling in or coming in over the retaining wall.

Mr. Alsuga believes the solution to the gang problem is Teen Groups. I tell him that's basically what a gang is, a Teen Group. But he says how can it be a Teen Group without an adult mentor with a special skill, like whittling? Mr. Alsuga whittles. Once he gave an Old Tyme Skills Seminar on it in the Black-smith Shoppe. It was poorly attended. All he got was two widowers and a chess-club type no gang would have wanted anyway. And myself. I attended. Evelyn called me a bootlicker, but I attended. She called me a bootlicker, and I told her she'd better bear in mind which side of the bread her butter was on. She said whichever side it was on it wasn't enough to shake a stick at. She's always denigrating my paystub. I came home from the Seminar with this kind of whittled duck. She threw it away the next day because she said she thought it was an acorn. It looked nothing like an acorn. As far as I'm concerned she threw it away out of spite. It made me livid and twice that night I had to step into a closet and perform my Hatred Abatement Breathing.

But that's neither here nor there.

Mr. Alsuga pulls out the summer stats. We're in the worst attendance decline in ten years. If it gets any worse, staff is going to be let go in droves. He gives me a meaningful look. I know full well I'm not one of his key players. Then he asks who we have that might be willing to fight fire with fire.

I say: I could research it.

He says: Why don't you research it?

So I go research it.

∞

Sylvia Loomis is the queen of info. It's in her personality. She enjoys digging up dirt on people. She calls herself an S&M buff in training. She's still too meek to go whole hog, so when she parties at the Make Me Club on Airport Road she limits herself to walking around talking mean while wearing kiddie hand-cuffs. But she's good at what she does, which is Security. It was Sylvia who identified the part-timer systematically crapping in the planters in the Gift

Acquisition Center and Sylvia who figured out it was Phil in Grounds leaving obscene messages for the Teen Belles on MessageMinder. She has access to all records. I ask can she identify current employees with a history of violence. She says she can if I buy her lunch.

We decide to eat in-Park. We go over to Nate's Saloon. Sylvia says don't spread it around but two of the nine can-can girls are knocked up. Then she pulls out her folder and says that according to her review of the data, we have a pretty tame bunch on our hands. The best she can do is Ned Quinn. His records indicate that while in high school he once burned down a storage shed. I almost die laughing. Quinn's an Adjunct Thespian and a world-class worry-wart. I can't count the times I've come upon him in Costuming, dwelling on the gory details of his Dread Disease Rider. He's a failed actor who won't stop trying. He says this is the only job he could find that would allow him to continue to develop his craft. Because he's ugly as sin he specializes in roles that require masks, such as Humpty-Dumpty during Mother Goose Days.

I report back to Mr. Alsuga and he says Quinn may not be much but he's all we've got. Quinn's dirt-poor with six kids and Mr. A says that's a plus, as we'll need someone between a rock and a hard place. What he suggests we do is equip the Desperate Patrol with live ammo and put Quinn in charge. The Desperate Patrol limps along under floodlights as the night's crowning event. We've costumed them to resemble troops who've been in the field too long. We used actual Gettysburg photos. The climax of the Patrol is a re-enacted partial rebellion, quelled by a rousing speech. After the speech the boys take off their hats and put their arms around each other and sing "I Was Born Under a Wandering Star." Then there's fireworks and the Parade of Old-Fashioned Conveyance. Then we clear the place out and go home.

"Why not confab with Quinn?" Mr. A says. "Get his input and feelings."

"I was going to say that," I say.

I look up the Thespian Center's SpeedDial extension and a few minutes later Quinn's bounding up the steps in the Wounded Grizzly suit.

"Desperate Patrol?" Mr. A says as Quinn sits down. "Any interest on your part?"

"Love it," Quinn says. "Excellent." He's been trying to get on Desperate Patrol for years. It's considered the pinnacle by the Thespians because of the wealth of speaking parts. He's so excited he's shifting around in his seat and getting some of his paw blood on Mr. A's nice cane chair.

"The gangs in our park are a damn blight," Mr. A says. "I'm talking about meeting force with force. Something in it for you? Oh yes."

"I'd like to see Quinn give the rousing speech myself," I say.

"Societal order," Mr. A says. "Sustaining the lifeblood of this goddamned park we've all put so much of our hearts into."

"He's not just free-associating," I say.

"I'm not sure I get it," Quinn says.

"What I'm suggesting is live ammo in your weapon only," Mr. A says. "Fire at your discretion. You see an unsavory intruder, you shoot at his feet. Just give him a scare. Nobody gets hurt. An additional two bills a week is what I'm talking."

"I'm an actor," Quinn says.

"Quinn's got kids," I say. "He knows the value of a buck."

"This is acting of the highest stripe," Mr. A says. "Act like a mercenary."

"Go for it on a trial basis," I say.

"I'm not sure I get it," Quinn says. "But jeez, that's good money."

"Superfantastic," says Mr. A.

∽

Next evening Mr. A and I go over the Verisimilitude Irregularities List. We've been having some heated discussions about our bird-species percentages. Mr. Grayson, Staff Ornithologist, has recently recalculated and estimates that to accurately approximate the 1865 bird population we'll need to eliminate a couple hundred orioles or so. He suggests using air guns or poison. Mr. A says that in his eyes, in fiscally troubled times, an ornithologist is a luxury, and this may be the perfect time to send Grayson packing. I like Grayson. He went way overboard on Howie's baseball candy. But I've got me and mine to think of. So I call Grayson in. Mr. A says did you botch the initial calculation or were you privy to new info. Mr. Grayson admits it was a botch. Mr. A sends him out into the hall and we confab.

"You'll do the telling," Mr. A says. "I'm getting too old for cruelty."

He takes his walking stick and beeper and says he'll be in the Great Forest if I need him.

I call Grayson back in and let him go, and hand him Kleenexes and fend off a few blows and almost before I know it he's reeling out the door and I go grab a pita.

Is this the life I envisioned for myself? My God no. I wanted to be a high jumper. But I have two of the sweetest children ever born. I go in at night and look at them in their fairly expensive sleepers and think: There are a couple of kids who don't need to worry about freezing to death or being cast out to the wolves. You should see their little eyes light up when I bring home a treat. They may not know the value of a dollar but it's my intention to see that they never need to.

I'm filling out Grayson's Employee Retrospective when I hear gunshots from the perimeter. I run out and there's Quinn and a few of his men tied to the cannon. The gangs took Quinn's pants and put some tiny notches in his penis with their knives. I free Quinn and tell him to get over to the Infirmary to guard against infection. He's absolutely shaking and can hardly walk, so I wrap him up in a Confederate flag and call over a hay cart and load him in.

When I tell Mr. A he says: Garbage in, garbage out, and that we were idiots for expecting a milquetoast to save our rears.

We decide to leave the police out of it because of the possible bad PR. So we give Quinn the rest of the week off and promise to let him play Grant now and then, and that's that.

∾

When visitors first come in there's this cornball part where they sit in this kind of spaceship and supposedly get blasted into space and travel faster than the speed of light and end up in 1865. The unit's dated. The helmets we distribute look like bowls and all the paint's peeling off. I've argued and argued that we need to update. But in the midst of a budget crunch one can't necessarily hang the moon.

When the tape of space sounds is over and the walls stop shaking, we pass out the period costumes. We try not to offend anyone, liability law being what it is. We distribute the slave and Native American roles equitably among racial groups. Anyone is free to request a different identity at any time. In spite of our precautions, there's a Herlicher in every crowd. He's the guy who sued us last fall for making him hangman. He claimed that for weeks afterwards he had nightmares and because he wasn't getting enough sleep botched a big contract by sending an important government buyer a load of torn pool liners. Big deal, is my feeling. But he's suing us for fifty grand for emotional stress because the buyer ridiculed him in front of his co-workers. Whenever he comes in we make him sheriff but he won't back down an inch.

Mr. A calls me into his office and says he's got bad news and bad news, and which do I want first. I say the bad news. First off, he says, the gangs have spraypainted a picture of Quinn's notched penis on the side of the Everly Mansion. Second, last Friday's simulated frontier hunt has got us in hot water, because apparently some of the beef we toughen up to resemble buffalo meat was tainted, and the story's going in the Sunday supplement. And finally, the verdict's come in on the Herlicher case and we owe that goofball a hundred grand instead of fifty because the pinko judge empathized.

I wait for him to say I'm fired but instead he breaks down in tears. I pat his back and mix him a drink. He says why don't I join him. So I join him.

"It doesn't look good," he says, "for men like you and I."

"No it doesn't," I say.

"All I wanted to do," he says, "was to give the public a meaningful perspective on a historical niche I've always found personally fascinating."

"I know what you mean," I say.

At eleven the phone rings. It's Maurer in Refuse Control calling to say that the gangs have set fire to the Anglican Church. That structure cost upwards of ninety thousand to transport from Clydesville and refurbish. We can see the flames from Mr. A's window.

"Oh Christ!" Mr. A says. "If I could kill those kids I would kill those kids. One shouldn't desecrate the dream of another individual in the fashion in which they have mine."

"I know it," I say.

We drink and drink and finally he falls asleep on his office couch.

∞

On the way to my car I keep an eye out for the ghostly McKinnon family. Back in the actual 1860s all this land was theirs. Their homestead's long gone but our records indicate that it was located near present-day Information Hoedown. They probably never saw this many buildings in their entire lives. They don't realize we're chronically slumming, they just think the valley's prospering. Something bad must have happened to them because their spirits are always wandering around at night looking dismayed.

Tonight I find the Mrs. doing wash by the creek. She sees me coming and asks if she can buy my boots. Machine stitching amazes her. I ask how are the girls. She says Maribeth has been sad because no appropriate boy ever died in the valley so she's doomed to loneliness forever. Maribeth is a homely sincere girl who glides around mooning and pining and reading bad poetry chapbooks. Whenever we keep the Park open late for high-school parties, she's in her glory. There was one kid who was able to see her and even got a crush on her, but when he finally tried to kiss her near Hostelry and found out she was spectral it just about killed him. I slipped him a fifty and told him to keep it under wraps. As far as I know he's still in therapy. I realize I should have come forward but they probably would have nut-hutted me, and then where would my family be?

The Mrs. says what Maribeth needs is choir practice followed by a nice quilting bee. In better times I would have taken the quilting-bee idea and run with it. But now there's no budget. That's basically how I finally moved up from Verisimilitude Inspector to Special Assistant, by lifting ideas from the McKinnons. The Mrs. likes me because after she taught me a few obscure 1800s ballads and I parlayed them into Individual Achievement Awards, I bought her a Rubik's Cube. To her, colored plastic is like something from Venus. The Mr. has kind of warned me away from her a couple of times. He doesn't trust me. He thinks the Rubik's Cube is the devil's work. I've brought him lighters and *Playboy*s and once I even dragged out Howie's little synth and the mobile battery pak. I set the synth for carillon and played it from behind a bush. I could tell he was tickled, but he stonewalled. It's too bad I can't make an inroad because he was at Antietam and could be a gold mine of war info. He came back from the war and a year later died in his cornfield, which is now Parking. So he spends most of his time out there calling the cars Beelzebubs and kicking their tires.

Tonight he's walking silently up and down the rows. I get out to my KCar and think oh jeez, I've locked the keys in. The Mr. sits down at the base of the

A3 light-pole and asks did I see the fire and do I realize it was divine retribution for my slovenly moral state. I say thank you very much. No way I'm telling him about the gangs. He can barely handle the concept of women wearing trousers. Finally I give up on prying the window down and go call Evelyn for the spare set. While I wait for her I sit on the hood and watch the stars. The Mr. watches them too. He says there are fewer than when he was a boy. He says that even the heavens have fallen into disrepair. I think about explaining smog to him but then Evelyn pulls up. She's wearing her bathrobe and as soon as she gets out starts with the lip. Howie and Marcus are asleep in the back. The Mr. says it's part and parcel of my fallen state that I allow a woman to speak to me in such a tone. He suggests I throttle her and lock her in the woodshed. Meanwhile she's going on and on so much about my irresponsibility that the kids are waking up. I want to get out before the gangs come swooping down on us. The Parking Area's easy pickings. She calls me a thoughtless oaf and sticks me in the gut with the car keys.

Marcus wakes up all groggy and says: Hey, our daddy.

Evelyn says: Yes, unfortunately he is.

∾

Just after lunch next day a guy shows up at Personnel looking so completely Civil War they immediately hire him and send him out to sit on the porch of the old Kriegal place with a butter churn. His name's Samuel and he doesn't say a word going through Costuming and at the end of the day leaves on a bike. I do the normal clandestine New Employee Observation from the O'Toole gazebo and I like what I see. He seems to have a passable knowledge of how to pretend to churn butter. At one point he makes the mistake of departing from the list of Then-Current Events to discuss the World Series with a Visitor, but my feeling is, we can work with that. All in all he presents a positive and convincing appearance, and I say so in my review.

Sylvia runs her routine check on him and calls me at home that night and says boy do we have a hot prospect on our hands if fucking with the gangs is still on our agenda. She talks like that. I've got her on speakerphone in the rec room and Marcus starts running around the room saying fuck. Evelyn stands there with her arms crossed, giving me a drop-dead look. I wave her off and she flips me the bird.

Sylvia's federal sources indicate that Samuel got kicked out of Vietnam for participating in a bloodbath. Sylvia claims this is oxymoronic. She sounds excited. She suggests I take a nice long look at his marksmanship scores. She says his special combat course listing goes on for pages.

I call Mr. A and he says it sounds like Sam's our man. I express reservations at arming an alleged war criminal and giving him free rein in a family-oriented facility. Mr. A says if we don't get our act together there won't be any family-oriented facility left in a month. Revenues have hit rock bottom and his investors are frothing at the mouth. There's talk of outright closure and liquidation of assets.

He says: Now get off your indefensible high horse and give me Sam's home phone.

So I get off my indefensible high horse and give him Sam's home phone.

∽

Thursday after we've armed Samuel and sent him and the Patrol out, I stop by the Worship Center to check on the Foley baptism. Baptisms are an excellent revenue source. We charge three hundred dollars to rent the Center, which is the former lodge of the Siala utopian free-love community. We trucked it in from downstate, a redbrick building with a nice gold dome. In the old days if one of the Sialians was overeating to the exclusion of others or excessively masturbating, he or she would be publicly dressed down for hours on end in the lodge. Now we put up white draperies and pipe in Stephen Foster and provide at no charge a list of preachers of various denominations.

The Foleys are an overweight crew. The room's full of crying sincere large people wishing the best for a baby. It makes me remember our own sweet beaners in their little frocks. I sit down near the wood-burning heater in the Invalid area and see that Justin in Prep has forgotten to remove the mannequin elderly couple clutching rosaries. Hopefully the Foleys won't notice and withhold payment.

The priest dips the baby's head into the fake marble basin and the door flies open and in comes a racially mixed gang. They stroll up the aisle tousling hair and requisition a Foley niece, a cute redhead of about sixteen. Her dad stands up and gets a blackjack in the head. One of the gang guys pushes her down the aisle with his hands on her breasts. As she passes she looks right at me. The gang guy spits on my shoe and I make my face neutral so he won't get hacked off and drag me into it.

The door slams and the Foleys sit there stunned. Then the baby starts crying and everyone runs shouting outside in time to see the gang dragging the niece into the woods. I panic. I try to think of where the nearest pay phone is. I'm weighing the efficiency of running to Administration and making the call from my cubicle when six fast shots come from the woods. Several of the oldest Foleys assume the worst and drop weeping to their knees in the churchyard.

I don't know the first thing about counseling survivors, so I run for Mr. A.

He's drinking and watching his bigscreen. I tell him what happened and he jumps up and calls the police. Then he says let's go do whatever little we can for these poor people who entrusted us with their sacred family occasion only to have us drop the ball by failing to adequately protect them.

When we get back to the churchyard the Foleys are kicking and upbraiding six gang corpses. Samuel's having a glass of punch with the niece. The niece's dad is hanging all over Sam trying to confirm his daughter's virginity. Sam says it wasn't even close and goes on and on about the precision of his scope.

Then we hear sirens.

Sam says: I'm going into the woods.

Mr. A says: We never saw you, big guy.

The niece's dad says: Bless you, sir.

Sam says: Adios.

Mr. A stands on the hitching post and makes a little speech, the gist of which is, let's blame another gang for killing these dirtbags so Sam can get on with his important work.

The Foleys agree.

The police arrive and we all lie like rugs.

∾

The word spreads on Sam and the gangs leave us alone. For two months the Park is quiet and revenues start upscaling. Then some high-school kid pulls a butter knife on Fred Moore and steals a handful of penny candy from the

General Store. As per specs, Fred alerts Mr. A of a Revenue-Impacting Event. Mr. A calls Security and we perform Exit Sealage. We look everywhere, but the kid's gone. Mr. A says what the hell, Unseal, it's just candy, profit loss is minimal. Sam hears the Unseal Tone on the PA and comes out of the woods all mad with his face painted and says that once the word gets out we've gone soft the gangs will be back in a heartbeat. I ask since when do gangs use butter knives. Sam says a properly trained individual can kill a wild boar with a butter knife. Mr. A gives me a look and says why don't we let Sam run this aspect of the operation since he possesses the necessary expertise. Then Mr. A offers to buy him lunch and Sam says no, he'll eat raw weeds and berries as usual.

I go back to my Verisimilitude Evaluation on the Cimarron Brothel. Everything looks super. As per my recommendations they've replaced the young attractive simulated whores with uglier women with a little less on the ball. We were able to move the ex-simulated whores over to the Sweete Shoppe, so everybody's happy, especially the new simulated whores, who were for the most part middle-aged women we lured away from fast-food places via superior wages.

When I've finished the Evaluation I go back to my office for lunch. I step inside and turn on the fake oil lamp and there's a damn human hand on my chair, holding a note. All around the hand there's penny candy. The note says: Sir, another pig disciplined who won't mess with us anymore and also I need more ammo. It's signed: Samuel the Rectifier.

I call Mr. A and he says Jesus. Then he tells me to bury the hand in the marsh behind Refreshments. I say shouldn't we call the police. He says we let it pass when it was six dead kids, why should we start getting moralistic now over one stinking hand?

I say: But sir, he killed a high-schooler for stealing candy.

He says: That so-called high-schooler threatened Fred Moore, a valued old friend of mine, with a knife.

A butter knife, I say.

He asks if I've seen the droves of unemployed huddled in front of Personnel every morning.

I ask if that's a threat and he says no, it's a reasonable future prognostication.

"What's done is done," he says. "We're in this together. If I take the fall on this, you'll eat the wienie as well. Let's just put this sordid ugliness behind us and get on with the business of providing an enjoyable living for those we love."

I hang up and sit looking at the hand. There's a class ring on it.

Finally I knock it into a garbage sack with my phone and go out to the marsh.

As I'm digging, Mr. McKinnon glides up. He gets down on his knees and starts sniffing the sack. He starts talking about bloody wagon wheels and a boy he once saw sitting in a creek slapping the water with his own severed arm. He tells how the dead looked with rain on their faces and of hearing lunatic singing from all corners of the field of battle and of king-sized rodents gorging themselves on the entrails of his friends.

It occurs to me that the Mr.'s a loon.

I dig down a couple feet and drop the hand in. Then I backfill and get out of there fast. I look over my shoulder and he's rocking back and forth over the hole mumbling to himself.

As I pass a sewer cover the Mrs. rises out of it. Seeing the Mr. enthralled by blood she starts shrieking and howling to beat the band. When she finally calms down she comes to rest in a tree branch. Tears run down her see-through cheeks. She says there's been a horrid violent seed in him since he came home from the war. She says she can see they're going to have to go away. Then she blasts over my head elongate and glowing and full of grief and my hat gets sucked off.

All night I have bad dreams about severed hands. In one I'm eating chili and a hand comes out of my bowl and gives me the thumbs-down. I wake up with a tingling wrist. Evelyn says if I insist on sleeping uneasily would I mind doing it on the couch, since she has a family to care for during the day and this requires a certain amount of rest. I think about confessing to her but then I realize if I do she'll nail me.

The nights when she'd fall asleep with her cheek on my thigh are certainly long past.

I lie there awhile watching her make angry faces in her sleep. Then I go for a walk. As usual Mr. Ebershom's practicing figure-skating moves in his foyer. I sit down by our subdivision's fake creek and think. First of all, burying a hand isn't murder. It doesn't say anywhere thou shalt not bury some guy's hand. By the time I got involved the kid was dead. Where his hand ended up is inconsequential.

Then I think: What am I saying? I did a horrible thing. Even as I sit here I'm an accomplice and an obstructor of justice.

But then I see myself in the penitentiary and the boys waking up scared in the night without me, and right then and there with my feet in the creek I decide to stay clammed up forever and take my lumps in the afterlife.

∾

Halloween's special in the Park. Our brochure says: Lose Yourself in Eerie Autumnal Splendor. We spray cobwebs around the Structures and dress up Staff in ghoul costumes and hand out period-authentic treats. We hide holograph generators in the woods and project images of famous Americans as ghosts. It's always a confusing time for the McKinnons. Last year the Mr. got in a head-to-head with the image of Jefferson Davis. He stood there in the woods yelling at it for hours while the Mrs. and the girls begged him to come away. Finally I had to cut power to the unit.

I drive home at lunch and pick the boys up for trick-or-treating. Marcus is a rancher and Howie's an accountant. He's wearing thick fake lips and carrying a ledger. The Park's the only safe place to trick-or-treat anymore. Last year some wacko in a complex near our house laced his Snickers with a virus. I drove by the school and they were CPRing this little girl in a canary suit. So forget it.

I take them around to the various Structures and they pick up their share of saltwater taffy and hard tasteless frontier candy and wooden whistles and toy soldiers made of soap.

Then just as we start across the Timeless Green a mob of teens bursts out of the Feinstein Memorial Conifer Grove.

"Gangs!" I yell to the boys. "Get down!"

I hear a shot and look up and there's Samuel standing on a stump at tree line. Thank God, I think. He lets loose another round and one of the teens drops. Marcus is down beside me whimpering with his nose in my armpit. Howie's always been the slow one. He stands there with his mouth open, one hand in his plastic pumpkin. A second teen drops. Then Howie drops and his pumpkin goes flying.

I crawl over and beg him to be okay. He says there's no pain. I check him over and check him over and all that's wrong is his ledger's been shot. I'm so relieved I kiss him on the mouth and he yells at me to quit.

Samuel drops a third teen, then runs yipping into the woods.

The ambulance shows up and the paramedics load up the wounded teens. They're all still alive and one's saying a rosary. I take the boys to City Hall and confront Mr. A. I tell him I'm turning Sam in. He asks if I've gone daft and suggests I try putting food on the table from a jail cell while convicts stand in line waiting to have their way with my rear.

At this point I send the boys out to the foyer.

"He shot Howie." I say. "I want him put away."

"He shot Howie's ledger," Mr. A says. "He shot Howie's ledger in the process of saving Howie's life. But whatever. Let's not mince hairs. If Sam gets put away, we get put away. Does that sound to you like a desirable experience?"

"No," I say.

"What I'm primarily saying," he says, "is that this is a time for knowledge assimilation, not backstabbing. We learned a lesson, you and I. We personally grew. Gratitude for this growth is an appropriate response. Gratitude, and being careful never to make the same mistake twice."

He gets out a Bible and says let's swear on it that we'll never hire a crazed maniac to perform an important security function again. Then the phone rings. Sylvia's cross-referenced today's Admissions data and found that the teens weren't a gang at all but a bird-watching-group who made the mistake of being male and adolescent and wandering too far off the trail.

"Ouch," Mr. A says. "This could be a serious negative."

In the foyer the kids are trying to get the loaches in the corporate tank to eat bits of Styrofoam. I phone Evelyn and tell her what happened and she calls me a butcher. She wants to know how on earth I could bring the boys to the Park knowing what I knew. She says she doesn't see how I'm going to live with myself in light of how much they trusted and loved me and how badly I let them down by leaving their fates to chance.

I say I'm sorry and she seems to be thinking. Then she tells me just get them home without putting them in further jeopardy, assuming that's within the scope of my mental powers.

∾

At home she puts them in the tub and sends me out for pizza. I opt for Melvin's Pasta Lair. Melvin's a religious zealot who during the Depression worked five jobs at once. Sometimes I tell him my troubles and he says I should stop whining and count my blessings. Tonight I tell him I feel I should take some responsibility for eliminating the Samuel problem but I'm hesitant because of the discrepancy in our relative experience in violence. He says you mean you're scared. I say not scared, just aware of the likelihood of the possibility of failure. He gives me a look. I say it must have been great to grow up when men were men. He says men have always been what they are now, namely incapable of coping with life without the intervention of God the Almighty. Then in the oven behind him my pizza starts smoking and he says case in point.

He makes me another and urges me to get in touch with my Lord personally. I tell him I will. I always tell him I will.

When I get home they're gone.

Evelyn's note says: I could never forgive you for putting our sons at risk. Goodbye forever, you passive flake. Don't try to find us. I've told the kids you sent us away in order to marry a floozy.

Like an idiot I run out to the street. Mrs. Schmidt is prodding her automatic sprinkler system with a rake, trying to detect leaks in advance. She asks how I am and I tell her not now. I sit on the lawn. The stars are very near. The phone rings. I run inside prepared to grovel, but it's only Mr. A. He says come down to the Park immediately because he's got big horrific news.

When I get there he's sitting in his office half-crocked. He tells me we're unemployed. The investors have gotten wind of the bird-watcher shootings and withdrawn all support. The Park is no more. I tell him about Evelyn and the kids. He says that's the least of his worries because he's got crushing debt. He asks if I have any savings he could have. I say no. He says that just for the record and my own personal development, he's always found me dull and has kept me around primarily for my yes-man capabilities and because sometimes I'm so cautious I'm a hoot.

Then he says: Look, get your ass out, I'm torching this shithole for insurance purposes.

I want to hit or at least insult him, but I need this week's pay to find my kids. So I jog off through the Park. In front of Information Hoedown I see the McKinnons cavorting. I get closer and see that they're not cavorting at all, they've inadvertently wandered too close to their actual death site and are being compelled to act out again and again the last minutes of their lives. The girls are lying side by side on the ground and the Mr. is whacking at them with an invisible scythe. The Mrs. is belly-up with one arm flailing in what must have been the parlor. The shrieking is mind-boggling. When he's killed everyone the Mr. walks out to his former field and mimes blowing out his brains. Then he gets up and starts over. It goes on and on, through five cycles. Finally he sits down in the dirt and starts weeping. The Mrs. and the girls backpedal away. He gets up and follows them, pitifully trying to explain.

Behind us the Visitor Center erupts in flames.

The McKinnons go off down the hill, passing through bushes and trees. He's shouting for forgiveness. He's shouting that he's just a man. He's shouting that hatred and war made him nuts. I start running down the hill agreeing with him. The Mrs. gives me a look and puts her hands over Maribeth's ears. We're all running. The Mrs. starts screaming about the feel of the scythe as it opened her up.

The girls bemoan their unborn kids. We make quite a group. Since I'm still alive I keep clipping trees with my shoulders and falling down.

At the bottom of the hill they pass through the retaining wall and I run into it. I wake up on my back in the culvert. Blood's running out of my ears and a transparent boy's kneeling over me. I can tell he's no McKinnon because he's wearing sweatpants.

"Get up now," he says in a gentle voice. "Fire's coming."

"No," I say. "I'm through. I'm done living."

"I don't think so," he says. "You've got amends to make."

"I screwed up." I say. "I did bad things."

"No joke," he says, and holds up his stump.

I roll over into the culvert muck and he grabs me by the collar and sits me up.

"I steal four jawbreakers and a Slim Jim and your friend kills and mutilates me?" he says.

"He wasn't my friend," I say.

"He wasn't your enemy," the kid says.

Then he cocks his head. Through his clear skull I see Sam coming out of the woods. The kid cowers behind me. Even dead he's scared of Sam. He's so scared he blasts straight up in the air shrieking and vanishes over the retaining wall.

Sam comes for me with a hunting knife.

"Don't take this too personal," he says, "but you've got to go. You know a few things I don't want broadcast."

I'm madly framing calming words in my head as he drives the knife in. I can't believe it. Never again to see my kids? Never again to sleep and wake to their liquid high voices and sweet breaths?

Sweet Evelyn, I think, I should have loved you better.

Possessing perfect knowledge I hover above him as he hacks me to bits. I see his rough childhood. I see his mother doing something horrid to him with a broomstick. I see the hate in his heart and the people he has yet to kill before pneumonia gets him at eighty-three. I see the dead kid's mom unable to sleep, pounding her fists against her face in grief at the moment I was burying her son's hand. I see the pain I've caused. I see the man I could have been, and the man I was, and then everything is bright and new and keen with love and I sweep through Sam's body, trying to change him, trying so hard, and feeling only hate and hate, solid as stone.

~ 1997

John Updike

～ A & P

John Updike was born in 1932 and raised in Shillington, Pennsylvania. He attended Harvard University, where he studied English and wrote and drew cartoons for the *Harvard Lampoon* humor magazine. After graduating, he worked as a staff writer for *The New Yorker* for two years, and then he and his family moved to Massachusetts. Over his long and productive career, he

> *"The trick about fiction, as I see it, is to make an unadventurous circumstance seem adventurous, to make it excite the reader, either with its truth or with the fact that there's always a little more that goes on."*
>
> ～ from an interview with the Academy of Achievement, June 12, 2004

published more than fifty books, including story collections, novels, poetry, and literary criticism. He won nearly every major literary award: the National Book Award, the National Book Critics Circle Award for Fiction, a Guggenheim Fellowship, and—twice—the Pulitzer Prize for Fiction. Updike died in 2009 at the age of seventy-six. His last book, published in 2008, was the novel *The Widows of Eastwick*, a sequel to his 1984 novel *The Witches of Eastwick*.

In walks these three girls in nothing but bathing suits. I'm in the third checkout slot, with my back to the door, so I don't see them until they're over by the bread. The one that caught my eye first was the one in the plaid green two-piece. She was a chunky kid, with a good tan and a sweet broad soft-looking can with those two crescents of white just under it, where the sun never seems to hit, at the top of the backs of her legs. I stood there with my hand on a box of HiHo crackers trying to remember if I rang it up or not. I ring it up again and the customer starts giving me hell. She's one of these cash-register-watchers, a witch about fifty with rouge on her cheekbones and no eyebrows, and I know it made her day to trip me up. She'd been watching cash registers for fifty years and probably never seen a mistake before.

By the time I got her feathers smoothed and her goodies into a bag—she gives me a little snort in passing, if she'd been born at the right time they would have burned her over in Salem—by the time I get her on her way the girls had circled around the bread and were coming back, without a pushcart, back my way along the counters, in the aisle between the checkouts and the Special bins. They didn't even have shoes on. There was this chunky one, with the two-piece—it was bright green and the seams on the bra were still sharp and her belly was still pretty pale so I guessed she just got it (the suit)—there was this one, with one of those chubby berry-faces, the lips all bunched together under her nose, this one, and a tall one, with black hair that hadn't quite frizzed right, and one of these sunburns right across under the eyes, and a chin that was too long—you know, the kind of girl other girls think is very "striking" and "attractive" but never quite makes it, as they very well know, which is why they like her so much—and then the third one, that wasn't quite so tall. She was the queen. She kind of led them, the other two peeking around and making their shoulders round. She didn't look around, not this queen, she just walked straight on slowly, on these long white prima-donna legs. She came down a little hard on her heels, as if she didn't walk in her bare feet that much, putting down her heels and then letting the weight move along to her toes as if she was testing the floor with every step, putting a little deliberate extra action into it. You never know for sure how girls' minds work (do you really think it's a mind in there or just a little buzz like a bee in a glass jar?) but you got the idea she had talked the other two into coming in here with her, and now she was showing them how to do it, walk slow and hold yourself straight.

She had on a kind of dirty-pink—beige maybe, I don't know—bathing suit with a little nubble all over it and, what got me, the straps were down. They were off her shoulders looped loose around the cool tops of her arms, and I guess as a result the suit had slipped a little on her, so all around the top of the cloth there was this shining rim. If it hadn't been there you wouldn't have known there could have been anything whiter than those shoulders. With the straps pushed off, there was nothing between the top of the suit and the top of her head except just *her*, this clean bare plane of the top of her chest down from the shoulder bones like a dented sheet of metal tilted in the light. I mean, it was more than pretty.

She had sort of oaky hair that the sun and salt had bleached, done up in a bun that was unraveling, and a kind of prim face. Walking into the A & P with your straps down, I suppose it's the only kind of face you *can* have. She held her head so high her neck, coming up out of those white shoulders, looked kind of stretched, but I didn't mind. The longer her neck was, the more of her there was.

She must have felt in the corner of her eye me and over my shoulder Stokesie in the second slot watching, but she didn't tip. Not this queen. She kept her eyes moving across the racks, and stopped, and turned so slow it made my stomach rub the inside of my apron, and buzzed to the other two, who kind of huddled against her for relief, and then they all three of them went up the cat-and-dogfood-breakfast-cereal-macaroni-rice-raisins-seasonings-spreads-spaghetti-soft-drinks-crackers-and-cookies aisle. From the third slot I look straight up this aisle to the meat counter, and I watched them all the way. The fat one with the tan sort of fumbled with the cookies, but on second thought she put the package back. The sheep pushing their carts down the aisle—the girls were walking against the usual traffic (not that we have one-way signs or anything)—were pretty hilarious. You could see them, when Queenie's white shoulders dawned on them, kind of jerk, or hop, or hiccup, but their eyes snapped back to their own baskets and on they pushed. I bet you could set off dynamite in an A & P and the people would by and large keep reaching and checking oatmeal off their lists and muttering "Let me see, there was a third thing, began with A, asparagus, no, ah, yes, applesauce!" or whatever it is they do mutter. But there was no doubt, this jiggled them. A few houseslaves in pin curlers even looked around after pushing their carts past to make sure what they had seen was correct.

You know, it's one thing to have a girl in a bathing suit down on the beach, where what with the glare nobody can look at each other much anyway, and another thing in the cool of the A & P, under the fluorescent lights, against all those stacked packages, with her feet paddling along naked over our checkerboard green-and-cream rubber-tile floor.

"Oh Daddy," Stokesie said beside me. "I feel so faint."

"Darling," I said. "Hold me tight." Stokesie's married, with two babies chalked up on his fuselage already, but as far as I can tell that's the only difference. He's twenty-two, and I was nineteen this April.

"Is it done?" he asks, the responsible married man finding his voice. I forgot to say he thinks he's going to be manager some sunny day, maybe in 1990 when it's called the Great Alexandrov and Petrooshki Tea Company or something.

What he meant was, our town is five miles from a beach, with a big summer colony out on the Point, but we're right in the middle of town, and the women generally put on a shirt or shorts or something before they get out of the car into the street. And anyway these are usually women with six children and varicose veins mapping their legs and nobody, including them, could care less. As I say, we're right in the middle of town, and if you stand at our front doors you can see two banks and the Congregational church and the newspaper store and three real-estate offices and about twenty-seven old freeloaders tearing up Central Street because the sewer broke again. It's not as if we're on the Cape, we're north of Boston and there's people in this town haven't seen the ocean for twenty years.

The girls had reached the meat counter and were asking McMahon something. He pointed, they pointed, and they shuffled out of sight behind a pyramid of Diet Delight peaches. All that was left for us to see was old McMahon patting his mouth and looking after them sizing up their joints. Poor kids, I began to feel sorry for them, they couldn't help it.

∞

Now here comes the sad part of the story, at least my family says it's sad, but I don't think it's so sad myself. The store's pretty empty, it being Thursday afternoon, so there was nothing much to do except lean on the register and wait for the girls to show up again. The whole store was like a pinball machine and I didn't know which tunnel they'd come out of. After a while they come around out of the far aisle, around the light bulbs, records at discount of the Caribbean Six or Tony Martin Sings or some such gunk you wonder they waste the wax on, sixpacks of candy bars, and plastic toys done up in cellophane that fall apart when a kid looks at them anyway. Around they come, Queenie still leading the way, and holding a little gray jar in her hands. Slots Three through Seven are unmanned and I could see her wondering between Stokes and me, but Stokesie with his usual luck draws an old party in baggy gray pants who stumbles up with four giant cans of pineapple juice (what do these bums *do* with all that pineapple juice? I've often asked myself). So the girls come to me. Queenie puts down the jar and I take it into my fingers icy cold. Kingfish Fancy Herring Snacks in Pure Sour Cream: 49¢. Now her hands are empty, not a ring or a bracelet, bare as God made them, and I wonder where the money's coming from. Still with that prim look she lifts a folded dollar bill out of the hollow at the center of her nubbled pink top. The jar went heavy in my hand. Really, I thought that was so cute.

Then everybody's luck begins to run out. Lengel comes in from haggling with a truck full of cabbages on the lot and is about to scuttle into that door marked MANAGER behind which he hides all day when the girls touch his eye. Lengel's pretty dreary, teaches Sunday school and the rest, but he doesn't miss that much. He comes over and says, "Girls, this isn't the beach."

Queenie blushes, though maybe it's just a brush of sunburn I was noticing for the first time, now that she was so close. "My mother asked me to pick up a jar of herring snacks." Her voice kind of startled me, the way voices do when you see the people first, coming out so flat and dumb yet kind of tony, too, the way it ticked over "pick up" and "snacks." All of a sudden I slid right down her voice into the living room. Her father and the other men were standing around in ice-cream coats and bow ties and the women were in sandals picking up herring snacks on toothpicks off a big glass plate and they were all holding drinks the color of water with olives and sprigs of mint in them. When my parents have somebody over they get lemonade and if it's a real racy affair Schlitz in tall glasses with "They'll Do It Every Time" cartoons stenciled on.

"That's all right," Lengel said. "But this isn't the beach." His repeating this struck me as funny, as if it had just occurred to him, and he had been thinking all these years the A & P was a great big dune and he was the head lifeguard. He didn't like my smiling — as I say he doesn't miss much — but he concentrates on giving the girls that sad Sunday-school-superintendent stare.

Queenie's blush is no sunburn now, and the plump one in plaid, that I liked better from the back — a really sweet can — pipes up, "We weren't doing any shopping. We just came in for the one thing."

"That makes no difference," Lengel tells her, and I could see from the way his eyes went that he hadn't noticed she was wearing a two-piece before. "We want you decently dressed when you come in here."

"We *are* decent," Queenie says suddenly, her lower lip pushing, getting sore now that she remembers her place, a place from which the crowd that runs the A & P must look pretty crummy. Fancy Herring Snacks flashed in her very blue eyes.

"Girls, I don't want to argue with you. After this come in here with your shoulders covered. It's our policy." He turns his back. That's policy for you. Policy is what the kingpins want. What the others want is juvenile delinquency.

All this while, the customers had been showing up with their carts but, you know, sheep, seeing a scene, they had all bunched up on Stokesie, who shook open a paper bag as gently as peeling a peach, not wanting to miss a word. I could feel in the silence everybody getting nervous, most of all Lengel, who asks me, "Sammy, have you rung up their purchase?"

I thought and said "No" but it wasn't about that I was thinking. I go through the punches, 4, 9, GROC. TOT — it's more complicated than you think, and after you do it often enough, it begins to make a little song, that you hear words to, in my case "Hello (*bing*) there, you (*gung*) hap-py *pee*-pul (*splat*)!" — the *splat* being the drawer flying out. I uncrease the bill, tenderly as you may imagine, it just having come from between the two smoothest scoops of vanilla I had ever known were there, and pass a half and a penny into her narrow pink palm, and nestle the herrings in a bag and twist its neck and hand it over, all the time thinking.

The girls, and who'd blame them, are in a hurry to get out, so I say "I quit" to Lengel quick enough for them to hear, hoping they'll stop and watch me, their unsuspected hero. They keep right on going, into the electric eye; the door flies open and they flicker across the lot to their car, Queenie and Plaid and Big Tall Goony-Goony (not that as raw material she was so bad), leaving me with Lengel and a kink in his eyebrow.

"Did you say something, Sammy?"

"I said I quit."

"I thought you did."

"You didn't have to embarrass them."

"It was they who were embarrassing us."

I started to say something that came out "Fiddle-de-doo." It's a saying of my grandmother's, and I know she would have been pleased.

"I don't think you know what you're saying," Lengel said.

"I know you don't," I said. "But I do." I pull the bow at the back of my apron and start shrugging it off my shoulders. A couple customers that had been heading for my slot begin to knock against each other, like scared pigs in a chute.

Lengel sighs and begins to look very patient and old and gray. He's been a friend of my parents for years. "Sammy, you don't want to do this to your Mom and Dad," he tells me. It's true, I don't. But it seems to me that once you begin a gesture it's fatal not to go through with it. I fold the apron, "Sammy" stitched in red on the pocket, and put it on the counter, and drop the bow tie on top of it. The bow tie is theirs, if you've ever wondered. "You'll feel this for the rest of your life," Lengel says, and I know that's true, too, but remembering how he made the pretty girl blush makes me so scrunchy inside I punch the No Sale tab and the machine whirs "pee-pul" and the drawer splats out. One advantage to this scene taking place in summer, I can follow this up with a clean exit, there's no fumbling around getting your coat and galoshes, I just saunter into the electric eye in my white shirt that my mother ironed the night before, and the door heaves itself open, and outside the sunshine is skating around on the asphalt.

I look around for my girls, but they're gone, of course. There wasn't anybody but some young married screaming with her children about some candy they didn't get by the door of a powder-blue Falcon station wagon. Looking back in the big windows, over the bags of peat moss and aluminum lawn furniture stacked on the pavement, I could see Lengel in my place in the slot, checking the sheep through. His face was dark gray and his back stiff, as if he'd just had an injection of iron, and my stomach kind of fell as I felt how hard the world was going to be to me hereafter.

~ 1961

Tobias Wolff

∼ Bullet in the Brain

"The most radical political writing of all is that which makes you aware of the reality of another human being. Self-absorbed as we are, self-imprisoned even, we don't feel that often enough."

∼ from *The Paris Review*, Fall 2004

Tobias Wolff was born in 1945 in Alabama and raised near Seattle, Washington. After a turbulent childhood (which he later depicted in his memoir *This Boy's Life*), he enlisted in the Army, where he trained in Special Forces and was sent to Vietnam. After leaving the military, he attended Oxford University and then Stanford University, where he was awarded a Wallace Stegner Fellowship in creative writing. His short stories have appeared in periodicals including *The New Yorker*, *The Atlantic*, and *Harper's*, and he has been the editor of *Best American Short Stories*, *The Vintage Book of Contemporary American Short Stories*, and *A Doctor's Visit: The Short Stories of Anton Chekhov*. The author of eight works of fiction and memoir, Wolff has received the PEN/ Faulkner Award for Fiction, a Guggenheim Fellowship, the Rea Award for the Short Story, the Story Prize, and three O. Henry awards. He is now the Priscilla B. Woods Professor in the Humanities at Stanford University.

A nders couldn't get to the bank until just before it closed, so of course the line was endless and he got stuck behind two women whose loud, stupid conversation put him in a murderous temper. He was never in the best of tempers anyway, Anders—a book critic known for the weary, elegant savagery with which he dispatched almost everything he reviewed.

With the line still doubled around the rope, one of the tellers stuck a "POSITION CLOSED" sign in her window and walked to the back of the bank, where she leaned against a desk and began to pass the time with a man shuffling papers. The women in front of Anders broke off their conversation and watched the teller with hatred. "Oh, that's nice," one of them said. She turned to Anders and added, confident of his accord, "One of those little human touches that keep us coming back for more."

Anders had conceived his own towering hatred of the teller, but he immediately turned it on the presumptuous crybaby in front of him. "Damned unfair," he said. "Tragic, really. If they're not chopping off the wrong leg, or bombing your ancestral village, they're closing their positions."

She stood her ground. "I didn't say it was tragic," she said. "I just think it's a pretty lousy way to treat your customers."

"Unforgivable," Anders said. "Heaven will take note."

She sucked in her cheeks but stared past him and said nothing. Anders saw that the other woman, her friend, was looking in the same direction. And then the tellers stopped what they were doing, and the customers slowly turned, and silence came over the bank. Two men wearing black ski masks and blue business suits were standing to the side of the door. One of them had a pistol pressed against the guard's neck. The guard's eyes were closed, and his lips were moving. The other man had a sawed-off shotgun. "Keep your big mouth shut!" the man with the pistol said, though no one had spoken a word. "One of you tellers hits the alarm, you're all dead meat. Got it?"

The tellers nodded.

"Oh, bravo," Anders said. "*Dead meat.*" He turned to the woman in front of him. "Great script, eh? The stern, brass-knuckled poetry of the dangerous classes."

She looked at him with drowning eyes.

The man with the shotgun pushed the guard to his knees. He handed the shotgun to his partner and yanked the guard's wrists up behind his back and locked them together with a pair of handcuffs. He toppled him onto the floor with a kick between the shoulder blades. Then he took his shotgun back and went over to the security gate at the end of the counter. He was short and heavy and moved with peculiar slowness, even torpor. "Buzz him in," his partner said. The man with the shotgun opened the gate and sauntered along the line of tellers, handing each of them a Hefty bag. When he came to the empty position he looked over at the man with the pistol, who said, "Whose slot is that?"

Anders watched the teller. She put her hand to her throat and turned to the man she'd been talking to. He nodded. "Mine," she said.

"Then get your ugly ass in gear and fill that bag."

"There you go," Anders said to the woman in front of him. "Justice is done."

"Hey! Bright boy! Did I tell you to talk?"

"No," Anders said.

"Then shut your trap."

"Did you hear that?" Anders said. " 'Bright boy.' Right out of 'The Killers.' "

"Please be quiet," the woman said.

"Hey, you deaf or what?" The man with the pistol walked over to Anders. He poked the weapon into Anders' gut. "You think I'm playing games?"

"No," Anders said, but the barrel tickled like a stiff finger and he had to fight back the titters. He did this by making himself stare into the man's eyes, which were clearly visible behind the holes in the mask: pale blue and rawly red-rimmed. The man's left eyelid kept twitching. He breathed out a piercing, ammoniac smell that shocked Anders more than anything that had happened, and he was beginning to develop a sense of unease when the man prodded him again with the pistol.

"You like me, bright boy?" he said. "You want to suck my dick?"

"No," Anders said.

"Then stop looking at me."

Anders fixed his gaze on the man's shiny wing-tip shoes.

"Not down there. Up there." He stuck the pistol under Anders' chin and pushed it upward until Anders was looking at the ceiling.

Anders had never paid much attention to that part of the bank, a pompous old building with marble floors and counters and pillars, and gilt scrollwork over the tellers' cages. The domed ceiling had been decorated with mythological figures whose fleshy, toga-draped ugliness Anders had taken in at a glance many years earlier and afterward declined to notice. Now he had no choice but to scrutinize the painter's work. It was even worse than he remembered, and all of it executed with the utmost gravity. The artist had a few tricks up his sleeve and used them again and again—a certain rosy blush on the underside of the clouds, a coy backward glance on the faces of the cupids and fauns. The ceiling was crowded with various dramas, but the one that caught Anders' eye was Zeus and Europa—portrayed, in this rendition, as a bull ogling a cow from behind a haystack. To make the cow sexy, the painter had canted her hips suggestively and given her long, droopy eyelashes through which she gazed back at the bull with sultry welcome. The bull wore a smirk and his eyebrows were arched. If there'd been a bubble coming out of his mouth, it would have said, "Hubba hubba."

"What's so funny, bright boy?"

"Nothing."

"You think I'm comical? You think I'm some kind of clown?"

"No."

"You think you can fuck with me?"

"No."

"Fuck with me again, you're history. *Capiche?*"

Anders burst out laughing. He covered his mouth with both hands and said, "I'm sorry, I'm sorry," then snorted helplessly through his fingers and said, "*Capiche*—oh, God, *capiche*," and at that the man with the pistol raised the pistol and shot Anders right in the head.

∞

The bullet smashed Anders' skull and ploughed through his brain and exited behind his right ear, scattering shards of bone into the cerebral cortex, the corpus callosum, back toward the basal ganglia, and down into the thalamus. But before all this occurred, the first appearance of the bullet in the cerebrum set off a crackling chain of ion transports and neuro-transmissions. Because of their peculiar origin these traced a peculiar pattern, flukishly calling to life a summer afternoon some forty years past, and long since lost to memory. After striking the cranium the bullet was moving at 900 feet per second, a pathetically sluggish, glacial pace compared to the synaptic lightning that flashed around it. Once in the brain, that is, the bullet came under the mediation of brain time, which gave Anders plenty of leisure to contemplate the scene that, in a phrase he would have abhorred, "passed before his eyes."

It is worth noting what Anders did not remember, given what he did remember. He did not remember his first lover, Sherry, or what he had most madly loved about her, before it came to irritate him—her unembarrassed carnality, and especially the cordial way she had with his unit, which she called Mr. Mole, as in, "Uh-oh, looks like Mr. Mole wants to play," and, "Let's hide Mr. Mole!" Anders did not remember his wife, whom he had also loved before she exhausted him with her predictability, or his daughter, now a sullen professor of economics at Dartmouth. He did not remember standing just outside his daughter's door as she lectured her bear about his naughtiness and described the truly appalling punishments Paws would receive unless he changed his ways. He did not remember a single line of the hundreds of poems he had committed to memory in his youth so that he could give himself the shivers at will—not "Silent, upon a peak in Darien," or "My God, I heard this day," or "All my pretty ones? Did you say all? O hell-kite! All?" None of these did he remember; not one. Anders did not remember his dying mother saying of his father, "I should have stabbed him in his sleep."

He did not remember Professor Josephs telling his class how Athenian prisoners in Sicily had been released if they could recite Aeschylus, and then reciting Aeschylus himself, right there, in the Greek. Anders did not remember how his eyes had burned at those sounds. He did not remember the surprise of seeing a college classmate's name on the jacket of a novel not long after they graduated, or the respect he had felt after reading the book. He did not remember the pleasure of giving respect.

Nor did Anders remember seeing a woman leap to her death from the building opposite his own just days after his daughter was born. He did not remember shouting, "Lord have mercy!" He did not remember deliberately crashing his father's car into a tree, or having his ribs kicked in by three policemen at an anti-war rally, or waking himself up with laughter. He did not remember when he began to regard the heap of books on his desk with boredom and dread, or when he grew angry at writers for writing them. He did not remember when everything began to remind him of something else.

This is what he remembered. Heat. A baseball field. Yellow grass, the whirr of insects, himself leaning against a tree as the boys of the neighborhood gather for a pickup game. He looks on as the others argue the relative genius of Mantle and Mays. They have been worrying this subject all summer, and it has become tedious to Anders: an oppression, like the heat.

Then the last two boys arrive, Coyle and a cousin of his from Mississippi. Anders has never met Coyle's cousin before and will never see him again. He says hi with the rest but takes no further notice of him until they've chosen sides and someone asks the cousin what position he wants to play. "Shortstop," the boy says. "Short's the best position they is." Anders turns and looks at him. He wants to hear Coyle's cousin repeat what he's just said, but he knows better than to ask. The others will think he's being a jerk, ragging the kid for his grammar. But that isn't it, not at all — it's that Anders is strangely roused, elated, by those final two words, their pure unexpectedness and their music. He takes the field in a trance, repeating them to himself.

The bullet is already in the brain; it won't be outrun forever, or charmed to a halt. In the end it will do its work and leave the troubled skull behind, dragging its comet's tail of memory and hope and talent and love into the marble hall of commerce. That can't be helped. But for now Anders can still make time. Time for the shadows to lengthen on the grass, time for the tethered dog to bark at the flying ball, time for the boy in right field to smack his sweat-blackened mitt and softly chant, *They is, they is, they is.*

~ 1996

ACKNOWLEDGMENTS

Sherman Alexie. "This Is What It Means to Say Phoenix, Arizona" from *The Lone Ranger and Tonto Fistfight in Heaven* by Sherman Alexie. Copyright © 1993 and 2005 by Sherman Alexie. Used by permission of Grove/Atlantic, Inc.

Richard Bausch. "Tandolfo the Great." Copyright © 1992 by Richard Bausch as taken from *The Stories of Richard Bausch* by Richard Bausch. Copyright © 2003 by Richard Bausch. Reprinted by permission of HarperCollins Publishers.

Kevin Brockmeier. "A Fable with Slips of White Paper Spilling from the Pockets" from *The View from the Seventh Layer,* p. 260. Copyright © 2008 by Kevin Brockmeier. Used by permission of Pantheon Books, a division of Random House, Inc.

Percival Everett. "The Appropriation of Cultures" from *Damned If I Do: Stories,* p. 91. Copyright © 2004 by Percival Everett. Reprinted with the permission of The Permissions Company, Inc., on behalf of Graywolf Press, Minneapolis, Minnesota. www.graywolfpress.org

Becky Hagenston. "Midnight, Licorice, Shadow" appeared in *Strange Weather* by Becky Hagenston (Press 53, 2010) and in *Crazyhorse* (Fall 2008). Copyright © 2008 by Becky Hagenston. Reproduced by permission.

Barry Hannah. "Water Liars," from *Airships.* Copyright © 1970, 1974, 1975, 1976, 1977, 1978 by Barry Hannah. Used by permission of Grove/Atlantic, Inc.

Jesse Lee Kercheval. *Building Fiction: How to Develop Plot and Structure,* University of Wisconsin Press, Copyright © 2003 by the Regents of the University of Wisconsin System. Reprinted by permission of The University of Wisconsin Press.

Jhumpa Lahiri. "This Blessed House" from *Interpreter of Maladies* by Jhumpa Lahiri. Copyright © 1999 by Jhumpa Lahiri. Reprinted by permission of Houghton Mifflin Harcourt Publishing Company. All rights reserved.

Jill McCorkle. "Magic Words" from *Going Away Shoes* by Jill McCorkle. © 2009 by Jill McCorkle. Reprinted by permission of Algonquin Books of Chapel Hill. All rights reserved.

Lorrie Moore. "How to Become a Writer" from *Self-Help* by Lorrie Moore. Copyright © 1985 by M. L. Moore. Used by permission of Alfred A. Knopf, a division of Random House, Inc.

Tim O'Brien. "On the Rainy River" from *The Things They Carried* by Tim O'Brien. Copyright © 1990 by Tim O'Brien. Reprinted by permission of Houghton Mifflin Harcourt Publishing Company. All rights reserved.

ZZ Packer. "Drinking Coffee Elsewhere" from *Drinking Coffee Elsewhere* by ZZ Packer, copyright © 2003 by ZZ Packer. Used by permission of Riverhead Books, an imprint of Penguin Group (USA) Inc.

index